For my parents, and Ambu

Contents

Preface.. vii

Introduction.. ix

1 Federal Judicial Power 2

2 State Action Doctrine... 36

3 Foreign Affairs 47

4 Taxing and Spending Powers...................................... 51

5 Federal Commerce Power.. 55

6 Federal Property Power... 63

7 Congressional Power to Enforce Civil Rights............. 65

8 State Power 67

9 Intergovernmental Immunity...................................... 93

10 Separation of Powers Doctrine.................................. 100

11 Due Process 116

12 Taking Clause (Eminent Domain) 138

13 Contract Clause.. 145

14 Equal Protection Clause 149

15 Ex Post Facto Laws 169

16 Bills of Attainder 172

17 Freedom of Speech—General Considerations........... 174

18 Freedom of Speech—Restricted Speech 190

19 Freedom of Speech—Public and Nonpublic Forums.... 241

20 Freedom of Association 255

21 Freedom of Press 267

22 Freedom of Religion 274

23 The Second Amendment... 310

Preface

I wrote this book to remove some of the confusion surrounding constitutional law, and also some of the frustration involved in learning it. Even law students struggle with this subject; they often complain that there is no "law" in constitutional law, and that it's all a matter of "analysis." This isn't true, of course, but it speaks to the difficulty in understanding it.

The truth is that constitutional law is comprised of many clear, specific, and understandable rules of law, but with the added benefit of the U.S. Supreme Court as our teacher. There are many very well written opinions in which the Court explains constitutional law to us within the context of different cases. In this way, the Court brings the Constitution to life for us, so we can see how it applies in our daily lives.

The format of this book is unlike that of any other book on constitutional law in that it is not a history book, so there is little historical information about the Constitution, and because my personal opinions are not law, there is no commentary either. Instead, there are clear and concise rule statements, followed by brief but informative summaries of the most important and relevant U.S. Supreme Court cases. While each chapter deals with a different topic of constitutional law, the format remains the same.

Researching and writing this book has been a joy for me. In the course of twelve years, I have read hundreds of cases and many books and treatises on this subject, but my purpose has always remained steadfast: to explain constitutional law in the most thorough, organized, concise, and understandable manner possible.

Introduction

The purpose of this book is to offer an intense study of and foster an appreciation for one of the most important documents in human history… the U.S. Constitution. Using this book as a guide should help in understanding constitutional law at a very high level, quickly and easily. In order to accomplish this goal most effectively, reading the book through, from beginning to end, and avoiding jumping from chapter to chapter is recommended. The chapters have been organized very carefully, each laying the groundwork for the next, making the learning process incremental.

Every day, laws are passed and executive actions are taken, and afterwards, people argue about whether these laws or actions are constitutional. Without an understanding of constitutional law, their arguments are weak and unproductive, but with an understanding of constitutional law, the arguments become informed, legal, and persuasive — arguments that can be shared with government representatives at the local, county, state, or national level, or with the media and fellow Americans.

THE CONSTITUTION

The Constitution consists of seven Articles, adopted on September 17, 1787, and twenty-seven Amendments, enacted between 1791 and 1992. The first three Articles are very important because they establish the three independent and coequal branches of government: legislative, executive, and judicial. Briefly, the legislative branch makes laws; the executive branch executes laws; and the judicial branch interprets laws. Here is a brief look at the Articles and Amendments.

Articles

- Article I: Defines the legislative power of the U.S. Congress.
- Article II: Defines the executive power of the president.
- Article III: Defines the judicial power of the courts.
- Article IV: Contains the "full faith and credit" and "privileges and immunities" clauses, and rules regarding federal property power and the republican form of government.
- Article V: Deals with amendments to the Constitution.
- Article VI: Provides that the Constitution "shall be the supreme Law of the Land."
- Article VII: Deals with ratification of the Constitution.

Amendments

- 1st Amendment: Freedoms of religion, speech, press, assembly, and petition.
- 2nd Amendment: Right to keep and bear arms.
- 3rd Amendment: Bans forces quartering of soldiers.
- 4th Amendment: Prohibits unreasonable searches and seizures.
- 5th Amendment: Contains the "due process" and "takings" clauses; prohibits double jeopardy; protects against self-incriminating statements.
- 6th Amendment: Rights to counsel, speedy and fair public trial by jury, confrontation of accusers, and pleas, in criminal cases.
- 7th Amendment: Right to trial by jury in civil cases.
- 8th Amendment: Prohibits excessive bail and cruel and unusual punishment.
- 9th Amendment: Unenumerated rights.
- 10th Amendment: Powers not delegated to the United States are reserved to the states.
- 11th Amendment: Immunity of states from certain suits.
- 12th Amendment: Revises presidential election procedures.
- 13th Amendment: Abolishes slavery and involuntary servitude.

- 14th Amendment: Contains the "equal protection," "due process," and "privileges or immunities" clauses; defines citizenship.

- 15th Amendment: Prohibits the denial of the right to vote based on race, color, or previous condition of servitude.

- 16th Amendment: Allows the federal government to collect income tax.

- 17th Amendment: Allows senators to be directly elected.

- 18th Amendment: Prohibition of alcohol (repealed by 21st Amendment).

- 19th Amendment: Allows for women's right to vote.

- 20th Amendment: Fixes the dates of term commencements for Congress (January 3) and the president (January 20).

- 21st Amendment: Repeals the 18th Amendment.

- 22nd Amendment: Limits the president to two terms, or a maximum of 10 years (i.e., if a vice president serves not more than one half of a president's term, he can be elected to two further terms).

- 23rd Amendment: Provides for representation of Washington, D.C., in the Electoral College.

- 24th Amendment: Prohibits the revocation of voting rights due to non-payment of poll taxes.

- 25th Amendment: Defines the process of presidential succession.

- 26th Amendment: Establishes 18 as the national voting age.

- 27th Amendment: Prevents laws affecting Congressional salary from taking effect until the beginning of the next session of Congress.

UNITED STATES SUPREME COURT

The U.S. Supreme Court is the highest court in the Nation for cases arising under the Constitution or the laws of the United States. The Court decides cases by interpreting and applying the Constitution to the facts of the case at hand. The Court has the authority to invalidate legislation or executive actions that, in the Court's judgment, conflict with the Constitution.

When the Court decides a case, it issues a written opinion. The Court's opinion explains the facts of the case, the Court's interpretation of the Constitution, and the Court's reasoning as it applied the Constitution to the facts of the case. The Court is the final authority in interpreting the Constitution and determining what the law is. So the Court's opinions are virtually final; its decisions can be altered only by a constitutional amendment or a new ruling of the Court.

The Court consists of the Chief Justice and eight Associate Justices.

READING CASES

Parties

A party is a person involved in a lawsuit. For example, the plaintiff and defendant are parties. If a party loses a lawsuit and appeals to a higher court, that party is referred to as the "appellant," or sometimes "petitioner." The opposing party, who won in the lower court and wants the higher court to uphold the lower court judgment, is referred to as the "appellee," or sometimes "respondent" or "defendant." For example, in *Doremus v. Board of Education*, 342 U.S. 429 (1952), *Doremus* was the appellant and Board of Education was the appellee; in *Jackson v. Metropolitan Edison Co.*, 419 U.S. 345 (1974), Jackson was the petitioner and Metropolitan Edison Co. was the respondent.

Citation Format

When arguing a point of law, it helps to refer to (or "cite") a case as support (or "authority") for your argument. A case citation allows the reader (or listener) to find the case quickly and easily.

The case citation, *Doremus v. Board of Education*, 342 U.S. 429 (1952), is an example. Doremus was the appellant and Board of Education was the appellee. 342 U.S. 429 indicates the case can be found in the 342nd volume of a publication (or "reporter") called U.S. Reports, starting at page 429. The year in parentheses (1952) is the year the case was decided.

Injunctions

Sometimes a plaintiff asks a court to command that a defendant perform a certain act. Or, a plaintiff may ask a court to "enjoin" or forbid a defendant from performing an act. If the court grants the plaintiff's request, it issues an injunction. An injunction is a court order that commands, or forbids, the performance of an act.

Decisions

In addition to having the power to uphold or invalidate legislation or executive actions, the Court may also

- "Remand," or send back, a case to a lower court for further determinations.
- "Reverse," or change to the contrary, a lower court decision.
- "Overrule," or void, the ruling (or "holding") of a prior U.S. Supreme Court case, and thus destroy the prior case's value as authority or precedent.

Opinions

A unanimous opinion is supported by all nine justices. A majority opinion is supported or "joined" by a majority (at least five) of the justices. Justices who did not support the majority opinion may write a dissenting opinion or concurring opinion. A dissenting opinion disagrees with the majority opinion, and explains why. A concurring opinion agrees with the conclusion of the majority, but may state different reasons for reaching the conclusion than those provided by the majority. If less than five justices agree on an opinion, than the controlling opinion, called the "plurality" opinion, is the opinion in which more justices join than in any concurring opinion.

The Elements of Constitutional Law

CHAPTER 1

Federal Judicial Power

THIS CHAPTER EXAMINES THE SOURCE AND SCOPE OF THE SUPREME COURT'S POWER, and several important rules the Court uses to decide whether it will hear a particular case.

SOURCE OF JUDICIAL POWER

Article III, Section 1, of the U.S. Constitution provides, "The judicial Power of the United States, shall be vested in one supreme Court, and in such inferior Courts as the Congress may from time to time ordain and establish." Thus, the Constitution establishes the Supreme Court, while Congress has discretion to establish lower federal courts such as district courts (trial courts) and circuit courts of appeal.

SCOPE OF JUDICIAL POWER

The Constitution is the supreme law of the land, and the Supreme Court is the final authority in interpreting the Constitution and determining what the law is [*Marbury v. Madison*, 5 U.S. (1 Cranch) 137 (1803)]. Thus, the Supreme Court has the power to

* Invalidate federal laws found to violate the Constitution [*Marbury v. Madison* (invalidating a federal jurisdictional statute found to violate the Constitution)];

- Review acts of the executive branch under the Constitution [*Marbury v. Madison* (holding that the executive was subject to constitutional restraints that could be enforced by the judiciary)];

- Invalidate state laws found to violate the Constitution [*Fletcher v. Peck*, 10 U.S. (6 Cranch) 87 (1810) (holding that a state statute annulling earlier land conveyances to private persons was an impairment of the obligation of contract under Article I)]; and

- Review state acts under the Constitution [*Martin v. Hunter's Lessee*, 14 U.S. (1 Wheat.) 304 (1816) (reversing the judgment of the Virginia Court of Appeals)].

SUPREME COURT JURISDICTION

The Supreme Court has two types of jurisdiction over cases: original and appellate.

Original Jurisdiction (Trial Jurisdiction)

The Supreme Court has original jurisdiction, in which it acts as a trial court, of all cases affecting ambassadors, other public ministers and consuls, and cases in which a state is a party [U.S. Const. art. III, § 2, cl. 2]. The Court's original jurisdiction is "exclusive" in controversies between two or more states, so only the Supreme Court may hear these cases (28 U.S.C. § 1251). The Court's original jurisdiction is not exclusive in cases affecting ambassadors, other public ministers and counsels, cases between the United States and a state, and cases brought by a state against citizens of another state or aliens; so federal district courts may also hear these cases (28 U.S.C.A. § 1251). Hence, the Supreme Court rarely accepts original jurisdiction in these cases because federal district courts can hear them. Finally, Congress cannot expand the Supreme Court's original jurisdiction beyond these limitations [*Marbury v. Madison*, 5 U.S. (1 Cranch) 137 (1803)].

Appellate Jurisdiction

The Supreme Court has two types of appellate jurisdiction: direct appeal and certiorari.

Direct Appeal (Mandatory)

Direct appeal allows the appellant to bypass the courts of appeal and have the Supreme Court review the case directly, as a matter of right (i.e., review is mandatory). Federal jurisdictional statutes provide the right of direct appeal only from decisions of three-judge federal district courts (28 U.S.C.A. § 1253). The appellant must file a jurisdictional statement, and there must be a substantial federal question involved. The Court considers the jurisdictional statement, and if at least four justices would like to review it, the Court accepts the case for review (the "rule of four"). A decision to affirm summarily or dismiss for lack of a substantial federal question is a vote on the merits of the case, and binding as precedent on lower courts.

Certiorari (Discretionary)

Certiorari allows the Supreme Court to review federal court of appeals cases and judgments from the highest state court in which a judgment could be had. The appellant must file a petition for writ of certiorari, and there must be "special and important" reasons for the Court to review the case. "Special and important" reasons include, for example, where a federal court of appeals decision conflicts with another federal court of appeals decision, where a state court of last resort decides a federal question in conflict with the decision of another state court of last resort, or where a state court or federal court of appeals decides an important federal question not yet settled by the Supreme Court. If at least four justices would like to review it, the Court accepts the case for review (rule of four). A decision to deny certiorari and not review a case has no precedential value [*Maryland v. Baltimore Radio Show*, 338 U.S. 912 (1950)].

Federal Court of Appeals Cases

Any party to a civil or criminal case may file a petition for writ of certiorari before or after the final judgment (28 U.S.C.A. § 1254). Also, a court of appeals may at any time certify any question of law in a civil or criminal case as to which it desires instructions. The Supreme Court may give binding instructions or require the entire record to be sent up for decision of the entire case.

State Cases

The Supreme Court may review a final judgment rendered by the highest state court in which a decision could be had if either

- The validity of a federal statute or treaty is drawn into question on constitutional grounds;

- The validity of a state statute is drawn into question on the ground of its being repugnant to a federal statute or treaty or the Constitution; or

- A title, right, privilege, or immunity is claimed under a federal statute or treaty or the Constitution (28 U.S.C.A. § 1257).

Limiting Appellate Jurisdiction

Congress may limit the Supreme Court's appellate jurisdiction [U.S. Const. art. III, § 2, cl. 2; *Ex parte McCardle*, 74 U.S. (7 Wall.) 506 (1869) (complying with Congress's withdrawal of one avenue of appeal to the Supreme Court)]. However, Congress may not eliminate an area of jurisdiction to control the results in a particular case [*United States v. Klein*, 80 U.S. (13 Wall.) 128 (1871) (holding that Congress's withdrawal of jurisdiction improperly denied presidential pardons the effect the Court previously held them to have, thus prescribing a rule for the Court and deciding the merits of the case)].

"CASE OR CONTROVERSY" RULE

Article III, Section 2, of the Constitution limits federal court jurisdiction to "cases" and "controversies" ("cases" and "controversies" mean the same thing). This provision prevents the Court from invalidating executive or legislative action merely because it is unconstitutional. That is, the dispute must be more than hypothetical, abstract, or academic. The dispute must be "definite and concrete, touching the legal relations of parties having adverse legal interests." It must be a "real and substantial controversy admitting of specific relief through a decree of a conclusive character, as distinguished from an opinion advising what the law would be upon a hypothetical state of facts" [*Aetna Life Insurance Co. v. Haworth*, 300 U.S. 227 (1937)].

RIPENESS DOCTRINE (CASE BROUGHT TOO EARLY)

The Court may decide only "ripe" cases. A case is ripe for decision when the plaintiff shows he suffered an actual injury, or is in immediate danger of sustaining an actual injury [*Laird v. Tatum*, 408 U.S. 1 (1972)].

A case is not ripe, for example, where a criminal statute is challenged before a prosecution is initiated. A mere hypothetical threat of injury is not enough, for the Court does not want to get involved in abstract disagreements. Also, until a case is ripe, it is difficult for the Court to evaluate the merits of the parties' positions. Finally, if the Court waits until a case is ripe, it may be able to avoid constitutional issues, for example, by interpreting a statute a certain way.

- *United Public Workers v. Mitchell*, 330 U.S. 75 (1947). The Hatch Act barred executive branch employees from participating in political campaigns. Plaintiffs sought declaratory relief and an injunction to prevent enforcement of the Act. The Court held the case was not ripe as to plaintiffs who had not been charged with violating the Act.

- *Poe v. Ullman*, 367 U.S. 497 (1961). Connecticut law prohibited the use of contraceptives and the giving of medical advice on their use. Two married women sought contraceptive advice from a physician. The physician did not provide the advice because the State's Attorney might have claimed it violated Connecticut law. The women and physician challenged the constitutionality of the law under the Fourteenth Amendment. The Court dismissed the cases because they were not ripe. The Court explained that the law had "been on the State's books since 1879," and contraceptives were "commonly and notoriously sold in Connecticut drug stores." Yet, "no prosecutions are recorded." Thus, "The fact that Connecticut has not chosen to press the enforcement of this statute deprives these controversies of the immediacy which is an indispensable condition of constitutional adjudication."

MOOTNESS DOCTRINE (CASE BROUGHT TOO LATE)

The Court may not decide moot cases [*Aetna Life Insurance Co. v. Haworth*, 300 U.S. 227 (1937)]. A case is moot if after the lawsuit is filed, events occur that resolve the issues or deprive the plaintiff of an interest in the outcome. Thus, the Court may decide a case only if an actual controversy exists at every stage of the proceeding, from trial to appeals [*United States v. Munsingwear, Inc.*, 340 U.S. 36 (1950)].

A case may become moot where, for example, (1) the law has changed; (2) the defendant paid the money owed and no longer wants to appeal; (3) the wrongful behavior stopped and cannot reasonably be expected to recur; or (4) the challenged statute no longer affects the litigant (e.g., a statute regulating the rights of minors becomes moot when the complaining party, through lapse of time, ages beyond the age limit of the statute). There are four exceptions to the mootness doctrine: voluntary cessation, repetition, collateral consequences, and class actions.

Voluntary Cessation

A case is not moot if a party voluntarily stops the alleged illegal conduct but is "free to return to his old ways" [*United States v. W.T. Grant Co.*, 345 U.S. 629 (1953)]. A case is moot only if "there is no reasonable expectation that the wrong will be repeated" [*W.T. Grant Co.*].

Repetition Exception ("Same Injury, Same Plaintiff")

A case is not moot if the injury is "capable of repetition, yet evading review" [*Murphy v. Hunt*, 455 U.S. 478 (1982)]. Two elements must be satisfied for the repetition exception to apply: (1) the challenged injury must be so short in duration that it cannot be fully litigated before it stops, and (2) there must be a reasonable expectation that the same injury will happen again to the same plaintiff [*Weinstein v. Bradford*, 423 U.S. 147 (1975)].

Examples of short duration injuries include where the challenged order is so short that it will normally expire before review may be had, such as short-term sentences [*Sibron v. New York*, 392 U.S. 40 (1968)] and short-term injunctions [*Carroll v. President and Commissioners of Princess Anne*, 393 U.S. 175 (1968)]; where an election statute is challenged but the election will likely pass before review may be had [*Moore v. Ogilvie*, 394 U.S. 814 (1969)]; and where a pregnant woman challenges the constitutionality of abortion legislation but will likely not be pregnant by the time of review [*Roe v. Wade*, 410 U.S. 113 (1973)].

- *DeFunis v. Odegaard*, 416 U.S. 312 (1974). A law student claimed his denial of admission to a state law school was racial discrimination. The trial court ordered him admitted, and the state Supreme Court reversed. By the time the U.S. Supreme Court considered his certiorari petition, he was in the last quarter of his third year, and the school said his registration would not be cancelled regardless of the case's outcome. The Court held the case was moot because the student will likely never be subjected again to the state's allegedly discriminatory law school admission policy. Thus, the repetition exception did not apply.

Collateral Consequences

A case is not moot, even if some of the original relief requested is moot, if there are collateral consequences. Examples include where a codefendant pays a joint judgment and then demands contribution from the other defendant [Bank of Marin v. England, 385 U.S. 99 (1966)]; and where a criminal defendant serves his sentence and is released but the conviction could still be used to deny voting privileges or professional licenses, impeach his testimony in a future proceeding, or be used in a persistent felony prosecution [Evitts v. Lucey, 469 U.S. 387 (1985); Sibron v. New York, 392 U.S. 40 (1968)].

Class Actions

A case is not moot between a defendant and a class member represented by the named plaintiff even though the named plaintiff's claim resolves and becomes moot [Sosna v. Iowa, 419 U.S. 393 (1975)]. If members of the class still have a controversy, the case can continue.

ADVISORY OPINIONS

An advisory opinion is a court opinion that does not decide a specific "case or controversy," but merely advises on the interpretation of a law. The Supreme Court may not give advisory opinions [Muskrat v. United States, 219 U.S. 346 (1911) (holding that Congress may not grant the Court jurisdiction to decide the constitutionality of an act of Congress without regard to the "case or controversy" requirement)]. One reason for the rule against advisory opinions is that when the Court waits until a real controversy develops before deciding a case it is sometimes able to avoid constitutional issues by deciding the case on narrower grounds (e.g., jurisdiction).

DECLARATORY JUDGMENTS

Though there must be a "case or controversy," there need not be coercive relief such as fines or imprisonment. The Court may also issue "declaratory relief" establishing the rights of the parties without granting a remedy or ordering anything to be done [Aetna Life Insurance Co. v. Haworth, 300 U.S. 227 (1937)].

Collusive Cases ("Friendly" Cases)

The Court may not decide "collusive" cases in which the controversy is feigned and not real. There must be an "honest and actual antagonistic assertion of rights." [*Chicago & G.T.R. Co. v. Wellman*, 143 U.S. 339 (1892)]

- *United States v. Johnson*, 319 U.S. 302 (1943), dismissing a case as collusive where plaintiff brought suit under a fictitious name at defendant's request; defendant selected and paid for plaintiff's counsel, who never met plaintiff; defendant assured plaintiff he would incur no expenses in connection with the suit; and plaintiff never read the complaint and had no knowledge of the judgment he asked for, outside of reading about it in the paper.

- *Moore v. Charlotte-Mecklenburg Board of Education*, 402 U.S. 47 (1971), dismissing a case where both sides argued and agreed that an antibusing law was constitutional, and urged that a desegregation order be set aside.

Standing

"In essence the question of standing is whether the litigant is entitled to have the court decide the merits of the dispute or of particular issues" [*Warth v. Seldin*, 422 U.S. 490 (1975)]. If a plaintiff has no standing, the court cannot decide his case. Standing is closely related to the questions of ripeness and mootness.

There are several types of standing. Personal standing is the most common. Other types of standing include taxpayer standing, third-party standing, association standing, state standing, citizen standing, legislator standing, and congressional conferral of standing.

Personal Standing

Article III of the Constitution requires that the plaintiff show (1) he personally suffered an "actual or imminent" injury; (2) there is a causal connection between his injury and defendant's conduct; and (3) his injury is likely to be redressed by a favorable decision [*Lujan v. Defenders of Wildlife*, 504 U.S. 555 (1992)]. So, the plaintiff must show injury, causation, and redressability.

Injury

The plaintiff must show he personally suffered an "actual or imminent" injury. Injuries sufficient for standing include, for example, injuries to common law rights (e.g., torts, contracts, and property), injuries to constitutional rights (e.g., freedom of speech or due process of law), injuries to statutory rights (e.g., the Civil Rights Act of 1968), and economic, aesthetic, and environmental injuries [*United States v. Students Challenging Regulatory Agency Procedures*, 412 U.S. 669 (1973)].

However, an abstract, conjectural, or hypothetical injury is not enough. Also, a mere "ideological interest" in having the government act according to law is not enough [*S. v. D.*, 410 U.S. 614 (1973) (holding that a private citizen lacks a judicially cognizable interest in the prosecution or nonprosecution of another)].

- *Sierra Club v. Morton*, 405 U.S. 727 (1972). The Sierra Club sought to restrain federal officials from approving a proposed ski resort in a national forest, the Mineral King Valley in the Sierra Nevada Mountains of California. The Court held the Sierra Club did not have standing because "The Sierra Club failed to allege that it or its members would be affected in any of their activities or pastimes by the Disney development. Nowhere in the pleadings or affidavits did the Club state that its members use Mineral King for any purpose, much less that they use it in any way that would be significantly affected by the proposed actions of the respondents."

- *Trafficante v. Metropolitan Life Insurance Co.*, 409 U.S. 205 (1972). Tenants of an apartment complex alleged that because of a landlord's discrimination against nonwhites, the tenants lost the social benefits of living in an integrated community, missed business and professional advantages that would have accrued from living with members of minority groups, and suffered from being "stigmatized" as residents of a "white ghetto." The Court held the tenants had standing to sue because they had been injured by a discriminatory housing practice and thus came within the definition of "persons aggrieved" in the Civil Rights Act of 1968.

- *Laird v. Tatum*, 408 U.S. 1 (1972). In response to civil disorders it helped control in 1967 and 1968, Army intelligence established a data-gathering system described as the "surveillance of lawful civilian political activity." Plaintiffs sought to enjoin the surveillance, alleging their First Amendment rights were chilled because of the mere existence of this data-gathering system. The Court held that plaintiffs did not have standing because they made "no showing of objective harm or threat of specific future harm."

- *City of Los Angeles v. Lyons*, 461 U.S. 95 (1983). Plaintiff sued the city of Los Angeles and certain police officers, alleging that in 1976 he was stopped for a traffic violation, and though he offered no resistance, the officers, without provocation or justification, seized him and applied a "chokehold," rendering him unconscious and damaging his larynx. In addition to seeking damages, plaintiff sought injunctive relief against the city, barring the use of choke-holds except in situations where the proposed victim reasonably appeared to be threatening the immediate use of deadly force. The Court held that plaintiff did not have standing to seek the injunction because he did not "establish a real and immediate threat that he would again be stopped for a traffic violation, or for any other offense, by an officer or officers who would illegally choke him into unconsciousness without any provocation or resistance on his part."

- *Quinn v. Millsap*, 491 U.S. 95 (1989). Citizens who did not own real property had standing to challenge, under the equal protection clause, a state law requirement that one own real property in order to serve on a government board.

- *Lujan v. Defenders of Wildlife*, 504 U.S. 555 (1992). Defenders of Wildlife (DW) challenged a regulation of the secretary of the interior that applied the Endangered Species Act only to actions within the United States, and not to actions in foreign nations. However, affidavits of two DW members stated only that they "had visited" and "intended" to revisit foreign places where they would presumably be deprived of the opportunity to observe animals of the endangered species. The Court held that they did not assert a sufficiently "imminent" injury to have standing to challenge the regulation.

Causation

The plaintiff must show a causal connection between his injury and the defendant's conduct. The Court can redress only injury that "fairly can be traced to the challenged action of the defendant, and not injury that results from the independent action of some third party not before the court" [*Simon v. Eastern Kentucky Welfare Rights Organization*, 426 U.S. 26 (1976)].

- *Simon v. Eastern Kentucky Welfare Rights Organization*, 426 U.S. 26 (1976). The government granted tax exemptions to hospitals that offered only emergency room service to indigents. Several indigent plaintiffs claimed they were denied treatment at these hospitals because of indigency. So, they challenged the tax exemptions, alleging that by extending tax benefits to hospitals that refused to fully serve the indigent, the government "encouraged" the hospitals to deny services to indigents. The Court held the plaintiffs had no standing because it was "purely speculative" whether the alleged denials of service were caused by the government's "encouragement," or instead resulted from decisions made by the hospitals without regard to the tax implications.

- *Allen v. Wright*, 468 U.S. 737 (1984). Parents of black children attending public schools undergoing desegregation claimed that their children had a diminished ability to receive an education in a racially integrated school because of a federal tax exemption granted to some racially discriminatory private schools. The Court held the parents did not have standing to challenge the tax exemption because they did not allege that there were enough racially discriminatory private schools receiving tax exemptions in their communities for withdrawal of those exemptions to make an appreciable difference in public school integration. Also, it was speculative whether withdrawal of a particular school's tax exemption would lead the school to change its policies, and whether any given parent of a child attending such a private school would decide to transfer the child to public school as a result. So, "The links in the chain of causation between the challenged Government conduct and the asserted injury are far too weak for the chain as a whole to sustain respondents' standing."

Redressability

The plaintiff must show his injury is likely to be redressed by a favorable decision. He must show that he personally would benefit in a tangible way from the court's intervention, or that prospective relief will remove the harm. The "redressability" requirement assures that judicial action will have real consequences, and not be a mere forum for debate.

- *S. v. D.*, 410 U.S. 614 (1973). A Texas criminal statute provided that any "parent" who fails to support his "children" is subject to prosecution. Texas courts construed the statute to apply only to parents of legitimate children. The mother of an illegitimate child did not receive support payments from the child's father, so she challenged the statute and sought to have the local district attorney prosecute the father. The Court held the mother did not have standing. Although she "no doubt suffered an injury stemming from the failure of her child's father to contribute support payments," if the Court granted the requested relief it "would not result in support but only in the father's incarceration." Hence, "The prospect that prosecution will, at least in the future, result in payment of support can, at best, be termed only speculative."

- *Warth v. Seldin*, 422 U.S. 490 (1975). Low-income residents of Rochester, New York, claimed a zoning ordinance of Penfield, a suburb of Rochester, effectively excluded low-income persons from living in Penfield. The Court held the plaintiffs did not have standing because they did not show a "reasonable probability" that they would have been able to purchase or lease in Penfield if the Court provided the requested relief and invalidated Penfield's zoning ordinance. Plaintiffs' descriptions of their individual financial situations and housing needs suggested that their inability to reside in Penfield was the consequence of the "economics of the area housing market," rather than Penfield's zoning ordinance.

Taxpayer Standing

There are three types of taxpayer standing: federal, state, and municipal.

Federal Taxpayers
General Rule (No Standing)

A federal taxpayer has no standing to challenge federal expenditures if the only interest he asserts is that he is a federal taxpayer, because his interest in treasury money is "shared with millions of others" and thus is "comparatively minute and indeterminable" [*Frothingham v. Mellon*, 262 U.S. 447 (1923)]. So, a taxpayer may not "employ a federal court as a forum in which to air his generalized grievances about the conduct of government or the allocation of power in the Federal System."

- *Frothingham v. Mellon*, 262 U.S. 447 (1923). A taxpayer challenged the Maternity Act of 1921. The Act provided federal grants to states that would undertake programs to reduce maternal and infant mortality. The taxpayer complained that the Act would increase her future federal tax liability and "thereby take her property without due process of law." The Court held the taxpayer had no standing because a federal taxpayer's interest in treasury money is "shared with millions of others" and thus "comparatively minute and indeterminable." Also, the effect upon future taxation of any payment out of the Treasury's funds is "remote, fluctuating and uncertain."

Exception (*Flast* "Nexus" Test)
A federal taxpayer may challenge a federal expenditure if he shows (1) the spending is a substantial expenditure of funds under the taxing and spending clause of Article I, Section 8, of the Constitution (an incidental expenditure of tax funds under a regulatory statute is insufficient), and (2) the challenged enactment exceeds a specific constitutional limitation on congressional taxing and spending power (an allegation that the enactment is simply "beyond Congress' powers" is insufficient).

- *Flast v. Cohen*, 392 U.S. 83 (1968). Federal taxpayers challenged the spending of federal funds, under the Elementary and Secondary Education Act of 1965, to finance teaching and textbooks in religious schools, alleging it violated the establishment clause of the First Amendment. The government appropriated almost $1 billion to implement the Act in 1965. The Court held the plaintiffs had standing because (1) "the challenged program involves a substantial expenditure of federal tax funds" by Congress of its power under the taxing and spending clause to spend for the general welfare, and (2) plaintiffs alleged the expenditures violated the establishment clause, which "operates as specific constitutional limitation upon exercise by Congress of taxing and spending power." The Court distinguished *Frothingham*, as plaintiff there "lacked standing because her constitutional attack was not based on an allegation that Congress, in enacting the Maternity Act of 1921, had breached a specific limitation upon its taxing and spending power." (Mrs. Frothingham relied, not on a specific limitation on the power to tax and spend, but on a more general claim based on the due process clause.)

- *United States v. Richardson*, 418 U.S. 166 (1974). Federal statutes regulated the CIA's accounting and reporting procedures, and permitted the CIA to withhold from the public detailed information about its expenditures. A federal taxpayer challenged the statutes, claiming they violated the accounts clause of the Constitution, and asked the Court to compel the government to give him information on precisely how the CIA spends its funds. The Court held he had no standing because "his challenge is not addressed to the taxing or spending power, but to the statutes regulating the CIA." There was "no claim that appropriated funds are being spent in violation of a specific constitutional limitation upon the taxing and spending power."

- *Valley Forge Christian College v. Americans United for Separation of Church and State, Inc.*, 454 U.S. 464 (1982). The secretary of health, education, and welfare (HEW) transferred to a Christian college, without any financial payment, a 77-acre tract of "surplus" federal property worth $577,500. Federal taxpayers claimed the transfer violated the establishment clause. The Court held the plaintiffs had no standing because they did not satisfy the first prong of the *Flast* "nexus" test. The challenged action was not an expenditure of funds by Congress under the taxing and spending clause; it was a transfer of property by HEW under the property clause of Article IV, Section 3.

State Taxpayers

A state taxpayer may challenge a state act in federal court if he shows "not only that the statute is invalid, but that he has sustained or is immediately in danger of sustaining some direct injury as the result of its enforcement, and not merely that he suffers in some indefinite way in common with people generally" [*Doremus v. Board of Education of Hawthorne*, 342 U.S. 429 (1952); *ASARCO Inc. v. Kadish*, 490 U.S. 605 (1989) (holding, "we have likened state taxpayers to federal taxpayers, and thus we have refused to confer standing upon a state taxpayer absent a showing of "direct injury," pecuniary or otherwise)].

Municipal Taxpayers

A municipal taxpayer may challenge a municipal expenditure in federal court if it is a "measurable expenditure." A municipal taxpayer's interest in municipal expenditures is "direct and immediate and the remedy by injunction to prevent their misuse is not inappropriate" [*Commonwealth of Massachusetts v. Mellon*, 262 U.S. 447 (1923) (explaining, "The reasons which support the extension of the equitable remedy to a single taxpayer in such cases are based upon the peculiar relation of the corporate taxpayer to the corporation, which is not without some resemblance to that subsisting between stockholder and private corporation")].

* *Doremus v. Board of Education*, 342 U.S. 429 (1952). A municipal taxpayer challenged a New Jersey statute that provided for reading, without comment, five verses of the Old Testament at the opening of each public school day. The Court held the plaintiff had no standing because he did not show a measurable expenditure of school-district funds caused by the Bible reading. The Court explained, "There is no allegation that this activity is supported by any separate tax or paid for from any particular appropriation or that it adds any sum whatever to the cost of conducting the school. No information is given as to what kind of taxes are paid by appellants and there is no averment that the Bible reading increases any tax they do pay or that as taxpayers they are, will, or possibly can be out of pocket because of it."

Third-Party Standing (Also Called *Jus Tertii* Standing)

General Rule (No Standing)

A plaintiff must assert his own legal rights and interests and cannot base his claim to relief on the legal rights or interests of third parties who are not parties to the lawsuit; injured parties must bring their own claims. First, it may be that the third party either wishes to assert his own rights, or will be able to enjoy his rights regardless of whether the plaintiff is successful. Second, third parties themselves are usually the best proponents of their own rights.

* *Tileston v. Ullman*, 318 U.S. 44 (1943). Connecticut statutes prohibited a physician from prescribing the use of contraceptive devices for married women. A doctor challenged the statutes,

alleging they prevented him from giving advice about contraceptive use to three patients whose lives would be endangered by childbearing. The Court held the doctor did not have standing because there was no allegation or proof that his life was in danger. Although his patients' lives may have been in danger, they "are not parties to this proceeding and there is no basis on which we can say that he has standing to secure an adjudication of his patients' constitutional right to life, which they do not assert in their own behalf."

Exception

If a plaintiff has suffered an injury, the Court may allow him to assert the rights of a third party after considering (1) the importance of the relationship between the plaintiff and the third party; (2) the ability of the third party to assert his own rights; and (3) the risk that the third party's rights will be diluted if third-party standing is denied.

- *Barrows v. Jackson*, 346 U.S. 249 (1953). Barrows, a white person, signed a racially restrictive covenant, and was sued for $11,600 in damages for breaching the covenant by selling realty to a black buyer. Barrow's defense was that the covenant denied equal protection to prospective black purchasers, who were not parties to the covenant or the lawsuit. The Court held that Barrows had third-party standing to assert the rights of blacks because "we are faced with a unique situation in which it is the action of the state court which might result in a denial of constitutional rights and in which it would be difficult if not impossible for the persons whose rights are asserted to present their grievance before any court." So, Barrows "is the only effective adversary of the unworthy covenant."

- *Griswold v. Connecticut*, 381 U.S. 479 (1965). A Connecticut statute prohibited the use of contraceptives. Planned Parenthood League's executive director and a doctor were convicted under the law as accessories for giving information, instruction, and medical advice to married persons about preventing conception. They argued the statute intruded on the right of marital privacy of their patients and was unconstitutional. The Court held the director and doctor had third-party standing to assert in their defense the constitutional rights of the married people with whom they had a professional relationship, because "The rights of husband and wife, pressed here, are likely to be diluted or adversely affected unless those rights are considered in a suit involving those who have this kind of confidential relation to them."

• *Warth v. Seldin*, 422 U.S. 490 (1975). Low-income residents of Rochester, New York, claimed a zoning ordinance of Penfield, a suburb of Rochester, effectively excluded low-income persons from living in Penfield, and therefore caused Rochester to raise taxes because it had to provide more low-income housing than it otherwise would. They claimed that Penfield's zoning ordinance violated the constitutional and statutory rights of third parties, namely, persons of low and moderate income who were excluded from Penfield, and were not parties to the lawsuit. The Court held the plaintiffs did not have third-party standing because they were not themselves subject to Penfield's ordinances. No relationship existed between the plaintiffs and the persons whose rights were allegedly violated, and the plaintiffs did not show that the persons actually excluded from Penfield were unable to assert their own rights.

Association Standing

Associations have two types of standing: (1) an association may sue on its own behalf and assert the association's rights, or (2) an association may sue on behalf of its members in a representative capacity and assert its members' rights.

Suing on Its Own Behalf

An association may sue on its own behalf and assert the association's rights if the association suffered an injury.

• *Havens Realty Corp. v. Coleman*, 455 U.S. 363 (1982). Housing Opportunities Made Equal (HOME) was an organization whose purpose was "to make equal opportunity in housing a reality." HOME sued an apartment complex, alleging that it violated the Fair Housing Act by giving false information about the availability of apartments in a discriminatory manner ("racial steering"). The Court held that HOME had standing, because if the apartment's "steering" practices impaired HOME's ability to provide counseling and referral services for low- and moderate-income home seekers, thereby draining the organization's resources, "there can be no question that the organization has suffered the requisite injury in fact."

Suing on Behalf of Members

An association may also sue on behalf of its members in a representative capacity and assert its members' rights, even if the association is not injured, if (1) its members would otherwise have standing to sue in their own right; (2) the interests it seeks to protect are germane to the organization's purpose; and (3) neither the claim asserted nor relief requested requires participation of individual members in the suit.

* *Hunt v. Washington State Apple Advertising Commission*, 432 U.S. 333 (1977). A North Carolina law required that all apples sold or shipped into the state in closed containers bear on the container "no grade other than the applicable U.S. grade or standard." Washington State had its own apple grading system that was the equivalent of, or superior to, the grades used by the United States Department of Agriculture (USDA). The North Carolina law prohibited the display of Washington State grades on containers of apples shipped into North Carolina. To comply with the law, Washington growers would have to either obliterate the printed labels on containers shipped to North Carolina, thus giving their product a damaged appearance; repack apples to be shipped to North Carolina in containers bearing only the USDA grade; or discontinue the use of the preprinted containers entirely. These options were costly, and would diminish the efficiency of their marketing efforts.

  The Washington State Apple Advertising Commission promoted and protected the state's apple industry, and was composed of thirteen Washington apple growers and dealers. The Commission sued on behalf of its members under the interstate commerce clause and sought declaratory and injunctive relief. The Court held the commission had "associational standing" to sue on behalf of its members because (1) the North Carolina law injured Washington apple producers, so they had standing; (2) the commission's attempt to remedy these injuries and to secure the industry's right to publicize its grading system was central to the commission's purpose of protecting and enhancing the market for Washington apples; and (3) neither the interstate commerce claim nor the request for declaratory and injunctive relief required individualized proof, so the members' individual participation in the lawsuit was unneeded.

State Standing

States have two types of standing: (1) a state may sue on its own behalf and assert its own rights, or (2) a state may sue another state on behalf of its citizens in a representative capacity (parens patriae) and assert its citizens' rights. A state does not have standing to sue the federal government and assert its citizens' rights as "parens patriae" [*Massachusetts v. Mellon*, 262 U.S. 447 (1923)].

Suing on Its Own Behalf

A state may sue on its own behalf and assert its own rights if the state suffered an injury.

* *Wyoming v. Oklahoma*, 502 U.S. 437 (1992). Oklahoma law required that Oklahoma coal-fired electric generating plants producing power for sale in Oklahoma burn a mixture of coal containing at least 10 percent Oklahoma-mined coal. Wyoming imposed a tax on the severance or extraction of coal from land within its boundaries. So, the Oklahoma law deprived Wyoming of severance tax revenues by causing a decline in total purchases of Wyoming-mined coal. The Court held that Wyoming had standing to challenge, under the commerce clause, the Oklahoma law because "Wyoming's loss of severance tax revenues 'fairly can be traced' to the Act."

Suing on Behalf of Citizens (Parens Patriae)

A state may sue another state on behalf of its citizens in a representative capacity (parens patriae) and assert its citizens' rights if "the injury affects the general population of a state in a substantial way."

* *Maryland v. Louisiana*, 451 U.S. 725 (1981). Several states challenged the constitutionality of Louisiana's "First-Use Tax" imposed on certain uses of natural gas brought into Louisiana. The tax, while imposed on the pipelines, was passed on to the ultimate consumer. Citizens in each state were consumers of natural gas

and were faced with increased costs aggregating millions of dollars per year. The Court held that the states had standing as parens patriae because of the "States' interest in protecting its citizens from substantial economic injury presented by imposition of the First-Use Tax."

Citizen Standing

Mere citizenship does not confer standing.

- *Schlesinger v. Reservists Committee to Stop the War*, 418 U.S. 208 (1974). The incompatibility clause provides that "no Person holding any Office under the United States, shall be a Member of either House during his Continuance in Office" (U.S. Const. art. I, § 6, cl. 2). So, the incompatibility clause prohibits members of Congress from holding certain offices. Several members of Congress were also members of the Armed Forces Reserve. Several citizens sued the government on behalf of all citizens, alleging that Reserve membership of members of Congress violated the incompatibility clause by depriving citizens of the faithful discharge of the legislative duties of reservist members of Congress. The Court held that the citizens lacked standing as citizens because "[t]o support standing there must be concrete injury," but their claim implicated only a generalized interest of all citizens and was thus a mere abstract injury. The Court explained, "In some fashion, every provision of the Constitution was meant to serve the interests of all. Such a generalized interest, however, is too abstract to constitute a 'case or controversy' appropriate for judicial resolution. The proposition that all constitutional provisions are enforceable by any citizen simply because citizens are the ultimate beneficiaries of those provisions has no boundaries."

Legislator Standing

Legislators whose votes would have been sufficient to defeat (or enact) a specific legislative act have standing to sue if that act goes into effect (or does not go into effect), on the ground that their votes have been completely nullified.

- *Coleman v. Miller*, 307 U.S. 433 (1939). In 1924, Congress proposed an amendment to the Constitution known as the Child

Labor Amendment. In 1925, the legislature of Kansas adopted a resolution rejecting the proposed amendment. In 1937, a resolution known as "Senate Concurrent Resolution No. 3" was introduced in the Senate of Kansas ratifying the proposed amendment. There were forty senators. When the resolution came up for consideration, twenty senators voted in favor of its adoption and twenty voted against it. The lieutenant governor, the presiding officer of the Senate, then cast his vote in favor of the resolution. The resolution was later adopted by the House of Representatives. The twenty senators who voted against the resolution sued and challenged the right of the lieutenant governor to cast the deciding vote in the Senate. The Court held the senators had standing because their "votes against ratification have been overridden and virtually held for naught although if they are right in their contentions their votes would have been sufficient to defeat ratification. We think that these senators have a plain, direct and adequate interest in maintaining the effectiveness of their votes."

- *Raines v. Byrd*, 521 U.S. 811 (1997). Individual members of Congress who voted against the Line Item Veto Act sued executive branch officials to challenge the Act's constitutionality. The Act gave the president the authority to cancel certain spending and tax benefit measures after he has signed them into law. The members claimed that the Act diminished legislative power by changing the "meaning" and "effectiveness" of their vote for appropriations bills. The Court held that the members did not have standing because they alleged no injury to themselves as individuals but rather alleged an abstract, widely dispersed institutional injury from dilution of legislative power. In contrast to *Coleman*, "They have not alleged that they voted for a specific bill, that there were sufficient votes to pass the bill, and that the bill was nonetheless deemed defeated. In the vote on the Act, their votes were given full effect. They simply lost that vote."

POLITICAL QUESTION DOCTRINE

Some issues are political in nature and inappropriate for judicial consideration. Under the separation of powers doctrine, these "political questions" are best resolved by the political branches of government (Congress and the executive branch). The *Baker* test is used to determine whether a case involves a political question and is therefore not "judiciable" [*Baker v. Carr*, 369 U.S. 186 (1962)].

Baker Test

The Court considers five factors:

1. Whether there is a "textually demonstrable constitutional commitment of the issue to a coordinate political department." The Court interprets the Constitution to determine whether it gives to one of the political branches a power that is judicially unreviewable. If it does, then the issue is a political question. For example, Article I, Section 3, clause 6, provides the Senate shall have the sole power to try all impeachments.

2. Whether there is "a lack of judicially discoverable and manageable standards" for resolving the issue. The Court examines the relevant constitutional provision to determine if it sets out criteria for assessing the plaintiff's legal claim. If it does not, then the issue is a political question.

3. Whether deciding the issue requires "an initial policy determination of a kind clearly for nonjudicial discretion." The Court considers whether it would have to determine the wisdom of any policy. If it would, then the issue is a political question.

4. Whether judicial determination of the issue would express "lack of the respect due" coordinate branches of government. If it would, then the issue is a political question.

5. Whether judicial determination of the issue would result in embarrassing "multifarious pronouncements by various departments" on one question. The Court considers whether the political branches have made any "pronouncements" on the issue, and whether a judicial determination would cause potential embarrassment because it would be inconsistent with those "pronouncements." If so, then the issue is a political question.

Examples

* *Luther v. Borden*, 48 U.S. (7 How.) 1 (1849). The guaranty clause of Article IV, Section 4, provides, "The United States shall guarantee to every State in this Union a Republican Form of Government."

In the 1840s, Rhode Island did not have a state constitution and governed under a charter granted by King Charles II in 1663. In 1841, a constitution was proposed and ratified, but the existing government passed a law to prohibit the constitution from going into effect. In 1842, Sheriff Luther Borden, acting under the charter government, broke into the house of Election Commissioner Martin Luther to search for evidence of illegal participation in elections under the new constitution. Luther sued Borden for trespassing, alleging that Borden acted under orders of an unconstitutional government because the charter government was not a republican form of government and violated the guaranty clause. The Court held the case posed a political question because the Constitution committed decision of the issue to Congress. The Court explained, "Under this article of the Constitution it rests with Congress to decide what government is the established one in a State. For as the United States guarantee to each State a republican government, Congress must necessarily decide what government is established in the State before it can determine whether it is republican or not." The Court also noted a lack of judicially discoverable and manageable standards for resolving the issue.

- *Pacific States Telephone & Telegraph Co. v. Oregon*, 223 U.S. 118 (1912). Oregon amended its constitution to authorize amendment of its constitution and enactment of laws by the method known as voter initiative and referendum. Using voter initiative, a law taxing certain classes of corporations was passed. The Pacific States Telephone & Telegraph Company, an Oregon corporation, was assessed a tax. Oregon sued the corporation to enforce payment of the tax. The corporation's defense was that the voter initiative process violated the right to a republican form of government guaranteed by Article IV, Section 4, of the U.S. Constitution. The Court held the case posed a political question, "[a]s the issues presented, in their very essence, are, and have long since by this court been, definitely determined to be political and governmental, and embraced within the scope of the powers conferred upon Congress, and not, therefore, within the reach of judicial power."

- *Coleman v. Miller*, 307 U.S. 433 (1939). In 1924, Congress proposed an amendment to the constitution known as the Child

Labor Amendment. In 1925, the Legislature of Kansas adopted a resolution rejecting the proposed amendment. In 1937, a resolution known as "Senate Concurrent Resolution No. 3" was introduced in the Senate of Kansas ratifying the proposed amendment. Senators who voted against the resolution sued. They alleged that the proposed amendment lost its vitality through lapse of time, and could not be ratified by the Kansas legislature in 1937. Nearly thirteen years elapsed between the proposal in 1924 and the ratification in 1937. When proposing an amendment, Congress may fix a reasonable time for ratification, but no time limitation was provided in this case. The senators claimed that, in the absence of a limitation by Congress, the Court should decide what a reasonable time is for ratification. The Court held this issue was a nonjusticiable political question because of a lack of judicially discoverable and manageable standards for resolving the issue. The Court explained, "Where are to be found the criteria for such a judicial determination? None are to be found in Constitution or statute." The question of a reasonable time would involve "an appraisal of a great variety of relevant conditions, political, social and economic, which can hardly be said to be within the appropriate range of evidence receivable in a court of justice." These questions are "political and not justiciable. They can be decided by the Congress."

- *Baker v. Carr*, 369 U.S. 186 (1962). A 1901 Tennessee apportionment statute described the manner of apportioning senators and representatives among the state's ninety-five counties. Between 1901 and 1961, Tennessee experienced substantial growth and redistribution of its population. Certain Tennessee citizens alleged that the statute violated the equal protection clause because it apportioned senators and representatives "arbitrarily and capriciously," debasing their votes. The Court held the issue was justiciable, and not a political question. The Court explained, "The question here is the consistency of state action with the Federal Constitution. We have no question decided, or to be decided, by a political branch of government coequal with this Court. Nor do we risk embarrassment of our government abroad, or grave disturbance at home if we take issue with Tennessee as to the constitutionality of her action here challenged. Nor need the appellants, in order to succeed in this action, ask the Court to enter upon policy determinations for which judicially manageable standards are lacking. Judicial standards under the Equal Protection Clause are well developed and familiar, and it has been open to courts since the enactment of the Fourteenth Amendment to determine, if on the particular facts they must, that a discrimination reflects no policy, but simply arbitrary and capricious action."

- *Powell v. McCormack*, 395 U.S. 486 (1969). Article I, Section 5, provides that each house of Congress shall be the judge of the "Qualifications of its own Members." Article II, Section 2, provides age, citizenship, and residence requirements for members. In 1966, Adam Clayton Powell, Jr. was duly elected to serve in the House of Representatives, but the House refused to seat him because of a subcommittee report that he had deceived House authorities about travel expenses. Powell sued, claiming that the House excluded him unconstitutionally because all parties agreed he met the age, citizenship, and residence qualifications of Article II, Section 2. Defendants argued the case posed a political question because Article I, Section 5, was a "textually demonstrable commitment" of the issue to Congress. The Court held the issue was justiciable, and not a political question, because Article I, Section 5, gives the House power to judge only whether elected members possess the age, citizenship, and residence qualifications of Article II, Section 2, which Powell met. The Court explained, "the Constitution leaves the House without authority to exclude any person, duly elected by his constituents, who meets all the requirements for membership expressly prescribed in the Constitution," and Article I, Section 5, "is at most a 'textually demonstrable commitment' to Congress to judge only the qualifications expressly set forth in the Constitution" (the age, citizenship, and residence qualifications).

- *Goldwater v. Carter*, 444 U.S. 996 (1979). When President Carter announced that he planned to terminate a mutual defense treaty with Taiwan without the Senate's consent, several senators sued for injunctive relief. The Constitution empowers the president to make treaties with the advice and consent of two-thirds of the senators present, but it is silent as to the Senate's participation in the termination of a treaty. Senator Goldwater argued that termination of a treaty requires approval of two-thirds of the Senate.

Justice Rehnquist, writing for a plurality of four justices, said the case presented a nonjusticiable political question because of "the absence of any constitutional provision governing the termination of a treaty" (i.e., a lack of judicially discoverable and manageable standards). Also, the case involved "the authority of the President in the conduct of our country's foreign relations and the extent to which the Senate or the Congress is authorized to negate the action of the President."

- *Davis v. Bandemer*, 478 U.S. 109 (1986). Indiana Democrats sued state officials, alleging that a reapportionment plan constituted a political gerrymander intended to disadvantage Democrats, and that the particular district lines that were drawn and the mix of single-member and multimember districts violated Democrats' equal protection rights. The Court held that the political gerrymandering claim was justiciable, and not a political question. The Court explained, "Disposition of this question does not involve us in a matter more properly decided by a coequal branch of our Government. There is no risk of foreign or domestic disturbance, and in light of our cases since Baker we are not persuaded that there are no judicially discernible and manageable standards by which political gerrymander cases are to be decided."

- *Nixon v. United States*, 506 U.S. 224 (1993). Article I, Section 3, clause 6, the impeachment trial clause, provides, "The Senate shall have the sole Power to try all Impeachments." A former chief judge of the United States District Court was impeached in a proceeding during which the Senate used a committee to take testimony and gather evidence. The former judge sought a declaratory judgment that the Senate's failure to give a full evidentiary hearing before the entire Senate violated its constitutional duty to "try" all impeachments. The Court held that the issue was a nonjusticiable political question because the language of the impeachment trial clause demonstrates a textual commitment of impeachment to the Senate. The Court explained, "The commonsense meaning of the word 'sole' is that the Senate alone shall have authority to determine whether an individual should be acquitted or convicted." And, the word "try" in the impeachment trial clause "lacks sufficient precision to afford any judicially manageable standard of review." Based on the variety of definitions of "try," "we cannot say that the Framers used the word 'try' as an implied limitation on the method by which the Senate might proceed in trying impeachments."

SOVEREIGN IMMUNITY
AND THE ELEVENTH AMENDMENT

Background

When the Constitution was ratified, English law provided that the Crown could not be sued in its own courts without its consent, because the King was sovereign. No court could have jurisdiction or power over the King.

When the states ratified the Constitution, they surrendered a portion of their sovereign immunity by consenting to suits brought by other states or the federal government. So, one state can sue another state, and the federal government can sue a state. However, as sovereign entities, states maintained their immunity from private suits.

Then *Chisholm v. Georgia*, 2 Dall. 419 (1793), was decided, a decision that "fell upon the country with a profound shock" [1 C. Warren, The Supreme Court in United States History 96 (rev. ed. 1926)]. *Chisholm* held that citizens of one state could sue another state in federal court. This holding placed state sovereign immunity in peril. So, Congress passed the Eleventh Amendment to reverse *Chisholm*.

The Eleventh Amendment provides, "The Judicial power of the United States shall not be construed to extend to any suit in law or equity, commenced or prosecuted against one of the United States by Citizens of another State, or by Citizens or Subjects of any Foreign State."

The Eleventh Amendment addressed only the concerns raised by *Chisholm*. Hence, "the Eleventh Amendment does not define the scope of the States' sovereign immunity; it is but one particular exemplification of that immunity" [*Federal Maritime Commission v. South Carolina State Ports Authority*, 535 U.S. 743, 753 (2002)]. This is because "sovereign immunity derives not from the Eleventh Amendment but from the structure of the original Constitution itself" [*Alden v. Maine*, 527 U.S. 706, 728]. Thus, the Court "has repeatedly held that the sovereign immunity enjoyed by the States extends beyond the literal text of the Eleventh Amendment" [*Federal Maritime Commission v. South Carolina State Ports Authority*, 535 U.S. 743, 754 (2002)].

Rule

The Eleventh Amendment bars private suits against a state in a federal court unless the state waives immunity, a federal statute overrides the state's immunity, or the suit is against a state officer to enjoin violations of federal law.

Private Suits

The Eleventh Amendment bars private parties from suing states in federal court without their consent. The text of the Eleventh Amendment bars only citizens of another state or citizens of a foreign state from suing a state in federal court without its consent [*Ex Parte State of New York*, 256 U.S. 490 (1921)]. But the Court has held the Eleventh Amendment also bars suits by citizens against their own state [*Hans v. Louisiana*, 134 U.S. 1 (1890)], by Indian tribes [*Blatchford v. Native Village of Noatak*, 501 U.S. 775 (1991)], by foreign nations [*Principality of Monaco v. Mississippi*, 292 U.S. 313 (1934)], and by federal corporations [*Smith v. Reeves*, 178 U.S. 436 (1900)]. And, though the text of the Eleventh Amendment speaks only about suits in law or equity, the Court has held the Eleventh Amendment also bars admiralty suits [*Ex Parte New York*, 256 U.S. 490 (1921)].

However, the Eleventh Amendment does not bar suits by a state against a private person [*Cohens v. Virginia*, 19 U.S. (6 Wheat.) 264 (1821)], a state against another state [*South Dakota v. North Carolina*, 192 U.S. 286 (1904)], a state against the United States [*United States v. Mississippi*, 380 U.S. 128 (1965)], or the United States against a state [*United States v. Texas*, 143 U.S. 621 (1892)]. Also, the Eleventh Amendment does not bar Supreme Court appellate jurisdiction over cases brought against states that arise from state courts [*McKesson Corporation v. Division of Alcoholic Beverages and Tobacco, Department of Business Regulation of Florida*, 496 U.S. 18 (1990)].

State Defendant (Protecting State Treasury)

The Eleventh Amendment bars private suits in federal court against a state or state agency. The Eleventh Amendment also bars a suit against a state officer in his "official capacity" if money damages will be paid from the state treasury [*Ford Motor Co. v. Department of Treasury of the State of Indiana*, 323 U.S. 459 (1945) (barring a suit for return of improperly collected state taxes); *Kentucky v. Graham*, 473 U.S. 159 (1985)]. Similarly, the Eleventh Amendment bars a suit against a state officer for an injunction that orders retroactive payment of money damages for past injuries if the money is to be paid from the state treasury [*Edelman v. Jordan*, 415 U.S. 651 (1974) (invalidating an injunction that ordered retroactive payment of past-due welfare checks)]. The Eleventh Amendment bars suits against state officers in federal court for prospective injunctive relief where the relief sought is the functional equivalent of a quiet title action [*Idaho v. Coeur d'Alene Tribe of Idaho*, 521 U.S. 261 (1997) (holding a suit by the Coeur d'Alene Tribe, alleging ownership of submerged lands of Lake Coeur d'Alene and various rivers and streams, was barred because it would "diminish, even extinguish, the State's control over a vast reach of lands and waters long deemed by the State to be an integral part of its territory," and "if the Tribe were to prevail, Idaho's sovereign interest in its lands and waters would be affected in a degree fully as intrusive as almost any conceivable retroactive levy upon funds in its Treasury")]. Finally, the Eleventh Amendment bars a suit against a state officer to enjoin violations of state law [*Pennhurst State School and Hospital v. Halderman*, 465 U.S. 89 (1984)].

However, the Eleventh Amendment does not bar suits against a state's political subdivisions such as counties [*Lincoln County v. Luning*, 133 U.S. 529 (1890)], municipal corporations, and local school boards [*Mt. Healthy City School District Board of Education v. Doyle*, 429 U.S. 274 (1977)]. The Eleventh Amendment does not bar a suit against a state officer in his "official capacity" to enjoin violations of federal law [*Ex Parte Young*, 209 U.S. 123 (1908) (allowing prospective injunctive relief)]. Such suits are allowed, even if complying with the injunction will require money to be paid from the state treasury in the future, because the relief is prospective, not retroactive [*Graham v. Richardson*, 403 U.S. 365 (1971)]. For example, if a state official acts in bad faith in failing to comply with an injunction, a federal court may impose attorney fees [*Hutto v. Finney*, 437 U.S. 678 (1978)]. Finally, the Eleventh Amendment does not bar a suit against a state official in his "personal capacity" if money damages will be paid from the officer's own pocket, even if the conduct was part of his official duties [*Scheuer v. Rhodes*, 416 U.S. 232 (1974)].

Federal Court

The Eleventh Amendment bars private suits against states in federal court. However, the Court has held that "sovereign immunity" bars private suits against a state in its own state court [*Alden v. Maine*,

527 U.S. 706 (1999)], and private complaints filed against a state with a federal administrative agency [*Federal Maritime Commission v. South Carolina State Ports Authority*, 535 U.S. 743 (2002)].

Neither the Eleventh Amendment nor sovereign immunity bars a private suit against a state in the court of another state [*Nevada v. Hall*, 440 U.S. 410 (1979)].

Waiver

A state can waive its Eleventh Amendment immunity by clearly and expressly consenting to federal court suits against the state [*Port Authority Trans-Hudson Corp. v. Feeney*, 495 U.S. 299 (1990) (finding express waiver of Eleventh Amendment immunity where state law provided that it consented to suits "of any form or nature at law, in equity or otherwise," and that venue shall be "within a county or a judicial district, established by one of said States or by the United States")]. A state waives its Eleventh Amendment immunity when it voluntarily removes a case to federal court and invokes the federal court's jurisdiction [*Lapides v. Board of Regents of University System of Georgia*, 535 U.S. 613 (2002)].

However, a state statute authorizing the state to be sued "in any court of competent jurisdiction" is only a general waiver of sovereign immunity and is insufficient to waive Eleventh Amendment immunity because it does not expressly authorize federal court suits [*Kennecott Copper Corp. v. State Tax Commission*, 327 U.S. 573 (1946)]. A "constructive" or "implied" waiver is also insufficient to waive Eleventh Amendment immunity [*College Savings Bank v. Florida Prepaid Postsecondary Education Expense Board*, 527 U.S. 666 (1999) (holding, in a suit against Florida for unfair competition, that Florida did not waive its sovereign immunity merely by engaging in interstate commerce); *Edelman v. Jordan*, 415 U.S. 651 (1974) (holding, in a suit against Illinois over its welfare program, that Illinois did not waive immunity by voluntarily choosing to receive federal funds for its welfare program)]. Finally, a waiver is not implied by a state's failure to plead immunity at the trial level, because a state may raise the Eleventh Amendment as a bar on appeal [*Edelman v. Jordan*, 415 U.S. 651 (1974)].

Congressional Authorization

The Fourteenth Amendment was enacted after the Eleventh Amendment, and limits state authority. Section 5 of the Fourteenth

Amendment gives Congress the power to enforce the Fourteenth Amendment by passing appropriate legislation. Thus, Congress may override Eleventh Amendment immunity and authorize private suits against states or state officials in federal court if it acts pursuant to Section 5 of the Fourteenth Amendment [*Fitzpatrick v. Bitzer*, 427 U.S. 445 (1976) (holding that state governments may be sued for violating Title VII of the 1964 Civil Rights Act, which prevents employment discrimination, because the Act was enacted by Congress pursuant to § 5 of the Fourteenth Amendment and overrides Eleventh Amendment immunity); *Hutto v. Finney*, 437 U.S. 678 (1978) (holding that successful plaintiffs in civil rights cases may sue a state for attorney fees "as part of the costs" because Congress, acting pursuant to § 5 of the Fourteenth Amendment, enacted the Civil Rights Attorney's Fees Awards Act of 1976, overriding Eleventh Amendment immunity); *Quern v. Jordan*, 440 U.S. 332 (1979) (holding that 42 U.S.C. § 1983, the basic civil rights law enacted pursuant to Section 5 of the Fourteenth Amendment, does not override Eleventh Amendment immunity because "§ 1983 does not explicitly and by clear language indicate on its face an intent to sweep away the immunity of the States")].

However, Congress cannot use any other provision of the Constitution, other than Section 5 of the Fourteenth Amendment, to override Eleventh Amendment immunity [*Seminole Tribe of Florida v. Florida*, 517 U.S. 44 (1996) (holding that Congress cannot use the Indian commerce clause to override Eleventh Amendment immunity); *Florida Prepaid Postsecondary Education Expense Board v.College Savings Bank*, 527 U.S. 627 (1999) (holding that Congress cannot use the Trademark Remedy Clarification Act to override Eleventh Amendment immunity)].

ABSTENTION DOCTRINE

Under the abstention doctrine, a federal court may decline or postpone exercising jurisdiction where the federal constitutional issue rests on an unsettled interpretation of state law. The federal court defers to the state court and gives it a chance to determine uncertain issues of state law, because the state court may interpret the state law in a way that would avoid or modify the necessity of deciding a federal constitutional question. Thus, abstention avoids unnecessary friction in federal-state relations, interference with important state functions, tentative decisions on questions of state law, and premature constitutional adjudication. Abstention assures that federal courts will decide a constitutional issue only if there is no other basis on which the case can be decided.

However, abstention is not appropriate where the challenged state statute is clear and unambiguous [*New Motor Vehicle Bd. v. Orrin W. Fox Co.*, 439 U.S. 96 (1978); *Harman v. Forssenius*, 380 U.S. 528 (1965)].

- *Railroad Commission v. Pullman Co.*, 312 U.S. 496 (1941). In parts of Texas where railroad passenger traffic was light, trains carried only one sleeping car known as a "Pullman sleeper." These trains, unlike trains having two or more sleepers, did not have a Pullman conductor. Instead, a Pullman porter was in charge of the sleeper, and he was subject to the train conductor's control. Pullman porters were black, and conductors were white. The Texas Railroad Commission ordered that no sleeping car shall be operated on any line of railroad in Texas unless it was in the charge of a Pullman conductor. This order increased job opportunities for whites (conductors) and decreased them for blacks (porters). The Pullman Company and railroads sued in a federal district court to enjoin the commission's order. The commission claimed the order was justified because of a Texas statute that empowered the commission to adopt regulations to prevent "unjust discrimination" and to prevent "any and all other abuses" in the conduct of railroads.

  The Court held that federal courts should abstain from exercising jurisdiction until the Texas Supreme Court interpreted the scope of the Texas statute, because if the statute did not authorize the commission's order, "there is an end of the litigation; the constitutional issue does not arise." The Court explained, "Whether arrangements pertaining to the staffs of Pullman cars are covered by the Texas concept of 'discrimination' is far from clear. What practices of the railroads may be deemed to be 'abuses' subject to the Commission's correction is equally doubtful. Reading the Texas statutes and the Texas decisions as outsiders without special competence in Texas law, we would have little confidence in our independent judgment regarding the application of that law to the present situation."

ADEQUATE AND INDEPENDENT STATE GROUNDS

The Court's only power over state court judgments is to correct them to the extent they incorrectly judge federal rights. So, when the Court reviews state court judgments it reviews only federal questions, not state law questions. Thus, when a state court decides a state law question that is sufficient to support the outcome of the case, regardless of how the federal question is decided, the Court will not review the state court judgment. The federal question becomes moot, and the Court's opinion on the federal question would be merely advisory. Hence, the Court will not review a state court judgment that rests on "adequate and independent state grounds" [*Herb v. Pitcairn*, 324 U.S. 117 (1945)].

Adequate State Grounds

The state court judgment must rest on a "fair or substantial basis." If it does not, the Court will review the federal questions [*Lawrence v. State Tax Commission*, 286 U.S. 276 (1932) (holding if the basis is "unsubstantial, constitutional obligations may not be thus avoided")]. For example, Supreme Court review is not prevented where the state court judgment rests on a new rule for appellate procedure that was created during the litigant's case and bars the litigant [*NAACP v. Alabama ex rel. Patterson*, 357 U.S. 449 (1958) (holding that new procedural requirements cannot thwart review in the U.S. Supreme Court applied for by those who rely on prior decisions and seek vindication of their federal constitutional rights in state courts)].

Independent State Grounds

The state court judgment must clearly indicate that it is based on independent state grounds. Independent state grounds exist where a state court holds that a state law violates the state constitution, and provides an alternative, independent holding that the state law violates the U.S. Constitution; even if the Court disagrees with the state court's interpretation of the U.S. Constitution, it cannot reverse the state court judgment that a state law violates the state constitution. Independent state grounds also exist where a state court is presented with state and federal grounds for a decision but decides the case only on state grounds and chooses not to review the federal ground [*Wood v. Chesborough*, 228 U.S. 672 (1913)].

Independent state grounds do not exist where a state court holds that a state law is valid under the state and federal constitutions. If the Court disagrees with the state court's interpretation of the U.S. Constitution, it will reverse the state court's judgment regardless of its interpretation of the state law. Nor do independent state grounds exist where a state court holds that a state law violates the state and federal constitutions but does not intend its decision to rest independently on the state ground [*Delaware v. Prouse*, 440 U.S. 648 (1979) (holding the Court had jurisdiction, even though the Delaware Supreme Court held an automobile stop and detention violated the Delaware and U.S. Constitutions, because the Delaware court's opinion showed it did not intend to rest its decision independently on the state constitution, but instead rested on its view of the reach of the Fourth and Fourteenth Amendments)].

Ambiguous Cases

If a state court judgment does not clearly indicate that its decision rested on an adequate and independent state ground, the Court will exercise jurisdiction and review the federal questions [*Michigan v. Long*, 463 U.S. 1032 (1983) (holding "when the adequacy and independence of any possible state law ground is not clear from the face of the opinion, we will accept as the most reasonable explanation that the state court decided the case the way it did because it believed that federal law required it to do so")].

CHAPTER 2

State Action Doctrine

Generally, the Constitution protects individual rights and liberties against actions by federal, state, and local government (i.e., "state action"), but not against actions by private individuals. For example, the First Amendment protects freedom of speech against interference by federal, state, and local government, but not against interference by private individuals. Also, the Fourteenth Amendment applies only to state action, and not to private action [*U.S. v. Morrison*, 529 U.S. 598 (2000)]. The only provision of the Constitution that directly regulates private action is the Thirteenth Amendment, which prohibits the practice of slavery anywhere in the United States, whether by government or a private individual [*Jones v. Alfred H. Mayer Co.*, 392 U.S. 409 (1968) (holding that Congress can prohibit private racial discrimination under the Thirteenth Amendment to eliminate the "badges and incidents" of slavery)].

There are two exceptions to the general rule that the Constitution protects individual rights and liberties only against actions by federal, state, and local government: the "public function" exception, and the "state involvement" exception. In each case, private action constitutes state action, and must comply with the Constitution.

GENERAL RULE: GOVERNMENT ACTION REQUIRED

Government action includes, for example, enactments by federal, state, and local legislative bodies; rules and decisions of government agencies at all levels; actions by corporations that are created and controlled by the government to further governmental objectives; and actions by government officials at all levels acting in their official capacity, even if their conduct is not authorized by law. All of these government actions are state action and must comply with the Constitution.

- *Nixon v. Herndon*, 273 U.S. 536 (1927) ("White Primary Case"). A Texas statute provided that "in no event shall a negro be eligible to participate in a Democratic party primary election held in the State of Texas." Nixon was a black man, a citizen of the United States and Texas, and qualified to vote except for the statute. The judges of elections applied the statute and denied Nixon the right to vote in a Texas primary election because he was black. The Court invalidated the statute under the Fourteenth Amendment's equal protection clause. Under the statute, Nixon was shut out from the primary election "by the command of the State itself, speaking by the voice of its chosen representatives" [*Nixon v. Condon*, 286 U.S. 73 (1932), discussing *Nixon v. Herndon*]. So, there was state action.

- *Screws v. United States*, 325 U.S. 91 (1945). Screws, a sheriff of Baker County, Georgia, a policeman, and a special deputy arrested Robert Hall, a thirty-year-old black man, for theft of a tire. They handcuffed him and drove him to the courthouse. As Hall exited the car at the courthouse, the officers began beating him with their fists and a solid-bar blackjack about eight inches long and weighing two pounds. After Hall was knocked to the ground, still handcuffed, the officers continued beating him from fifteen to thirty minutes until he was unconscious. Hall died hours later without regaining consciousness. The Court held the officers were "state actors" and their actions were state action. Although they exceeded their authority under state law, they were performing official duties under "color of law." The Court explained, "Here the state officers were authorized to make an arrest and to take such steps as were necessary to make the arrest effective. They acted without authority only in the sense that they used excessive force in making the arrest effective." When officers perform their official duties their actions are state action "whether they hew to the line of their authority or overstep it."

- *Polk County v. Dodson*, 454 U.S. 312 (1981). Iowa employed a public defender to represent an indigent criminal defendant in an appeal of a conviction. The defendant sued, claiming the public defender failed to represent him adequately because she sought to withdraw as counsel on the ground that defendant's claims were legally frivolous. The Court held that a public defender is not a state actor and does not act under color of state law when performing the traditional functions of counsel to a criminal defendant. The public defender's function was "in no way dependent on state authority." Except for the source of payment, the relationship between public defender and defendant "became identical to that existing between any other lawyer and client." This is essentially a "private function, traditionally filled by retained counsel, for which state office and authority are not needed." In fact, a public defender's responsibility is to *oppose* the government in adversary litigation while exercising independent judgment on behalf of the client. Finally, "a public defender is not amenable to administrative direction in the same sense as other employees of the State."

- *West v. Atkins*, 487 U.S. 42 (1988). North Carolina contracted with a private physician to provide medical services to inmates at a state prison on a part-time basis. An inmate sued the physician, claiming the physician gave inadequate treatment for a leg injury. The Court held the physician's actions in treating the inmate were state action, under color of state law, because the state has an obligation under the Eighth Amendment and state law to provide adequate medical care to inmates, and it delegated that function to the physician.

- *Lebron v. National Railroad Passenger Corp.*, 513 U.S. 374 (1995). Mr. Lebron wanted to display, on a billboard at Amtrak's Penn Station in New York City, an advertisement that criticized Coors beer company's political activities. Amtrak refused to allow the advertisement because political advertising was not allowed at Penn Station. The Court held that Amtrak is part of the government for state action purposes and must comply with the Constitution. Although the statute creating Amtrak declares it "will not be an agency or establishment of the United States government," the government created Amtrak to further the government objective of providing railroad passenger service and retained authority to appoint a majority of Amtrak directors.

"PUBLIC FUNCTION" EXCEPTION

If a private entity performs an activity that is "traditionally exclusively reserved to the State," for example operating an election system, or governing a town, the activity is a "public function" constituting state action. So the private entity must comply with the Constitution. However, if a private entity merely performs an activity that serves the public, for example operating a shopping center, or a school for special education, the activity is not a "public function," and there is no state action. Private action is a "public function" only if it has traditionally exclusively been done by the government.

- *Nixon v. Condon*, 286 U.S. 73 (1932) ("White Primary Case"). After *Nixon v. Herndon*, 273 U.S. 536 (1927), Texas enacted a new statute that provided "every political party in this State through its State Executive Committee shall have the power to prescribe the qualifications of its own members and shall in its own way determine who shall be qualified to vote." The State Executive Committee of the Democratic Party then adopted a resolution that "all white democrats" could vote in the Democratic primary election. The judges of elections followed the resolution and denied Nixon the right to vote in a primary election because he was black. The Court declared this unconstitutional under the Fourteenth Amendment's equal protection clause. Although the Democratic Party was a voluntary association, the committee's power to exclude blacks came from the Texas statute, not from any inherent power that voluntary associations have to determine their own membership. So the committee became an organ of the state, a governmental instrument, and a delegate of the state's power. The committee's action was therefore state action.

- *Smith v. Allwright*, 321 U.S. 649 (1944). Texas statutes authorized the Democratic Party of Texas, a private association, to hold primary elections and decide who may participate. The party held a primary election and purposefully excluded blacks from voting ("white primary" system). The Court held there was state action. The Constitution protects the right to vote in a primary election without discrimination by the state because primaries are part of the "machinery" for choosing state and national officials. And this right "is not to be nullified by a State through casting its electoral process in a form which permits a private organization to practice racial discrimination in the election." Although no Texas law directed the exclusion of blacks from voting, an extensive statutory system controlled primary elections and authorized the Democratic Party of Texas to hold them. Thus the Democratic Party of Texas was "an agency of the State in so far as it determines the participants in a primary election." So the Democratic Party of Texas performed a public function constituting state action.

- *Marsh v. Alabama*, 326 U.S. 501 (1946). A private corporation, Gulf Shipbuilding, owned and governed a town, Chickasaw, Alabama. The town had "all the characteristics of any other American town," including "residential buildings, streets, a system of sewers, a sewage disposal plant and a 'business block' on which business places are situated." The corporation refused to allow a Jehovah's Witness to distribute religious literature in the "company town," thus raising a First Amendment issue. The Court held that owning and governing a town is a public function, constituting state action. So the corporation had to comply with the Constitution.

- *Terry v. Adams*, 345 U.S. 461 (1953). The Jaybird Democratic Association, a private group, held a primary election each year and purposefully excluded blacks from voting ("white primary" system). The Jaybird primary elections were not governed by state laws and did not use state election machinery or funds. But for more than fifty years successful Jaybird candidates had invariably run and won, usually unopposed, in the official Democratic primaries and general elections that followed.

  Without a majority opinion, the Court held there was state action. Justice Black wrote "The only election that has counted in this Texas county for more than fifty years has been that held by the Jaybirds from which Negroes were excluded." The Democratic primary and general election were no more than "perfunctory ratifiers" of the choice that had already been made in the Jaybird elections from which blacks were excluded. So "It is immaterial that the state does not control that part of this elective process which it leaves for the Jaybirds to manage." The "combined Jaybird-Democratic-general election machinery has deprived these petitioners of their right to vote on account of their race and color."

- *Evans v. Newton*, 382 U.S. 296 (1966). A testamentary trust in the will of Senator Augustus Bacon established a park in Macon, Georgia. The trust required that the park be used only by white persons, and designated the city as the trustee. To avoid desegregating the park, the city resigned as trustee and requested appointment of private trustees. The Court held that operating a park was a public function constituting state action, even if done by a private entity, because a park "traditionally serves the community." So the park had to comply with the Constitution.

- *Jackson v. Metropolitan Edison Co.*, 419 U.S. 345 (1974). A privately owned electric utility company terminated a woman's service without a hearing. The woman claimed the utility performed a public function that constituted state action, and therefore should have provided due process before terminating her service. The Court held that the utility company did not perform a public function because there have long been private utility companies, so running a utility is "not traditionally the exclusive prerogative of the State." Thus, the utility did not have to provide due process.

- *Hudgens v. National Labor Relations Board*, 424 U.S. 507 (1976). Striking union members picketed in front of their employer's store in a privately owned shopping center. The shopping center's manager threatened them with arrest for criminal trespass if they did not leave. The Court held that operating a privately owned shopping center was not a public function. So the First Amendment does not create a right to use privately owned shopping centers for speech.

- *Flagg Brothers, Inc. v. Brooks*, 436 U.S. 149 (1978). A "self-help" provision of the New York Uniform Commercial Code permitted, but did not compel, the private sale by a warehouseman of goods entrusted to him for storage if storage fees were not paid. The Court held that a warehouseman's proposed private sale of goods, as permitted by the Code, was not "state action." The Court explained that "settlement of disputes between debtors and creditors is not traditionally an exclusive public function." And other remedies for settlement of such disputes remained available to the parties. For example, the debtor could have asked the creditor to waive his right to sell the goods, or sought to replevy the goods. Also, there was no allegation that any public officials participated in the proposed sale.

- *Rendell-Baker v. Kohn*, 457 U.S. 830 (1982). A private school for special education received most of its funding from the state and was regulated by the state. The school fired a teacher because of her speech activities. The Court held the decision to fire the teacher, made by private management, was not state action. So the school did not have to provide due process. The Court explained that the legislative policy "in no way makes these services the exclusive province of the State. Indeed, the Court of Appeals noted that until recently the State had not undertaken to provide education for students who could not be served by traditional public schools."

"STATE INVOLVEMENT" EXCEPTION

Private action constitutes "state action," and must comply with the Constitution, if the government authorized, encouraged, or facilitated the unconstitutional conduct [*Reitman v. Mulkey*, 387 U.S. 369 (1967) (holding a state must have "significantly involved itself with invidious discriminations" for there to be state action)].

- *Shelley v. Kraemer*, 334 U.S. 1 (1948). A white property owner attempted to sell to a black person property that was subject to a covenant that prohibited sales to racial minorities. Persons with an interest in the racially restrictive covenant sued to enforce it and enjoin the sale. The Court held that although the covenant was a private contractual agreement, judicial action is state action. So a court order to enforce the covenant would be state action because the government, through the judicial branch, would facilitate discrimination. Thus, the courts cannot enforce racially restrictive covenants.

- *Burton v. Wilmington Parking Authority*, 365 U.S. 715 (1961). A privately owned restaurant, Eagle Coffee Shoppe, leased space in a government parking facility, the Wilmington Parking Authority. The land and building were publicly owned, and public funds were used for building maintenance. The restaurant denied service to a person because he was black. The parking authority could have but did not require the restaurant to serve all persons.

The Court held that the restaurant's actions were state action. The Court explained, "It cannot be doubted that the peculiar relationship of the restaurant to the parking facility in which it is located confers on each an incidental variety of mutual benefits. Guests of the restaurant are afforded a convenient place to park their automobiles, even if they cannot enter the restaurant directly from the parking area. Similarly, its convenience for diners may well provide additional demand for the Authority's parking facilities." The Court concluded, "The State has so far insinuated itself into a position of interdependence with Eagle that it must be recognized as a joint participant in the challenged activity, which, on that account, cannot be considered to have been so 'purely private' as to fall without the scope of the Fourteenth Amendment."

- *Reitman v. Mulkey*, 387 U.S. 369 (1967). A voter initiative amended the California Constitution (Article I, § 26) by repealing a law that prohibited private racial discrimination. The Court invalidated the amendment because it was state action. The Court explained, "Here we are dealing with a provision which does not just repeal an existing law forbidding private racial discriminations. Section 26 was intended to authorize, and does authorize, racial discrimination in the housing market. The right to discriminate is now one of the basic policies of the State. The California Supreme Court believes that the section will significantly encourage and involve the State in private discriminations. We have been presented with no persuasive considerations indicating that these judgments should be overturned."

- *Moose Lodge Number 107 v. Irvis*, 407 U.S. 163 (1972). A private club, the Moose Lodge, restricted membership to whites. A black guest of a club member was refused service at the club's dining room and bar solely because of his race. He claimed the licensing of the club to serve liquor by the Pennsylvania Liquor Control Board amounted to such state involvement with the club's activities as to make its discriminatory practices state action. The Court held the club's actions were not state action. The Court explained that the regulatory scheme of the Liquor Control Board "cannot be said to in any way foster or encourage racial discrimination. Nor can it be said to make the State in any realistic sense a partner or even a joint venturer in the club's enterprise." So "the regulatory scheme enforced by the Pennsylvania Liquor Control Board does not sufficiently implicate the State in the discriminatory guest policies of Moose Lodge to make the latter 'state action.'" The Court distinguished *Burton* by noting "while Eagle was a public restaurant in a public building, Moose Lodge is a private social club in a private building."

- *Jackson v. Metropolitan Edison Co.*, 419 U.S. 345 (1974). A customer sued a heavily regulated and privately owned utility, Metropolitan Edison Co., seeking damages because her electric service was terminated without notice, a hearing, and an opportunity to pay any amounts due. The Court held there was no state action. The Court explained, "The mere fact that a business is subject to state regulation does not by itself convert its action into that of the State for purposes of the Fourteenth Amendment. Nor does the fact that the regulation is extensive and detailed, as in the case of most public utilities, do so." The Court concluded, "All of petitioner's arguments taken together show no more than that Metropolitan was a heavily regulated, privately owned utility, enjoying at least a partial monopoly in the providing of electrical service within its territory, and that it elected to terminate service to petitioner in a manner which the Pennsylvania Public Utility Commission found permissible under state law. Under our decision this is not sufficient to connect the State of Pennsylvania with respondent's action so as to make the latter's conduct attributable to the State."

- *Lugar v. Edmonson Oil Co.*, 457 U.S. 922 (1982). Edmonson, a creditor, sued a debtor on a debt. Edmonson filed an *ex parte* petition under a Virginia statute, alleging the debtor might dispose of his property to defeat his creditors. This allowed Edmonson to obtain a pretrial writ of attachment against the debtor's property, executed by the County Sheriff. The Court held there was state action because the statutory scheme "obviously is the product of state action," and "a private party's joint participation with state officials in the seizure of disputed property is sufficient to characterize that party as a 'state actor' for purposes of the Fourteenth Amendment." So the attachment procedure had to satisfy due process.

- *Rendell-Baker v. Kohn*, 457 U.S. 830 (1982). A private school for special education received most of its funding from the state and was regulated by the state. The school fired several teachers because of their speech activities. The Court held the decisions to fire the teachers, made by private management, were not state action. So the school did not have to provide due process. The Court explained, "the school's receipt of public funds does not make the discharge decisions acts of the State," and, "the decisions to discharge the petitioners were not compelled or even influenced by any state regulation. Indeed, in contrast to the extensive regulation of the school generally, the various regulators showed relatively little interest in the school's personnel matters."

- *Edmonson v. Leesville Concrete Co.*, 500 U.S. 614 (1991). A black construction worker was injured in a job-site accident at a federal enclave and sued a concrete company for negligence. During voir dire, the private defendant used two of its three peremptory challenges to remove black persons from the prospective jury. The Court held that defendant's use of peremptory challenges was state action. The Court explained, "a private party could not exercise its peremptory challenges absent the overt, significant assistance of the court. The government summons jurors, constrains their freedom of movement, and subjects them to public scrutiny and examination. The party who exercises a challenge invokes the formal authority of the court, which must discharge the prospective juror, thus effecting the 'final and practical denial' of the excluded individual's opportunity to serve on the petit jury. Without the direct and indispensable participation of the judge, who beyond all question is a state actor, the peremptory challenge system would serve no purpose." The Court concluded the government created the "legal framework" governing the challenged conduct, "and in a significant way has involved itself with invidious discrimination."

- *Georgia v. McCollum*, 505 U.S. 42 (1992). White defendants were charged with assaulting two African Americans. Before jury selection began, the prosecution moved to prohibit the defendants from exercising peremptory challenges in a racially discriminatory manner. The trial judge denied the prosecution's motion. The Court reversed and held that a criminal defendant's exercise of peremptory challenges constitutes state action. The Court followed the reasoning of *Edmonson*, and explained, "the defendant in a Georgia criminal case relies on 'governmental assistance and benefits' that are equivalent to those found in the civil context in *Edmonson*." Thus, the Constitution prohibits a criminal defendant from engaging in purposeful discrimination on the ground of race in the exercise of peremptory challenges.

CHAPTER 3

Foreign Affairs

THE PRESIDENT AND CONGRESS SHARE FOREIGN AFFAIRS POWER. HOWEVER, INDIVIDUAL states have no foreign affairs power because foreign affairs power passed directly to the federal government from the sovereign nation of Great Britain [*United States v. Curtiss-Wright Export Corp.*, 299 U.S. 304 (1936)].

EXECUTIVE POWER

The Court has explained the president's power over foreign affairs as follows: "In this vast external realm, with its important, complicated, delicate and manifold problems, the President alone has the power to speak or listen as a representative of the nation. He makes treaties with the advice and consent of the Senate; but he alone negotiates. Into the field of negotiation the Senate cannot intrude; and Congress itself is powerless to invade it. As Marshall said in his great argument of March 7, 1800, in the House of Representatives, 'The President is the sole organ of the nation in its external relations, and its sole representative with foreign nations'" [*United States v. Curtiss-Wright Export Corp.*, 299 U.S. 304 (1936)].

Ambassadors

The president is empowered to appoint ambassadors, public ministers, and consuls with the Senate's advice and consent (U.S. Const.

art. II, § 2), and to receive ambassadors and public ministers as the representative of the United States (U.S. Const. art. II, § 3).

Commander in Chief

The president is the commander in chief of the armed forces (U.S. Const. art. II, § 2). Presidents have used this power to send troops to foreign countries in wars without express congressional approval. However, the Court has not addressed the constitutionality of this since the Civil War [*Prize Cases* 67 U.S. (2 Black) 635 (1863) (holding President Lincoln could impose a blockade on southern states without a congressional declaration of war, because the president is authorized "to use the military and naval forces of the United States in case of invasion by foreign nations, and to suppress insurrection against the government of a State or of the United States")].

A challenge to the president's use of troops in a foreign country is likely to be dismissed as a nonjusticiable political question.

Treaties (Senate Approval Required)

The president is empowered to make treaties with the advice and consent of two-thirds of the senators present (U.S. Const. art. II, § 2).

Treaties are the supreme law of the land, superior to the laws and constitutions of the states, and are binding on the states so long as they are not contrary to the Constitution (e.g., the Bill of Rights) [U.S. Const. art. VI, § 2; *Hauenstein v. Lynham*, 100 U.S. (10 Otto) 483 (1879) (holding a treaty between the United States and Switzerland that allowed aliens to inherit property prevailed over a Virginia law that denied aliens inheritance rights); *Reid v. Covert*, 354 U.S. 1 (1957) (reversing a conviction of a U.S. military dependent who was convicted in Great Britain without a jury trial under a treaty between the United States and Great Britain, because "no agreement with a foreign nation can confer power on the Congress, or on any other branch of government, which is free from the restraints of the Constitution")].

States are prohibited from entering into treaties (U.S. Const. art. I, § 10). Also, the Tenth Amendment, which reserves to the states powers that are not delegated to the federal government, does not limit the president's treaty power because the treaty power is delegated to the federal government [*Missouri v. Holland*, 252 U.S. 416 (1920) (upholding a treaty between the United States and Great Britain protecting migratory birds in danger of extinction, despite Missouri's claim that it interfered with its Tenth Amendment rights)].

"Self-executory" treaties take effect immediately upon ratification. "Executory" treaties require implementing legislation before they take effect [*Whitney v. Robertson*, 124 U.S. 190 (1888)]. Where a "self-executing" treaty conflicts with an act of Congress, the one adopted last in time controls (*Whitney*, "Last Expression of the Sovereign Rule").

Executive Agreements (Senate Approval Not Required)

The president is empowered to make executive agreements with foreign countries without senatorial approval so long as they do not violate the Bill of Rights [*United States v. Pink*, 315 U.S. 203 (1942)]. Executive agreements can be used for any purpose, and they often cover the same subjects as treaties. The agreement is effective when signed by the president and the head of the foreign nation. Executive agreements are the supreme law of the land, superior to the laws and constitutions of the states, and are binding on the states (*Pink*). It is unclear whether an executive agreement can override an earlier act of Congress.

CONGRESSIONAL POWER

Congress is empowered to provide for the common defense; regulate foreign commerce; define and punish piracies and felonies committed on the high seas and offenses against the law of nations; declare war; make rules of war; grant letters of marque and reprisal; raise, support, and regulate an army and navy; and regulate naturalization of aliens (U.S. Const. art. I, § 8).

JUDICIAL POWER

Federal courts are empowered to exercise jurisdiction in all cases arising under the Constitution, the laws of the United States and treaties made, or that shall be made under their authority; in all cases affecting ambassadors, other public ministers, and consuls; in controversies to which the United States shall be a party; and in controversies between a state or citizen thereof and foreign states, citizens, or subjects (U.S. Const. art. III, § 2).

WAR POWER

Congress

Congress has the power to provide for the defense of the United States, declare war, tax and finance expenditures necessary for defense, create and maintain land and naval military forces, regulate the armed forces and militia (i.e., state National Guard units), and make all laws necessary and proper for exercising the war power (U.S. Const. art. I, § 8). Congress may also impose economic regulations during times of war, and even after hostilities have ended, to "remedy the evils" that arise from a war [*Woods v. Cloyd W. Miller Co.*, 333 U.S. 138 (1948) (holding Congress could regulate rent after World War II under the Housing and Rent Act of 1947)].

Executive

The president is the commander in chief of the armed forces (U.S. Const. art. 2, § 2), and may use military force to protect national interests [*Brig Amy Warwick*, 67 U.S. (2 Black) 635 (1863) (holding President Lincoln had the right, during the Civil War, to impose a blockade of ports in possession of the States in rebellion, because "If a war be made by invasion of a foreign nation, the President is not only authorized but bound to resist force by force. He does not initiate the war, but is bound to accept the challenge without waiting for any special legislative authority. And whether the hostile party be a foreign invader, or States organized in rebellion, it is none the less a war"]. The Court has rarely discussed the constitutionality of a president waging war without a congressional declaration of war, partly because of the political question doctrine.

The War Powers Resolution restricts the president's power to involve the United States in foreign controversies without Congress's approval. But the resolution allows the president to send the military into combat without requesting Congress's approval if the United States or one of its territories is attacked (50 U.S.C.A. §§ 1541–1548). The resolution requires the president to (1) consult with Congress, where possible, before introducing troops into hostilities; (2) report to Congress within forty-eight hours after introducing troops into hostilities; and (3) withdraw troops after sixty days unless Congress declares war or authorizes a sixty-day extension. The Court has not decided the constitutionality of the War Powers Resolution, and may consider it a nonjusticiable political question.

CHAPTER 4

Taxing and Spending Powers

"THE CONGRESS SHALL HAVE POWER TO LAY AND COLLECT TAXES, DUTIES, IMPOSTS and Excises, to pay the Debts and provide for the common Defence and general Welfare of the United States" (U.S. Const. art. 1, § 8).

TAXING POWER

Taxes often have an indirect regulatory effect by discouraging the taxed activity. For example, a cigarette tax may discourage smoking. If Congress has the power to regulate the taxed activity directly (e.g., under the commerce clause), the tax's regulatory effect is not a constitutional problem because the tax may be upheld as a "necessary and proper" exercise of Congress's regulatory power [*Veazie Bank v. Fenno*, 75 U.S. (8 Wall.) 533 (1869) (holding constitutional a federal tax on bank notes, even though the tax effectively drove the bank notes out of existence, because Congress had the power to regulate currency through taxation under Article 1, § 8)].

If Congress has no power to regulate the taxed activity directly (a rare occurrence under the Court's expansive interpretation of the commerce clause), the Court determines whether the tax is intended to raise revenue, and thus valid under the taxing power, or whether the tax is intended to punish certain actions, and thus invalid as an unauthorized regulatory measure [McCray v. United States, 195 U.S. 27 (1904) (holding constitutional as a "revenue tax" a ten-cent per pound tax on yellow oleomargarine, even though the corresponding tax on white oleomargarine was only one-fourth of a cent per pound); United States v. Constantine, 296 U.S. 287 (1935) (holding unconstitutional as a "penal tax" a heavy federal tax on liquor dealers not operating in compliance with state laws); Bailey v. Drexel Furniture Co., 259 U.S. 20 (1922) (holding unconstitutional as a "penal tax" a tax imposed on an employer for failing to comply with federal child labor law)].

SPENDING POWER (DOLE TEST)

Congress may attach conditions on the receipt of federal funds. So, spending programs often have an indirect regulatory effect by encouraging certain activity. For example, when Congress grants money to a state on certain conditions, the grant encourages state action.

If Congress has no power to regulate the activity directly (a rare occurrence under the Court's expansive interpretation of the commerce clause), the four-part Dole test applies: (1) the spending must be for the general welfare; (2) conditions must be unambiguous; (3) conditions must be related to the federal interest; and (4) there must be no independent constitutional bar to the grant of funds [South Dakota v. Dole, 483 U.S. 203 (1987)].

General Welfare

The spending must be for the "general welfare" of the public (i.e., for the common good rather than a local purpose). The Court gives Congress substantial deference in determining which expenditures will promote the general welfare, and will uphold Congress's decision unless there is "no reasonable possibility" the challenged legislation falls within the wide range of discretion permitted to Congress [Helvering v. Davis, 301 U.S. 672 (1937) (explaining, "The discretion belongs to Congress, unless the choice is clearly wrong, a display of arbitrary power, not an exercise of judgment")].

Unambiguous Conditions

Congress must express clearly its intent to impose conditions on the grant of federal funds so that the states can knowingly decide whether or not to accept those funds.

* *Pennhurst State School and Hospital v. Halderman*, 451 U.S. 1 (1981). A federal grant program gave states money to provide better care for the developmentally disabled, and included a "bill of rights" provision. The "bill of rights" provision stated that "The treatment, services, and habilitation for a person with developmental disabilities should be designed to maximize the developmental potential of the person and should be provided in the setting that is least restrictive of the person's personal liberty." A state accepted the federal money and was sued for violating the "bill of rights." The Court held, in favor of the state, that the program failed to require that states meet the "bill of rights" as a condition to accepting the federal money. The Court explained that the lack of conditional language in the "bill of rights" provision and the legislative history indicated that "Congress intended to encourage, rather than mandate, the provision of better services to the developmentally disabled."

Related Conditions

Conditions on federal grants might be illegitimate if they are unrelated to the federal interest in particular national projects or programs.

* *South Dakota v. Dole*, 483 U.S. 203 (1987). A presidential commission appointed to study alcohol-related accidents and fatalities on the nation's highways concluded that the lack of uniformity in the states' drinking ages created an incentive to drink and drive because young persons commute to border states where the drinking age is lower. To encourage states to adopt a uniform, minimum drinking age, Congress passed a statute conditioning the states' receipt of a portion of federal highway funds on adoption of a minimum drinking age of twenty-one. The Court held "the condition imposed by Congress is directly related to one of the main purposes for which highway funds are expended—safe interstate travel."

"Independent Constitutional Bar"

The Court must determine whether any other constitutional provisions provide an independent bar to the conditional grant of federal funds. Congress has "wide latitude to attach conditions to the receipt of federal assistance in order to further its policy objectives" [*United States v. American Library Association, Inc.*, 123 S.Ct. 2297 (2003)]. However, Congress may not induce states "to engage in activities that would themselves be unconstitutional" [*South Dakota v. Dole*, 483 U.S. 203 (1987)]. For example, "a grant of federal funds conditioned on invidiously discriminatory state action or the infliction of cruel and unusual punishment would be an illegitimate exercise of the Congress' broad spending power" (*Dole*).

CHAPTER 5

Federal Commerce Power

UNDER THE COMMERCE CLAUSE, CONGRESS MAY REGULATE INTERSTATE COMMERCE and commerce with foreign nations and Indian tribes (U.S. Const. art. 1, § 8). The commerce clause creates a common market among the states and prevents states from engaging in economic protectionism by discriminating against interstate and foreign commerce.

INTERSTATE COMMERCE

Congress may regulate the "channels and instrumentalities" of interstate commerce and intrastate activities that have a "substantial effect" on interstate commerce [*United States v. Lopez*, 514 U.S. 549 (1995)].

"Channels and Instrumentalities" of Interstate Commerce

Congress may regulate transactions, activities, persons, and things that cross state lines.

- *Champion v. Ames*, 188 U.S. 321 (1903) (the Lottery Case). The Federal Lottery Act of 1895 prohibited interstate shipment of lottery tickets. The Court upheld the Act, and explained "the carrying from state to state of lottery tickets constitutes interstate commerce, and…the regulation of such commerce is within the power of Congress under the Constitution."

- *Hipolite Egg Co. v. United States*, 220 U.S. 45 (1911). The Pure Food and Drug Act of 1906 prohibited interstate shipment of any article of food or drugs that is adulterated, and authorized its confiscation. The Court upheld the Act, and explained the power to confiscate adulterated food or drugs "is certainly appropriate to the right to bar them from interstate commerce, and completes its purpose, which is not to prevent merely the physical movement of adulterated articles, but the use of them, or rather to prevent trade in them between the states by denying to them the facilities of interstate commerce."

- *Hoke v. United States*, 227 U.S. 308 (1913). The White Slave Act of 1910 prohibited interstate transportation of women for immoral purposes. The Court upheld the Act, and explained "It is misleading to say that men and women have rights. Their rights cannot fortify or sanction their wrongs; and if they employ interstate transportation as a facility of their wrongs, it may be forbidden to them to the extent of the act of July 25, 1910, and we need go no farther in the present case."

- *Kentucky Whip & Collar Co. v. Illinois Central R. Co.*, 299 U.S. 334 (1937). The Ashurst-Sumners Act of 1935 prohibited interstate transportation of goods made by convict labor into states that prohibited their use. The Court upheld the Act. The Court explained where the subject of commerce is one that the state may constitutionally prohibit to prevent harmful consequences, "Congress may, if it sees fit, put forth its power to regulate interstate commerce so as to prevent that commerce from being used to impede the carrying out of the state policy."

- *United States v. Darby*, 312 U.S. 100 (1941). The Fair Labor Standards Act of 1938 prohibited interstate transportation of goods made by employees whose wages and hours of employment did not conform to the requirements of the Act. The Court upheld the Act because "While manufacture is not of itself interstate commerce the shipment of manufactured goods interstate is such commerce and the prohibition of such shipment by Congress is indubitably a regulation of the commerce."

- *United States v. South-Eastern Underwriters Association*, 322 U.S. 533 (1944). The Court held that an insurance company that conducted a substantial part of its business across state lines was engaged in interstate commerce and thereby was subject to the antitrust laws.

- *Reno v. Condon*, 528 U.S. 141 (2000). The Driver's Privacy Protection Act restricted the ability of the states to sell or release a driver's personal information without the driver's consent. The Court upheld the Act. The Court explained that the information is used by insurers, manufacturers, direct marketers, and others engaged in interstate commerce to contact drivers with customized solicitations, and by public and private entities for matters related to interstate motoring. So, "Because drivers' personal, identifying information is, in this context, an article of commerce, its sale or release into the interstate stream of business is sufficient to support congressional regulation."

Intrastate Activities That Have a "Substantial Effect" on Interstate Commerce

Congress may regulate intrastate activities (activities within a single state) that have a "substantial effect" on interstate commerce. If the regulated activity is "commercial," the Court gives great deference to Congress's judgment. The Court affords the regulation a presumption of constitutionality so long as there is a rational basis on which Congress could have concluded that the activity substantially affects interstate commerce. If the regulated activity is "noncommercial" (e.g., *Lopez* and *Morrison*, mentioned later), the Court gives less deference to Congress's judgment. So, the government must show a factual basis, rather than mere theoretical argument, for finding that the regulated activity substantially affects interstate commerce.

- *Houston, East & West Texas Railway Company v. United States*, 234 U.S. 342 (1914) (the Shreveport Rate Case). The Interstate Commerce Commission regulated railroad rates charged for shipments made entirely within the state of Texas (intrastate activities), and required that they not be higher than rates charged for shipments of similar distance made to Texas from Louisiana (interstate activities). The Court upheld the regulations on intrastate activities because they had a substantial relation to interstate traffic. The Court explained that the rates charged for shipments from Dallas and Houston eastward to other Texas cities were much less, according to distance, than from Shreveport, Louisiana, westward to the same Texas cities. For example, a rate of 60 cents carried first-class traffic a distance of 160 miles eastward from Dallas, while the same rate would carry the same class of traffic only 55 miles into Texas from Shreveport. Thus, low intrastate rates discriminated against interstate traffic, and had a "close and substantial relation to interstate traffic."

The Court explained, "It is immaterial, so far as the protecting power of Congress is concerned, that the discrimination arises from intrastate rates as compared with interstate rates. The use of the instrument of interstate commerce in a discriminatory manner so as to inflict injury upon that commerce, or some part thereof, furnishes abundant ground for Federal intervention."

- *NLRB v. Jones & Laughlin Steel Corp.*, 301 U.S. 1 (1937). The National Labor Relations Act of 1935 created the National Labor Relations Board and provided the right of employees to self-organization and to bargain collectively through representatives of their own choosing (intrastate activities). The Court upheld the Act. The Court explained, "Although activities may be intrastate in character when separately considered, if they have such a close and substantial relation to interstate commerce that their control is essential or appropriate to protect that commerce from burdens and obstructions, Congress cannot be denied the power to exercise that control." The Court noted that work stoppage caused by industrial strife "would have a most serious effect upon interstate commerce." The Court added, "When industries organize themselves on a national scale, making their relation to interstate commerce the dominant factor in their activities, how can it be maintained that their industrial labor relations constitute a forbidden field into which Congress may not enter when it is necessary to protect interstate commerce from the paralyzing consequences of industrial war?"

- *United States v. Darby*, 312 U.S. 100 (1941). The Fair Labor Standards Act of 1938 set the minimum wage and maximum hours (intrastate activities) for employees engaged in the production of goods for interstate commerce. The Court upheld the Act because "the power of Congress to regulate interstate commerce extends to the regulation through legislative action of activities intrastate which have a substantial effect on the commerce." Although substandard labor conditions are intrastate activities, they have a substantial effect on interstate commerce because competition for goods causes substandard labor conditions to spread through interstate commerce. The Court explained that the Act sought to stop the spread of substandard labor conditions through interstate commerce not only by prohibiting interstate transportation of the proscribed product, but also by stopping "the initial step toward transportation, production with the purpose of so transporting it."

- *Wickard v. Filburn*, 317 U.S. 111 (1942). The Agricultural Adjustment Act of 1938 allowed the secretary of agriculture to limit the amount of wheat produced on individual farms (intrastate activities). The purpose of the Act was to increase the market price of wheat by limiting the volume of wheat in interstate commerce. Farmer Filburn owned and operated a small farm in Ohio. His practice was to raise a small acreage of winter wheat, sown in the fall and harvested in the following July; to sell a portion of the crop; to feed part to poultry and livestock on the farm, some of which was sold; to use some in making flour for home consumption; and to keep the rest for the following seeding. The quota for his 1941 crop was 223 bushels, but he produced 462 bushels and was fined $117 for the excess production.

   The Court upheld the Act as applied to Filburn because "It can hardly be denied that a factor of such volume and variability as home-consumed wheat would have a substantial influence on price and market conditions." When homegrown wheat supplies the needs of the person who grows it, that person will not buy wheat in the open market. So, "Home-grown wheat in this sense competes with wheat in commerce." The Court explained, "That appellee's own contribution to the demand for wheat may be trivial by itself is not enough to remove him from the scope of federal regulation where, as here, his contribution, taken together with that of many others similarly situated, is far from trivial."

- *Heart of Atlanta Motel Inc. v. United States*, 379 U.S. 241 (1964). Title II of the Civil Rights Act of 1964 prohibited discrimination in public accommodations (intrastate activities). The Heart of Atlanta Motel refused to provide lodging for transient blacks because of their race. The Court upheld the Act and Congress's power to prohibit racial discrimination by motels serving interstate travelers. Although their operations may appear "local," there was "overwhelming evidence" that discrimination by hotels and motels discouraged interstate travel and impaired the traveler's pleasure. The Court concluded, "If it is interstate commerce that feels the pinch, it does not matter how local the operation which applies the squeeze."

- *Katzenbach v. McClung*, 379 U.S. 294 (1964). Title II of the Civil Rights Act of 1964 prohibited discrimination in public accommodations (intrastate activities). Ollie's Barbecue, a family-owned restaurant in Birmingham, Alabama, refused to serve blacks in its dining accommodations since its original opening in 1927. The restaurant also purchased locally approximately $150,000 worth of food, $69,683 (or 46 percent) of which was meat that it bought from a local supplier who had procured it from outside the state. The Court upheld the Act because "Congress prohibited discrimination only in those establishments having a close tie to interstate commerce, i.e., those, like the McClungs', serving food that has come from out of the State. We think in so doing that Congress acted well within its power to protect and foster commerce in extending the coverage of Title II only to those restaurants offering to serve interstate travelers or serving food, a substantial portion of which has moved in interstate commerce."

- *Perez v. United States*, 402 U.S. 146 (1971). Title II of the Consumer Credit Protection Act prohibited "loan sharking" activities (intrastate activities). The Court upheld the Act because "Extortionate credit transactions, though purely intrastate, may in the judgment of Congress affect interstate commerce." The Court explained that "loan sharking in its national setting is one way organized interstate crime holds its guns to the heads of the poor and the rich alike and syphons funds from numerous localities to finance its national operations."

- *United States v. Lopez*, 514 U.S. 549 (1995). The Gun-Free School Zones Act of 1990 made it a federal crime to knowingly possess a firearm in a school zone (intrastate activities). The

Court invalidated the Act because "The possession of a gun in a local school zone is in no sense an economic activity that might, through repetition elsewhere, substantially affect any sort of interstate commerce." The Court explained that "Section 922(q) [of the Act] is a criminal statute that by its terms has nothing to do with 'commerce' or any sort of economic enterprise, however broadly one might define those terms. Section 922(q) is not an essential part of a larger regulation of economic activity, in which the regulatory scheme could be undercut unless the intrastate activity were regulated. It cannot, therefore, be sustained under our cases upholding regulations of activities that arise out of or are connected with a commercial transaction, which viewed in the aggregate, substantially affects interstate commerce." Also, the Act had no "jurisdictional element" or language that limited its application to cases where firearm possession had "an explicit connection with or effect on interstate commerce."

- *United States v. Morrison*, 529 U.S. 598 (2000). A provision of the Violence Against Women Act of 1994 allowed the victims of gender-motivated violence to sue for money damages. The Court invalidated the provision because "Gender-motivated crimes of violence are not, in any sense of the phrase, economic activity. While we need not adopt a categorical rule against aggregating the effects of any noneconomic activity in order to decide these cases, thus far in our Nation's history our cases have upheld Commerce Clause regulation of intrastate activity only where that activity is economic in nature."

  The Court explained, "We accordingly reject the argument that Congress may regulate noneconomic, violent criminal conduct based solely on that conduct's aggregate effect on interstate commerce. The Constitution requires a distinction between what is truly national and what is truly local." Also, "Like the Gun-Free School Zones Act at issue in Lopez, § 13981 [of the Act] contains no jurisdictional element establishing that the federal cause of action is in pursuance of Congress' power to regulate interstate commerce."

- *Gonzales v. Raich*, 545 U.S. 1 (2005). The federal Controlled Substances Act (CSA) criminalized the manufacture, distribution, or possession of marijuana. California's Compassionate Use

Act authorized limited marijuana use for medicinal purposes. Raich and Monson were California residents who used doctor-recommended marijuana, grown locally, for serious medical conditions. They claimed that enforcing the CSA against them would violate the commerce clause.

The Court upheld the CSA. The Court explained, "The similarities between this case and *Wickard* are striking. Like the farmer in *Wickard*, respondents are cultivating, for home consumption, a fungible commodity for which there is an established, albeit illegal, interstate market. Just as the Agricultural Adjustment Act was designed "to control the volume [of wheat] moving in interstate and foreign commerce in order to avoid surpluses . . ." and consequently control the market price, a primary purpose of the CSA is to control the supply and demand of controlled substances in both lawful and unlawful drug markets. In *Wickard*, we had no difficulty concluding that Congress had a rational basis for believing that, when viewed in the aggregate, leaving home-consumed wheat outside the regulatory scheme would have a substantial influence on price and market conditions. Here too, Congress had a rational basis for concluding that leaving home-consumed marijuana outside federal control would similarly affect price and market conditions." Moreover, "Unlike those at issue in *Lopez* and *Morrison*, the activities regulated by the CSA are quintessentially economic." The Court concluded, "In both cases, the regulation is squarely within Congress' commerce power because production of the commodity meant for home consumption, be it wheat or marijuana, has a substantial effect on supply and demand in the national market for that commodity."

COMMERCE WITH FOREIGN NATIONS AND INDIAN TRIBES

Congress has exclusive and plenary (complete) power to regulate commerce with foreign nations and Indian tribes [*Japan Line, Ltd. v. County of Los Angeles*, 441 U.S. 434 (1979) (holding that a state tax on instrumentalities was unconstitutional because it could subject foreign commerce to multiple burdens and impair federal uniformity)].

CHAPTER 6

Federal Property Power

ARTICLE I POWER

CONGRESS MAY ACQUIRE IMMEDIATE, EXCLUSIVE JURISDICTION OVER LAND WITHIN A state with the state's consent (U.S. Const. art. I, § 8, cl. 17). For example, Virginia and Maryland ceded jurisdiction of some land to the federal government in 1791 to establish the District of Columbia as the capital of the United States.

ARTICLE IV POWER

Congress has the power to "dispose of and make all needful Rules and Regulations respecting the Territory or other Property belonging to the United States" [U.S. Const. art. IV, § 3, cl. 2; *Kleppe v. New Mexico*, 426 U.S. 529 (1976) (upholding the Wild Free-roaming Horses and Burros Act, which protected "all unbranded and unclaimed horses and burros on public lands of the United States" from "capture, branding, harassment, or death"); *Hunt v. United States*, 278 U.S. 96 (1928) (holding the United States had authority to kill deer in the Kaibab National Forest and the Grand Canyon National Game Preserve to protect the lands from overbrowsing and killing of valuable young trees, shrubs, bushes, and forage plants)].

Congress's Article IV property power is plenary, without significant judicial restriction, so federal legislation enacted under this power overrides conflicting state laws under the supremacy clause.

CHAPTER 7

Congressional Power to Enforce Civil Rights

THE FOURTEENTH AMENDMENT CONTAINS THE DUE PROCESS, EQUAL PROTECTION, and privileges or immunities clauses. Section 5 of the Fourteenth Amendment provides that Congress "shall have power to enforce, by appropriate legislation, the provisions of this article."

The Fifteenth Amendment provides that "The right of citizens of the United States to vote shall not be denied or abridged by the United States or by any State on account of race, color, or previous condition of servitude." Section 2 of the Fifteenth Amendment provides that Congress "shall have power to enforce this article by appropriate legislation."

Section 5 of the Fourteenth Amendment and Section 2 of the Fifteenth Amendment raise the issue of whether Congress has the power to interpret the Constitution and thus expand or contract Fourteenth or Fifteenth Amendment rights, or whether Congress has power only to enforce these rights by enacting laws to prevent or remedy violations. The Court has held that Congress has power only to enforce these rights, and may not expand or contract them.

- *South Carolina v. Katzenbach*, 383 U.S. 301 (1966). In response to some states using literacy tests to deny blacks the right to vote, Congress passed the Voting Rights Act of 1965. The Act empowered the attorney general to suspend literacy tests for voting in states where less than 50 percent of the citizens had voted or were registered to vote. The Court upheld the Act because it was a proper exercise of Congress's power, under Section 2 of the Fifteenth Amendment, to provide a remedy for proven violations of the Fifteenth Amendment.

- *City of Boerne v. Flores*, 521 U.S. 507 (1997). In *Employment Division v. Smith*, 494 U.S. 872 (1990), the Court upheld an Oregon law that prohibited use of peyote, a hallucinogenic substance, even though such use was required by some Native American religions, because it was a religiously neutral and generally applicable criminal law. In response to *Smith*, Congress enacted the Religious Freedom Restoration Act (RFRA) to overturn the *Smith* decision and restore strict scrutiny for free exercise clause analysis, thus expanding constitutional rights. The Court invalidated the RFRA and held that Congress exceeded its powers under Section 5 of the Fourteenth Amendment when it enacted the RFRA. Section 5 gives Congress power only to enforce the free exercise clause, and "Legislation which alters the meaning of the Free Exercise Clause cannot be said to be enforcing the Clause."

CHAPTER 8

State Power

IF CONGRESS PASSES A LAW, IT MAY PREEMPT STATE OR LOCAL LAW. IF CONGRESS HAS
not passed a law, or federal law does not preempt state or local law,
state or local law may still be challenged under the dormant commerce
clause, the privilege and immunities clause, or the privilege or immunities clause. States also have regulatory power over liquor under the
Twenty-first Amendment.

PREEMPTION

The preemption doctrine derives from the supremacy clause (U.S.
Const. art. VI, cl. 2) and provides that federal law preempts, or overrides, state or local law where Congress expressly or impliedly preempts state or local regulation in an area.

Express Preemption

Where Congress has power to regulate, Congress can make federal law
exclusive by expressly preempting state or local regulation in an area.
A court then determines "the domain expressly preempted by that
language" (i.e., the scope of preemption) [*Medtronic, Inc. v. Lohr*, 518
U.S. 470 (1996)].

- *Jones v. Rath Packing Co.*, 430 U.S. 519 (1977). The Federal Meat
  Inspection Act (FMIA), as amended by the Wholesome Meat Act,

required meat packaging to accurately state net weight, but permitted "reasonable variations" caused by manufacturing variations or moisture loss during distribution. The FMIA also prohibited "(m)arking, labeling, packaging, or ingredient requirements" different than those made under the Act (express preemption). The California Business and Professions Code also required meat packaging to accurately state net weight, but permitted "reasonable variations" caused only by manufacturing variations, and made no allowance for weight variations caused by moisture loss during distribution.

The Court held that the FMIA preempted the California law. The Court explained that the express preemption provision in the FMIA "dictates the result in the controversy between *Jones* and *Rath*" because "the state law's requirement that the label accurately state the net weight, with implicit allowance only for reasonable manufacturing variations is 'different than' the federal requirement, which permits manufacturing deviations and variations caused by moisture loss during good distribution practice."

Implied Preemption

There are three types of implied preemption: field preemption, conflict preemption, and interference preemption.

Field Preemption

Field preemption exists when a scheme of federal regulation is so pervasive that it is reasonable to infer that Congress intended federal law to "occupy the field" exclusively, with no room for state or local regulation. The Court is more likely to find preemption where there is a traditional federal interest (e.g., foreign policy and immigration) and less likely to find preemption where there is a traditional state or local interest (e.g., health and safety).

- *Hines v. Davidowitz*, 312 U.S. 52 (1941). The Pennsylvania Alien Registration Act of 1939 required aliens eighteen years of age and over to register with the state, pay a fee, and carry a registration card. The federal Alien Registration Act of 1940 required a single registration of aliens fourteen years of age and over, and did not require aliens to carry a card. The Court held that federal law preempted Pennsylvania law because "the treatment of aliens, in whatever state they may be located, [is] a matter of national moment" (traditional federal interest). Also, Congress "provided a standard for alien registration in a single integrated and all-embracing system in order to obtain the information deemed to be desirable in connection with aliens. When it made this addition to its uniform naturalization and immigration laws, it plainly manifested a purpose to do so in such a way as to protect the personal liberties of law-abiding aliens through one uniform national registration system" (pervasive federal regulation).

- *Pennsylvania v. Nelson*, 350 U.S. 497 (1956). The Pennsylvania Sedition Act prohibited the knowing advocacy of the overthrow of the U.S. government by force and violence. The federal Smith Act of 1940 prohibited the same conduct. The Court held that federal law preempted Pennsylvania law because "we find that Congress has occupied the field to the exclusion of parallel state legislation [pervasive federal regulation], that the dominant interest of the Federal Government precludes state intervention [traditional federal interest], and that administration of state Acts would conflict with the operation of the federal plan."

- *Hillsborough County, Florida v. Automated Medical Laboratories, Inc.*, 471 U.S. 707 (1985). Under the Public Health Service Act, the Food and Drug Administration (FDA) established standards for the collection of blood plasma. A Hillsborough County ordinance incorporated by reference the FDA's blood plasma regulations, but also imposed donor testing and record-keeping requirements beyond those contained in the federal regulations. The Court held that federal regulations did not preempt local ordinances because "the FDA explained in a statement [in 1973] accompanying the regulations that 'these regulations are not intended to usurp the powers of State or local authorities to regulate plasmapheresis procedures in their localities.'" Also, "even in the absence of the 1973 statement, the comprehensiveness of the FDA's regulations would not justify pre-emption." Finally, "the regulation of health and safety matters is primarily, and historically, a matter of local concern" (traditional state or local interest).

Conflict Preemption

Conflict preemption exists when "compliance with both federal and state regulations is a physical impossibility" [*Florida Lime & Avocado Growers, Inc. v. Paul*, 373 U.S. 132 (1963)].

- *Florida Lime & Avocado Growers, Inc. v. Paul*, 373 U.S. 132 (1963). California's Agricultural Code gauged the maturity of avocados by oil content, and prohibited the transportation or sale in California of avocados that contained less than 8 percent of oil. Federal marketing regulations adopted pursuant to the Agricultural Adjustment Act gauged the maturity of avocados grown in Florida by standards that attributed no significance to oil content. The Court held that federal law did not preempt California law because although the two laws used different standards, there was no actual conflict that made it impossible to comply with both. The Court explained that it would be impossible to comply with both laws if, for example, federal law prohibited the sale of any avocado with more than 7 percent oil content, and the California law prohibited the sale of any avocado with less than 8 percent oil content. However, the Court explained "No such impossibility of dual compliance is presented on this record."

- *Hisquierdo v. Hisquierdo*, 439 U.S. 572 (1979). The federal Railroad Retirement Act of 1974 provided that benefits resulting from employment during marriage were not community property subject to division in the event of dissolution of marriage. California has a form of community property law in which community property includes the property earned by either spouse during marriage. The Court held that federal law preempted state law because "the community property interest that respondent seeks conflicts with [the Act], promises to diminish that portion of the benefit Congress has said should go to the retired worker alone, and threatens to penalize one whom Congress has sought to protect. It thus causes the kind of injury to federal interests that the Supremacy Clause forbids."

Interference Preemption

Interference preemption exists when state law "stands as an obstacle to the accomplishment and execution of the full purposes or objectives of Congress" [*Hines v. Davidowitz*, 312 U.S. 52 (1941)].

- *Nash v. Florida Industrial Commission*, 389 U.S. 235 (1967). The National Labor Relations Act authorized the National Labor Relations Board to initiate unfair labor practice proceedings whenever some person charged that another person had committed such practices. Florida Unemployment Compensation Law denied unemployment compensation to any person who filed an unfair labor practice charge. The Court held that federal law preempted state law.

The Court explained, "The action of Florida here, like the coercive actions which employers and unions are forbidden to engage in, has a direct tendency to frustrate the purpose of Congress to leave people free to make charges of unfair labor practices to the Board. Florida has applied its Unemployment Compensation Law so that an employee who believes he has been wrongly discharged has two choices: (1) he may keep quiet and receive unemployment compensation until he finds a new job or (2) he may file an unfair labor practice charge, thus under Florida procedure surrendering his right to unemployment compensation, and risk financial ruin if the litigation is protracted. Even the hope of a future award of back pay may mean little to a man of modest means and heavy responsibilities faced with the immediate severance of sustaining funds. It appears obvious to us that this financial burden which Florida imposes will impede resort to the Act and thwart congressional reliance on individual action. A national system for the implementation of this country's labor policies is not so dependent on state law. Florida should not be permitted to defeat or handicap a valid national objective by threatening to withdraw state benefits from persons simply because they cooperate with the Government's constitutional plan."

- *Perez v. Campbell*, 402 U.S. 637 (1971). Arizona's Motor Vehicle Safety Responsibility Act provided that a discharge in bankruptcy did not relieve an individual from having his driver's license suspended if he failed to satisfy a judgment entered against him in an action arising out of operation of a motor vehicle. The federal Bankruptcy Act provided that a discharge in bankruptcy fully discharged all but certain specified judgments. The Court held that federal law preempted state law because the state law frustrated the full effectiveness of federal law. The Court explained that one of the primary purposes of the Bankruptcy Act is to give debtors "a new opportunity in life and a clear field for future effort, unhampered by the pressure and discouragement of pre-existing debt."

DORMANT COMMERCE CLAUSE
(NEGATIVE COMMERCE CLAUSE)

The commerce clause does two things: It authorizes congressional action, as described in Chapter 5, and it limits state and local authority, as described here. The terms "dormant commerce clause" and "negative commerce clause" are interchangeable, and describe the principle that state and local regulations or taxes are unconstitutional if they place an undue burden on interstate commerce.

State Regulation of Interstate Commerce

If Congress has not used its commerce power to regulate a certain item or activity regarding interstate commerce, its commerce power is "dormant" in that subject area. If Congress's commerce power is "dormant" in a subject area, and a state or local regulation concerning the same subject unduly burdens interstate commerce, the Court may strike down the law under the dormant commerce clause. By striking down the state or local law, the Court preserves Congress's unused power and prevents states from discriminating against interstate commerce and engaging in economic protectionism.

In deciding the state law's constitutionality, the Court considers whether the law is discriminatory or nondiscriminatory, and exceptions to the dormant commerce clause.

Discriminatory Law

Discriminatory law is usually invalidated, and will be upheld only if it is necessary (i.e., the least discriminatory means) to achieve a legitimate local purpose that is unrelated to economic protectionism. State law may be discriminatory in one of two ways: (1) It may be "facially" discriminatory, or (2) it may be "facially" neutral, yet have a discriminatory "purpose or effect." State law is "facially" discriminatory if it expressly draws a distinction between in-staters and out-of-staters. State law that is "facially" neutral, in that it treats in-staters and out-of-staters alike, may still be discriminatory if it has a discriminatory purpose or effect.

- *Dean Milk Co. v. City of Madison*, 340 U.S. 349 (1951). A Madison, Wisconsin, ordinance prohibited the sale of milk as pasteurized unless it was processed and bottled at an approved pasteurization plant within five miles from the central square of Madison (facially discriminatory). The ordinance had the effect of excluding from distribution in Madison milk produced and pasteurized in Illinois. The Court invalidated the ordinance because it placed a "discriminatory burden on interstate commerce," and "reasonable and adequate alternatives" were available. Madison could have achieved its goal of safe milk (legitimate local purpose) by less discriminatory means such as sending its own inspectors to importing producers and processors, or relying on federal inspectors (least discriminatory means).

- *Hunt v. Washington State Apple Advertising Commission*, 432 U.S. 333 (1977). A North Carolina law required all closed containers of apples shipped into or sold in the state to display either the applicable USDA grade or none at all. State grades were expressly prohibited (facially neutral because it applied to all apples sold in the state, whether produced in state or out of state). Washington had a different and more stringent grading system for apples than the USDA standard. So the law would cause Washington growers to lose the competitive advantage they gained from Washington's superior grading system. And Washington growers would suffer increased costs because they would have to obliterate the printed labels on containers shipped to North Carolina, thus giving their product a damaged appearance (discriminatory effects).

  The Court invalidated the statute. The Court explained that although protecting citizens from "confusion and deception in the marketing of foodstuffs" is a legitimate local purpose, "it appears that nondiscriminatory alternatives to the outright ban of Washington State grades are readily available. For example, North Carolina could effectuate its goal by permitting out-of-state growers to utilize state grades only if they also marked their shipments with the applicable USDA label. In that case, the USDA grade would serve as a benchmark against which the consumer could evaluate the quality of the various state grades" (least discriminatory means).

- *City of Philadelphia v. New Jersey*, 437 U.S. 617 (1978). A New Jersey statute prohibited the importation of solid or liquid waste that originated or was collected outside the state (facially discriminatory). The Court invalidated the law. The Court said it did not matter whether the statute's goal was to reduce the waste disposal costs of New Jersey residents or to save remaining open lands from pollution, because "the evil of protectionism can reside in legislative means as well as legislative ends."

The Court explained, "The New Jersey law blocks the importation of waste in an obvious effort to saddle those outside the State with the entire burden of slowing the flow of refuse into New Jersey's remaining landfill sites. That legislative effort is clearly impermissible under the Commerce Clause of the Constitution. Today, cities in Pennsylvania and New York find it expedient or necessary to send their waste into New Jersey for disposal, and New Jersey claims the right to close its borders to such traffic. Tomorrow, cities in New Jersey may find it expedient or necessary to send their waste into Pennsylvania or New York for disposal, and those States might then claim the right to close their borders. The Commerce Clause will protect New Jersey in the future, just as it protects her neighbors now, from efforts by one State to isolate itself in the stream of interstate commerce from a problem shared by all."

- *Hughes v. Oklahoma*, 441 U.S. 322 (1979). An Oklahoma statute prohibited the transportation of natural minnows out of the state for purposes of sale (facially discriminatory). The Court invalidated the law because it discriminated against interstate commerce "on its face." And although Oklahoma's interest in conserving minnows was "a legitimate local purpose," equally effective nondiscriminatory conservation measures were available. Oklahoma could have limited the number of minnows taken by licensed minnow dealers, or limited how minnows were disposed of within the state (least discriminatory means).

- *Maine v. Taylor*, 477 U.S. 131 (1986). A Maine statute prohibited importing live baitfish into the state (facially discriminatory). The Court upheld the statute. The Court explained that the statute served a legitimate local purpose, protecting native fisheries from parasitic infection and adulteration by nonnative species. And that purpose could not be served as well by available nondiscriminatory means. Experts testified "there was no satisfactory way to inspect shipments of live baitfish for parasites or commingled species" (no less discriminatory means). Inspecting live baitfish for commingled species was "a physical impossibility," and inspecting the fish for parasites "required destruction of the fish."

- *Granholm v. Heald*, 544 U.S. 460 (2005). Michigan and New York regulated the sale and importation of wine. The regulations allowed in-state wineries to sell wine directly to consumers in that state, but prohibited out-of-state wineries from doing so, or at least made direct sales impractical from an economic standpoint (facially discriminatory). The Court invalidated the regulations. The states argued that restricting direct shipments from out-of-state wineries was necessary to prevent underage drinking; they argued minors had easy access to credit cards and the Internet and were likely to take advantage of direct wine shipments as a means of obtaining alcohol illegally. However, the Court explained, "The States provide little evidence that the purchase of wine over the Internet by minors is a problem." Also, "Even were we to credit the States' largely unsupported claim that direct shipping of wine increases the risk of underage drinking, this would not justify regulations limiting only out-of-state direct shipments. As the wineries point out, minors are just as likely to order wine from in-state producers as from out-of-state ones."

Nondiscriminatory ("Even-Handed") Law

State law is nondiscriminatory if it treats in-staters and out-of-staters alike ("facially" neutral) and has no discriminatory purpose or effect. Nondiscriminatory law is usually upheld, and will be struck down only if the law's burdens on interstate commerce outweigh its local benefits. The extent of the burden tolerated depends on the nature of the local interest and whether it could be promoted by less discriminatory means.

- *South Carolina State Highway Department v. Barnwell*, 303 U.S. 177 (1938). A South Carolina law prohibited the use on state highways of motor trucks whose width exceeded 90 inches (7 1/2 feet) and whose weight exceeded 20,000 pounds (facially neutral and nondiscriminatory). The Court upheld the statute. From 85 to 90 percent of the motor trucks used in interstate transportation were 96 inches (8 feet) wide and of a gross weight, when loaded, of more than 20,000 pounds, and thus were excluded from South Carolina highways by the law (burden). However, "a large part of the [South Carolina] highways in question are from 18 to 20 feet in width, approximately 100 miles are only 16 feet wide. On all the use of a 96-inch truck leaves but a narrow margin for passing. On the road

16 feet wide it leaves none." Also, many South Carolina roads were old and liable to crack from heavy weight (local benefits of law).

- *Southern Pacific Co. v. Arizona*, 325 U.S. 761 (1945). The Arizona Train Limit Law of 1912 made it unlawful to operate within the state a railroad train of more than fourteen passenger or seventy freight cars (facially neutral and nondiscriminatory). The Court invalidated the law. The Court explained that the law imposed a "serious burden" on interstate commerce because "limiting train lengths requires interstate trains of a length lawful in other states to be broken up and reconstituted as they enter each state." The alternative was for the carrier to conform to the lowest train limit restriction of any of the states through which its trains passed (burdens). Moreover, "We think, as the trial court found, that the Arizona Train Limit Law, viewed as a safety measure, affords at most slight and dubious advantage, if any, over unregulated train lengths, because it results in an increase in the number of trains and train operations and the consequent increase in train accidents of a character generally more severe than those due to slack action" (no local benefits).

- *Bibb v. Navajo Freight Lines*, 359 U.S. 520 (1959). An Illinois statute required trucks and trailers operating in the state to use curved mudguards that followed the contour of the rear wheels, instead of the usual straight mudguards (facially neutral and non-discriminatory). The Court invalidated the statute. The Court explained that straight mudguards were legal in at least forty-five other states. So if a truck or trailer was to be operated in another state and Illinois, "mudguards would have to be interchanged, causing a significant delay in an operation where prompt move-ment may be of the essence. It was found that from two to four hours of labor are required to install or remove a contour mud-guard. Moreover, the contour guard is attached to the trailer by welding and if the trailer is conveying a cargo of explosives (e.g., for the United States Government) it would be exceedingly dan-gerous to attempt to weld on a contour mudguard without unload-ing the trailer" (burden). Also, curved mudguards "tended to cause an accumulation of heat in the brake drum, thus decreasing the effectiveness of brakes," and "were susceptible of being hit and bumped when the trucks were backed up and of falling off on the highway" (no local benefits).

- *Exxon Corp. v. Governor of Maryland*, 437 U.S. 117 (1978). Evidence indicated that during the 1973 petroleum shortage, oil producers or refiners favored company-operated gasoline stations. So, Maryland enacted a statute prohibiting producers or refiners from operating retail service stations within the state (facially neutral and nondiscriminatory). The Court upheld the statute because it placed no burdens on interstate commerce. The Court explained, "there are several major interstate marketers of petroleum that own and operate their own retail gasoline stations. These interstate dealers, who compete directly with the Maryland independent dealers, are not affected by the Act because they do not refine or produce gasoline. In fact, the Act creates no barriers whatsoever against interstate independent dealers; it does not prohibit the flow of interstate goods, place added costs upon them, or distinguish between in-state and out-of-state companies in the retail market."

- *Minnesota v. Clover Leaf Creamery Co.*, 449 U.S. 456 (1981). A Minnesota statute banned retail sale of milk in plastic nonreturnable, nonrefillable containers, but allowed such sale in paperboard nonreturnable, nonrefillable containers (facially neutral and nondiscriminatory). The Court upheld the statute. The Court held, "The burden imposed on interstate commerce by the statute is relatively minor. Milk products may continue to move freely across the Minnesota border, and since most dairies package their products in more than one type of containers, the inconvenience of having to conform to different packaging requirements in Minnesota and the surrounding States should be slight."

  The Court explained that plastic resin, the raw material used for making plastic nonreturnable milk jugs, is produced entirely by non-Minnesota firms, while pulpwood, used for making paperboard, is a major Minnesota product. However, the degree of this burden on out-of-state interests was minor, "both because plastics will continue to be used in the production of plastic pouches, plastic returnable bottles, and paperboard itself, and because out-of-state pulpwood producers will presumably absorb some of the business generated by the Act." Moreover, "Even granting that the out-of-state plastics industry is burdened relatively more heavily than the Minnesota pulpwood industry, we find that this burden is not "clearly excessive" in light of the substantial state interest in promoting conservation of energy and other natural resources and easing solid waste disposal problems" (local benefits). Finally, the Court found no approach with "a lesser impact on interstate activities" was available (no less discriminatory means).

- *Kassel v. Consolidated Freightways Corp.*, 450 U.S. 662 (1981). An Iowa statute prohibited the use of 65-foot double-trailer trucks within its borders, and allowed the use of 55-foot single-trailer trucks and 60-foot double-trailer trucks (facially neutral and nondiscriminatory). No other state in the West or Midwest had a similar prohibition. The Court invalidated the statute because it substantially burdened interstate commerce "without any significant countervailing safety interest." The Court explained, "Trucking companies that wish to continue to use 65-foot doubles must route them around Iowa or detach the trailers of the doubles and ship them through separately. Alternatively, trucking companies must use the smaller 55-foot singles or 60-foot doubles permitted under Iowa law. Each of these options engenders inefficiency and added expense" (burden). Also, although Iowa argued the statute promoted safety, "The evidence showed, and the District Court found, that the 65-foot double was at least the equal of the 55-foot single in the ability to brake, turn, and maneuver" (no local benefits).

Exceptions

There are two exceptions to the dormant commerce clause: congressional approval, and the "market participant exception."

Congressional Approval

If Congress authorizes the states to regulate an aspect of interstate commerce, state regulation within the scope of the congressional authorization does not violate the dormant commerce clause, even if it burdens interstate commerce. However, congressional approval does not excuse the violation of other constitutional provisions such as equal protection or the privileges and immunities clause.

- *Prudential Insurance Co. v. Benjamin*, 328 U.S. 408 (1946). South Carolina imposed a tax on foreign insurance companies as a condition of receiving authority to do business in South Carolina. The federal McCarran Act authorized state regulation and taxation of the insurance business by "removing obstructions which might be thought to flow from its own power, whether dormant or exercised," and by declaring expressly that the insurance business and all who engage in it "'shall be subject to' the laws of the several states." The Court upheld the South Carolina tax, and explained that the Act "was a determination by Congress that state taxes, which in its silence might be held invalid as discriminatory, do not place on interstate insurance business a burden which it is unable generally to bear or should not bear in the competition with local business."

- *Metropolitan Life Insurance Co. v. Ward*, 470 U.S. 869 (1985). Alabama's domestic preference tax statute taxed out-of-state insurance companies at a higher rate than domestic insurance companies. The Court held that the statute did not violate the dormant commerce clause because federal law allowed such taxes. However, the Court invalidated the statute under the equal protection clause. The Court explained, "Although the McCarran-Ferguson Act exempts the insurance industry from Commerce Clause restrictions, it does not purport to limit in any way the applicability of the Equal Protection Clause."

Market Participant Exception

If a state buys or sells in a particular interstate market, it is allowed to favor its own citizens and discriminate against out-of-staters (thus imposing a burden on interstate commerce) because it acts as a "market participant" rather than a "market regulator." As a participant in the market, the state may choose with whom it deals the same as any private trader or manufacturer.

However, just as a seller has no say in how a product is used after sale, the state may not impose conditions that have a regulatory effect outside the particular market in which it participates; this is "downstream" regulation, and it violates the dormant commerce clause.

- *Hughes v. Alexandria Scrap Corp.*, 426 U.S. 794 (1976). A Maryland statute provided that anyone in possession of an inoperable automobile over eight years old ("hulk") could transfer it to a licensed scrap processor, who then could claim a "bounty" from the state for its destruction. Out-of-state scrap processors were required to submit a certificate of title or a bill of sale from a police auction to receive a bounty; in-state scrap processors were not required to do so. This discouraged hulk suppliers from taking their hulks out of state for processing and reduced the movement of hulks in interstate commerce.

The Court upheld the statute because Maryland was a market participant rather than a market regulator. The Court explained, "Maryland has not sought to prohibit the flow of hulks, or to regulate the conditions under which it may occur. Instead, it has entered into the market itself to bid up their price. There has been an impact upon the interstate flow of hulks only because [under the statute] Maryland effectively has made it more lucrative for unlicensed suppliers to dispose of their hulks in Maryland rather than take them outside the State." So hulks will tend to be processed inside the state of Maryland, not because the statute imposed a trade barrier, but "in response to market forces, including that exerted by money from the State." The Court noted that "Nothing in the purposes animating the Commerce Clause prohibits a State, in the absence of congressional action, from participating in the market and exercising the right to favor its own citizens over others."

- *Reeves, Inc. v. Stake*, 447 U.S. 429 (1980). For more than fifty years, South Dakota operated a cement plant that produced cement for both state residents and out-of-state buyers. In 1978, because of a cement shortage, the State Cement Commission announced a policy to confine the sale of cement by the state plant to residents of the state. The Court upheld the state policy because "South Dakota, as a seller of cement, unquestionably fits the 'market participant' label." The Court explained that the distinction between states as market participants and states as market regulators "makes good sense and sound law," and "[t]here is no indication of a constitutional plan to limit the ability of the States themselves to operate freely in the free market."

- *New England Power Co. v. New Hampshire*, 455 U.S. 331 (1982). A New Hampshire statute prohibited companies engaged in the generation of electrical energy by water power from transmitting such energy out of the state unless approval was first obtained from the New Hampshire Public Utilities Commission. The commission could prohibit the exportation of such energy when it determined that the energy was "reasonably required for use within this state." After an investigation and hearings, the commission withdrew such approval and ordered New England Power to arrange to sell the previously exported hydroelectric energy within New Hampshire.

The Court invalidated the statute. New Hampshire claimed it owned the Connecticut River, the source of New England Power's hydroelectricity, and therefore acted as a market participant. However, the Court explained, "New Hampshire has done more than regulate use of the resource it assertedly owns; it has restricted the sale of electric energy, a product entirely distinct from the river waters used to produce it. This product is manufactured by a private corporation using privately owned facilities." So, New Hampshire engaged in downstream regulation.

- *White v. Massachusetts Council of Construction Employers*, 460 U.S. 204 (1983). An executive order of the mayor of Boston required that all construction projects funded in whole or in part by city funds be performed by a workforce consisting of at least 50 percent city residents. The Court upheld the order because "Insofar as the city expended only its own funds in entering into construction contracts for public projects, it was a market participant and entitled to be treated as such under the rule of *Hughes v. Alexandria Scrap Corp.*"

- *South-Central Timber Development, Inc. v. Wunnicke*, 467 U.S. 82 (1984). An Alaska law required that buyers of state-owned timber process the timber in Alaska before shipping it out of state. The Court invalidated the law because although Alaska was a market participant in the timber market, the law imposed conditions "downstream" in the timber-processing market, in which it was not a participant. The Court explained, "In the commercial context, the seller usually has no say over, and no interest in, how the product is to be used after sale; in this case, however, payment for the timber does not end the obligations of the purchaser, for, despite the fact that the purchaser has taken delivery of the timber and has paid for it, he cannot do with it as he pleases. Instead, he is obligated to deal with a stranger to the contract after completion of the sale." The Court concluded, "The limit of the market-participant doctrine must be that it allows a State to impose burdens on commerce within the market in which it is a participant, but allows it to go no further. The State may not impose conditions, whether by statute, regulation, or contract, that have a substantial regulatory effect outside of that particular market."

State Taxation of Interstate Commerce

As with state regulation of interstate commerce, if Congress has not used its commerce power to tax an activity regarding interstate commerce, its commerce power is "dormant" in that subject area. If Congress's commerce power is "dormant" in a subject area, and a state or local tax concerning the same subject unduly burdens interstate commerce, the Court may strike down the tax under the dormant commerce clause. By striking down the state or local tax, the Court preserves Congress's unused power and prevents states from discriminating against interstate commerce and engaging in economic protectionism.

A state tax is valid under the dormant commerce clause if (1) the taxed activity has a "substantial nexus" to the taxing state; (2) the tax is "fairly apportioned" by taxing only the activities connected to the taxing state; (3) the tax does not discriminate against interstate commerce; and (4) the tax is "fairly related" to services provided by the taxing state [*Complete Auto Transit, Inc. v. Brady*, 430 U.S. 274 (1977)]. If a state tax discriminates against interstate commerce, but Congress exercises its power and approves the tax, the tax does not violate the dormant commerce clause.

"Substantial Nexus"

The dormant commerce clause requires that the taxed activity or property have a "substantial nexus" (i.e., a significant connection) to the taxing state. In addition, due process requires that a company have "minimum contacts" with the taxing state for the state to have jurisdiction to tax.

- *Braniff Airways, Inc. v. Nebraska State Board of Equalization and Assessment*, 347 U.S. 590 (1954). Nebraska statutes authorized a personal property tax on flight equipment of an interstate air carrier. The Court upheld the tax. The airline claimed its aircraft never attained a taxable situs within Nebraska. The Court explained, "the situs issue devolves into the question of whether eighteen stops per day by appellant's aircraft is sufficient contact with Nebraska to sustain that state's power to levy an apportioned

ad valorem tax on such aircraft. We think such regular contact is
sufficient to establish Nebraska's power to tax even though the
same aircraft do not land every day and even though none of the
aircraft is continuously within the state."

The Court added that the airline "rents its ground facilities
and pays for fuel it purchases in Nebraska. This leaves it in the
position of other carriers such as rails, boats and motors that pay
for the use of local facilities so as to have the opportunity to exploit
the commerce, traffic, and trade that originates in or reaches
Nebraska. Approximately one-tenth of appellant's revenue is produced by the pickup and discharge of Nebraska freight and pas-
sengers. Nebraska certainly affords protection during such stops
and these regular landings are clearly a benefit to appellant."

- *Quill Corporation v. North Dakota*, 504 U.S. 298 (1992). North
Dakota required an out-of-state mail-order house with no outlets
or sales representatives in the state to collect a tax on goods purchased for use in the state. The Court invalidated the tax. The
Court explained that a vendor with no physical presence in the
taxing state, and whose only contacts with the taxing state are by
mail or common carrier, lacks the "substantial nexus" required by
the commerce clause.

"Fairly Apportioned"
If the taxed activity has a "substantial nexus" to the taxing state, it
does not follow that the state may tax the entirety of a company's business. The state tax must be "fairly apportioned" by applying only to the
portion of a company's business that is connected to the taxing state.

- *Moorman Manufacturing Co. v. Bair*, 437 U.S. 267 (1978). Iowa
imposed an income tax on foreign and domestic corporations
doing business in the state. If a corporation's business was not
conducted entirely within Iowa, the statute imposed a tax only on
the portion of its income "reasonably attributable" to the business
within the state. Moorman was an Illinois corporation that sold
animal feed it manufactured in Illinois to Iowa customers through
Iowa salesmen and warehouses. Moorman claimed that both Iowa
and Illinois imposed a tax on its income from the Iowa sales and
that Iowa's tax statute was responsible for the duplication. The
Court upheld Iowa's tax statute.

The Court explained, "The only conceivable constitutional basis for invalidating the Iowa statute would be that the Commerce Clause prohibits any overlap in the computation of taxable income by the States. If the Constitution were read to mandate such precision in interstate taxation, the consequences would extend far beyond this particular case. For some risk of duplicative taxation exists whenever the States in which a corporation does business do not follow identical rules for the division of income."

- *Container Corp. v. Franchise Tax Board*, 463 U.S. 159 (1983). California imposed a corporate tax that employed a "unitary business" principle in applying the tax to corporations doing business both inside and outside the state. The tax used a "three-factor" formula based, in equal parts, on the proportion of a unitary business's total payroll, property, and sales that are located in the state. Container Corporation did business in California and had a number of overseas subsidiaries, but in calculating the share of its net income that was apportionable to California, it omitted all of its subsidiaries' payroll, property, and sales. The Franchise Tax Board issued notices that Container Corporation should have included its overseas subsidiaries as part of its unitary business. The Court upheld the tax. The Court explained that "California's application of the unitary business principle to appellant and its foreign subsidiaries was proper, and ... its use of the standard three-factor formula to apportion the income of that unitary business was fair."

Nondiscriminatory

A state tax must not discriminate against interstate commerce by providing a commercial advantage to local business.

- *Commonwealth Edison v. Montana*, 453 U.S. 609 (1981). Montana imposed a severance tax on each ton of coal mined in the state. Edison claimed the tax discriminated against interstate commerce because 90 percent of Montana coal was shipped to other states under contracts that shifted the tax burden primarily to non-Montana utility companies and thus to citizens of other states. The Court upheld the tax. The Court explained "the Montana tax is computed at the same rate regardless of the final destination of the coal." So, "there is no real discrimination in this case; the tax burden is borne according to the amount of coal consumed and not according to any distinction between in-state and out-of-state consumers." The Court concluded, "We are not, therefore, confronted here with the type of differential tax treatment of interstate and intrastate commerce that the Court has found in other 'discrimination' cases."

- *New Energy Co. of Indiana v. Limbach*, 486 U.S. 269 (1988). An Ohio law awarded a tax credit for each gallon of ethanol sold by fuel dealers, but only if the ethanol was produced in Ohio or in a state that granted similar tax advantages to ethanol produced in Ohio. The Court invalidated the law. Ohio claimed the law promoted health by encouraging ethanol use to reduce harmful exhaust emissions. However, the Court explained "there is no reason to suppose that ethanol produced in a State that does not offer tax advantages to ethanol produced in Ohio is less healthy, and thus should have its importation into Ohio suppressed by denial of the otherwise standard tax credit." Ohio also claimed the law increased commerce in ethanol by encouraging other states to enact ethanol subsidies. However, the Court explained, "What is encouraged is not ethanol subsidies in general, but only favorable treatment for Ohio-produced ethanol. In sum, appellees' health and commerce justifications amount to no more than implausible speculation, which does not suffice to validate this plain discrimination against products of out-of-state manufacture."

- *Associated Industries of Missouri v. Lohman*, 511 U.S. 641 (1994). Missouri imposed a 1.5 percent use tax on the privilege of storing, using, or consuming within Missouri any article of personal property purchased outside Missouri. Missouri claimed the use tax compensated for the state's inability to collect a sales tax on these goods, as they were not purchased in Missouri. The Court invalidated the tax. The Court explained, "Where the use tax exceeds the sales tax, the discrepancy imposes a discriminatory burden on interstate commerce."

"Fairly Related"

States provide services such as police and fire protection, the benefit of a trained workforce, and the advantages of a civilized society. A state tax is "fairly related" to services provided by the taxing state if it is assessed in proportion to a taxpayer's activities or presence in the state, because a taxpayer may be made to bear a just share of the state tax burden based on his activities or presence in the state.

- *Commonwealth Edison v. Montana*, 453 U.S. 609 (1981). Montana imposed a severance tax on each ton of coal mined in the state. Edison claimed that coal mining caused Montana to incur additional costs for schools, roads, police, fire and health protection, and environmental protection amounting to approximately $.02 per ton. However, revenues from the severance tax were more than $2 per ton. So Edison argued the amount collected under the Montana tax was not "fairly related" to the additional costs the state incurred because the amount Montana received in taxes far exceeded the value of the services provided to the coal mining industry. The Court upheld the tax.

   The Court explained, "Because it is measured as a percentage of the value of the coal taken, the Montana tax is in 'proper proportion' to appellants' activities within the State and, therefore, to their 'consequent enjoyment of the opportunities and protections which the State has afforded' in connection with those activities. When a tax is assessed in proportion to a taxpayer's activities or presence in a State, the taxpayer is shouldering its fair share of supporting the State's provision of police and fire protection, the benefit of a trained work force, and the advantages of a civilized society."

PRIVILEGES AND IMMUNITIES CLAUSE (PROTECTS RIGHTS OF STATE CITIZENSHIP)

The privileges and immunities clause, sometimes called the "comity" clause, states "The Citizens of each State shall be entitled to all Privileges and Immunities of Citizens in the several States" (U.S. Const. art. IV, § 2). This clause was intended to fuse a collection of independent, sovereign states into one nation, and create a national economic union. The clause does this by guaranteeing to a citizen of State A who temporarily enters State B the same privileges that citizens of State B enjoy. For example, the clause guarantees to citizens of State A the privilege of doing business in State B on substantially equal terms with citizens of State B.

The clause prohibits states from discriminating against citizens of other states with regard to fundamental rights unless the law is closely related to a substantial state interest and less discriminatory means are not available.

Citizens

The privileges and immunities clause protects only citizens or residents of a state [*United Bldg. & Constr. Trades Council v. Camden,* 465 U.S. 208 (1984) (holding, "it is now established that the terms 'citizen' and 'resident' are essentially interchangeable for purposes of analysis of most cases under the Privileges and Immunities Clause")]. Corporations and aliens cannot sue under the privileges and immunities clause [Blake v. McClung, 172 U.S. 239 (1898) (holding, "a corporation is not a citizen within the meaning of the constitutional provision that 'the citizens of each State shall be entitled to all privileges and immunities of citizens in the several States'")].

Fundamental Rights

Fundamental rights include important economic activities (usually the ability to earn a livelihood, the most common basis for a privileges and immunities challenge), and constitutional rights (i.e., rights expressly protected by the Constitution and its amendments, such as First Amendment rights).

- *Toomer v. Witsell,* 334 U.S. 385 (1948). A South Carolina statute required a $25 license fee for each shrimp boat owned by a resident, and a $2,500 license fee for each one owned by a nonresident. The Court invalidated the statute. South Carolina argued the statute's purpose was to conserve its shrimp supply and head off an impending threat of excessive trawling. However, the Court explained "Nothing in the record indicates that nonresidents use larger boats or different fishing methods than residents, that the cost of enforcing the laws against them is appreciably greater, or that any substantial amount of the State's general funds is devoted to shrimp conservation" (no substantial state interest).

  Moreover, the statute was not closely related to the state's purported interest because less discriminatory means were available. The Court explained that South Carolina had the power "to restrict the type of equipment used in its fisheries, to graduate license fees according to the size of the boats, or even to charge non-residents a differential which would merely compensate the State for any added enforcement burden they may impose."

- *Doe v. Bolton*, 410 U.S. 179 (1973). Georgia law prohibited abortion except under certain circumstances, and required that a woman who sought an abortion be a Georgia resident. The Court invalidated the residency requirement. The Court explained "Just as the Privileges and Immunities Clause, Const. Art. IV, § 2, protects persons who enter other States to ply their trade, so must it protect persons who enter Georgia seeking the medical services that are available there. A contrary holding would mean that a State could limit to its own residents the general medical care available within its borders. This we could not approve" (constitutional right involved). Moreover, the Court explained the law was "not based on any policy of preserving state-supported facilities for Georgia residents, for the bar also applies to private hospitals and to privately retained physicians. There is no intimation, either, that Georgia facilities are utilized to capacity in caring for Georgia residents" (law not closely related to a substantial state interest).

- *Baldwin v. Fish and Game Commission of Montana*, 436 U.S. 371 (1978). A Montana elk-hunting license scheme imposed substantially higher (at least 7 1/2 times) license fees on nonresidents of the state than on residents. The Court upheld the license scheme. The Court explained, "Elk hunting by nonresidents in Montana is a recreation and a sport. In itself—wholly apart from license fees—it is costly and obviously available only to the wealthy nonresident or to the one so taken with the sport that he sacrifices other values in order to indulge in it and to enjoy what it offers. It is not a means to the nonresident's livelihood." Thus, the Court held, "Whatever rights or activities may be 'fundamental' under the Privileges and Immunities Clause, we are persuaded, and hold, that elk hunting by nonresidents in Montana is not one of them."

- *Supreme Court of New Hampshire v. Piper*, 470 U.S. 274 (1985). Rule 42 of the New Hampshire Supreme Court limited bar admission to state residents. The Court invalidated the rule. The Court held that the practice of law is a "fundamental right" protected by the privilege and immunities clause because "the practice of law is important to the national economy." Moreover, "Out-of-state lawyers may—and often do—represent persons who raise unpopular federal claims. In some cases, representation by nonresident counsel may be the only means available for the vindication of federal rights."

Closely Related to Substantial State Interest and Less Discriminatory Means Are Not Available

A state may discriminate against citizens of other states, even with regard to fundamental rights, if the law is closely related (i.e., sufficiently tailored so the degree of discrimination is not excessive) to a substantial state interest (i.e., a substantial reason for treating nonresidents differently than residents), and less discriminatory means are not available.

- *Hicklin v. Orbeck*, 437 U.S. 518 (1978). An "Alaska Hire" statute required that all Alaskan oil and gas leases contain a requirement that qualified Alaska residents be hired in preference to nonresidents. The Court invalidated the statute because it was not "closely related" to the purported state interest. Alaska argued the statute was enacted to reduce unemployment in the state. However, the Court explained "the major cause of Alaska's high unemployment was not the influx of nonresidents seeking employment, but rather the fact that a substantial number of Alaska's jobless residents—especially the unemployed Eskimo and Indian residents—were unable to secure employment either because of their lack of education and job training or because of their geographical remoteness from job opportunities."

  Moreover, "Alaska Hire simply grants all Alaskans, regardless of their employment status, education, or training, a flat employment preference for all jobs covered by the Act. A highly skilled and educated resident who has never been unemployed is entitled to precisely the same preferential treatment as the unskilled, habitually unemployed Arctic Eskimo enrolled in a job-training program."

- *Supreme Court of New Hampshire v. Piper*, 470 U.S. 274 (1985). Rule 42 of the New Hampshire Supreme Court limited bar admission to state residents. The Court invalidated the rule. The Court held the rule was not closely related to a substantial state interest. The Supreme Court of New Hampshire claimed that nonresident members of the bar would be less likely to become familiar with local rules and procedures, to behave ethically, to be available for court proceedings, and to do pro bono work in the state.

  However, the Court explained "There is no evidence to support appellant's claim that nonresidents might be less likely to keep abreast of local rules and procedures," and "there is no reason to believe that a nonresident lawyer will conduct his practice in a dishonest manner" (no substantial state interest). Regarding availability for court proceedings, the Court explained "in those cases where the nonresident counsel will be unavailable on short notice, the State can protect its interests through less restrictive means. The trial court, by rule or as an exercise of discretion, may require any lawyer who resides at a great distance to retain a local attorney who will be available for unscheduled meetings and hearings" (less discriminatory means available). Regarding pro bono work, the Court explained, "We think it is reasonable to believe, however, that most lawyers who become members of a state bar will endeavor to perform their share of these services."

PRIVILEGES OR IMMUNITIES CLAUSE (PROTECTS RIGHTS OF NATIONAL CITIZENSHIP)

The privileges or immunities clause states, "No State shall make or enforce any law which shall abridge the privileges or immunities of citizens of the United States" (U.S. Const. amend. XIV, § 1). This clause prohibits states from terminating certain federal rights that derive from being a citizen of the federal government (i.e., "national citizenship"). These rights include the right to vote in federal elections, the right to interstate travel or commerce, the right to enter federal lands, and the rights of a citizen while in the custody of federal officers [*Slaughter-House Cases*, 83 U.S. (16 Wall.) 36 (1873)]. However, the clause does not protect any of the rights found in the first ten Amendments to the Constitution (the Bill of Rights).

- *Saenz v. Roe*, 526 U.S. 489 (1999). A California statute limited the amount of welfare benefits payable to a family that had resided in the state for less than twelve months to the amount payable by the state of the family's prior residence. The Court invalidated the statute. California argued the statute would save the state approximately $10.9 million a year. However, the Court explained that the privileges or immunities clause protects the right to interstate travel, and the right to interstate travel includes "the right of the newly arrived citizen to the same privileges and immunities enjoyed by other citizens of the same State." In other words, "the right to travel embraces the citizen's right to be treated equally in her new State of residence." The statute discriminated against newly arrived citizens so it was invalid.

TWENTY-FIRST AMENDMENT

From 1919 until 1933, the Eighteenth Amendment to the Constitution totally prohibited "the manufacture, sale, or transportation of intoxicating liquors" in the United States. Section 1 of the Twenty-first Amendment repealed that prohibition, and Section 2 delegated to the states the power to prohibit commerce in, or the use of, alcoholic beverages. Section 2 states "The transportation or importation into any State, Territory, or possession of the United States for delivery or use therein of intoxicating liquors, in violation of the laws thereof, is hereby prohibited" (U.S. Const., amend. XXI, § 2). Thus, the Twenty-first Amendment gives the states power to prohibit the importation of liquor into a state for delivery or use in the state [*44 Liquormart, Inc. v. Rhode Island*, 517 U.S. 484 (1996)]. However, the Court has held that state laws that violate other provisions of the Constitution (e.g., the First Amendment, establishment clause, equal protection clause, commerce clause, and due process clause) are not saved by the Twenty-first Amendment.

- *Hostetter v. Idlewild Bon Voyage Liquor Corp.*, 377 U.S. 324 (1964). Idlewild was in the business of selling bottled wines and liquors to departing international airline travelers at the John F. Kennedy Airport in New York. The liquor purchased was not delivered to the customer until he arrived at his foreign destination. New York law prohibited the sales. The Court invalidated the law because it violated the commerce clause. New York claimed the law was valid under the Twenty-first Amendment. However, the Court explained that the Twenty-first Amendment did not empower New York to prohibit the passage of liquor through its territory in this case because, "Here, ultimate delivery and use is not in New York, but in a foreign country." Thus, "The State has not sought to regulate or control the passage of intoxicants through her territory in the interest of preventing their unlawful diversion into the internal commerce of the State."

- *Bacchus Imports, Ltd. v. Dias*, 468 U.S. 263 (1984). The Hawaii Liquor Tax imposed a 20 percent excise tax on sales of liquor at wholesale, but exempted from the tax certain locally produced alcoholic beverages. The Court invalidated the tax exemption because it violated the commerce clause. Hawaii adopted the tax exemption to encourage the development of the Hawaiian liquor industry, in particular, pineapple wine and okolehao, a brandy distilled from the root of the ti plant, an indigenous shrub of Hawaii. When Hawaii prepared its brief on the merits in the U.S. Supreme Court, it claimed for the first time that the tax exemption was valid under the Twenty-first Amendment.

However, the Court explained "The central purpose of the [Twenty-first Amendment] was not to empower States to favor local liquor industries by erecting barriers to competition." Moreover, "the State does not seek to justify its tax on the ground that it was designed to promote temperance or to carry out any other purpose of the Twenty-first Amendment, but instead acknowledges that the purpose was 'to promote a local industry.' Consequently, because the tax violates a central tenet of the Commerce Clause but is not supported by any clear concern of the Twenty-first Amendment, we reject the State's belated claim based on the Amendment."

- *Granholm v. Heald*, 544 U.S. 460 (2005). Michigan and New York regulated the sale and importation of wine. The regulations allowed in-state wineries to sell wine directly to consumers in that state, but prohibited out-of-state wineries from doing so, or at least made direct sales impractical from an economic standpoint (facially discriminatory). The Court invalidated the regulations. The states argued the regulations were valid under the Twenty-first Amendment. However, the Court explained, "Bacchus forecloses any contention that § 2 of the Twenty-first Amendment immunizes discriminatory direct-shipment laws from Commerce Clause scrutiny." For, "State policies are protected under the Twenty-first Amendment when they treat liquor produced out of state the same as its domestic equivalent. The instant cases, in contrast, involve straightforward attempts to discriminate in favor of local producers. The discrimination is contrary to the Commerce Clause and is not saved by the Twenty-first Amendment."

CHAPTER 9

Intergovernmental Immunity

THE SUPREMACY CLAUSE LIMITS STATE TAXATION AND REGULATION OF THE FEDERAL government, and state sovereignty principles limit federal taxation and regulation of state governments.

STATE TAXATION OF THE FEDERAL GOVERNMENT (LEGAL INCIDENCE TEST)

A state tax is unconstitutional if it imposes a duty to pay on the federal government, or on an "agency or instrumentality" so closely connected to the government that the two cannot realistically be viewed as separate entities, unless Congress expressly allows the tax. However, a state tax is constitutional if it imposes a duty to pay on a private entity (e.g., a contractor), even if the tax ultimately increases costs for the federal government. This is called the "legal incidence" test because the issue is whether the legal incidence of the tax (i.e., the obligation to pay) falls on the federal government or a private entity.

- *McCulloch v. Maryland*, 17 U.S. (4 Wheat.) 316 (1819). A Maryland law imposed a tax on a branch of the Bank of the United States that was located in Maryland. The Court invalidated the tax. The Court explained that (1) Congress had the power to create the Bank of the United States; (2) the power to create implies the power to preserve; and (3) "the power to tax involves the power to destroy." Thus, the Court held the tax was unconstitutional because it could tax the Bank of the United States out of existence. The Court concluded, "the states have no power, by taxation or otherwise, to retard, impede, burden, or in any manner control, the operations of the constitutional laws enacted by congress to carry into execution the powers vested in the general government. This is, we think, the unavoidable consequence of that supremacy which the constitution has declared. We are unanimously of opinion, that the law passed by the legislature of Maryland, imposing a tax on the Bank of the United States, is unconstitutional and void."

- *James v. Dravo Contracting Co.*, 302 U.S. 134 (1937). West Virginia imposed a tax on the gross receipts of an independent contractor who had construction contracts with the federal government. The Court upheld the tax. The Court explained that even if the tax increased the cost to the federal government, it was imposed on the earnings of the contractor, a private entity, and not upon the federal government, its officers or property, or upon the contract of federal government. Thus, the tax "did not interfere in any substantial way with the performance of federal functions."

- *United States v. New Mexico*, 455 U.S. 720 (1982). New Mexico imposed a tax on the gross receipts of companies that contracted with the federal government to build and manage government-owned atomic laboratories in New Mexico. The government gave the contractors "advanced funding" so they could pay their creditors and employees from a bank account in which U.S. Treasury funds were deposited. The Court upheld the tax. The Court explained that the "legal incidence" of the tax fell on the contractors, who were privately owned corporations, and not upon the federal government. Also, federal funding of the contracts did not make the contractors part of the federal government because "If receipt of advanced funding is coextensive with status as a federal instrumentality, virtually every federal contractor is, or could easily become, immune from state taxation."

STATE REGULATION OF THE FEDERAL GOVERNMENT

State regulation of the federal government is unconstitutional if it interferes with federal law, activities, or policy, unless Congress expressly allows the regulation.

- *Johnson v. Maryland*, 254 U.S. 51 (1920). A U.S. Post Office employee drove a government truck through Maryland to transport mail, but he did not have a Maryland driver's license. Maryland arrested, tried, and convicted him for driving without a license. The Court reversed the conviction. The Court explained that requiring a state driver's license is an attempt to regulate an act the person was employed by the government to do, and "requires qualifications in addition to those that the Government has pronounced sufficient."

- *Mayo v. United States*, 319 U.S. 441 (1943). The Florida Commercial Fertilizer Law regulated the sale and distribution of commercial fertilizer and required that every bag of fertilizer have a stamp showing an inspection fee was paid. The United States, acting under the direction of the secretary of agriculture and the Soil Conservation and Domestic Allotment Act, bought commercial fertilizer and distributed it to consumers in Florida without the inspection stamps required by Florida law. The Court held that Florida could not require inspection fees in this case because of federal immunity from state regulation. The Court explained that "These inspection fees are laid directly upon the United States. They are money exactions the payment of which, if they are enforceable, would be required before executing a function of government. Such a requirement is prohibited by the supremacy clause."

- *Sperry v. Florida*, 373 U.S. 379 (1963). Sperry was a nonlawyer registered to practice before the U.S. Patent Office, but not admitted to practice law before the Florida bar. Florida enjoined him from preparing and prosecuting patent applications in Florida based on Florida law prohibiting the unauthorized practice of law. The Court vacated the order enjoining Sperry. The Court explained that federal law "expressly permits the Commissioner [of Patents] to authorize practice before the Patent Office by non-lawyers, and the Commissioner has explicitly granted such authority. If the authorization is unqualified, then, by virtue of the

Supremacy Clause, Florida may not deny to those failing to meet its own qualifications the right to perform the functions within the scope of the federal authority."

FEDERAL TAXATION OF STATE GOVERNMENTS

Federal taxation of state governments is unconstitutional if it interferes unduly with a state's performance of traditional governmental functions.

- *Ohio v. Helvering*, 292 U.S. 360 (1934). Federal statutes imposed a tax on every person selling liquors. Ohio was engaged in the sale of liquor in state-owned liquor stores. Helvering, as Commissioner of Internal Revenue, threatened to levy and collect taxes on the agencies and operations of Ohio in the conduct of its department of liquor control. Ohio claimed it was immune from the tax because it was an attempt to tax a sovereign state that was performing a "governmental function." However, the Court upheld the tax. The Court explained, "Whenever a state engages in a business of a private nature, it exercises nongovernmental functions, and the business, though conducted by the state, is not immune from the exercise of the power of taxation which the Constitution vests in the Congress."

- *New York v. United States*, 326 U.S. 572 (1946). The 1932 Revenue Act imposed a tax on mineral waters. The United States used the Act to assess taxes against New York on the sale of mineral waters taken from Saratoga Springs, New York. New York claimed immunity from the tax. However, the Court upheld the tax. The Court explained that New York "is engaged in an enterprise in which the State sells mineral waters in competition with private waters, the sale of which Congress has found necessary to tap as a source of revenue for carrying on the National Government. To say that the States cannot be taxed for enterprises generally pursued, like the sale of mineral water, because it is somewhat connected with a State's conservation policy, is to invoke an irrelevance to the federal taxing power."

- *Massachusetts v. United States*, 435 U.S. 444 (1978). Congress enacted the Airport and Airway Revenue Act. The Act imposed an annual "flat fee" registration tax on all civil aircraft, including those owned by the states and the federal government, that flew in the navigable airspace of the United States. The registration tax was collected under protest from the Commonwealth of Massachusetts with respect to a helicopter it used exclusively for patrolling highways and other police functions. Massachusetts claimed the tax was invalid under the doctrine of implied immunity of state government from federal taxation. However, the Court upheld the tax.

The Court explained the tax did not unduly interfere with the state's ability to perform essential services because (1) the tax did not discriminate against state functions, as it applied not only to private users of the airways but also to civil aircraft operated by the United States; (2) the tax merely recovered the costs of federal aviation programs from those who use the national air system and was a fair approximation of those costs; and (3) the tax was not excessive in relation to the cost of the government benefits supplied.

- *South Carolina v. Baker*, 485 U.S. 505 (1988). An Internal Revenue code provision imposed federal income tax liability on interest earned from unregistered state and local government bonds. South Carolina claimed the tax was invalid under the doctrine of intergovernmental tax immunity. However, the Court upheld the tax. The Court explained that the tax "imposes no direct tax on the States. The tax is imposed on and collected from bondholders, not States, and any increased administrative costs incurred by States in implementing the registration system are not 'taxes' within the meaning of the tax immunity doctrine."

FEDERAL REGULATION OF STATE GOVERNMENTS

Federal commercial regulation of state governments is constitutional if it regulates state governments and private entities equally and is otherwise valid. The states are represented in Congress, so "[t]he political process ensures that the laws that unduly burden the States will not be promulgated" [*Garcia v. San Antonio Metropolitan Transit Authority*, 469 U.S. 528 (1985)]. However, the federal government may not require state or local governments to enact laws, or require state or local executive officers to enforce federal law.

- *Garcia v. San Antonio Metropolitan Transit Authority*, 469 U.S. 528 (1985). Congress enacted the Fair Labor Standards Act (FLSA), which provided minimum-wage and overtime requirements. The Department of Labor applied the Act to the San Antonio Metropolitan Transit Authority (SAMTA), a public mass-transit authority. The Court upheld the application of the FLSA to SAMTA. The Court explained "we need go no further than to state that we perceive nothing in the overtime and minimum-wage requirements of the FLSA, as applied to SAMTA, that is destructive of state sovereignty or violative of any constitutional provision. SAMTA faces nothing more than the same minimum-wage and overtime obligations that hundreds of thousands of other employers, public as well as private, have to meet."

- *New York v. United States*, 505 U.S. 144 (1992). Congress enacted the Low-Level Radioactive Waste Policy Amendments Act of 1985. A provision of the Act gave states the "option" of either regulating the disposal of waste in conformity with federal guidelines, or in the alternative taking title to and possession of the waste and becoming liable for damages caused by the waste. The Court invalidated this provision because both options were "unconstitutionally coercive." The Court explained, "The Federal Government may not compel the States to enact or administer a federal regulatory program." So Congress could not simply direct the states to regulate the disposal of radioactive waste. And forcing states to "take title" to waste and become liable for damages would "commandeer" state governments into the service of federal regulatory purposes, and would be "inconsistent with the Constitution's division of authority between federal and state governments."

- *Printz v. United States*, 521 U.S. 898 (1997). Congress enacted the Brady Handgun Violence Prevention Act. A provision of the Act commanded the chief law enforcement officer (CLEO) of each local jurisdiction to conduct background checks on prospective handgun purchasers until a national system for background checks became operative. The Court invalidated the provision. The Court explained "the Federal Government may not compel the States to implement, by legislation or executive action, federal regulatory programs," and "The mandatory obligation imposed on CLEOs to perform background checks on prospective handgun purchasers plainly runs afoul of that rule."

- *Reno v. Condon*, 528 U.S. 141 (2000). Congress enacted the Driver's Privacy Protection Act, which restricted the ability of the states to sell or release a driver's personal information without the driver's consent. The Court upheld the Act. The Court explained the Act did not require the South Carolina legislature to enact any laws or regulations, as did the statute at issue in *New York*. Nor did the act require state officials to assist in the enforcement of federal statutes regulating private individuals, as did the law considered in *Printz*. The act simply regulated the states as the owners of databases.

CHAPTER 10

Separation of Powers Doctrine

Articles I, II, and III of the Constitution define legislative, executive, and judicial power, respectively, and separate federal power among three branches of government. The separation of powers prevents tyranny by dispersing federal power among three branches.

However, the three branches of government are not completely separate. For example, the president participates in the law-making process by virtue of his authority to veto bills enacted by Congress. And the Senate participates in the appointment process by virtue of its authority to refuse to confirm persons nominated to office by the president. Some interaction between the branches of government is necessary.

The separation of powers doctrine generally provides that one branch of the government may not intrude on the central prerogatives of another branch, or impair another branch in the performance of its constitutional duties.

LEGISLATIVE POWER

Delegation of Legislative Power (Nondelegation Doctrine)

The Constitution provides that "All legislative Powers herein granted shall be vested in a Congress of the United States" (U.S. Const.

art. I, § 1). This provision gave rise to the nondelegation doctrine, which provides that Congress generally cannot delegate its legislative power to another branch. Yet Congress sometimes delegates some of its power to the executive or judicial branches (e.g., to executive agencies such as the FCC, SEC, FDA, and EPA). This raises a separation of powers issue because it conflicts with the idea that Congress alone possesses federal legislative power.

However, Congress may delegate some of its power to another branch so long as Congress provides "intelligible principles" (i.e., specific and detailed criteria) to guide the delegated branch in exercising its discretion.

- *A.L.A. Schechter Poultry Corporation v. United States*, 295 U.S. 495 (1935). Section 3 of the National Industrial Recovery Act authorized the president to prescribe "codes of fair competition" for certain industries to promote industrial recovery and rehabilitation. The Court invalidated the provision.

  The Court explained "Section 3 of the Recovery Act is without precedent. It supplies no standards for any trade, industry, or activity. It does not undertake to prescribe rules of conduct to be applied to particular states of fact determined by appropriate administrative procedure. Instead of prescribing rules of conduct, it authorizes the making of codes to prescribe them. For that legislative undertaking, section 3 sets up no standards, aside from the statement of the general aims of rehabilitation, correction, and expansion described in section 1. In view of the scope of that broad declaration and of the nature of the few restrictions that are imposed, the discretion of the President in approving or prescribing codes, and thus enacting laws for the government of trade and industry throughout the country, is virtually unfettered. We think that the code-making authority thus conferred is an unconstitutional delegation of legislative power." Justice Cardozo (concurring) added, "The delegated power of legislation which has found expression in this code is not canalized within banks that keep it from overflowing. It is unconfined and vagrant."

- *Mistretta v. United States*, 488 U.S. 361 (1989). Congress passed the Sentencing Reform Act of 1984. The Act created the United States Sentencing Commission as an independent body in the judicial branch with power to promulgate binding sentencing guidelines for federal offenses and defendants according to specific and detailed factors. The Court upheld Congress's delegation of power. The Court explained, "we harbor no doubt that Congress' delegation of authority to the Sentencing Commission is sufficiently specific and detailed to meet constitutional requirements."

- *Loving v. United States*, 116 S. Ct. 1737 (1996). The Uniform Code of Military Justice allowed for the death penalty in military cases for premeditated and felony murder, but did not specifically identify the aggravating factors required for imposing the death penalty, as required by the Constitution. Congress delegated its constitutional authority to the president to define the aggravating factors required for the death penalty. The president issued an executive order promulgating a rule that enumerated 11 categories of aggravating factors sufficient for imposing the death penalty, and required that at least one aggravating factor be present. The Court upheld Congress's delegation of power.

  The Court noted that the Constitution gives Congress the power "To make Rules for the Government and Regulation of the land and naval Forces" (U.S. Const. art. I, § 8, cl. 14). However, the Court explained, "we discern no reasons why Congress should have less capacity to make measured and appropriate delegations of this power than of any other." The Court added, "we give Congress the highest deference in ordering military affairs." The Court concluded, "We decline to import into Clause 14 a restrictive nondelegation principle that the Framers left out."

- *Whitman v. American Trucking Associations*, 531 U.S. 457 (2001). The Clean Air Act delegated authority to the Environmental Protection Agency to set national ambient air quality standards at levels "requisite to protect public health." The Court upheld Congress's delegation of power. The Court explained the Act contained an "intelligible principle" for setting air quality standards, and there was no necessity that the Act set precise upper limits for pollutants. The Court concluded, "The scope of discretion [the Act] allows is in fact well within the outer limits of our nondelegation precedents."

"Legislative Veto" (Unconstitutional)

Congress sometimes delegates some of its power to the executive branch (e.g., to executive agencies). To maintain some control over how the executive branch used this power, Congress sometimes included a "legislative veto" provision in the legislation that delegated the power. A legislative veto provision allowed Congress, or one of its houses or committees, to reject a regulation proposed by the executive branch before it took effect.

However, the presentment requirement provides that all legislation be presented to the president before becoming law (U.S. Const. art. I, § 7, cl. 2). And the bicameral requirement provides that no law take effect without the concurrence of the prescribed majority of the members of both houses (U.S. Const. art. I, §§ 1, 7). Thus, Congress may legislate only if there is presentment and bicameralism.

Legislative vetoes are, in effect, legislation without presentment or bicameralism, and are therefore unconstitutional.

- *Immigration and Naturalization Service v. Chadha*, 462 U.S. 919 (1983). The Immigration and Nationality Act delegated to the attorney general the power to suspend the deportation of aliens in certain situations. The Act also included a "legislative veto" provision that allowed either house of Congress to pass a resolution to "veto" the attorney general's decision. The Court invalidated the legislative veto provision. The Court explained that the legislative veto provision had "the purpose and effect of altering the legal rights, duties and relations of persons." So it was "essentially legislative in purpose and effect." Because it was legislative, the legislative veto provision was required to satisfy the procedural requirements of passage by a majority of both houses (bicameralism) and presentation to the president (presentment). The legislative veto provision did not satisfy these requirements, so it was unconstitutional.

Appointment Power (Appointments Clause)

Any appointee exercising significant authority pursuant to the laws of the United States is an "officer of the United States" and must be appointed according to the appointments clause (U.S. Const. art. II, § 2).

Only the president may nominate, and with the Senate's advice and consent, appoint, "principal" federal officers (e.g., ambassadors, other public ministers and consuls, judges of the Supreme Court, and cabinet officers).

Congress may allow the president, the heads of departments, or the judiciary to appoint "inferior" federal officers (e.g., election supervisors or "independent counsel"). Congress itself may not appoint any federal officers, principal or inferior.

Congress may appoint "employees" to exercise powers of an investigative or informative nature. "Employees" are "lesser functionaries subordinate to officers of the United States" [*Buckley v. Valeo*, 424 U.S. 1 (1976)].

* *Buckley v. Valeo*, 424 U.S. 1 (1976). The Federal Election Campaign Act of 1971, as amended in 1974, created an eight-member commission with extensive rule-making, adjudicatory, and enforcement powers. The commission included two members appointed by the president pro tempore of the Senate, two members appointed by the Speaker of the House, two members appointed by the president (all appointments subject to confirmation by both houses of Congress), and the secretary of the Senate and clerk of the House as nonvoting members. The Court invalidated the commission because Congress may not appoint federal officers.

  The Court explained that "Although two members of the Commission are initially selected by the President, his nominations are subject to confirmation not merely by the Senate, but by the House of Representatives as well. The remaining four voting members of the Commission are appointed by the President pro tempore of the Senate and by the Speaker of the House. While the second part of the [Appointments] Clause authorizes Congress to vest the appointment of the officers described in that part in 'the Courts of Law, or in the Heads of Departments,' neither the Speaker of the House nor the President pro tempore of the Senate comes within this language."

* *Morrison v. Olson*, 487 U.S. 654 (1988). The Ethics in Government Act created a special court ("Special Division") with authority to appoint an "independent counsel" to investigate and, if

appropriate, prosecute certain high-ranking government officials for violations of federal criminal laws. The Court upheld the Act. The Court explained that independent counsel is an "inferior" officer because (1) he is "subject to removal by a higher Executive Branch official," the attorney general; (2) his role "is restricted primarily to investigation and, if appropriate, prosecution for certain federal crimes"; and (3) "the office of independent counsel is 'temporary' in the sense that an independent counsel is appointed essentially to accomplish a single task, and when that task is over the office is terminated." Also, the appointments clause "seems clearly to give Congress significant discretion to determine whether it is 'proper' to vest the appointment of, for example, executive officials in the 'courts of Law.'"

Removal Power

Only the president may remove executive officers. Congress may not remove an executive officer except by impeachment. However, Congress can limit the president's power to remove an executive officer if there is good reason why the office should be independent of the president and removal power is limited to where "good cause" is shown for the removal.

* *Humphrey's Executor v. United States*, 295 U.S. 602 (1935). A provision of the Federal Trade Commission Act allowed the president to remove members of the Federal Trade Commission only for inefficiency, neglect of duty, or malfeasance in office. The Court upheld the provision. The Court explained, "The authority of Congress, in creating quasi legislative or quasi judicial agencies, to require them to act in discharge of their duties independently of executive control cannot well be doubted; and that authority includes, as an appropriate incident, power to fix the period during which they shall continue, and to forbid their removal except for cause in the meantime."

* *Bowsher v. Synar*, 478 U.S. 714 (1986). The Balanced Budget and Emergency Deficit Control Act of 1985 set a maximum deficit amount for federal spending per year for five years. Provisions of the Act required the comptroller general to review deficit estimates and budget reduction calculations and report his conclusions to

the president. The Act also provided that Congress could remove the comptroller general not only by impeachment but also for "inefficiency," "neglect of duty," and "malfeasance." The Court invalidated these provisions.

First, the Court explained that the comptroller general was an executive officer because "the Comptroller General must exercise judgment concerning facts that affect the application of the Act. He must also interpret the provisions of the Act to determine precisely what budgetary calculations are required. Decisions of that kind are typically made by officers charged with executing a statute." Second, the Court explained "Congress cannot reserve for itself the power of removal of an officer charged with the execution of the laws except by impeachment. To permit the execution of the laws to be vested in an officer answerable only to Congress would, in practical terms, reserve in Congress control over the execution of the laws."

- *Morrison v. Olson*, 487 U.S. 654 (1988). The Ethics in Government Act created a special court ("Special Division") with authority to appoint an "independent counsel" to investigate and, if appropriate, prosecute certain high-ranking government officials for violations of federal criminal laws. A provision of the Act allowed the attorney general to remove the independent counsel only in instances in which he could show "good cause." The Court upheld the provision.

  The Court distinguished *Bowsher*, explaining that unlike *Bowsher*, "this case does not involve an attempt by Congress itself to gain a role in the removal of executive officials other than its established powers of impeachment and conviction. The Act instead puts the removal power squarely in the hands of the Executive Branch." The Court concluded "the congressional determination to limit the removal power of the Attorney General was essential, in the view of Congress, to establish the necessary independence of the office. We do not think that this limitation as it presently stands sufficiently deprives the President of control over the independent counsel to interfere impermissibly with his constitutional obligation to ensure the faithful execution of the laws."

- *Free Enter. Fund v. Pub. Co. Accounting Oversight Bd.*, 177 L. Ed. 2d 706 (2010). After "a series of celebrated accounting debacles," Congress enacted the Sarbanes-Oxley Act of 2002, which created the Public Company Accounting Oversight Board. The Board was composed of five members appointed by the Securities and Exchange Commission. The Commission could remove a Board member only "for good cause." The president could remove a commissioner only for "inefficiency, neglect of duty, or malfeasance in office" (the *Humphrey's Executor* standard). So, the president was restricted in his ability to remove a principal officer (a commissioner), who was in turn restricted in his ability to remove an inferior officer (a Board member). The Court invalidated this "multilevel protection" from removal of Board members.

  The Court explained, "we have previously upheld limited restrictions on the President's removal power. In those cases, however, only one level of protected tenure separated the President from an officer exercising executive power. It was the President—or a subordinate he could remove at will—who decided whether the officer's conduct merited removal under the good-cause standard. The Act before us does something quite different. It not only protects Board members from removal except for good cause, but withdraws from the President any decision on whether that good cause exists. That decision is vested instead in other tenured officers—the Commissioners—none of whom is subject to the President's direct control. The result is a Board that is not accountable to the President, and a President who is not responsible for the Board."

  The Court added, "if allowed to stand, this dispersion of responsibility could be multiplied. If Congress can shelter the bureaucracy behind two layers of good-cause tenure, why not a third? . . . The officers of such an agency—safely encased within a Matryoshka doll of tenure protections—would be immune from Presidential oversight, even as they exercised power in the people's name."

  The Court concluded, "By granting the Board executive power without the Executive's oversight, this Act subverts the President's ability to ensure that the laws are faithfully executed—as well as the public's ability to pass judgment on his efforts.

The Act's restrictions are incompatible with the Constitution's separation of powers."

Legislative Immunity

The "speech or debate" clause provides members of Congress and their aides immunity from civil or criminal liability for "legislative acts" and the motives for those acts (U.S. Const. art. I, § 6). The clause also provides the right not to be questioned about those acts and motives. Congressional aides are protected by legislative immunity when they perform acts that would be protected if performed by a member of Congress. Legislative immunity reinforces legislative independence and separation of powers.

State legislators are not protected by the speech or debate clause; only federal legislators are protected [*United States v. Gillock*, 445 U.S. 360 (1980)].

Legislative Acts and Motives (Protected)

Legislative acts, and the motivation for those acts, are protected by legislative immunity. Legislative acts include speech and debate in either house, preparation of internal reports, voting, and other matters that are "an integral part of the deliberative and communicative processes by which Members participate in committee and House proceedings." [*Gravel v. United States*, 408 U.S. 606 (1972)]

- *Gravel v. United States*, 408 U.S. 606 (1972). A U.S. senator read to a subcommittee from classified documents (the Pentagon Papers) that he then placed in the public record. An aide, Dr. Rodberg, assisted the senator in preparing for and conducting the hearing. A grand jury investigating possible violations of federal law subpoenaed the aide. The Court held that the senator and his aide were immune from grand jury questioning about their investigatory acts in preparation for the subcommittee hearing. The speech or debate clause prohibited inquiry into things done by Dr. Rodberg as the senator's aide that would have been legislative acts, and therefore privileged, if performed by the senator personally.

  The Court explained "it is literally impossible, in view of the complexities of the modern legislative process, with Congress almost constantly in session and matters of legislative concern constantly proliferating, for Members of Congress to perform their legislative tasks without the help of aides and assistants; that the day-to-day work of such aides is so critical to the Members' performance that they must be treated as the latter's alter egos; and that if they are not so recognized, the central role of the Speech or Debate Clause—to prevent intimidation of legislators by the Executive and accountability before a possibly hostile judiciary— will inevitably be diminished and frustrated."

• *United States v. Helstoski*, 442 U.S. 477 (1979). While Helstoski was a member of the House, the Department of Justice began investigating reported political corruption, including allegations that aliens had paid money for the introduction of private bills that would suspend the application of the immigration laws so as to allow them to remain in this country. The government sought to introduce evidence of past legislative acts to show motive. Helstoski asserted his privilege under the speech or debate clause. The Court upheld the privilege. The Court explained "the Speech or Debate Clause was designed to preclude prosecution of Members for legislative acts." Thus, "references to past legislative acts of a Member cannot be admitted without undermining the values protected by the Clause."

Political Acts and Promises (Not Protected)

Political acts are not protected by legislative immunity because they are political in nature rather than legislative (e.g., errands performed for constituents, making appointments with governmental agencies, assistance in securing government contracts, preparing newsletters to constituents, news releases, and speeches delivered outside Congress) [*United States v. Brewster*, 408 U.S. 501 (1972)].

Similarly, a promise by a member of Congress to perform an act in the future is not protected by legislative immunity because it is not a legislative act (e.g., a promise to deliver a speech, introduce a bill, vote a particular way on a bill, or solicit other votes at some future date) [*United States v. Brewster*, 408 U.S. 501 (1972) (holding a former senator could be indicted for accepting a bribe because "Taking a bribe is, obviously, no part of the legislative process or function; it is not a legislative act," and "no inquiry into legislative acts or motivation for legislative acts is necessary for the Government to make out a prima facie case"); *United States v. Helstoski*, 442 U.S. 477 (1979)].

Republication of Materials (Not Protected)

Although voting and preparing committee reports are legislative acts and are protected by the speech or debate clause, republishing (e.g., in press releases or newsletters) statements originally made in Congress is not protected by the speech or debate clause [*Hutchinson v. Proxmire*, 443 U.S. 111 (1979) (holding, "Valuable and desirable as it may be in broad terms, the transmittal of such information by individual Members in order to inform the public and other Members is not a part of the legislative function or the deliberations that make up the legislative process. As a result, transmittal of such information by press releases and newsletters is not protected by the Speech or Debate Clause")].

- *Doe v. McMillan*, 412 U.S. 306 (1973). Parents of District of Columbia (DC) school children sought damages and declaratory and injunctive relief for the public distribution of a congressional report on the DC school system that identified students, by name, in derogatory contexts. The Court held that the speech or debate clause provided immunity for the congressional committee members, members of their staff, the consultant, and the investigator for conducting hearings, preparing the report, and voting for its publication because these were legislative acts.

  However, there was no immunity for others such as the superintendent of documents or public printer, who, with congressional authorization distributed actionable materials to the public, because these were not legislative acts. The Court explained, "we cannot accept the proposition that in order to perform its legislative function Congress not only must at times consider and use actionable material but also must be free to disseminate it to the public at large, no matter how injurious to private reputation that material might be."

- *Hutchinson v. Proxmire*, 443 U.S. 111 (1979). Senator Proxmire gave his "Golden Fleece of the Month Award," an award publicizing wasteful government spending, to federal agencies that funded a scientist's study of aggressive monkey behavior, and publicized the award nationwide in press releases and newsletters. The scientist sued the senator for defamation. The Court held the speech or debate clause did not provide the senator immunity. The Court explained that "A speech by Proxmire in the Senate would be wholly immune and would be available to other Members of Congress and the public in the Congressional Record. But neither the newsletters nor the press release was 'essential to the deliberations of the Senate' and neither was part of the deliberative process." Thus, the Court concluded that "a Member may be held liable for republishing defamatory statements originally made in either House."

Congressional Power to Investigate

Congress's power to conduct investigations is broad, as "It encompasses inquiries concerning the administration of existing laws as well as proposed or possibly needed statutes. It includes surveys of defects in our social, economic or political system for the purpose of enabling the Congress to remedy them. It comprehends probes into departments of the Federal Government to expose corruption, inefficiency or waste" [*Watkins v. United States*, 354 U.S. 178 (1957)].

- *Barenblatt v. United States*, 360 U.S. 109 (1959). While investigating alleged Communist infiltration into the field of education, a subcommittee of the House Committee on Un-American Activities asked a college professor about his membership in the Communist Party. The professor refused to answer and was convicted for contempt of Congress. The Court upheld the conviction. The Court explained that "in pursuance of its legislative concerns in the domain of 'national security' the House has clothed the Un-American Activities Committee with pervasive authority to investigate Communist activities in this country." The Court concluded "legislative authority to conduct the inquiry presently under consideration is unassailable."

- *Gibson v. Florida Legislative Investigation Committee*, 372 U.S. 539 (1963). A state legislative committee investigating Communist infiltration into organizations asked the president of the Miami branch of the NAACP to produce the association's membership lists. The president refused and was convicted for contempt. The Court reversed the conviction because there was no substantial relation between the NAACP Miami branch and Communist activities. The Court distinguished *Barenblatt* by explaining "the Committee was not here seeking from the petitioner or the records of which he was custodian any information as to whether he, himself, or even other persons were members of the Communist Party, Communist front or affiliated organizations, or other allegedly subversive groups; instead, the entire thrust of the demands on the petitioner was that he disclose whether other persons were members of the N.A.A.C.P., itself a concededly legitimate and nonsubversive organization."

EXECUTIVE POWER

Lawmaking Power

The president cannot make laws; he can only execute the laws, recommend laws he thinks are wise, and veto laws he thinks are bad.

* *Youngstown Sheet & Tube Co. v. Sawyer*, 343 U.S. 579 (1952). The president ordered the secretary of commerce to seize and operate most of the nation's steel mills to keep labor disputes from stopping steel production during the Korean War. No statute expressly authorized the order, but the government argued the president's authority should be implied by the president's powers as the commander in chief and chief executive. The Court invalidated the seizure order.

    The Court explained the commander in chief does not have the power to take possession of private property to keep labor disputes from stopping production because "This is a job for the Nation's lawmakers, not for its military authorities." Also, the order was not merely an exercise of the president's power as chief executive to "take Care that the Laws be faithfully executed." It was an attempt to exercise lawmaking power. The Court noted "The preamble of the order itself, like that of many statutes, sets out reasons why the President believes certain policies should be adopted, proclaims these policies as rules of conduct to be followed, and again, like a statute, authorizes a government official to promulgate additional rules and regulations consistent with the policy proclaimed and needed to carry that policy into execution." The Court explained that Congress alone has the power to adopt such policies and make such laws, and concluded "The Constitution did not subject this law-making power of Congress to presidential or military supervision or control."

Justice Jackson's concurring opinion described three zones of presidential authority. First, "When the President acts pursuant to an express or implied authorization of Congress, his authority is at its maximum, for it includes all that he possesses in his own right plus all that Congress can delegate." Second, "When the President acts in absence of either a congressional grant or denial of authority, he can only rely upon his own independent powers, but there is a zone of twilight in which he and Congress may have concurrent authority, or in which its distribution is uncertain." In this area, "any actual test of power is likely to depend on the imperatives of events and contemporary imponderables rather than on abstract theories of law." Third, "When the President takes measures incompatible with the expressed or implied will of Congress, his power is at its lowest ebb, for then he can rely only upon his own constitutional powers minus any constitutional powers of Congress over the matter."

War Power

Congress alone has the power to declare war (U.S. Const. art. I, § 8). However, the president, as commander in chief of the armed forces, may use military force to protect national interests. The War Powers Resolution restricts the president's power to involve the United States in foreign controversies without Congress's approval. But the resolution allows the president to send the military into combat without requesting Congress's approval if the United States or one of its territories is attacked (50 U.S.C.A. §§ 1541–1548). The resolution requires the president to (1) consult with Congress, where possible, before introducing troops into hostilities; (2) report to Congress within forty-eight hours after introducing troops into hostilities; and (3) withdraw troops after sixty days unless Congress declares war or authorizes a sixty-day extension. The Court has not decided the constitutionality of the War Powers Resolution, and may consider it a nonjusticiable political question.

Executive Privilege

The president has a qualified privilege protecting confidential communications between himself and his immediate advisers. However, the privilege may be overridden by a demonstrated, specific need for the evidence in a pending criminal trial [*United States v. Nixon*, 418 U.S. 683 (1974) (holding President Nixon had to comply with a subpoena issued by the Watergate Special Prosecutor for certain papers and tape recordings to be used as evidence in an upcoming criminal trial in which seven administration officials were indicted for obstruction of justice and conspiracy to defraud)]. Courts must give "utmost deference" to claims of secrecy for military or diplomatic matters. A former president may also assert executive privilege [*Nixon v. Administrator of General Services*, 433 U.S. 425 (1977) (holding that a former president, as well as an incumbent president, may assert the presidential privilege of confidentiality)].

Executive Immunity

Official Acts (Absolute Immunity)

A president, or former president, has absolute immunity from being sued for money damages for his "official acts" (i.e., "acts within the 'outer perimeter' of his official responsibility") [*Nixon v. Fitzgerald*, 457 U.S. 731 (1982) (holding an Air Force analyst was barred from suing the president for money damages based on a claim that his job was eliminated in retaliation for his exposing cost overruns in the Defense Department)].

Unofficial Acts (No Immunity)

A president has no immunity from being sued for money damages for his "unofficial acts" (i.e., personal, private acts not part of the president's official duties) [*Clinton v. Jones*, 520 U.S. 681 (1997) (holding that a private citizen could sue President Clinton for damages for an alleged sexual harassment committed while Clinton was governor of Arkansas, and that the separation of powers doctrine does not require a federal court to stay all private actions against the president until he leaves office)].

Other Executive Officials (Qualified Immunity)

Other executive officials (e.g., presidential aides and cabinet officials) generally have qualified immunity from being sued for money damages, and will be liable for civil damages only if their conduct violates a clearly established statutory or constitutional right that a reasonable person would know [*Harlow v. Fitzgerald*, 457 U.S. 800 (1982)]. An executive official does not derive any absolute immunity from the president unless he can show the function he performed was so sensitive that it demands absolute immunity (e.g., foreign policy or national security).

CHAPTER 11

Due Process

THE FIFTH AND FOURTEENTH AMENDMENTS, RESPECTIVELY, PROHIBIT THE FEDERAL government and state and local governments from depriving any person of "life, liberty, or property, without due process of law" (U.S. Const. amend. V; amend. XIV). These amendments provide two limits on government: substantive due process and procedural due process.

Substantive due process requires that government have adequate reason for depriving a person of life, liberty, or property. Thus, in substantive due process the Court reviews the substance of a law and whether it is constitutional.

Procedural due process requires that government follow certain procedures before it deprives a person of life, liberty, or property. Thus, in procedural due process the Court reviews the process by which government takes a person's life, liberty, or property, and whether it is constitutional.

SUBSTANTIVE DUE PROCESS

If a law deprives persons of life, liberty, or property, the Court determines whether the government has adequate reason to support the law. The standard of review used by the Court depends on whether the law regulates and impairs nonfundamental rights or fundamental rights.

If a law regulates and impairs nonfundamental rights such as social welfare or economic matters (e.g., laws regulating business and employment practices) the Court defers to the legislature's judgment, presumes the law valid, and upholds it so long as it is rationally related to a legitimate government purpose (rational basis test).

If a law regulates and impairs a fundamental right, the Court reviews the law with "strict scrutiny" and invalidates it unless it is necessary to achieve a compelling state interest.

Regulation of Nonfundamental Rights (Rational Basis Test)

If a law regulates and impairs nonfundamental rights such as social welfare or economic matters (e.g., laws regulating business and employment practices), the Court defers to the legislature's judgment, presumes the law valid, and upholds it so long as it is rationally related to a legitimate government purpose (rational basis test). "Rationally related" means the law must seem a reasonable way of achieving the government's purpose. A "legitimate government purpose" can be any conceivable goal that is not prohibited by the Constitution (e.g., goals within federal powers, or state "police powers" of protecting public health, safety, welfare, and morals). The government's purpose need not be the legislature's actual purpose, for the Court can hypothesize possible legitimate purposes for the law.

- *West Coast Hotel v. Parrish*, 300 U.S. 379 (1937). Washington had a minimum wage law for women. The Court upheld the law. The Court explained that women's health, protecting women from "unscrupulous and overreaching employers," and redressing their unequal bargaining power were in the public interest (legitimate government purpose). Also, a minimum wage set to meet "the very necessities of existence" was not an "arbitrary or capricious" response (i.e., the law was "rationally related" to the purpose).

- *United States v. Carolene Products Co.*, 304 U.S. 144 (1938). The Filled Milk Act of 1923 prohibited "filled milk," a product created by replacing natural milk fat with vegetable oil. The Court upheld the Act. The Court explained that Congress had investigated and concluded that "the use of filled milk as a substitute for pure milk is generally injurious to health and facilitates fraud on the public" (legitimate government purpose for the Act). The Court noted that even without such legislative findings, "the existence of facts supporting the legislative judgment is to be presumed," because the law affected only "ordinary commercial transactions" (i.e., nonfundamental rights).

- *Williamson v. Lee Optical*, 348 U.S. 483 (1955). An Oklahoma statute prohibited an optician from fitting or duplicating lenses without a prescription from an ophthalmologist or optometrist. The Court upheld the statute. The Court hypothesized possible legitimate government purposes for the statute. For example, "The legislature might have concluded that the frequency of occasions when a prescription is necessary was sufficient to justify this regulation of the fitting of eyeglasses. Likewise, when it is necessary to duplicate a lens, a written prescription may or may not be necessary. But the legislature might have concluded that one was needed often enough to require one in every case." The Court concluded "It is enough that there is an evil at hand for correction, and that it might be thought that the particular legislative measure was a rational way to correct it."

- *Lawrence v. Texas*, 539 U.S. 558 (2003). A Texas statute prohibited same-sex sodomy. The Court invalidated the statute because it violated the due process clause. First, the Court reconsidered the Court's holding in *Bowers v. Hardwick* [478 U.S. 186 (1986)]. *Bowers* upheld a Georgia statute that prohibited sodomy, same-sex or not, because there is no fundamental right to engage in homosexual sodomy, even between consenting adults in private. In *Bowers*, Justice Stevens stated in dissent, "the fact that the governing majority in a State has traditionally viewed a particular practice as immoral is not a sufficient reason for upholding a law prohibiting the practice." Moreover, individual decisions by married and unmarried persons "concerning the intimacies of their physical relationship, even when not intended to produce offspring, are a form of 'liberty' protected by the Due Process Clause of the Fourteenth Amendment."

The *Lawrence* Court adopted Justice Steven's analysis and overruled *Bowers*, as "Its continuance as precedent demeans the lives of homosexual persons." However, in overruling *Bowers* the Court did not hold that there is a "fundamental right" to engage in homosexual sodomy. Instead, the Court applied the rational basis test. The Court explained "The Texas statute furthers no legitimate state interest which can justify its intrusion into the personal and private life of the individual." Substantive due process protects the liberty of consenting adult homosexuals to engage in sodomy in private, "without intervention of the government."

Regulation of Fundamental Rights (Strict Scrutiny Test)

"Fundamental" rights include interstate travel, marriage, procreation, childrearing, contraceptives, abortion, freedom of speech and religion, and voting. Generally, if a law regulates and impairs a fundamental right, the Court reviews the law with "strict scrutiny" and invalidates it unless it is necessary to achieve a compelling state interest. "Necessary" means the law is the least-restrictive alternative means to achieve the goal. Thus, the government must show that there is no less discriminatory alternative means to achieve the goal. The government purpose is "compelling" if it is truly vital.

Interstate Travel

The right to interstate travel is a fundamental right [*United States v. Guest*, 383 U.S. 745 (1966) (holding, "The constitutional right to travel from one State to another, and necessarily to use the highways and other instrumentalities of interstate commerce in doing so, occupies a position fundamental to the concept of our Federal Union."); *Shapiro v. Thompson*, 394 U.S. 618 (1969) (invalidating a statute that denied welfare assistance to individuals who had not resided in the state for at least one year because the law deterred the migration of indigent persons into the state)]. However, a state may prevent a person who committed a crime from leaving the state [*Jones v. Helms*, 452 U.S. 412 (1981) (upholding a Georgia statute that made willful abandonment of a child a misdemeanor if the parent remained in the state and a felony if the parent left the state after the abandonment, because it served the legislative purpose of causing parents to support their children and did not infringe on the right to interstate travel)].

International Travel

The right to international travel is not a fundamental right [*Califano v. Aznavorian*, 439 U.S. 170 (1978) (upholding a Social Security Act provision that denied benefits to a person who had been residing outside of the United States for thirty days until the person returned to the United States for thirty days because it was rationally related to the congressional objective of providing benefits only to residents of the United States); *Haig v. Agee*, 453 U.S. 280 (1981) (upholding the secretary of state's power to revoke former CIA agent Philip Agee's passport because he threatened to expose CIA officers and agents operating in foreign countries, and "no governmental interest is more compelling than the security of the Nation"); *Regan v. Wald*, 468 U.S. 222 (1984) (upholding the president's decision to restrict travel to Cuba because of the traditional deference to executive judgment in foreign policy and the national interest in curtailing the flow of hard currency to Cuba that could be used in support of Cuban adventurism)].

Marriage

The right to marry is a fundamental right.

- *Loving v. Virginia*, 388 U.S. 1 (1967). A Virginia statute prohibited interracial marriage. The Court invalidated the statute. The Court explained that "Marriage is one of the basic civil rights of man, fundamental to our very existence and survival. To deny this fundamental freedom on so unsupportable a basis as the racial classifications embodied in these statutes, classifications so directly subversive of the principle of equality at the heart of the Fourteenth Amendment, is surely to deprive all the State's citizens of liberty without due process of law."

Procreation

The right to procreate is a fundamental right.

- *Skinner v. Oklahoma*, 316 U.S. 535 (1942). Oklahoma's Habitual Criminal Sterilization Act authorized the sterilization of persons convicted two or more times of "felonies involving moral turpitude," which included grand larceny, but not embezzlement. The Court invalidated the Act. The Court explained, "We are dealing here with legislation which involves one of the basic civil rights of man. Marriage and procreation are fundamental to the very existence and survival of the race. The power to sterilize, if exercised, may have subtle, far-reaching and devastating effects. In evil or reckless hands it can cause races or types which are inimical to the dominant group to wither and disappear. There is no redemption for the individual whom the law touches. Any experiment which the State conducts is to his irreparable injury. He is forever deprived of a basic liberty."

Child Care, Custody, and Control

Parents have a fundamental right to make decisions concerning the care, custody, and control of their children.

- *Pierce v. Society of Sisters*, 268 U.S. 510 (1925). The Oregon Compulsory Education Act required children between eight and sixteen years to attend public rather than private schools. The Court invalidated the Act. The Court explained "The fundamental theory of liberty upon which all governments in this Union repose excludes any general power of the state to standardize its children by forcing them to accept instruction from public teachers only. The child is not the mere creature of the state; those who nurture him and direct his destiny have the right, coupled with the high duty, to recognize and prepare him for additional obligations."

- *Santosky v. Kramer*, 455 U.S. 745 (1982). The New York Family Court Act allowed the state to terminate, over parental objection, the rights of parents to their natural child upon a finding that the child was "permanently neglected," and required that only a "fair preponderance of the evidence" support that finding. The Court invalidated the "fair preponderance of the evidence" standard. The Court explained "The fundamental liberty interest of natural parents in the care, custody, and management of their child does not evaporate simply because they have not been model parents or have lost temporary custody of their child to the State."

  The Court added that in parental rights termination proceedings, "the risk of error from using a preponderance standard is substantial; and the countervailing governmental interest favoring that standard is comparatively slight." The Court concluded that "Before a State may sever completely and irrevocably the rights of parents in their natural child, due process requires that the State support its allegations by at least clear and convincing evidence."

- *Troxel v. Granville*, 530 U.S. 57 (2000). A Washington law allowed "[a]ny person" to petition for visitation rights "at any time" and authorized state superior courts to grant such rights whenever "visitation may serve the best interest of the child." The father of two young daughters committed suicide. The paternal grandparents petitioned for the right to visit their grandchildren. The girls' mother did not oppose all visitation but opposed the amount of visitation the grandparents sought. The Court, without a majority opinion, invalidated the law.

   The Court explained "The liberty interest at issue in this case—the interest of parents in the care, custody, and control of their children—is perhaps the oldest of the fundamental liberty interests recognized by this Court." The law unconstitutionally infringed on that fundamental parental right because it was "breathtakingly broad." The Court noted it "effectively permits any third party seeking visitation to subject any decision by a parent concerning visitation of the parent's children to state-court review." Also, the law contained "no requirement that a court accord the parent's decision any presumption of validity or any weight whatsoever."

Contraceptives

The right to use contraceptives is a fundamental right.

- *Griswold v. Connecticut*, 381 U.S. 479 (1965). A Connecticut statute prohibited the use of contraceptives. Planned Parenthood League's executive director and a doctor were convicted under the law as accessories for giving information, instruction, and medical advice to married persons about preventing conception. The Court invalidated the law. The Court explained, "The present case, then, concerns a relationship lying within the zone of privacy created by several fundamental constitutional guarantees. And it concerns a law which, in forbidding the use of contraceptives rather than regulating their manufacture or sale, seeks to achieve its goals by means having a maximum destructive impact upon that relationship."

- *Eisenstadt v. Baird*, 405 U.S. 438 (1972). A Massachusetts statute permitted married persons to obtain contraceptives to prevent pregnancy but prohibited distribution of contraceptives to single persons for that purpose. The Court invalidated the statute. The Court explained "If the right of privacy means anything, it is the right of the individual, married or single, to be free from unwarranted governmental intrusion into matters so fundamentally affecting a person as the decision whether to bear or beget a child."

- *Carey v. Population Services International*, 431 U.S. 678 (1977). A New York law made it a crime for anyone other than a licensed pharmacist to distribute contraceptives to persons sixteen or over. The Court invalidated the law. The Court explained "where a decision as fundamental as that whether to bear or beget a child is involved, regulations imposing a burden on it may be justified only by compelling state interests, and must be narrowly drawn to express only those interests." The Court concluded the law was not justified by a compelling state interest because, "Insofar as [the law] applies to nonhazardous contraceptives, it bears no relation to the State's interest in protecting health."

Abortion

The right to abortion is a fundamental right. The government may not prohibit abortion before viability (the time at which there is a realistic possibility of maintaining and nourishing life outside the womb). However, the government may regulate abortion before viability so long as the regulation does not impose an "undue burden" on a woman's ability to decide whether to terminate pregnancy. A regulation imposes an "undue burden," and is invalid, if it has the purpose or effect of placing a substantial obstacle in the path of a woman who seeks abortion of a nonviable fetus.

The government may prohibit abortion after viability, unless abortion is necessary, in appropriate medical judgment, for the preservation of the mother's life or health.

- *Roe v. Wade*, 410 U.S. 113 (1973). Texas criminal abortion statutes prohibited abortions at any stage of pregnancy except to save the life of the mother. The Court invalidated the statutes. The Court explained the right to abortion was a fundamental right, and where "fundamental rights are involved, the Court has held that regulation limiting these rights may be justified only by a compelling state interest."

The Court held the state did not have a compelling state interest during the first trimester; so the government could not prohibit abortion during the first trimester, but could require minimal medical safeguards, such as requiring that the abortion be performed by a licensed medical doctor. However, the state did have a compelling state interest in protecting the mother's health during the second trimester; so a state could "regulate the abortion procedure in ways that are reasonably related to maternal health" during the second trimester. Finally, the state had a compelling state interest in "the potentiality of human life" during the third trimester; so the government could "regulate, and even proscribe, abortion except where it is necessary, in appropriate medical judgment, for the preservation of the life or health of the mother" during the third trimester.

- *Planned Parenthood v. Casey*, 505 U.S. 833 (1992). The Pennsylvania Abortion Control Act of 1982 included requirements for informed consent, a twenty-four-hour waiting period, spousal notification and consent, parental notification and consent, and reporting and record-keeping requirements. A plurality opinion overruled *Roe*'s "trimester analysis" and use of strict scrutiny for evaluating abortion regulation, and articulated a new "undue burden" test for previability regulation.

  The plurality opinion said that the government may not prohibit abortion before viability (the time at which there is a realistic possibility of maintaining and nourishing life outside the womb). However, the government may, in promoting its interests in protecting the health of the woman and life of the fetus, regulate abortion before viability so long as the regulation does not impose an "undue burden" on a woman's ability to decide whether to terminate pregnancy. A regulation imposes an "undue burden" and is invalid if its "purpose or effect is to place a substantial obstacle in the path of a woman seeking an abortion before the fetus attains viability."

  After viability, a state may, in promoting its interest in potentiality of human life, regulate and even prohibit abortion, except where it is necessary in appropriate medical judgment for the preservation of the life or health of the mother.

The Court held that the informed consent requirements, twenty-four-hour waiting period, parental consent provision, medical emergency definition, and reporting and record-keeping requirements did not impose an undue burden. However, the spousal notification provision imposed an undue burden and was invalid. The Court explained, "For the great many women who are victims of abuse inflicted by their husbands, or whose children are the victims of such abuse, a spousal notice requirement enables the husband to wield an effective veto over his wife's decision."

- *Stenberg v. Carhart*, 530 U.S. 914 (2000). A Nebraska statute prohibited "partial birth abortion" unless it was necessary to save the mother's life. The statute defined partial birth abortion as "deliberately and intentionally delivering into the vagina a living unborn child, or a substantial portion thereof, for the purpose of performing a procedure that the person performing such procedure knows will kill the unborn child and does kill the unborn child." Dilation and evacuation (D&E) was the most commonly used abortion method during the second trimester of pregnancy. Dilation and extraction (D&X), or "partial birth abortion," was a less commonly used variation of D&E, but substantial medical authority showed that it was the safest method in certain cases. The statute did not distinguish between the D&E and D&X methods. The Court invalidated the law.

First, the Court expressly adopted the "undue burden" test for evaluating previability abortion regulation. Next, the Court explained that "the law lacks any exception for the preservation of the health of the mother." The Court explained "a statute that altogether forbids D&X creates a significant health risk. The statute consequently must contain a health exception." Finally, the Court explained the statute's failure to distinguish between the D&E and D&X methods imposed "an undue burden on a woman's ability to choose a D&E abortion, thereby unduly burdening the right to choose abortion itself." Some prosecutors "may choose to pursue physicians who use D&E procedures, the most commonly used method for performing previability second trimester abortions. All those who perform abortion procedures using that method must fear prosecution, conviction, and imprisonment. The result is an undue burden upon a woman's right to make an abortion decision."

- *Gonzales v. Carhart*, 550 U.S. 124 (2007). After the *Stenberg* decision, Congress passed the Partial-Birth Abortion Ban Act of 2003. The Act prohibited "partial-birth abortion" unless it was necessary to save the mother's life. The Act defined partial birth abortion as a procedure in which the person performing the abortion "deliberately and intentionally vaginally delivers a living fetus" for the purpose of performing an overt act the person knows will kill the partially delivered living fetus. D&E is the usual abortion method in the second trimester. In D&E, a doctor dilates the cervix to insert surgical instruments into the uterus and maneuver them to evacuate the fetus. The doctor grips a fetal part with the forceps and pulls it through the cervix and vagina, continuing to pull after meeting resistance from the cervix. The friction causes the fetus to tear apart. A doctor may make ten to fifteen passes with the forceps to evacuate the fetus in its entirety. The Act prohibited a variation of D&E, referred to as "intact D&E," or dilation and extraction (D&X). The main difference between the D&E and intact D&E procedures is that in intact D&E a doctor extracts the fetus intact or largely intact with only a few passes; thus, the abortion occurs when the fetus is partially outside the mother. The Court upheld the Act.

  First, the Court explained that unlike the statute in *Stenberg*, which did not distinguish between the D&E and D&X methods, the Act "prohibits intact D&E; and, notwithstanding respondents' arguments, it does not prohibit the D&E procedure in which the fetus is removed in parts." Next, the Court held the Act's failure to include a "health exception" that would allow the intact D&E procedure where necessary for the preservation of the health of the mother did not impose an undue burden on the abortion right. The Court explained, "There is documented medical disagreement whether the Act's prohibition [of intact D&E] would ever impose significant health risks on women." The Court concluded, "The medical uncertainty over whether the Act's prohibition creates significant health risks provides a sufficient basis to conclude in this facial attack that the Act does not impose an undue burden."

Informed Consent

A state may require that women be given truthful, nonmisleading information about the nature of the abortion procedure, health risks of abortion and childbirth, and probable gestational age of the fetus. A state may also require doctors to inform a woman about the availability of information related to fetal development, consequences to the fetus, and assistance available if the woman decides to carry the pregnancy to full term. These "informed consent" requirements are constitutional as they promote the state's interest in potential life and do not impose an undue burden on a woman's ability to decide whether to terminate pregnancy [*Planned Parenthood v. Casey*, 505 U.S. 833 (1992)].

Twenty-Four-Hour Waiting Period

A state may require a twenty-four-hour waiting period between the time the woman signs a consent form and the abortion. A twenty-four-hour waiting period is constitutional as it promotes the state's interest in potential life and does not impose an undue burden on a woman's ability to decide whether to terminate pregnancy [*Planned Parenthood v. Casey*, 505 U.S. 833 (1992)].

Parental Notification and Consent

A state may require parental notification and consent for an unemancipated minor seeking an abortion, provided there is a judicial bypass procedure. A judicial bypass procedure allows the minor to have an abortion without parental notification or consent if a judge approves the abortion by finding that the minor is mature enough to decide for herself or the abortion is in her best interests. Parental notification and consent requirements are constitutional because they reasonably further the state's legitimate interest in protecting the welfare of its minor citizens [*Ohio v. Akron Center for Reproductive Health*, 497 U.S. 502 (1990) (upholding a state law that required notification of at least one parent before an unmarried minor could have an abortion but allowed the minor to avoid the notice requirement by a judicial bypass procedure); *Planned Parenthood v. Danforth*, 428 U.S. 52 (1976) (invalidating a state law that required parental consent before an unmarried minor could have an abortion but did not provide the minor a judicial bypass procedure)].

Viability Tests

A state may require that a physician, before performing an abortion after the twentieth week of pregnancy, first determine if the unborn child is viable, and in making the viability determination, perform such medical examinations and tests as are necessary to make a finding of the unborn child's gestational age, weight, and lung maturity. A viability test requirement is constitutional as it furthers the state's interest in protecting potential human life [*Webster v. Reproductive Health Services*, 492 U.S. 490 (1989)].

Reporting and Recording

The government may require a report to be filed for each abortion performed that includes the physician's name, the woman's age and marital status, the number of pregnancies and abortions the woman had experienced, the fetus's weight and gestational age, the type of abortion procedure, and medical complications from the abortion [*Planned Parenthood v. Casey*, 505 U.S. 833 (1992)]. These reporting requirements do not impose an undue burden on a woman's ability to decide whether to terminate pregnancy, and they rationally further the state's legitimate interests in advancing the state of medical knowledge concerning maternal health and prenatal life.

Government Funding

The government is not required to fund abortion [*Williams v. Zbarez*, 448 U.S. 358 (1980) (upholding an Illinois statute that prohibited state medical assistance payments for all abortions except those necessary for the preservation of the life of the mother); *Webster v. Reproductive Health Services*, 492 U.S. 490 (1989) (upholding a Missouri statute that prohibited the use of public employees and facilities to perform or assist abortions not necessary to save the mother's life)].

Spousal Notification and Consent

The government cannot require either spousal notification or spousal consent for a married woman to have an abortion. Spousal notification and consent requirements are unconstitutional because they place an undue burden on a woman's ability to decide whether to terminate pregnancy [*Planned Parenthood v. Casey*, 505 U.S. 833 (1992) (invalidating a state law that required spousal notification before a married woman could have an abortion); *Planned Parenthood v. Danforth*, 428 U.S. 52 (1976) (invalidating a state law that required spousal consent before a married woman could have an abortion)].

Voting

The right to vote is a fundamental right [*Harper v. Virginia State Bd. of Elections*, 383 U.S. 663 (1966) (invalidating a Virginia poll tax of $1.50 per year because "wealth or fee paying has, in our view, no relation to voting qualifications; the right to vote is too precious, too fundamental to be so burdened or conditioned")].

Refusing Medical Care

Competent adults have a constitutional right to refuse medical care such as lifesaving hydration and nutrition, but it is not clear if this is a fundamental right [*Cruzan v. Director, Missouri Department of Health*, 497 U.S. 261 (1990)]. Nevertheless, a state may require that an incompetent person's wishes as to the withdrawal of life-sustaining medical treatment be proven by clear and convincing evidence. [Cruzan] Also, a state is not required to accept the "substituted judgment" of close family members of a patient in a persistent vegetative state as to the withdrawal of life-sustaining medical treatment absent substantial proof that their views reflected the views of the patient. [Cruzan] State interests include the protection and preservation of human life, and guarding against potential abuses by surrogates who may not act to protect the patient.

Suicide

There is no fundamental right to commit suicide [*Washington v. Glucksberg*, 521 U.S. 702 (1997) (upholding a state law that prohibited anyone from aiding another to commit suicide because the law reasonably served legitimate state interests in preserving life and protecting the integrity of the medical profession); *Vacco v. Quill*, 521 U.S. 793 (1997) (upholding a New York law similar to the one in *Glucksberg*)].

Involuntary Commitment

The Court has not defined this right precisely. However, a person who is mentally retarded and involuntarily committed to a state institution has constitutionally protected liberty interests, under the due process clause of the Fourteenth Amendment, to reasonably safe conditions of confinement, freedom from unreasonable bodily restraints, and such minimally adequate training as reasonably may be required by these interests [*Youngberg v. Romeo*, 457 U.S. 307 (1982)].

Procedural Due Process

Procedural due process requires that the government follow certain procedures before it deprives a person of life, liberty, or property. Thus, in procedural due process the Court reviews the process by which government takes a person's life, liberty, or property, and whether it is constitutional. The government may not intentionally deprive a person of life, liberty, or property without providing notice of the charges or issue, opportunity for a hearing, and an impartial decision maker.

Intentional Government Deprivation

First, a procedural due process violation exists only if the government intentionally deprives a person of life, liberty, or property. Mere negligent government conduct is not enough [*Daniels v. Williams*, 474 U.S. 327 (1986) (holding that "the Due Process Clause is simply not implicated by a negligent act of an official causing unintended loss of or injury to life, liberty, or property")].

Second, procedural due process generally protects people only against government conduct; the government has no duty to protect people from privately inflicted harms [*DeShaney v. Winnebago County Department of Social Services*, 489 U.S. 189 (1989) (holding no due process violation occurred where social workers and local officials received complaints that a child was being abused by his father but did not remove him from his father's custody, because the abuse was inflicted by a private party, not the government)].

Life

Claims involving government deprivation of life are usually litigated under constitutional provisions other than procedural due process, such as the Fourth and Eighth Amendments.

Liberty

Liberty interests require procedural due process. "Liberty" has a broad meaning, as "the term denotes not merely freedom from bodily restraint but also the right of the individual to contract, to engage in any of the common occupations of life, to acquire useful knowledge, to marry, establish a home and bring up children, to worship God according to the dictates of his own conscience, and generally to enjoy those privileges long recognized…as essential to the orderly pursuit of happiness by free men" [*Board of Regents v. Roth*, 408 U.S. 564 (1972)].

Parental Rights

Parents have a liberty interest in the care, custody, and management of their children [*Santosky v. Kramer*, 455 U.S. 745 (1982) (holding that the state may not terminate parental rights unless it provides notice and a hearing and it proves parental unfitness by "clear and convincing" evidence); *Stanley v. Illinois*, 405 U.S. 645 (1972) (holding that the state may not deny an unmarried father custody of his child without a hearing as to his fitness as a parent)].

Deportation and Exclusion

Deportation of a resident alien involves a loss of liberty, and therefore requires due process, including notice and a hearing [*Shaughnessy v. United States ex rel. Mezei*, 345 U.S. 206 (1953) (holding that "aliens who have once passed through our gates, even illegally, may be expelled only after proceedings conforming to traditional standards of fairness encompassed in due process of law"); *Chew v. Colding*, 344 U.S. 590 (1953)].

However, exclusion of a nonresident alien does not involve a loss of liberty, because there is no liberty interest in entering the country; so exclusion may be allowed without due process [*United States ex rel. Knauff v. Shaughnessy*, 338 U.S. 537 (1950) (holding that "an alien on the threshold of initial entry stands on a different footing: Whatever the procedure authorized by Congress is, it is due process as far as an alien denied entry is concerned"); *Shaughnessy v. United States ex rel. Mezei*, 345 U.S. 206 (1953)].

Prisoners

Prisoners have a liberty interest against restraint that "imposes atypical and significant hardship on the inmate in relation to the ordinary incidents of prison life" [*Sandin v. Conner*, 515 U.S. 472 (1995) (holding that a prisoner's discipline in segregated confinement "did not present the type of atypical, significant deprivation in which a State might conceivably create a liberty interest")].

Reputation

Harm to reputation alone does not implicate any "liberty" or "property" interests sufficient to invoke the procedural protection of the due process clause [*Paul v. Davis*, 424 U.S. 693 (1976) (holding no loss of "liberty" or "property" interests for a plaintiff whose name was on a list of "active shoplifters" distributed by police chiefs to merchants without a hearing as to guilt, though the plaintiff could sue in state court under tort law)].

Property

Property interests require procedural due process. Property interests include not only real and personal property, but also government benefits and government employment if one has a legitimate claim of entitlement to the benefits or employment. A legitimate claim of entitlement is a reasonable expectation of continued receipt of the benefit or continued employment [*Board of Regents v. Roth*, 408 U.S. 564 (1972)].

Government Employment

To have a property interest in a benefit, a person must have more than an abstract need or desire for it, or a unilateral expectation of it. One must have a "legitimate claim of entitlement" to it [*Board of Regents v. Roth*, 408 U.S. 564 (1972) (holding an assistant professor had no legitimate claim of entitlement to reemployment and thus no property interest sufficient to require a hearing when the university declined to renew his contract, because he was hired for a fixed term of one academic year)].

Welfare Benefits

Procedural due process requires that a pretermination evidentiary hearing be held when public assistance payments to welfare recipients are discontinued [*Goldberg v. Kelly*, 397 U.S. 254 (1970)].

Driver's License

Suspension of issued drivers' licenses involves state action that adjudicates important interests of licensees. So licenses may not be taken away without procedural due process [*Bell v. Burson*, 402 U.S. 535 (1971)].

Public Education

When a state creates a public school system and requires students to attend, the students have a legitimate claim of entitlement to, and thus a property interest in, continued receipt of a public education. So they may not be suspended or dismissed for misconduct without procedural due process [*Goss v. Lopez*, 419 U.S. 565 (1975)].

Public Utilities

Where state law does not permit a public utility to terminate service "at will," customers have a legitimate claim of entitlement to, and thus a property interest in, continued service from the utility. So service cannot be terminated without due process [*Memphis Light, Gas & Water Division v. Craft*, 436 U.S. 1 (1978) (holding that under state law, a utility could not terminate service "at will" but only "for cause," and hence respondents asserted a "legitimate claim of entitlement" within the protection of the due process clause of the Fourteenth Amendment)].

Notice, Opportunity for a Hearing, and Impartial Decision Maker (*Mathews* Test)

Where procedural due process is required, the government must provide three things: notice of the charges or issue; opportunity for a hearing; and an impartial decision maker.

In deciding what type of notice, hearing, and decision maker is required, the Court applies the *Mathews* test and balances three factors: (1) the private interest that will be affected by the official action (the more important the private interest, the more procedural safeguards the Court will require); (2) the ability of additional procedures to produce more accurate decisions (the higher the ability, the more likely it is that the Court will require the additional procedures); and (3) the government's interest, including the fiscal and administrative burdens that additional procedures would impose on the government (the higher the burdens, the less likely it is that the Court will require the additional procedures) [*Mathews v. Eldridge*, 424 U.S. 319 (1976)].

Government Employment

- *Cleveland Board of Education v. Loudermill*, 470 U.S. 532 (1985). The Court held a government employee had a property right in continued employment. So the employee could not be fired without being given notice and the opportunity to respond to charges against him in an informal pretermination proceeding, followed by a formal posttermination hearing. Applying the *Mathews* test, the Court held there was a significant private interest in retaining employment (factor one); a pretermination proceeding would help avoid erroneous terminations (factor two); and the cost and delay of pretermination proceedings did not outweigh the employee's interest in keeping his job and the need to avoid errors (factor three).

Welfare Benefits

- *Goldberg v. Kelly*, 397 U.S. 254 (1970). The Court held that the government may not terminate welfare benefits without providing the welfare beneficiary notice, an adversarial pretermination evidentiary hearing, the right to counsel, and an impartial decision maker. The Court explained that "termination of aid pending resolution of a controversy over eligibility may deprive an eligible recipient of the very means by which to live while he waits." Moreover, governmental interests in conserving fiscal and administrative resources were not sufficient to justify failure to provide a pretermination evidentiary hearing.

Social Security Benefits

- *Mathews v. Eldridge*, 424 U.S. 319 (1976). The Court held that an evidentiary hearing is not required prior to the termination of Social Security disability payments because the private interest adversely affected by an erroneous termination of benefits is likely to be less for a disabled worker than for a welfare recipient (factor one); the decision whether to discontinue disability benefits will normally depend on routine, standard, and unbiased medical reports by physician specialists (factor two); and requiring an evidentiary hearing upon demand in all cases prior to the termination of disability benefits would entail fiscal and administrative burdens out of proportion to any countervailing benefits (factor three).

Driver's License

- *Mackey v. Montrym*, 443 U.S. 1 (1979). The Court held that Massachusetts may suspend a driver's license for refusing to take a breath-analysis test upon arrest for operating a motor vehicle while under the influence of intoxicating liquor without providing a presuspension hearing. The Court explained that neither the nature nor the weight of the licensee's interest in the continued possession and use of his license pending the outcome of the hearing compels a presuspension hearing (factor one); the risk of erroneous observation or deliberate misrepresentation by the reporting police officer of the facts forming the basis for the suspension is insubstantial (factor two); and the compelling interest in highway safety justifies Massachusetts in making a summary suspension effective pending the outcome of a prompt postsuspension hearing (factor three).

Public Education

- *Goss v. Lopez*, 419 U.S. 565 (1975). The Court held that a high school student facing suspension of up to ten days must be given oral or written notice of the charges against him and, if he denies them, an explanation of the evidence the authorities have and an opportunity to present his side of the story. The student need not be given the opportunity to secure counsel, to confront and cross-examine witnesses supporting the charge, or to call his own witnesses to verify his version of the incident. The Court explained "To impose in each such case even truncated trial-type procedures might well overwhelm administrative facilities in many places and, by diverting resources, cost more than it would save in educational effectiveness."

Public Utilities

- *Memphis Light, Gas & Water Division v. Craft*, 436 U.S. 1 (1978). The Court held that a public utility may not terminate a customer's service without providing notice of the availability of an administrative procedure to consider their complaint of erroneous billing, and an opportunity to present their complaint to a designated employee empowered to review disputed bills and rectify error. The Court explained the customer's interest in not having services terminated is "self-evident" (factor one); "the risk of an erroneous deprivation, given the necessary reliance on computers, is not insubstantial" (factor two); and "the utility's interests are not incompatible with affording the notice and procedure described above" (factor three).

Children's Rights

- *Schall v. Martin*, 467 U.S. 253 (1984). A New York statute permitted a brief pretrial detention of an arrested juvenile based on a finding of a "serious risk" that he may commit a crime before his return date. The Court upheld the statute. The Court explained that detention is a substantial deprivation of liberty for the juvenile (factor one). However, the statutory procedures protected against erroneous deprivation of liberty (factor two). The procedures provided an initial informal appearance where the accused juvenile is given notice of the charges and informed of his rights to remain silent and be represented by counsel, and a formal, adversarial probable-cause hearing within three days of the initial appearance. Finally, the state has an important interest in "protecting both the community and the juvenile himself from the consequences of future criminal conduct" (factor three).

Creditor's Claims

- *Connecticut v. Doehr*, 501 U.S. 1 (1991). A Connecticut statute authorized the prejudgment attachment of real estate, without prior notice or hearing, upon the plaintiff's verification that there is probable cause to sustain the validity of his or her claim. The Court invalidated the statute. The Court explained that the property interests that attachment affects are significant because "attachment ordinarily clouds title; impairs the ability to sell or otherwise alienate the property; taints any credit rating; reduces the chance of obtaining a home equity loan or additional mortgage; and can even place an existing mortgage in technical default where there is an insecurity clause" (factor one).

  Moreover, without preattachment notice and a hearing, the statute presents too great a risk of erroneous deprivation because it permits a court to authorize attachment "merely because the plaintiff believes the defendant is liable" (factor two). Finally, "the State cannot seriously plead additional financial or administrative burdens involving predeprivation hearings when it already claims to provide an immediate post-deprivation hearing" (factor three).

CHAPTER 12

Taking Clause (Eminent Domain)

THE FIFTH AND FOURTEENTH AMENDMENTS, RESPECTIVELY, PROVIDE THE FEDERAL and state governments power to take private property for public use if the government pays just compensation. This is the power of eminent domain.

"TAKING"

There are two types of taking: possessory taking and regulatory taking.

Possessory Taking

A possessory taking occurs if the government authorizes the permanent confiscation or physical occupation of property, even if a relatively insubstantial amount of space is occupied.

- *Pumpelly v. Green Bay & Mississippi Canal Co.*, 80 U.S. (13 Wall.) 166 (1871). The government built a dam that permanently flooded Pumpelly's land. The Court held this was a taking. The Court explained "where real estate is actually invaded by superinduced additions of water, earth, sand, or other material, or by having any artificial structure placed on it, so as to effectually destroy or impair its usefulness, it is a taking, within the meaning of the Constitution."

- *United States v. Causby*, 328 U.S. 256 (1946). Army and Navy aircraft, including heavy bombers, transports, and fighters, conducted frequent and regular takeoffs and landings at an airport 2,275 feet from Causby's house and chicken farm. The aircraft flew 83 feet over his land, 67 feet above his house, 63 feet above his barn, and 18 feet above the highest tree. The aircraft disturbed Causby's sleep and caused him to give up his chicken business because chickens were killed by flying into the walls from fright. The Court held this was a taking. The Court explained the flights were "so low and so frequent as to be a direct and immediate interference with the enjoyment and use of the land."

- *Loretto v. Teleprompter Manhattan CATV Corp.*, 458 U.S. 419 (1982). A New York statute provided that a landlord must permit a cable television (CATV) company to install its CATV facilities on his property. The Court held this was a taking because it was a permanent physical occupation of property. The Court explained "The installation involved a direct physical attachment of plates, boxes, wires, bolts, and screws to the building, completely occupying space immediately above and upon the roof and along the building's exterior wall."

Regulatory Taking

A regulatory taking occurs if a land-use regulation denies an owner all economically viable use of land or does not substantially advance legitimate state interests.

- *Penn Central Transportation Co. v. City of New York*, 438 U.S. 104 (1978). Under New York City's Landmarks Preservation Law, the city designated Grand Central Terminal, owned by the Penn Central Transportation Co., a "landmark" and denied Penn Central permission to build a fifty-five-story office building above the station, calling such a proposal "an aesthetic joke." The Court held there was no taking. The Court explained the law permitted Penn Central "not only to profit from the Terminal but also to obtain a "reasonable return" on its investment" (economically viable use). Also, the restrictions imposed were substantially related to the promotion of general welfare interests in "preserving structures and areas with special historic, architectural, or cultural significance" (state interests).

- *Lucas v. South Carolina Coastal Council*, 505 U.S. 1003 (1992). In 1986, Lucas bought two residential lots on a South Carolina barrier island, intending to build single-family homes such as those on immediately adjacent parcels. However, in 1988, the state legislature enacted the Beachfront Management Act, which barred Lucas from erecting any permanent habitable structures on his parcels. The Court held that because the Act eliminated all economically beneficial use of the land, it was a taking, unless the state could show that state law had already eliminated all economically beneficial uses of the land before Lucas took title to it. The Court explained, "It seems unlikely that common-law principles would have prevented the erection of any habitable or productive improvements on petitioner's land; they rarely support prohibition of the 'essential use' of land. The question, however, is one of state law to be dealt with on remand."

- *Agins v. Tiburon*, 447 U.S. 255 (1980). After owners acquired five acres of unimproved land in Tiburon for residential development, the city adopted zoning ordinances with density restrictions permitting the owners to build between one and five single-family residences on their tract. The Court held there was no taking. First, the Court explained the zoning ordinances substantially advanced legitimate governmental goals of discouraging the "premature and unnecessary conversion of open-space land to urban uses" and protecting the residents of Tiburon from the "ill effects of urbanization." Second, the Court explained that although the ordinances limited development, they did not eliminate all economically beneficial use of land. The owners could still build as many as five houses on their five acres of prime residential property, and were "free to pursue their reasonable investment expectations by submitting a development plan to local officials" (economically viable use).

- *Keystone Bituminous Coal Association v. DeBenedictis*, 480 U.S. 470 (1987). Provisions of Pennsylvania's Bituminous Mine Subsidence and Land Conservation Act required that coal mine operators leave 50 percent of the coal in the ground underneath certain structures to prevent land subsidence. The Court held there was no taking. First, the Court explained that the Act was intended to serve legitimate public interests in health, the environment, and the fiscal integrity of the area by minimizing damage to surface areas. Second, the Court explained "petitioners have never claimed that their mining operations, or even any specific mines, have been unprofitable since the Subsidence Act was passed. Nor is there evidence that mining in any specific location affected by the 50 percent rule has been unprofitable." The Court concluded "Petitioners may continue to mine coal profitably even if they may not destroy or damage surface structures at will in the process" (economically viable use).

- *Nollan v. California Coastal Commission*, 483 U.S. 825 (1987). The California Coastal Commission granted a permit to the Nollans to replace a small bungalow on their beachfront lot with a larger house, upon the condition that they allow the public an easement to pass across their beach, which was located between two public beaches. The Court held the condition was a taking. The Court explained the easement had no relation to the original purposes of the building restriction, which were to protect the public's ability to see the beach, help the public overcome the "psychological barrier" to using the beach created by a developed shorefront, and prevent congestion on the public beaches (state interests). The Court explained, "It is quite impossible to understand how a requirement that people already on the public beaches be able to walk across the Nollans' property reduces any obstacles to viewing the beach created by the new house."

- *Dolan v. City of Tigard*, 512 U.S. 374 (1994). The city of Tigard granted a permit to Dolan to expand her store and pave her parking lot on the condition that she dedicate part of her land for (1) a public greenway along Fanno Creek to minimize flooding that would be exacerbated by her development and (2) a pedestrian/ bicycle pathway intended to relieve traffic congestion. The Court held these conditions were a taking. The Court provided a two-step process for determining whether a permit condition requiring dedication of private land for public use is a taking.

First, the Court must determine whether a "nexus" exists between the legitimate state interest and the permit condition. Second, the Court must determine whether the permit condition is "roughly proportionate" to the impact of the proposed development. The Court explained it was "obvious that a nexus exists between preventing flooding along Fanno Creek and limiting development," and between reducing traffic congestion and providing for alternative means of transportation such as biking.

However, requiring the owner to dedicate part of her land for a public greenway is not "roughly proportionate" to preventing flood damage as, "The city has never said why a public greenway, as opposed to a private one, was required in the interest of flood control." Moreover, the city did not show how requiring a bicycle path is "roughly proportionate" to the increased number of bicycle and vehicle trips generated by the larger store, beyond saying that it "could offset some of the traffic demand...and lessen the increase in traffic congestion."

PRIVATE PROPERTY

The power of eminent domain extends to tangible and intangible property interests.

- *Webb's Fabulous Pharmacies, Inc. v. Beckwith*, 449 U.S. 155 (1980). Acting under the authority of a Florida statute, a Florida county took the interest earned on an interpleader fund (a sum of money temporarily deposited with the court to which there are competing claims). The Court held this was a taking. The Court explained "any interest on an interpleaded and deposited fund follows the principal and is to be allocated to those who are ultimately to be the owners of that principal." Thus, a state may not "transform private property into public property without compensation, even for the limited duration of the deposit in court."

- *Ruckelshaus v. Monsanto Co.*, 467 U.S. 986 (1984). The Federal Insecticide, Fungicide, and Rodenticide Act (FIFRA) authorized the Environmental Protection Agency (EPA) to disclose publicly some of the trade secret data submitted by Monsanto for registration of a product. The Court held that trade secrets are property protected by the taking clause. The Court explained that despite their intangible nature, "Trade secrets have many of the characteristics of more tangible forms of property. A trade secret is assignable. A trade secret can form the res of a trust, and it passes to a trustee in bankruptcy."

Public Use

The taking must be for public use. A taking is for public use if it is rationally related to a conceivable public purpose. Public purposes include a state's "police powers," such as protecting the health, safety, welfare, or morals of its citizens. The concept of public welfare is broad, and represents spiritual values as well as physical, and aesthetic values as well as monetary. A taking for private use would be invalidated, and the government would have to return the property to the owner.

- *Berman v. Parker*, 348 U.S. 26 (1954). Acting under the District of Columbia Redevelopment Act of 1945, the District of Columbia used its eminent domain power to take slum properties and sell or lease them to private parties for redevelopment. The Court held the taking was for public use. The Court explained "It is within the power of the legislature to determine that the community should be beautiful as well as healthy, spacious as well as clean, well-balanced as well as carefully patrolled."

- *Hawaii Housing Authority v. Midkiff*, 467 U.S. 229 (1984). Hawaii's Land Reform Act of 1967 created a land condemnation scheme whereby title in real property was taken from lessors and transferred to lessees. The Hawaii legislature established the Act to reduce the concentration of land ownership and the perceived social and economic evils of a land oligopoly traceable to the early high chiefs of the Hawaiian Islands. The Court upheld the Act. The Court explained, "The Hawaii Legislature enacted its Land Reform Act not to benefit a particular class of identifiable individuals but to attack certain perceived evils of concentrated property ownership in Hawaii—a legitimate public purpose. Use of the condemnation power to achieve this purpose is not irrational."

- *Kelo v. City of New London*, 545 U.S. 469 (2005). The city of New London approved a development plan that was projected to create more than 1,000 jobs, increase tax and other revenues, and to revitalize an economically distressed city. The city's development agent purchased some of the property earmarked for the project from willing sellers, but initiated condemnation proceedings when the owners of the rest of the property refused to sell. The owners sued, claiming the taking of their properties would violate the "public use" restriction in the taking clause. The Court upheld the taking.

The Court explained, "as was true of the statute challenged in *Midkiff*, the City's development plan was not adopted 'to benefit a particular class of identifiable individuals.'" Rather, "The City has carefully formulated an economic development plan that it believes will provide appreciable benefits to the community, including—but by no means limited to—new jobs and increased tax revenue. As with other exercises in urban planning and development, the City is endeavoring to coordinate a variety of commercial, residential, and recreational uses of land, with the hope that they will form a whole greater than the sum of its parts. To effectuate this plan, the City has invoked a state statute that specifically authorizes the use of eminent domain to promote economic development. Given the comprehensive character of the plan, the thorough deliberation that preceded its adoption, and the limited scope of our review, it is appropriate for us, as it was in *Berman*, to resolve the challenges of the individual owners, not on a piecemeal basis, but rather in light of the entire plan. Because that plan unquestionably serves a public purpose, the takings challenged here satisfy the public use requirement of the Fifth Amendment."

JUST COMPENSATION

"Just compensation" for a taking is the fair market value of the property at the time when it is taken. Under this standard, the owner is entitled to receive "what a willing buyer would pay in cash to a willing seller" at the time of the taking [*United States v. 564.54 Acres of Land, More or Less, Situated in Monroe and Pike Counties, Pennsylvania*, 441 U.S. 506 (1979)].

CHAPTER 13

Contract Clause

THE CONTRACT CLAUSE PROVIDES THAT NO STATE SHALL PASS ANY LAW THAT impairs the "Obligation of Contracts" (U.S. Const. art. I, § 10). The clause prohibits states from passing a law that substantially impairs an existing contractual relationship in a government or private contract, unless the law is narrowly tailored and reasonably necessary to promote a significant and legitimate state interest [*Energy Reserves Group v. Kansas Power & Light*, 459 U.S. 400 (1983)]. The contract clause does not apply to the federal government; however, the due process clause limits the federal government's ability to interfere with government or private contracts.

- *Home Building & Loan Association v. Blaisdell*, 290 U.S. 398 (1934). The Minnesota Mortgage Moratorium Law of 1933, enacted during the Great Depression, provided a moratorium on mortgage foreclosures for existing mortgages from 1933 until no later than May 1, 1935. The Court upheld the law. The Court explained that although the law impaired mortgage contracts by modifying debtor obligations, it was an emergency measure of limited duration. The Court stated "the economic emergency which threatened the loss of homes and lands which furnish those in possession the necessary shelter and means of subsistence was a potent cause for the enactment of the statute." Thus, "The legislation was addressed to a legitimate end; that is, the legislation was not for the mere advantage of particular individuals but for the protection of a basic interest of society."

- *El Paso v. Simmons*, 379 U.S. 497 (1965). Texas sold land under a contract that provided the buyer would forfeit his rights to the property if he failed to make interest payments, but could reinstate his rights at any time by paying the overdue interest. Then Texas adopted a law that placed a five-year limit on the right of reinstatement. The Court upheld the law. The Court explained "The long shadow cast by perpetual reinstatement gave rise to a spate of litigation between forfeiting purchasers and the State or between one or more forfeiting purchasers and other forfeiting purchasers." So the law's purpose was to "restore confidence in the stability and integrity of land titles." The Court concluded, "The measure taken to induce defaulting purchasers to comply with their contracts, requiring payment of interest in arrears within five years, was a mild one indeed, hardly burdensome to the purchaser who wanted to adhere to his contract of purchase, but nonetheless an important one to the State's interest."

- *United States Trust Co. v. New Jersey*, 431 U.S. 1 (1977). In 1962, New York and New Jersey promised bondholders that toll revenues pledged as security for the bonds would not be used to subsidize unprofitable commuter railroad service. Then in 1974 the states passed laws that retroactively repealed the 1962 covenant and allowed the subsidies. The 1974 laws were intended to encourage users of private automobiles to shift to public transportation by raising bridge and tunnel tolls and using the extra revenue from those tolls to subsidize improved commuter railroad service. The Court invalidated the 1974 laws.

First, the Court explained that repealing the 1962 covenant eliminated an important security provision for the bondholders and thus impaired the obligation of the states' contract with the bondholders. Second, the impairment was not reasonably necessary to achieve the states' goals. Total repeal of the 1962 covenant was not essential because the states' plan could have been implemented with a less drastic modification of the covenant. Or the states could have adopted alternative means of achieving their twin goals of discouraging automobile use and improving mass transit without modifying the covenant at all.

- *Allied Structural Steel Co. v. Spannaus*, 438 U.S. 234 (1978). An employer had a pension plan that allowed termination of the plan at any time, and vested an employee's pension right if he satisfied certain length of service and age conditions. Then Minnesota enacted the Private Pension Benefits Protection Act. The Act provided that if a private employer terminated a pension plan or closed its Minnesota offices, it had to grant pension benefits to employees who had worked for the employer more than ten years, regardless of the length of service and age provisions of the employer's pension plan. The Court invalidated the Act.

  First, the Court explained the Act substantially impaired contractual relationships because it imposed "a sudden, totally unanticipated, and substantial retroactive obligation upon the company." Second, the Court explained the Act was not narrowly tailored and reasonably necessary to promote a significant and legitimate state interest. The Act had an "extremely narrow focus" as it applied only to private employers who had at least 100 employees and terminated their plans or closed their Minnesota offices, and "was not even purportedly enacted to deal with a broad, generalized economic or social problem."

- *Keystone Bituminous Coal Association v. DeBenedictis*, 480 U.S. 470 (1987). Coal mine operators and owners of surface rights entered into contracts that allowed mining even if it caused land subsidence. Then Pennsylvania passed the Bituminous Mine Subsidence and Land Conservation Act. The Act required that coal mine operators leave 50 percent of the coal in the ground underneath certain structures to prevent land subsidence, and authorized the revocation of a mining permit if coal removal caused damage to a protected structure or area and the operator had not repaired the damage within six months. The Court upheld the Act.

  The Court held the Act was as "a substantial impairment of a contractual relationship." However, the Court explained that the act was intended to serve legitimate public interests in health, the environment, and the fiscal integrity of the area by minimizing damage to surface areas. Also, "by requiring the coal companies either to repair the damage or to give the surface owner funds to repair the damage, the Commonwealth accomplishes both deterrence and restoration of the environment to its previous condition. We refuse to second-guess the Commonwealth's determinations that these are the most appropriate ways of dealing with the problem."

- *General Motors Corp. v. Romein*, 503 U.S. 181 (1992). A 1987 Michigan statute repudiated a state court interpretation of a workers' compensation statute and required employers to make retroactive payments to previously disabled workers. The Court held that the 1987 statute did not substantially impair an existing contractual relationship because there was "no contractual agreement regarding the specific workers' compensation terms allegedly at issue." Thus, "the 1987 statute did not change the legal enforceability of the employment contracts here. The parties still have the same ability to enforce the bargained-for terms of the employment contracts that they did before the 1987 statute was enacted."

CHAPTER 14

Equal Protection Clause

THE EQUAL PROTECTION CLAUSE PROVIDES THAT NO STATE SHALL DENY ANY PERSON within its jurisdiction the "equal protection of the laws" (U.S. Const. amend. XIV, § 1). Equal protection provides that the government cannot classify or discriminate among people unless it has a sufficient purpose. Whether a purpose is sufficient depends on the type of classification or discrimination made by the government.

Equal protection analysis is done in two parts. First, the Court determines if the law in question classifies or discriminates among people. A law may discriminate "on its face" by its own terms. Or a law may be facially neutral yet still be discriminatory if it has a discriminatory impact and purpose.

Second, if a law classifies or discriminates among people, then the Court determines whether the classification is constitutional by applying the test or level of scrutiny that is used for that particular type of classification. The three tests are the rational basis test, intermediate scrutiny, and strict scrutiny.

Equal protection applies to the federal government through the due process clause of the Fifth Amendment [*Bolling v. Sharpe*, 347 U.S. 497 (1954)]. Equal protection analysis is the same whether a state law is challenged under the Fourteenth Amendment or a federal law is challenged under the Fifth Amendment [*Buckley v. Valeo*, 424 U.S. 1, (1976)].

THE CLASSIFICATION

A facially discriminatory law classifies or discriminates among people expressly, on the face of the law. However, a facially neutral law that does not expressly classify people may still be discriminatory if it has a discriminatory impact and purpose.

Facially Discriminatory Law

A facially discriminatory law classifies or discriminates among people expressly, by its own terms.

- *Strauder v. West Virginia*, 100 U.S. (10 Otto) 303 (1879). A West Virginia statute provided, "All white male persons who are twenty-one years of age and who are citizens of this State shall be liable to serve as jurors." The Court invalidated the statute. The Court explained that the statute "singled out and expressly denied" blacks the right to participate in the administration of the law as jurors.

- *Brown v. Board of Education*, 347 U.S. 483 (1954). A Kansas statute permitted cities with a population of more than 15,000 to maintain separate school facilities for black and white students. In a prior case, *Plessy v. Ferguson* [163 U.S. 537 (1896)], the Court announced the "separate but equal" doctrine that upheld laws requiring blacks and whites to use separate but equal facilities. However, in *Brown* the Court overturned *Plessy* and invalidated the Kansas statute.

  The Court held that "in the field of public education the doctrine of 'separate but equal' has no place. Separate educational facilities are inherently unequal." The Court explained that to separate black children from others of similar age and qualifications solely because of their race "generates a feeling of inferiority as to their status in the community that may affect their hearts and minds in a way unlikely ever to be undone."

- *Anderson v. Martin*, 375 U.S. 399 (1964). A Louisiana statute required that each candidate's race appear on the ballot in all primary, general, and special elections. The Court invalidated the statute. The Court explained that "Race is the factor upon which the statute operates and its involvement promotes the ultimate discrimination which is sufficient to make it invalid." For "by directing the citizen's attention to the single consideration of race or color, the State indicates that a candidate's race or color is an important—perhaps paramount—consideration in the citizen's choice, which may decisively influence the citizen to cast his ballot along racial lines."

- *Craig v. Boren*, 429 U.S. 190 (1976). Oklahoma statutes prohibited the sale of 3.2 percent beer to males under the age of twenty-one and females under the age of eighteen. The Court invalidated the statutes. The Court explained that although protection of public health and safety represents an important function of state and local governments, statistics showed only that .18 percent of females and 2 percent of males in the eighteen- to twenty-year-old age group were arrested for driving while under the influence of liquor. The Court concluded, "While such a disparity is not trivial in a statistical sense, it hardly can form the basis for employment of a gender line as a classifying device."

- *United States v. Virginia*, 518 U.S. 515 (1996). Virginia Military Institute (VMI) excluded women from admission and was the sole single-sex school among Virginia's fifteen public institutions of higher learning. The Court held VMI's categorical exclusion of women from the educational opportunities VMI provided denied equal protection to women. The Court explained that Virginia "has shown no exceedingly persuasive justification for withholding from women qualified for the experience premier training of the kind VMI affords." The Court concluded, "There is no reason to believe that the admission of women capable of all the activities required of VMI cadets would destroy the Institute rather than enhance its capacity to serve the 'more perfect Union.'"

Facially Neutral Law

A facially neutral law does not expressly classify people by its terms. However, it may still classify or discriminate among people if it has a discriminatory impact and it is enacted or applied with a discriminatory purpose. Showing discriminatory purpose requires proof that the government desired to discriminate. Statistical evidence of the discriminatory impact of a law is relevant to prove discriminatory purpose, but statistics alone are not enough unless they show clearly and convincingly that the law was enacted or applied with a discriminatory purpose. If the plaintiff offers proof of a discriminatory purpose, the burden shifts to the government to show that the law would have been enacted or applied for constitutionally permissible reasons even if the discriminatory purpose had not been considered [*Village of Arlington Heights v. Metropolitan Housing Development Corp.*, 429 U.S. 252 (1977)].

- *Yick Wo v. Hopkins*, 118 U.S. 356 (1886). A San Francisco ordinance banned the operation of laundries in wood buildings unless an exemption was granted. The Court invalidated the ordinance. The Court noted that although the law was "fair on its face," 200 petitions for exemptions by Chinese persons were denied, while 80 petitions by non-Chinese persons were granted (discriminatory impact). Moreover, the ordinance was racially discriminatory because it was applied "with a mind so unequal and oppressive as to amount to a practical denial by the state of that equal protection of the laws which is secured to the petitioners" (discriminatory purpose).

- *Guinn v. United States*, 238 U.S. 347 (1915). An Oklahoma law required a literacy test for voting, but also included a "grandfather clause" that exempted persons, or their lineal descendents, who were qualified to vote on January 1, 1886, when blacks were ineligible to vote in the state. The Court invalidated the law. The Court explained that although the law was facially neutral with respect to race, the "grandfather clause" imposed the test on all black voters but few white voters (discriminatory impact). Moreover, the law was a racial classification because the obvious purpose was to disenfranchise blacks (discriminatory purpose).

- *Griffin v. School Board of Prince Edward County*, 377 U.S. 218 (1964). In response to desegregation orders, a county school board closed public schools and funded private schools that excluded black students. The Court invalidated the action. The Court explained that "Closing Prince Edward's schools bears more heavily on Negro children in Prince Edward County since white children there have accredited private schools which they can attend" (discriminatory impact). Moreover, the action was racially discriminatory because "the record in the present case could not be clearer that Prince Edward's public schools were closed and private schools operated in their place with state and county assistance, for one reason, and one reason only: to ensure, through measures taken by the county and the State, that white and colored children in Prince Edward County would not, under any circumstances, go to the same school" (discriminatory purpose).

- *Personnel Administrator of Massachusetts v. Feeney,* 442 U.S. 256 (1979). A Massachusetts veterans' preference statute provided that all veterans who qualify for state civil service positions must be considered for appointment ahead of any qualifying non-veterans. The Court upheld the law. The Court explained that although the law was facially neutral with respect to gender, the law operated overwhelmingly to the advantage of males, as more than 98 percent of veterans in the state were male (discriminatory impact). However, there was no gender classification because there was no proof that the state enacted the law for the purpose of discriminating against women (no discriminatory purpose). The Court explained "The statutory history shows that the benefit of the preference was consistently offered to 'any person' who was a veteran." Thus, the law was "a preference for veterans of either sex over nonveterans of either sex, not for men over women."

- *Hunter v. Underwood,* 471 U.S. 222 (1985). An Alabama law denied the right to vote to anyone convicted of a crime involving "moral turpitude." The Court invalidated the law. The Court explained that although the law was facially neutral with respect to race, statistics showed that the law disenfranchised a significantly greater percentage of black voters than white voters (discriminatory impact). Moreover, the law was unconstitutional race discrimination because records and testimony from historians showed conclusively that the law "was enacted with the intent of disenfranchising blacks," and would not have been enacted "in the absence of the racially discriminatory motivation" (discriminatory purpose).

- *McCleskey v. Kemp,* 481 U.S. 279 (1987). A black man was convicted in a Georgia trial court of armed robbery and murder, arising from the killing of a white police officer during the robbery of a store. Pursuant to a Georgia death penalty statute, the jury at the penalty hearing considered the mitigating and aggravating circumstances and recommended the death penalty on the murder charge. The Court upheld the statute and sentence. The Court noted a study indicating that black defendants who killed white victims had the greatest likelihood of receiving the death penalty (discriminatory impact). However, the Court explained there was no racial classification because the defendant offered no evidence that racial considerations played a part in his sentence. The study was "clearly insufficient to support an inference that any of the decision-makers in McCleskey's case acted with discriminatory purpose." Also, "There was no evidence then, and there is none now, that the Georgia Legislature enacted the capital punishment statute to further a racially discriminatory purpose."

THE TESTS

If a law classifies or discriminates among people, then the Court determines whether the classification is constitutional by applying the test or level of scrutiny that is used for that particular type of classification. The three tests are the rational basis test, intermediate scrutiny, and strict scrutiny.

Rational Basis Test (Minimum Scrutiny—Laws Presumed Valid)

The rational basis test applies to classifications regarding wealth, age, disability, and other social welfare or economic matters that do not involve a fundamental constitutional right. Under the rational basis test, a law is upheld if it is rationally related to a legitimate state interest.

"Rationally related" means that the law must be a rational way to accomplish the goal; a law is invalidated only if it is arbitrary and irrational. "Legitimate state interests" include the "police powers" of protecting public health, safety, welfare, and morals, and virtually any other goal that is not forbidden by the Constitution. The Court will accept any conceivable legitimate state interest regardless of whether it was the actual reason why the government enacted the law. Thus, the government's lawyer can conceive of legitimate state interests and is not limited to the actual purpose behind the law.

Under the rational basis test, the Court gives great deference to the government and rarely invalidates laws. The party challenging the law has the burden of proving that the law does not satisfy the test.

- *Railway Express Agency v. New York*, 336 U.S. 106 (1949). A New York City traffic regulation prohibited advertising on vehicles unless it was for the vehicle owner's business (classifying advertising for a vehicle owner's business differently than advertising for others). The Court upheld the regulation. The Court explained the regulation had an arguable relation (rationally related) to promoting public safety (legitimate state interest) by reducing distractions for drivers and pedestrians.

- *Dandridge v. Williams*, 397 U.S. 471 (1970). A Maryland regulation limited welfare benefits to $250 per month regardless of the size of the family and its actual need (reducing per capita benefits to children in larger families). The Court upheld the regulation. The Court explained the regulation was rationally related to the state's legitimate interests in encouraging employment and allocating limited public welfare funds.

- *San Antonio Independent School District v. Rodriguez*, 411 U.S. 1 (1973). Texas used local property taxes to fund public education, allowing wealthier areas to spend more on education than poorer areas. The Court upheld the tax system. The Court explained the tax system was rationally related to legitimate state interests in (1) assuring a basic education for every child in the state and (2) giving local school districts more control in deciding how local tax dollars will be spent so they could tailor local programs to local needs. The Court noted "It has simply never been within the constitutional prerogative of this Court to nullify statewide measures for financing public services merely because the burdens or benefits thereof fall unevenly depending upon the relative wealth of the political subdivisions in which citizens live."

- *New Orleans v. Dukes*, 427 U.S. 297 (1976). A New Orleans ordinance prohibited pushcart vendors from selling goods in the city's French Quarter unless a vendor had operated there continuously for eight or more years (classifying vendors differently based on length of work). The Court upheld the ordinance. The Court explained the ordinance rationally furthered the legitimate purpose of preserving the charm, beauty, and economic vitality of the area. The City could make the reasoned judgment that "street peddlers and hawkers tend to interfere with the charm and beauty of a historic area and disturb tourists and disrupt their enjoyment of that charm and beauty, and that such vendors in the Vieux Carre, the heart of the city's tourist industry, might thus have a deleterious effect on the economy of the city." Regarding the classification of vendors based on length of work, the Court explained that rather than abolishing all pushcart food vendors, the city could rationally choose initially to eliminate vendors "of more recent vintage." The city could reasonably decide that newer businesses were "less likely to have built up substantial reliance interests in continued operation."

- *Massachusetts Board of Retirement v. Murgia*, 427 U.S. 307 (1976). A Massachusetts law required police officers to retire at age fifty (classifying officers differently based on age). The Court upheld the law. The Court explained the age classification was rationally related to furthering a legitimate state interest in protecting the public by assuring the physical preparedness of its uniformed police. The Court said "Since physical ability generally declines with age, mandatory retirement at 50 serves to remove from police service those whose fitness for uniformed work presumptively has diminished with age. This clearly is rationally related to the State's objective."

- *Vance v. Bradley*, 440 U.S. 93 (1979). The Foreign Service Act of 1946 required foreign service officers to retire at age sixty (classifying officers differently based on age). The Court upheld the retirement provision. The Court explained the federal government had a legitimate interest in assuring "a vigorous and competent Foreign Service." Moreover, the retirement provision "could rationally be deemed to serve that end" because overseas duty is more demanding than stateside duty, and "those over age 60 often are less able to face the rigors of the Foreign Service."

- *Metropolitan Life Insurance Co. v. Ward*, 470 U.S. 869 (1985). An Alabama statute taxed out-of-state insurance companies at a higher rate than in-state companies (classifying out-of-state companies differently than in-state companies). The Court invalidated the law. The Court explained that "promotion of domestic business by discriminating against nonresident competitors is not a legitimate state purpose."

- *City of Cleburne, Texas v. Cleburne Living Center, Inc.*, 473 U.S. 432 (1985). A city of Cleburne ordinance required a special use permit to operate a group home for the mentally retarded. But it did not require a special use permit for apartment houses, multiple dwellings, fraternity or sorority houses, hospitals, sanitariums, nursing homes for convalescents, or private clubs (classifying housing for the mentally retarded differently than other housing). The Court invalidated the ordinance.

The Court explained there was no rational basis for believing the group home would pose any special threat to the city's legitimate interests, so the ordinance appeared to rest instead on "an irrational prejudice against the mentally retarded." The city was concerned with the negative attitude of property owners located within 200 feet of the group home. However the Court explained that "mere negative attitudes, or fear, unsubstantiated by factors which are properly cognizable in a zoning proceeding, are not permissible bases for treating a home for the mentally retarded differently from apartment houses, multiple dwellings, and the like." The city was also concerned that the group home was across the street from a junior high school, and that the students might harass the occupants of the home. However the Court explained that "the school itself is attended by about 30 mentally retarded students, and denying a permit based on such vague, undifferentiated fears is again permitting some portion of the community to validate what would otherwise be an equal protection violation."

- *Romer v. Evans*, 517 U.S. 620 (1996). An amendment to the Colorado Constitution prohibited all legislative, executive, or judicial action designed to protect homosexual persons from discrimination (classifying homosexuals differently than heterosexuals). The Court invalidated the amendment. The Court explained the amendment was not rationally related to a legitimate state interest. The primary rationale Colorado offered for the amendment was respecting other citizens' freedom of association, in particular the liberties of landlords or employers who had personal or religious objections to homosexuality.

However, the Court explained "The breadth of the amendment is so far removed from these particular justifications that we find it impossible to credit them. We cannot say that Amendment 2 is directed to any identifiable legitimate purpose or discrete objective." The Court concluded the amendment "classifies homosexuals not to further a proper legislative end but to make them unequal to everyone else. This Colorado cannot do. A State cannot so deem a class of persons a stranger to its laws."

Intermediate Scrutiny

Intermediate scrutiny is a middle-level standard of review between the rational basis test and strict scrutiny. Intermediate scrutiny applies to classifications regarding gender and nonmarital children. Under intermediate scrutiny a law is upheld if it is substantially related to an important state interest. The government has the burden of proving the law satisfies the test.

- *Craig v. Boren*, 429 U.S. 190 (1976). Oklahoma statutes prohibited the sale of 3.2 percent beer to males under the age of twenty-one and females under the age of eighteen (classifying women differently than men). The Court invalidated the statutes. The Court explained that although protection of public health and safety represents an important function of state and local governments, statistics showed only that .18 percent of females and 2 percent of males in the eighteen- to twenty-year-old age group were arrested for driving while under the influence of liquor (law not substantially related). The Court concluded, "While such a disparity is not trivial in a statistical sense, it hardly can form the basis for employment of a gender line as a classifying device."

- *Califano v. Webster*, 430 U.S. 313 (1977). A Social Security Act provision allowed women to exclude from the calculation of their retirement benefits three more low-earning years than men could exclude, thus calculating benefits for women with a more favorable formula than was used for men (classifying males differently than females). The Court upheld the provision. The Court explained, "Reduction of the disparity in economic condition between men and women caused by the long history of discrimination against women" was an important government interest. Moreover, the provision was substantially related to the government's interest because "allowing women, who as such have been unfairly hindered from earning as much as men, to eliminate additional low-earning years from the calculation of their retirement benefits works directly to remedy some part of the effect of past discrimination."

- *Lalli v. Lalli*, 439 U.S. 259 (1978). A New York statute provided that a nonmarital child could inherit from his or her father by intestate succession only if the child received a court order of paternity during the father's life (classifying nonmarital children who established paternity differently from those who had not). The Court upheld the law. The Court explained that preventing fraudulent claims of heirship and providing for the just and orderly disposition of property at death were important state interests. Moreover, the statute was substantially related to the state's interests because, "Fraudulent assertions of paternity will be much less likely to succeed, or even to arise, where the proof is put before a court of law at a time when the putative father is available to respond, rather than first brought to light when the distribution of the assets of an estate is in the offing."

- *Orr v. Orr*, 440 U.S. 268 (1979). An Alabama statute provided that husbands could be ordered to pay alimony but not wives (classifying men differently than women). The Court invalidated the statute. The Court explained that assisting needy spouses and compensating women for past economic discrimination were important state interests. However, the statute was not substantially related to achieving those objectives because, "Under the statute, individualized hearings at which the parties' relative financial circumstances are considered already occur." The Court concluded, "since individualized hearings can determine which women were in fact discriminated against vis-à-vis their husbands, as well as which family units defied the stereotype and left the husband dependent on the wife, Alabama's alleged compensatory purpose may be effectuated without placing burdens solely on husbands."

- *Caban v. Mohammed*, 441 U.S. 380 (1979). A New York law permitted an unwed mother, but not an unwed father, to block the adoption of their child simply by withholding her consent (classifying men differently than women). The Court invalidated the law. The Court explained that promoting the adoption of children born out of wedlock was an important state interest. However, the law was not substantially related to the state's interest. The

Court explained "It may be that, given the opportunity, some unwed fathers would prevent the adoption of their illegitimate children. This impediment to adoption usually is the result of a natural parental interest shared by both genders alike; it is not a manifestation of any profound difference between the affection and concern of mothers and fathers for their children. Neither the State nor the appellees have argued that unwed fathers are more likely to object to the adoption of their children than are unwed mothers; nor is there any self-evident reason why as a class they would be."

- *Kirchberg v. Feenstra*, 450 U.S. 455 (1981). A Louisiana statute gave a husband, as "head and master" of property jointly owned with his wife, the unilateral right to dispose of such property without his spouse's consent (classifying men differently than women). The Court invalidated the statute. The Court explained that neither party to the case identified an important government objective that was served by the statute.

- *Michael M. v. Superior Court*, 450 U.S. 464 (1981). California's "statutory rape" law punished men for having sexual intercourse with a woman under age eighteen, but did not punish a woman for having sexual intercourse with a man under age eighteen. The Court, without a majority opinion, upheld the law. Justice Rehnquist, writing for the plurality, explained that preventing teenage pregnancy out of wedlock was an important state interest. Moreover, the law's gender classification was substantially related to the state's interest. Justice Rehnquist explained, "Because virtually all of the significant harmful and inescapably identifiable consequences of teenage pregnancy fall on the young female, a legislature acts well within its authority when it elects to punish only the participant who, by nature, suffers few of the consequences of his conduct. It is hardly unreasonable for a legislature acting to protect minor females to exclude them from punishment."

- *Clark v. Jeter*, 486 U.S. 456 (1988). A Pennsylvania statute required that a nonmarital child seeking support file a support claim against the father before the child was six years old, while a marital child could file a support claim at any time (classifying nonmarital children differently than marital children). The Court invalidated the statute. The Court explained that the six-year statute of limitations was not substantially related to Pennsylvania's interest in avoiding the litigation of stale or fraudulent claims. The Court noted "increasingly sophisticated tests for genetic markers permit the exclusion of over 99% of those who might be accused of paternity, regardless of the age of the child. This scientific evidence is available throughout the child's minority, and it is an additional reason to doubt that Pennsylvania had a substantial reason for limiting the time within which paternity and support actions could be brought."

Strict Scrutiny

Strict scrutiny is the highest level of review, and it applies to classifications regarding race, national origin, and with some exceptions, alienage. Under strict scrutiny a law is upheld if it is necessary or narrowly tailored to achieve a compelling state interest. A law is "necessary" or "narrowly tailored" if it is the least restrictive means to achieve the goal. Thus, the government must show that there is no less discriminatory alternative means to achieve the goal. The government purpose is "compelling" if it is truly vital. The government has the burden of proving the law satisfies the test.

Race and National Origin Classification

- *Korematsu v. United States*, 323 U.S. 214 (1944). The government temporarily excluded all Japanese Americans from the West Coast during wartime (classifying Japanese Americans differently than other Americans). The Court upheld the action. The Court explained the United States was at war with the Japanese Empire, and military authorities, fearing an invasion of the West Coast and seeking to prevent espionage and sabotage, found it was impossible to segregate the disloyal from the loyal. The Court concluded, "We cannot—by availing ourselves of the calm perspective of hindsight—now say that at that time these actions were unjustified."

- *Regents of University of California v. Bakke* 438 U.S. 265 (1978). The Medical School of the University of California at Davis had a racial set-aside program that reserved 16 out of 100 seats in a medical school class for members of certain minority groups.

The Court invalidated the program, without a majority opinion. Justice Powell explained "attainment of a diverse student body" was a "constitutionally permissible goal for an institution of higher education." However, ethnic diversity "is only one element in a range of factors a university properly may consider in attaining the goal of a heterogeneous student body." Thus, "The diversity that furthers a compelling state interest encompasses a far broader array of qualifications and characteristics of which racial or ethnic origin is but a single though important element. Petitioner's special admissions program, focused solely on ethnic diversity, would hinder rather than further attainment of genuine diversity."

- *United States v. Paradise*, 480 U.S. 149 (1987). A federal court ordered that a qualified black person be promoted by the Alabama Department of Public Safety (ADPS) every time a white person was promoted. The Court upheld the order. The Court explained that for almost four decades the ADPS had excluded blacks from all positions, including jobs in the upper ranks. So, "The Government unquestionably has a compelling interest in remedying past and present discrimination by a state actor." Moreover, the order was temporary and applied only if qualified blacks were available and the department had an objective need to make promotions. So "the one-for-one promotion requirement was narrowly tailored to serve its several purposes."

- *Richmond v. J.A. Croson Co.*, 488 U.S. 469 (1989). The city of Richmond adopted a plan that required the primary contractor on city-funded construction contracts to subcontract at least 30 percent of the contract to minority-owned subcontractor businesses. The plan defined a minority-owned business to include a business from anywhere in the country at least 51 percent of which was owned and controlled by black, Spanish-speaking, Oriental, Indian, Eskimo, or Aleut citizens. The Court invalidated the plan.

  The Court explained the city failed to demonstrate a compelling interest in apportioning public contracting opportunities on the basis of race because "none of the evidence presented by the city points to any identified discrimination in the Richmond construction industry." Moreover, the plan was not narrowly tailored to remedy the effects of prior discrimination because under the plan "a successful black, Hispanic, or Oriental entrepreneur from anywhere in the country enjoys an absolute preference over other citizens based solely on their race." Finally, the city did not show there were no less discriminatory alternative means to achieve the goal because "There is no evidence in this record that the Richmond City Council has considered any alternatives to a race-based quota."

- *Miller v. Johnson*, 515 U.S. 900 (1995). After the Justice Department refused to approve, under the Voting Rights Act, two Georgia congressional districting plans that contained only two majority-black districts, Georgia drew the boundaries of an election district to provide three majority black districts. The Court invalidated the districting plan.

  The Court explained that where a plaintiff claims a state has drawn race-based district lines the plaintiff must show, either through circumstantial evidence of a district's shape and demographics, or direct evidence of legislative purpose, that race was the predominant factor motivating the legislature's decision to place a significant number of voters within or without a district. To make this showing the plaintiff must prove the legislature subordinated traditional race-neutral districting principles such as compactness, contiguity, and respect for communities defined by actual shared interests, to racial considerations. If race was the predominant factor in districting, strict scrutiny applies.

  The Court concluded that race was the predominant factor here because the legislature was motivated by a "predominant, overriding desire" to create a third majority-black district to comply with the Justice Department's demands. Moreover, Georgia did not create the election district to remedy past discrimination, but instead created it to satisfy the Justice Department's demands, and this was not a compelling state interest that would justify race-based districting.

- *Gratz v. Bollinger*, 539 U.S. 244 (2003). The University of Michigan's College of Literature, Science, and the Arts (LSA) admissions policy was based on a point system that automatically granted 20 points of the 100 needed to guarantee admission to applicants from underrepresented minority groups. The Court invalidated the admissions policy. The Court explained "the University's policy, which automatically distributes 20 points, or one-fifth of the points needed to guarantee admission, to every single 'underrepresented minority' applicant solely because of race, is not narrowly tailored to achieve the interest in educational diversity that respondents claim justifies their program."

The Court noted "Justice Powell's opinion in *Bakke* emphasized the importance of considering each particular applicant as an individual, assessing all of the qualities that individual possesses, and in turn, evaluating that individual's ability to contribute to the unique setting of higher education." However, "The current LSA policy does not provide such individualized consideration. The LSA's policy automatically distributes 20 points to every single applicant from an 'underrepresented minority' group, as defined by the University." Thus, "LSA's automatic distribution of 20 points has the effect of making the factor of race decisive for virtually every minimally qualified underrepresented minority applicant."

- *Grutter v. Bollinger* 539 U.S. 306 (2003). The University of Michigan Law School sought to have a diverse student body by enrolling a "critical mass" of students who were members of underrepresented minority groups such as African Americans, Hispanics, and Native Americans. When the law school denied admission to Grutter, a white Michigan resident with a 3.8 GPA and 161 LSAT score, she sued, alleging the law school discriminated against her on the basis of race. The Court held the law school's use of race in admissions decisions was not prohibited by the equal protection clause.

The Court explained "we hold that the Law School has a compelling interest in attaining a diverse student body. The Law School's educational judgment that such diversity is essential to its educational mission is one to which we defer." Moreover, "We find that the Law School's admissions program bears the hallmarks of a narrowly tailored plan. As Justice Powell made clear in *Bakke*, truly individualized consideration demands that race be used in a flexible, nonmechanical way. It follows from this mandate that universities cannot establish quotas for members of certain racial groups or put members of those groups on separate admissions tracks. Nor can universities insulate applicants who belong to certain racial or ethnic groups from the competition for admission. Universities can, however, consider race or ethnicity more flexibly as a 'plus' factor in the context of individualized consideration of each and every applicant."

The Court concluded, "Here, the Law School engages in a highly individualized, holistic review of each applicant's file, giving serious consideration to all the ways an applicant might contribute to a diverse educational environment. The Law School affords this individualized consideration to applicants of all races."

Alienage Classification

Alienage classifications discriminate against noncitizens. If state law discriminates against noncitizens for economic reasons, strict scrutiny applies (e.g., laws that concern the distribution of benefits, or the right to engage in private sector economic activity).

Under the "political function" exception to strict scrutiny, if state law discriminates against noncitizens for reasons relating to self-governance or the democratic process, the rational basis test applies (e.g., laws excluding noncitizens from elected government positions, positions that involve a significant policy-making function, or positions that require the exercise of important discretionary governmental powers over citizens).

If state law discriminates against "undocumented" noncitizens (aliens not legally admitted into the United States), intermediate scrutiny applies.

If federal law discriminates against noncitizens, the rational basis test applies. Here, the Court gives deference to the federal government because the federal government has important interests in foreign policy and immigration.

State Discrimination—Economic (Strict Scrutiny)

- *Graham v. Richardson*, 403 U.S. 365 (1971). A Pennsylvania law made noncitizens ineligible for public assistance, and an Arizona law restricted benefits to citizens or persons who had resided in the state for at least fifteen years. The Court invalidated the laws. The Court explained "a State's desire to preserve limited welfare benefits for its own citizens is inadequate to justify Pennsylvania's making noncitizens ineligible for public assistance, and Arizona's restricting benefits to citizens and longtime resident aliens." The Court added, the "justification of limiting expenses is particularly inappropriate and unreasonable when the discriminated class consists of aliens. Aliens like citizens pay taxes and may be called into the armed forces."

- *Sugarman v. Dougall*, 413 U.S. 634 (1973). A New York statute excluded aliens from permanent positions in the competitive class of the state civil service. The Court invalidated the statute. The Court explained "We recognize a State's interest in establishing its own form of government, and in limiting participation in that government to those who are within 'the basic conception of a political community.'" However, the statute "is neither narrowly confined nor precise in its application. Its imposed ineligibility may apply to the 'sanitation man, class B,' to the typist, and to the office worker, as well as to the person who directly participates in the formulation and execution of important state policy. The citizenship restriction sweeps indiscriminately." The Court concluded "a flat ban on the employment of aliens in positions that have little, if any relation to a State's legitimate interest, cannot withstand scrutiny under the Fourteenth Amendment."

- *Application of Griffiths*, 413 U.S. 717 (1973). A Connecticut court rule restricted admission to the bar to citizens of the United States. The Court invalidated the rule. The Court explained that "a State does have a substantial interest in the qualifications of those admitted to the practice of law." However, the Court noted that a lawyer's responsibilities "hardly involve matters of state policy or acts of such unique responsibility as to entrust them only to citizens." The Court concluded the bar committee "simply has not established that it must exclude all aliens from the practice of law in order to vindicate its undoubted interest in high professional standards."

State Discrimination—Political Function Exception (Rational Basis Test)

- *Foley v. Connelie*, 435 U.S. 291 (1978). A New York statute provided that one must be a U.S. citizen to be a police officer. The Court upheld the statute. The Court explained police officers "are clothed with authority to exercise an almost infinite variety of discretionary powers." Moreover, a state may presume that citizens are "more familiar with and sympathetic to American traditions." The Court concluded, "In the enforcement and execution of the laws the police function is one where citizenship bears a rational relationship to the special demands of the particular position. A State may, therefore, consonant with the Constitution, confine the performance of this important public responsibility to citizens of the United States."

- *Ambach v. Norwick*, 441 U.S. 68 (1979). A New York statute prohibited permanent certification as a public school teacher of any person who was not a U.S. citizen, unless that person had manifested an intention to apply for citizenship. The Court upheld the statute. The Court explained the state had a legitimate interest in promoting self-governance because, "Public education, like the police function, fulfills a most fundamental obligation of government to its constituency." And "a teacher has an opportunity to influence the attitudes of students toward government, the political process, and a citizen's social responsibilities." Moreover, the citizenship requirement was rationally related to the state's interest because "The restriction is carefully framed to serve its purpose, as it bars from teaching only those aliens who have demonstrated their unwillingness to obtain United States citizenship."

- *Cabell v. Chavez-Salido*, 454 U.S. 432 (1982). A California statute provided that one must be a U.S. citizen to be a probation officer. The Court upheld the statute. The Court explained the state had a legitimate interest in limiting the exercise of its coercive police powers to citizens because "the probation officer necessarily has a great deal of discretion that, just like that of the police officer and the teacher, must be exercised, in the first instance, without direct supervision." Moreover, the citizenship requirement was "sufficiently tailored" to the state's interest because it was "an appropriate limitation on those who would exercise and, therefore, symbolize this power of the political community over those who fall within its jurisdiction."

- *Bernal v. Fainter*, 467 U.S. 216 (1984). A Texas statute provided that one must be a U.S. citizen to be a notary public. The Court invalidated the statute. First, the Court explained the public function exception to strict scrutiny did not apply because notaries are not invested with "policymaking responsibility or broad discretion in the execution of public policy that requires the routine exercise of authority over individuals." Rather, their duties are "essentially clerical and ministerial."

  Second, the Court explained the statute failed strict scrutiny. The state asserted an interest in ensuring that notaries "be reasonably familiar with state law and institutions." However, the Court explained, "There is nothing in the record that indicates that resident aliens, as a class, are so incapable of familiarizing themselves with Texas law as to justify the State's absolute and classwide exclusion." Moreover, "if the State's concern with ensuring a notary's familiarity with state law were truly 'compelling,' one would expect the State to give some sort of test actually measuring a person's familiarity with the law. The State, however, administers no such test."

State Discrimination—Undocumented Aliens (Intermediate Scrutiny)

- *Plyler v. Doe*, 457 U.S. 202 (1982). A Texas statute withheld from local school districts any state funds for the education of children who were not "legally admitted" into the United States and authorized local school districts to deny enrollment to such children. The Court invalidated the statute. The Court explained, "While a State might have an interest in mitigating the potentially harsh economic effects of sudden shifts in population, [the statute] hardly offers an effective method of dealing with an urgent demographic or economic problem. There is no evidence in the record suggesting that illegal entrants impose any significant burden on the State's economy." Moreover, although the state claimed undocumented children imposed special burdens on the state's ability to provide high-quality public education, "the record in no way supports the claim that exclusion of undocumented children is likely to improve the overall quality of education in the State."

Federal Discrimination (Rational Basis Test)

- *Mathews v. Diaz*, 426 U.S. 67 (1976). A Social Security Act provision denied eligibility for Medicare to aliens unless they had been admitted for permanent residence and had resided in the United States for at least five years. The Court upheld the provision. The Court explained the federal government had a legitimate interest in maintaining the fiscal integrity of the Medicare program. Moreover, it was "unquestionably reasonable for Congress to make an alien's eligibility depend on both the character and the duration of his residence." The permanent residence and five-year duration requirements were not "wholly irrational."

CHAPTER 15

Ex Post Facto Laws

THE CONSTITUTION PROHIBITS THE FEDERAL AND STATE GOVERNMENTS FROM PASSING ex post facto laws (U.S. Const. art. I, §§ 9, 10). An ex post facto law makes an act punishable, retroactively, in a manner in which it was not punishable when it was committed. There are four types of ex post facto laws:

- Those that make criminal, and punish, an act that was not criminal when it was committed;
- Those that make a crime a greater offense than it was when committed;
- Those that impose greater punishment for a crime than was allowed when it was committed; and
- Those that change the rules of evidence to require less evidence to convict than was required when the crime was committed.

The prohibition against ex post facto laws applies only to criminal or penal laws (i.e., laws that involve criminal punishment), and not to civil laws (i.e., laws with only civil consequences).

- *Calder v. Bull*, 3 U.S. (3 Dall.) 386 (1798). A Connecticut statute overturned a probate court decision and ordered a new hearing on the validity of a will. The Court upheld the statute. The Court explained the statute was not an ex post facto law because the ex post facto prohibition applies "to penal statutes, and no further."

- *Hawker v. New York*, 170 U.S. 189 (1898). A physician was convicted of the crime of abortion and sentenced to imprisonment for ten years. New York later passed a statute prohibiting a convicted felon from practicing medicine. The Court upheld the statute. The Court explained the statute was not an ex post facto law because it simply defined the qualifications for practicing medicine. Thus, "The state is not seeking to further punish a criminal, but only to protect its citizens from physicians of bad character."

- *Malloy v. South Carolina*, 237 U.S. 180 (1915). Malloy was convicted of murder. Under the South Carolina laws effective when the crime was committed the punishment for one found guilty of murder was death by hanging. A subsequent South Carolina Act prescribed electrocution as the method of execution instead of hanging. The Court upheld the Act. The Court explained the Act was not an ex post facto law because "The statute under consideration did not change the penalty—death—for murder, but only the mode of producing this, together with certain nonessential details in respect of surroundings. The punishment was not increased, and some of the odious features incident to the old method were abated."

- *Dobbert v. Florida*, 432 U.S. 282 (1977). Dobbert was convicted of first-degree murder. At the time of the murder, Florida law provided that a person convicted of a capital felony was to be punished by death unless a majority of the jury recommended mercy. A jury verdict of death or life was binding and not reviewable. Before trial, Florida revised its death penalty statute to make a jury verdict of death or life reviewable, first by the trial judge and then by the state supreme court. Under the new statute, the jury recommended mercy. However, the trial judge overruled the jury's recommendation and sentenced the defendant to death. The state supreme court affirmed. The U.S. Supreme Court upheld the death sentence and the revised statute.

   The Court explained the revised statute was not an ex post facto law because "The new statute simply altered the methods employed in determining whether the death penalty was to be imposed; there was no change in the quantum of punishment attached to the crime." In fact, "the new statute affords significantly more safeguards to the defendant than did the old." The

Court concluded that "the changes in the law are procedural, and on the whole ameliorative, and...there is no ex post facto violation."

- *Weaver v. Graham*, 450 U.S. 24 (1981). Weaver was convicted of second-degree murder and sentenced to fifteen years in prison. Later, a Florida statute retroactively reduced the amount of "good time" or good behavior credits available to prisoners for early release. The Court invalidated the retroactive application of the statute. The Court explained the statute was an ex post facto law because "the new provision constricts the inmate's opportunity to earn early release, and thereby makes more onerous the punishment for crimes committed before its enactment. This result runs afoul of the prohibition against ex post facto laws."

- *Miller v. Florida*, 482 U.S. 423 (1987). When Miller committed the crime for which he was convicted, Florida's sentencing guidelines would have provided a sentence of 3 1/2 to 4 1/2 years in prison. When Miller was sentenced, revised sentencing guidelines provided a sentence of 5 1/2 to 7 years in prison. The trial court applied the new guidelines and imposed a 7-year sentence. The Court invalidated the retroactive application of the new sentencing law.

The Court explained the new sentencing law was an ex post facto law because, "The law at issue in this case, like the law in *Weaver*, 'makes more onerous the punishment for crimes committed before its enactment.' Accordingly, we find that Florida's revised guidelines law, 1984 Fla. Laws, ch. 84–328, is void as applied to petitioner, whose crime occurred before the law's effective date."

CHAPTER 16

Bills of Attainder

THE CONSTITUTION PROHIBITS THE FEDERAL AND STATE GOVERNMENTS FROM PASSING bills of attainder (U.S. Const. art. I, §§ 9, 10). A bill of attainder is a law that designates specific individuals or a particular group of people for punishment without a judicial trial (e.g., a law requiring a specific person to be executed). "Punishment" is defined broadly and includes, for example, death, imprisonment, fines, exclusion from employment, and confiscation of property. If a law does not designate specific individuals or a particular group of people for punishment but merely describes conduct that will be punished, it is not a bill of attainder (e.g., a law stating that any person who kills intentionally shall be punished). The prohibition against bills of attainder applies only to persons and not to states (i.e., states cannot raise bill of attainder claims for themselves or for their citizens).

- *United States v. Lovett*, 328 U.S. 303 (1946). Section 304 of the Urgent Deficiency Appropriation Act prohibited payment of further salary to three named federal employees because the House of Representatives believed they were subversives. The Court invalidated the law. The Court explained the law "clearly accomplishes the punishment of named individuals without a judicial trial."

- *United States v. Brown*, 381 U.S. 437 (1965). Section 504 of the Labor-Management Reporting and Disclosure Act made it a crime for a member of the Communist Party to serve as an officer or (except in clerical or custodial positions) as an employee of a labor union. The Court invalidated the law. The Court explained, "The statute does not set forth a generally applicable rule decreeing that any person who commits certain acts or possesses certain characteristics (acts and characteristics which, in Congress' view, make them likely to initiate political strikes) shall not hold union office, and leave to courts and juries the job of deciding what persons have committed the specified acts or possess the specified characteristics. Instead, it designates in no uncertain terms the persons who possess the feared characteristics and therefore cannot hold union office without incurring criminal liability—members of the Communist Party."

- *Nixon v. Administrator of General Services*, 433 U.S. 425 (1977). The Presidential Recordings and Materials Preservations Act provided for government custody of Richard Nixon's presidential papers. The Court upheld the Act. The Court explained that although the Act designated Richard Nixon by name, it merely ensured the preservation of presidential papers. Thus, the Court concluded, "the Act cannot fairly be read to inflict legislative punishment as forbidden by the Constitution."

- *Selective Service System v. Minnesota Public Interest Research Group*, 468 U.S. 841 (1984). Section 12(f) of the Military Selective Service Act denied federal financial assistance to male students between the ages of eighteen and twenty-six who failed to register for the draft. The Court upheld the law. The Court explained male students could receive financial assistance by registering for the draft at any time, so the law did not "single out an identifiable group" as ineligible for financial assistance. Moreover, "the legislative history provides convincing support for the view that, in enacting § 12(f), Congress sought, not to punish anyone, but to promote compliance with the draft registration requirement and fairness in the allocation of scarce federal resources. Section 12(f) clearly furthers nonpunitive legislative goals."

CHAPTER 17

Freedom of Speech— General Considerations

THE FIRST AMENDMENT STATES CONGRESS SHALL MAKE NO LAW "ABRIDGING THE freedom of speech, or of the press; or the right of the people peaceably to assemble." The First Amendment protection of freedom of speech applies to the states through the Fourteenth Amendment [Gitlow v. New York, 268 U.S. 652 (1925)]. So freedom of speech is protected from state and local interference as well as from federal interference.

This chapter explains general considerations when reviewing laws that restrict freedom of speech.

GENERAL CONSIDERATIONS

Any law that restricts freedom of speech may be reviewed to determine if it is content based or content neutral, unduly vague or overbroad, a "prior restraint," or violates the right not to speak or the unconstitutional condition doctrine.

Content-Based Regulation (Presumed Invalid)

If the government regulates speech based on its subject matter or view-point, the regulation is "content based." Generally, content-based reg-ulation is presumed invalid and must satisfy the strict scrutiny test (i.e., the law must be necessary to achieve a compelling state interest).

- *Simon & Schuster, Inc. v. Members of New York State Crime Victims Board*, 502 U.S. 105 (1991). New York's "Son of Sam" statute required that any income a person "accused or convicted of a crime" derived from the production of a book or other work describing the crime be deposited in an escrow account for the crime victims and criminal's creditors. The statute defined a "person convicted of a crime" to include "any person convicted of a crime in this state either by entry of a plea of guilty or by conviction after trial and any person who has voluntarily and intelligently admitted the commission of a crime for which such person is not prosecuted." The Court invalidated the law.

  The Court explained the statute was content based because it established "a financial disincentive to create or publish works with a particular content." Moreover, although the state had a compelling interest in compensating victims from the fruits of the crime, the stat-ute was not narrowly tailored to advance the state's interest because it applied "to works on any subject, provided that they express the author's thoughts or recollections about his crime, however tangen-tially or incidentally." Also, "the statute's broad definition of 'person convicted of a crime' enables the board to escrow the income of any author who admits in his work to having committed a crime, whether or not the author was ever actually accused or convicted."

- *R.A.V. v. City of St. Paul, Minnesota*, 505 U.S. 377 (1992). St. Paul's Bias-Motivated Crime Ordinance prohibited the display of a sym-bol that one knows or has reason to know "arouses anger, alarm or resentment in others on the basis of race, color, creed, reli-gion or gender." The Court invalidated the ordinance. The Court explained the ordinance was content based because it applied only to "fighting words" that insult or provoke violence "on the basis of race, color, creed, religion or gender." The Court noted "Displays containing abusive invective, no matter how vicious or severe, are permissible unless they are addressed to one of the specified disfavored topics. Those who wish to use 'fighting words' in connection with other ideas—to express hostility, for example, on the basis of political affiliation, union membership, or homosexuality—are not covered."

Although St. Paul had a compelling interest in ensuring "basic human rights of members of groups that have historically been subjected to discrimination," content discrimination was not reasonably necessary to advance those interests. "Adequate content-neutral alternatives" existed. The Court explained, "An ordinance not limited to the favored topics, for example, would have precisely the same beneficial effect. In fact the only interest distinctively served by the content limitation is that of displaying the city council's special hostility towards the particular biases thus singled out."

Content-Neutral Regulation (Intermediate Scrutiny)

If the government regulates speech regardless of its subject matter or viewpoint, the regulation is "content neutral." Generally, content neutral regulation must satisfy the intermediate scrutiny test (i.e., the law must be substantially related to an important state interest).

* *Members of City Council of City of Los Angeles v. Taxpayers for Vincent*, 466 U.S. 789 (1984). Section 28.04 of the Los Angeles Municipal Code prohibited the posting of signs on public property. The Court upheld the ordinance. The Court explained the ordinance was content neutral because, "There is no claim that the ordinance was designed to suppress certain ideas that the City finds distasteful or that it has been applied to appellees because of the views that they express. The text of the ordinance is neutral—indeed it is silent—concerning any speaker's point of view." Moreover, "municipalities have a weighty, essentially esthetic interest in proscribing intrusive and unpleasant formats for expression." And, "The ordinance curtails no more speech than is necessary to accomplish its purpose."

"Void for Vagueness" Doctrine

A law is void if it is so vague that people "of common intelligence must necessarily guess at its meaning and differ as to its application"

[*Connally v. General Construction Co.*, 269 U.S. 385 (1926)]. Thus, a law restricting speech is "void for vagueness" if a reasonable person cannot tell what speech is prohibited and what speech is allowed. The "void for vagueness" doctrine allows the Court to invalidate a law "on its face" (i.e., as it is written), even if the defendant's speech would otherwise be unprotected by the First Amendment (i.e., the "guilty" can go free).

- *Baggett v. Bullitt*, 377 U.S. 360 (1964). A 1931 Washington statute required teachers, as a condition of employment, to take a loyalty oath that they would promote respect for the flag and institutions of the state and the United States. A 1955 Washington statute required state employees, as a condition of employment, to take a loyalty oath that they were not subversive persons and were not members of the Communist Party or knowingly members of any other subversive organization. The Court invalidated the statutes.

  The Court explained the 1931 statute was void for vagueness because, "The range of activities which are or might be deemed inconsistent with the required promise is very wide indeed. The teacher who refused to salute the flag or advocated refusal because of religious beliefs might well be accused of breaching his promise." The 1955 statute was void for vagueness because it was susceptible "to require forswearing of an undefined variety of 'guiltless knowing behavior.'" For example, "Does the statute reach endorsement or support for Communist candidates for office? Does it reach a lawyer who represents the Communist Party or its members or a journalist who defends constitutional rights of the Communist Party or its members or anyone who supports any cause which is likewise supported by Communists or the Communist Party?"

- *Coates v. Cincinnati*, 402 U.S. 611 (1971). A Cincinnati ordinance made it a crime for "three or more persons to assemble…on any of the sidewalks…and there conduct themselves in a manner annoying to persons passing by." The Court invalidated the ordinance. The Court explained the ordinance was void for vagueness because, "Conduct that annoys some people does not annoy others. Thus, the ordinance is vague, not in the sense that it requires a person to conform his conduct to an imprecise but comprehensible normative standard, but rather in the sense that no standard of conduct is specified at all. As a result, 'men of common intelligence must necessarily guess at its meaning.'"

- *Smith v. Goguen*, 415 U.S. 566 (1974). A Massachusetts flag-misuse statute subjected anyone who publicly treated the flag of the United States "contemptuously" to criminal liability. Goguen was convicted under the statute for wearing a small U.S. flag sewn to the seat of his trousers. The Court invalidated the statute. The Court explained the statute was void for vagueness because it "fails to draw reasonably clear lines between the kinds of nonceremonial treatment that are criminal and those that are not." The Court concluded, "The language at issue is void for vagueness as applied to Goguen because it subjected him to criminal liability under a standard so indefinite that police, court, and jury were free to react to nothing more than their own preferences for treatment of the flag."

Overbreadth Doctrine

A law is void for being overbroad if it regulates substantially more speech than the Constitution allows to be regulated (e.g., where a law regulates both speech that may be constitutionally prohibited and speech that is constitutionally protected). Overbroad laws "chill" speech by causing people to refrain from expression rather than challenge the law. The Court once described an overbroad law by stating, "Surely, this is to burn the house to roast the pig" [*Butler v. Michigan*, 352 U.S. 380 (1957)].

The overbreadth doctrine allows the Court to invalidate a law "on its face" (i.e., as it is written), even if the defendant's speech would otherwise be unprotected by the First Amendment (i.e., the "guilty" can go free). The overbreadth doctrine does not apply to commercial speech regulation [*Village of Hoffman Estates v. Flipside, Hoffman Estates, Inc.*, 455 U.S. 489 (1982)].

- *Broadrick v. Oklahoma*, 413 U.S. 601 (1973). Section 818 of Oklahoma's Merit System of Personnel Administration Act prohibited a broad range of political activities and conduct by the state's classified civil servants. The Court upheld the law. The Court explained that although the law may prohibit constitutionally protected activities such as wearing political buttons or using bumper stickers, "Section 818 is not substantially overbroad," and "whatever overbreadth may exist should be cured through case-by-case analysis."

- *Schad v. Borough of Mount Emphraim*, 452 U.S. 61 (1981). A Mount Ephraim zoning ordinance prohibited all live entertainment, including nonobscene, nude dancing, in any establishment in the Borough of Mount Ephraim. The Court invalidated the ordinance. The Court explained the ordinance was overbroad because, "By excluding live entertainment throughout the Borough, the Mount Ephraim ordinance prohibits a wide range of expression that has long been held to be within the protections of the First and Fourteenth Amendments. Entertainment, as well as political and ideological speech, is protected; motion pictures, programs broadcast by radio and television, and live entertainment, such as musical and dramatic works fall within the First Amendment guarantee."

- *Houston v. Hill*, 482 U.S. 451 (1987). A city ordinance made it illegal to, in any manner, oppose, molest, abuse, or interrupt a police officer in the execution of his duty. The Court invalidated the ordinance. The Court explained the ordinance was substantially overbroad because "the First Amendment protects a significant amount of verbal criticism and challenge directed at police officers." And, "The freedom of individuals verbally to oppose or challenge police action without thereby risking arrest is one of the principal characteristics by which we distinguish a free nation from a police state." Thus, "Houston's ordinance criminalizes a substantial amount of constitutionally protected speech, and accords the police unconstitutional discretion in enforcement."

- *Board of Airport Commissioners of Los Angeles v. Jews for Jesus, Inc.*, 482 U.S. 569 (1987). A resolution of the board of airport commissioners banned all "First Amendment activities" within the "Central Terminal Area" at Los Angeles International Airport (LAX). The Court invalidated the resolution. The Court explained the resolution was substantially overbroad because, "On its face, the resolution at issue in this case reaches the universe of expressive activity, and, by prohibiting all protected expression, purports to create a virtual 'First Amendment Free Zone' at LAX." The Court noted the resolution prohibited "even talking and reading, or the wearing of campaign buttons or symbolic clothing. Under such a sweeping ban, virtually every individual who enters LAX may be found to violate the resolution by engaging in some 'First Amendment activit[y].'"

Prior Restraints (Presumed Invalid)

A prior restraint restricts speech before the speech occurs. Two classic forms of prior restraint are court injunctions and licensing systems. Prior restraints are presumed invalid, and the government carries a heavy burden to justify a prior restraint. Generally, the proper remedy for unprotected speech is to punish the speech after it occurs, not restrain the speech before it occurs.

Court Injunctions

An injunction that stops speech before it occurs is a prior restraint and is presumed invalid. However, the "collateral bar rule" provides that one must obey an injunction until it is set aside. So one who disobeys an injunction cannot defend against a resulting charge of contempt by claiming that the injunction was unconstitutional because it prohibited constitutionally protected speech; this is an impermissible "collateral attack" against an injunction. Instead, one must seek review of an injunction in court before violating it (i.e., one must attack an injunction "directly").

- *Near v. Minnesota*, 283 U.S. 697 (1931). A Minnesota statute permitted state courts to enjoin as a public nuisance any "malicious, scandalous and defamatory newspaper, magazine or other periodical." The statute was used to perpetually enjoin *The Saturday Press*, which had criticized local public officials, from publishing "malicious, scandalous and defamatory" matter. The Court invalidated the statute. The Court explained, "The fact that the liberty of the press may be abused by miscreant purveyors of scandal does not make any the less necessary the immunity of the press from previous restraint in dealing with official misconduct. Subsequent punishment for such abuses as may exist is the appropriate remedy, consistent with constitutional privilege."

- *New York Times v. United States*, 403 U.S. 713 (1971). The United States sought injunctions prohibiting the *New York Times* and *Washington Post* from publishing excerpts from a top secret forty-seven-volume Defense Department study of the Vietnam War, known as the "Pentagon Papers." The Court invalidated the injunctions. The Court explained, "Any system of prior restraints of expression comes to this Court bearing a heavy presumption against its constitutional validity," and "the Government had not met that burden."

- *Nebraska Press Association v. Stuart*, 427 U.S. 539 (1976). A Nebraska state trial judge, in anticipation of a trial for a multiple murder that had attracted widespread news coverage, entered a "gag order." The order restrained members of the press from publishing accounts of confessions made by the accused or facts strongly implicative of the accused. The Court invalidated the gag order.

  The Court explained "on the record now before us it is not clear that further publicity, unchecked, would so distort the views of potential jurors that 12 could not be found who would, under proper instructions, fulfill their sworn duty to render a just verdict exclusively on the evidence presented in open court. We cannot say on this record that alternatives to a prior restraint on petitioners would not have sufficiently mitigated the adverse effects of pretrial publicity so as to make prior restraint unnecessary. Nor can we conclude that the restraining order actually entered would serve its intended purpose."

Licensing Systems

If a law requires a license or permit before speech occurs, it is a prior restraint and presumed invalid. A licensing law is valid only if (1) there is an important reason for licensing; (2) there are clear standards for licensing that leave almost no discretion to the licensing authority; and (3) there are procedural safeguards (e.g., a prompt hearing).

If a licensing law is valid on its face, the defendant cannot proceed without a license and claim later that his speech is constitutionally protected (i.e., "collateral attack" against the licensing law not allowed). Instead, he must challenge the denial of the license through the available administrative or judicial means (i.e., attack the licensing law "directly").

If a licensing law is void on its face (e.g., for lack of clear standards or procedural safeguards), the defendant may ignore it and claim later that his speech is constitutionally protected (i.e., "collateral attack" against the licensing law allowed).

- *Lovell v. Griffin*, 303 U.S. 444 (1938). A city of Griffin ordinance prohibited the distribution of circulars, handbooks, advertising, or literature of any kind without a permit. The Court invalidated the ordinance on its face. The Court explained, "Whatever the motive which induced its adoption, its character is such that it strikes at the very foundation of the freedom of the press by subjecting it to license and censorship." The Court noted that because the ordinance was void on its face, the defendant did not have to apply for a permit and then challenge its denial in court ("direct attack" unneeded); she could ignore the ordinance and claim after her arrest that it was unconstitutional ("collateral attack" allowed).

- *Cox v. New Hampshire*, 312 U.S. 569 (1941). A New Hampshire statute prohibited a "parade or procession" upon a public street without a special license. The Court upheld the statute. The Court explained the city had an important reason for licensing because requiring an application for a permit gave "the public authorities notice in advance so as to afford opportunity for proper policing." Also, "the licensing board was not vested with arbitrary power or an unfettered discretion."

- *Saia v. New York*, 334 U.S. 558 (1948). A Lockport, New York, ordinance prohibited the use of sound amplification devices in public places except with the permission of the chief of police. The Court invalidated the ordinance. The Court explained the ordinance was void on its face because, "To use a loudspeaker amplifier, a permit was required from the police chief. There were no standards prescribed for the exercise of the chief's uncontrolled discretion."

- *Kunz v. New York*, 340 U.S. 290 (1951). A New York City ordinance made it unlawful to hold public worship meetings on the streets without first obtaining a permit from the city police commissioner. The ordinance contained no provision for revocation of such permits and no standard to guide administrative actions in granting or denying permits. The Court invalidated the ordinance. The Court explained, "It is sufficient to say that New York cannot vest restraining control over the right to speak on religious subjects in an administrative official where there are no appropriate standards to guide his action."

- *Poulos v. New Hampshire*, 345 U.S. 395 (1953). A city ordinance prohibited the holding of a religious meeting in a public park without a license. Poulos, a member of the Jehovah's Witnesses, was convicted for conducting religious services in a public park without the required license after his application for a license had been denied. The Court upheld the ordinance and conviction.

First, the Court explained the ordinance was valid on its face because it required "uniform, nondiscriminatory and consistent administration of the granting of licenses." Second, although the city wrongly denied Poulos a license, he could be convicted because he did not appeal the denial of the license in state court (a "direct" attack against the denial was required); instead he conducted the service without the license and claimed after his arrest that the license was wrongly denied (an improper "collateral attack" against the denial).

- *Freedman v. Maryland*, 380 U.S. 51 (1965). A Maryland motion-picture censorship statute made it unlawful to exhibit a motion picture without having first obtained a license. Freedman exhibited a film without first applying for a license and was subsequently convicted of violating the statute. The Court invalidated the statute and reversed the conviction. The Court held the statute lacked procedural safeguards designed to eliminate the dangers of censorship. The Court explained (1) the burden of proving a film is unprotected expression must rest on the censor; (2) the censor must make a prompt determination of a license request; and (3) there must be a "prompt final judicial decision." The Court concluded, "It is readily apparent that the Maryland procedural scheme does not satisfy these criteria."

- *Shuttlesworth v. City of Birmingham*, 394 U.S. 147 (1969). A Birmingham, Alabama, ordinance made it unlawful to participate in any parade or procession or other public demonstration without first obtaining a permit from the city commission. A minister was convicted for leading an orderly civil rights march for which a request for a permit had been denied. The Court invalidated the ordinance and reversed the conviction. The Court explained the ordinance was invalid on its face because it "conferred upon the City Commission virtually unbridled and absolute power to prohibit any 'parade,' 'procession,' or 'demonstration' on the city's streets or public ways." In deciding whether or not to withhold a permit, the members of the commission were to be guided only by their own ideas of "public welfare, peace, safety, health, decency, good order, morals or convenience." So, the minister could ignore the ordinance (i.e., "direct attack" against the ordinance unneeded), engage in the free expression, and claim after his arrest the ordinance was unconstitutional (i.e., "collateral attack" allowed).

- *City of Lakewood v. Plain Dealer Publishing Co.*, 486 U.S. 750 (1988). A city of Lakewood ordinance gave the mayor the authority to grant or deny applications to install newspaper dispensing machines on public property. The Court invalidated the ordinance. The Court explained the ordinance was invalid on its face because, "It is apparent that the face of the ordinance itself contains no explicit limits on the mayor's discretion. Indeed, nothing in the law as written requires the mayor to do more than make the statement 'it is not in the public interest' when denying a permit application."

- *Forsyth County v. The Nationalist Movement*, 505 U.S. 123 (1992). A Forsyth County, Georgia, ordinance required a permit for parades, assemblies, or demonstrations and imposed a fee for each day of activities. The fee depended on an administrator's measure of the amount of hostility likely to be created by the speech based on the speech's content. The Court invalidated the ordinance. The Court explained the ordinance was invalid on its face because, "The decision how much to charge for police protection or administrative time—or even whether to charge at all—is left to the whim of the administrator. There are no articulated standards either in the ordinance or in the county's established practice. The administrator is not required to rely on any objective factors. He need not provide any explanation for his decision, and that decision is unreviewable."

The Right Not to Speak

The First Amendment protects both the right to speak freely and the right to refrain from speaking at all.

- *West Virginia State Board of Education v. Barnette*, 319 U.S. 624 (1943). The board of education adopted a resolution requiring public school children to salute and pledge allegiance to the U.S. flag. The Court invalidated the resolution. The Court explained, "If there is any fixed star in our constitutional constellation, it is that no official, high or petty, can prescribe what shall be orthodox in politics, nationalism, religion, or other matters of opinion or force citizens to confess by word or act their faith therein. If there are any circumstances which permit an exception, they do not now occur to us."

- *Wooley v. Maynard*, 430 U.S. 705 (1977). A New Hampshire statute required that noncommercial motor vehicles bear license plates embossed with the state motto, "Live Free or Die," and made it a misdemeanor to obscure the motto. Maynard, a Jehovah's Witness, objected to the motto on religious and moral grounds, covered up the motto on the license plates of his car, and was subsequently convicted of violating the statute. The Court invalidated the statute. The Court explained, "Here, as in *Barnette*, we are faced with a state measure which forces an individual, as part of his daily life—indeed constantly while his automobile is in public view—to be an instrument for fostering public adherence to an ideological point of view he finds unacceptable. In doing so, the State invades the sphere of intellect and spirit which it is the purpose of the First Amendment to our Constitution to reserve from all official control."

- *PruneYard Shopping Center v. Robins*, 447 U.S. 74 (1980). Prune-Yard, a privately owned shopping center open to the public, prohibited any visitor or tenant from engaging in any publicly expressive activity, including the circulation of petitions, if the activity was not directly related to the center's commercial purposes. Several high school students set up a table in PruneYard's central courtyard to distribute leaflets and solicit signatures from passersby for petitions in opposition to a United Nations resolution against "Zionism." PruneYard asked the students to leave. The Court held PruneYard's owner's free speech rights were not violated by permitting individuals to exercise their free speech and petition rights on the property of the shopping center (i.e., the owner's right "not to speak" was not infringed).

The Court explained the views expressed by members of the public in passing out pamphlets or seeking signatures for a petition would not likely be identified with those of the owner because (1) the shopping center was "a business establishment that is open to the public to come and go as they please;" (2) "no specific message is dictated by the State to be displayed on appellants' property;" (3) the owner was not compelled to affirm his belief in any "governmentally prescribed position or view;" and (4) the owner could "expressly disavow any connection with the message by simply posting signs in the area where the speakers or handbillers stand." The Court distinguished *Wooley*, where the government itself prescribed the message, and *Barnette*, where persons were compelled to recite a message containing an affirmation of belief.

- *Pacific Gas & Electric Co. v. Public Utilities Commission*, 475 U.S. 1 (1986). The California Public Utilities Commission ordered Pacific Gas & Electric Co. to let Toward Utility Rate Normalization (TURN), a consumer organization, use the extra space in billing envelopes to raise funds and communicate with customers. Pacific opposed TURN's views. The Court invalidated the order. The Court explained that similar to *Wooley*, "the Commission's order requires appellant to use its property— the billing envelopes—to distribute the message of another." The Court concluded, "Such forced association with potentially hostile views burdens the expression of views different from TURN's and risks forcing appellant to speak where it would prefer to remain silent."

"Unconstitutional Condition" Doctrine

The unconstitutional condition doctrine provides the government may not grant a benefit on the condition the beneficiary surrender a constitutional right.

- *Speiser v. Randall*, 357 U.S. 513 (1958). A California statute required anyone who sought to take advantage of a property tax exemption to sign a declaration stating he did not advocate the forcible overthrow of the government of the United States. The Court invalidated the statute. The Court explained, "To deny an exemption to claimants who engage in certain forms of speech is in effect to penalize them for such speech." Thus, "the denial of a tax exemption for engaging in certain speech necessarily will have the effect of coercing the claimants to refrain from the proscribed speech."

- *Regan v. Taxation with Representation of Washington*, 461 U.S. 540 (1983). Section 501(c)(3) of the Internal Revenue Code of 1954 granted tax exempt status to nonprofit organizations on the condition that the organizations not engage in lobbying activities. Taxation With Representation of Washington (TWR), a nonprofit corporation, applied for tax-exempt status. But the Internal Revenue Service denied the application because it appeared a substantial part of TWR's activities would consist of lobbying. The Court upheld the code. The Court explained "The Code does not deny TWR the right to receive deductible contributions to support its nonlobbying activity, nor does it deny TWR any independent benefit on account of its intention to lobby. Congress has merely refused to pay for the lobbying out of public moneys. This Court has never held that Congress must grant a benefit such as TWR claims here to a person who wishes to exercise a constitutional right."

- *Federal Communications Commission v. League of Women Voters*, 468 U.S. 364 (1984). Section 399 of the Public Broadcasting Act of 1967 prohibited any noncommercial educational station receiving a grant from the Corporation for Public Broadcasting (CPB) from engaging in "editorializing." The Court invalidated section 399. The Court explained "unlike the situation faced by the charitable organization in *Taxation With Representation*, a noncommercial educational station that receives only 1% of its overall income from CPB grants is barred absolutely from all editorializing. Therefore, in contrast to the appellee in *Taxation With Representation*, such a station is not able to segregate its activities according to the source of its funding. The station has no way of limiting the use of its federal funds to all noneditorializing activities, and, more importantly, it is barred from using even wholly private funds to finance its editorial activity."

- *Rust v. Sullivan*, 500 U.S. 173 (1991). The secretary of health and human services issued regulations prohibiting those receiving federal funds for family-planning services under Title X of the Public Health Service Act from engaging in activities that encouraged, promoted, or advocated abortion as a method of family planning. The Court upheld the regulations. The Court explained that the government exercised its authority to fund family planning services, which would lead to conception and childbirth, and declined to "promote or encourage abortion." The Court concluded, "By requiring that the Title X grantee engage in abortion-related activity separately from activity receiving federal funding, Congress has, consistent with our teachings in *League of Women Voters* and *Regan*, not denied it the right to engage in abortion-related activities. Congress has merely refused to fund such activities out of the public fisc, and the Secretary has simply required a certain degree of separation from the Title X project in order to ensure the integrity of the federally funded program."

- *Legal Services Corporation v. Velazquez*, 531 U.S. 533 (2001). The Legal Services Corporation Act authorized the Legal Services Corporation (LSC) to fund organizations providing free legal assistance to indigent clients in welfare benefit claims. However, Congress prohibited LSC funding of any organization that represented clients in an effort to amend or otherwise challenge existing welfare law. The Court invalidated the funding condition.

  The Court explained, "viewpoint-based funding decisions can be sustained in instances in which the government is itself the speaker, or instances, like *Rust*, in which the government used private speakers to transmit information pertaining to its own program." However, "the LSC program was designed to facilitate private speech, not to promote a governmental message. Congress funded LSC grantees to provide attorneys to represent the interests of indigent clients." Thus, "The lawyer is not the government's speaker. The attorney defending the decision to deny benefits will deliver the government's message in the litigation. The LSC lawyer, however, speaks on the behalf of his or her private, indigent client." Moreover, "Restricting LSC attorneys in advising their clients and in presenting arguments and analyses to the courts distorts the legal system by altering the traditional role of the attorneys."

- *United States v. American Library Association, Inc.*, 539 U.S. 194 (2003). The Children's Internet Protection Act (CIPA) prohibited public libraries from receiving federal assistance for Internet access unless they installed software to block or filter obscene or pornographic computer images and to prevent minors from accessing material harmful to them. The Court upheld the Act. The Court explained that the federal assistance programs "were intended to help public libraries fulfill their traditional role of obtaining material of requisite and appropriate quality for educational and informational purposes. Congress may certainly insist that these public funds be spent for the purposes for which they were authorized. Especially because public libraries have traditionally excluded pornographic material from their other collections, Congress could reasonably impose a parallel limitation on its Internet assistance programs. As the use of filtering software helps to carry out these programs, it is a permissible condition under *Rust*."

- *Rumsfeld v. Forum for Academic & Institutional Rights, Inc.*, 547 U.S. 47 (2006). The Solomon Amendment (10 U.S.C. § 983) provided if any part of an institution of higher education denied military recruiters access equal to that provided other recruiters, the entire institution would lose certain federal funds. The Court upheld the amendment.

  The Court explained that Congress could have required campus access for military recruiters directly, using its "broad authority to legislate on matters of military recruiting." Congress chose instead to secure campus access for military recruiters "indirectly," through its spending clause power (conditioning funding on access for military recruiters). Nevertheless, "Congress' decision to proceed indirectly does not reduce the deference given to Congress in the area of military affairs." So the Court concluded, "It is clear that a funding condition cannot be unconstitutional if it could be constitutionally imposed directly. Because the First Amendment would not prevent Congress from directly imposing the Solomon Amendment's access requirement, the statute does not place an unconstitutional condition on the receipt of federal funds."

CHAPTER 18

Freedom of Speech— Restricted Speech

T~HE~ C~OURT~ ~HAS~ ~DEVELOPED~ ~DIFFERENT~ ~TESTS~ ~FOR~ ~CERTAIN~ ~TYPES~ ~OF~ ~SPEECH,~ ~REVIEWED~ in this chapter. However, when reviewing these specific types of speech, keep in mind the general considerations you reviewed earlier (e.g., content-based regulations, content-neutral regulations, vagueness, and overbreadth).

Advocacy of Unlawful Conduct

The government may prohibit speech that advocates the use of force or crime if (1) the advocacy is intended to cause imminent lawless action, and (2) the advocacy is likely to cause such action [*Brandenburg v. Ohio*, 395 U.S. 444 (1969)]. Thus, the government may not prohibit the mere teaching of abstract doctrines.

- *Brandenburg v. Ohio*, 395 U.S. 444 (1969). Ohio's criminal syndicalism statute prohibited (1) "advocat[ing]...the duty, necessity, or propriety of crime, sabotage, violence, or unlawful methods of terrorism as a means of accomplishing industrial or political reform" and (2) "voluntarily assembl[ing] with any society, group, or assemblage of persons formed to teach or advocate the doctrines of criminal syndicalism." Brandenburg, a leader of a Ku Klux Klan group, was convicted under the statute for appearing at a Klan rally and threatening "revengeance" if the "suppression" of the white race continued. The Court invalidated the statute and reversed the conviction.

The Court explained the statute punished mere advocacy, which is not punishable, as opposed to advocacy intended to cause imminent lawless action that is likely to occur, which is punishable. The Court noted, "Neither the indictment nor the trial judge's instructions to the jury in any way refined the statute's bald definition of the crime in terms of mere advocacy not distinguished from incitement to imminent lawless action. Accordingly, we are here confronted with a statute which, by its own words and as applied, purports to punish mere advocacy and to forbid, on pain of criminal punishment, assembly with others merely to advocate the described type of action."

- *Hess v. Indiana*, 414 U.S. 105 (1973). Hess said, "We'll take the fucking street later" during an antiwar demonstration on a university campus, and was convicted of violating Indiana's disorderly conduct statute. The Court reversed the conviction. The Court explained, "there was no evidence, or rational inference from the import of the language, that his words were intended to produce, and likely to produce, imminent disorder." The Court said Hess's statement "amounted to nothing more than advocacy of illegal action at some indefinite future time. This is not sufficient to permit the State to punish Hess' speech."

- *NAACP v. Claiborne Hardware Co.*, 458 U.S. 886 (1982). During an NAACP-sponsored boycott of white merchants in Claiborne County, Mississippi, an NAACP official, Charles Evers, stated in a public speech, "If we catch any of you going in any of them racist stores, we're gonna break your damn neck." A state court held the NAACP liable for damages that arose from the boycott, based in part on Evers's speech. The Court reversed the state court's imposition of liability. The Court explained, "The emotionally charged rhetoric of Charles Evers' speeches did not transcend the bounds of protected speech set forth in *Brandenburg*." The Court noted, "An advocate must be free to stimulate his audience with spontaneous and emotional appeals for unity and action in a common cause. When such appeals do not incite lawless action, they must be regarded as protected speech." The Court concluded, "there is no evidence—apart from the speeches themselves—that Evers authorized, ratified, or directly threatened acts of violence."

"Fighting Words"

The government may prohibit speech that is directed to a specific person and either inflicts immediate injury (e.g., emotional harm) or tends to incite an immediate breach of the peace. Examples include profane, obscene, lewd, libelous, and insulting or "fighting" words.

- *Chaplinsky v. New Hampshire*, 315 U.S. 568 (1942). A New Hampshire statute made it unlawful for any person to address "any offensive, derisive or annoying word to any other person who is lawfully in any street or other public place" or "call him by any offensive or derisive name." Chaplinsky, a Jehovah's Witness, was convicted under the statute for saying to the city marshal of Rochester, "You are a God damned racketeer" and "a damned Fascist and the whole government of Rochester are Fascists or agents of Fascists." The Court upheld the statute and conviction.

  The Court explained the statute was "narrowly drawn and limited to define and punish specific conduct lying within the domain of state power, the use in a public place of words likely to cause a breach of the peace." Moreover, "Argument is unnecessary to demonstrate that the appellations 'damned racketeer' and 'damned Fascist' are epithets likely to provoke the average person to retaliation, and thereby cause a breach of the peace."

- *Cohen v. California*, 403 U.S. 15 (1971). A California statute prohibited "maliciously and willfully disturb[ing] the peace or quiet of any neighborhood or person...by...offensive conduct." Cohen was convicted under the statute for wearing a jacket bearing the words "Fuck the Draft" in a corridor of a Los Angeles Courthouse. The Court reversed the conviction.

  The Court explained, "While the four-letter word displayed by Cohen in relation to the draft is not uncommonly employed in a personally provocative fashion, in this instance it was clearly not directed to the person of the hearer. No individual actually or likely to be present could reasonably have regarded the words on appellant's jacket as a direct personal insult." The Court noted, "while the particular four-letter word being litigated here is perhaps more distasteful than most others of its genre, it is nevertheless often true that one man's vulgarity is another's lyric."

- *R.A.V. v. City of St. Paul*, 505 U.S. 377 (1992). A St. Paul, Minnesota, ordinance made it unlawful to place on public or private property "a symbol, object, appellation, characterization or graffiti, including, but not limited to, a burning cross or Nazi swastika, which one knows or has reasonable grounds to know arouses anger, alarm or resentment in others on the basis of race, color, creed, religion or gender." A teenager who allegedly burned a cross inside the fenced yard of a black family was charged with violating the ordinance. The Court invalidated the ordinance because it was content-based discrimination.

    The Court explained, "the ordinance applies only to 'fighting words' that insult, or provoke violence, 'on the basis of race, color, creed, religion or gender.' Displays containing abusive invective, no matter how vicious or severe, are permissible unless they are addressed to one of the specified disfavored topics. Those who wish to use 'fighting words' in connection with other ideas— to express hostility, for example, on the basis of political affiliation, union membership, or homosexuality—are not covered. The First Amendment does not permit St. Paul to impose special prohibitions on those speakers who express views on disfavored subjects." The Court concluded, "Let there be no mistake about our belief that burning a cross in someone's front yard is reprehensible. But St. Paul has sufficient means at its disposal to prevent such behavior without adding the First Amendment to the fire."

- *Virginia v. Black*, 538 U.S. 343 (2003). A Virginia statute made it a felony "for any person…with the intent of intimidating any person or group…to burn…a cross on the property of another, a highway or other public place." The statute also included a "prima facie" provision that stated "any such burning…shall be prima facie evidence of an intent to intimidate a person or group." The Court upheld the part of the statute that banned cross burning with intent to intimidate.

    The Court explained, "The First Amendment permits Virginia to outlaw cross burnings done with the intent to intimidate because burning a cross is a particularly virulent form of intimidation. Instead of prohibiting all intimidating messages, Virginia may choose to regulate this subset of intimidating messages in light of cross burning's long and pernicious history as a signal of impending violence."

However, the Court invalidated the "prima facie" provision, without a majority opinion. Justice O'Connor stated, "a burning cross is not always intended to intimidate." Sometimes cross burning is "a statement of ideology, a symbol of group solidarity." And sometimes cross burning "does not intend to express either a statement of ideology or intimidation," for example cross burnings in movies and plays. Yet, "The prima facie provision makes no effort to distinguish among these different types of cross burnings." Instead, "The provision permits the Commonwealth to arrest, prosecute, and convict a person based solely on the fact of cross burning itself."

"Hostile Audience"

The government may prohibit speech that threatens imminent and uncontrolled violence by the audience.

- *Cantwell v. Connecticut*, 310 U.S. 296 (1940). Cantwell, a Jehovah's Witness, stopped two men on a public street. He then asked and received permission to play a phonograph record. The record attacked the religion and church of the two men, who were Catholics. Cantwell was convicted of inciting a breach of the peace. The Court overturned the conviction. The Court explained, "We find in the instant case no assault or threatening of bodily harm, no truculent bearing, no intentional discourtesy, no personal abuse. On the contrary, we find only an effort to persuade a willing listener to buy a book or to contribute money in the interest of what Cantwell, however misguided others may think him, conceived to be true religion." The Court concluded that in the fields of religious faith and political belief, "the tenets of one man may seem the rankest error to his neighbor."

- *Feiner v. New York*, 340 U.S. 315 (1951). Feiner stood on a sidewalk, addressed a crowd of about seventy-five people through a loud-speaker system, and made derogatory remarks concerning President Truman, the American Legion, the mayor of Syracuse, and other local political officials. He also urged blacks to "rise up in arms and fight for equal rights." This caused "a little excitement" and at least one onlooker to threaten violence if the police did not act. A police officer twice requested Feiner to stop, but Feiner continued talking. Feiner was convicted of disorderly conduct. The Court upheld the conviction. The Court explained, "the imminence of greater disorder coupled with petitioner's deliberate defiance of the police officers convince us that we should not reverse this conviction in the name of free speech."

- *Edwards v. South Carolina*, 372 U.S. 229 (1963). High school and college students peaceably assembled at the site of the state government, expressed their grievances "to the citizens of South Carolina, along with the Legislative Bodies of South Carolina," sang religious and patriotic songs while stamping their feet and clapping their hands, and were convicted for breach of the peace. The Court overturned the convictions. The Court explained, "There was no violence or threat of violence on their part, or on the part of any member of the crowd watching them." Also, "Police protection at the scene was at all times sufficient to meet any foreseeable possibility of disorder." The Court concluded, "This, therefore, was a far cry from the situation in *Feiner*," where at least one member of the crowd "threatened violence if the police did not act."

- *Cox v. Louisiana*, 379 U.S. 536 (1965). Reverend Cox, a civil rights leader, led a demonstration of about 2,000 college students. The students assembled peaceably at the state capitol building and marched to the courthouse where they sang, prayed, and listened to a speech by Cox objecting to racial segregation at lunch counters and urging students to sit in at the lunch counters. Cox was convicted for disturbing the peace. The Court overturned the conviction.

  The Court explained, "the students themselves were not violent and threatened no violence," and "the entire meeting from the beginning until its dispersal by tear gas was orderly." Also, the police present "could have handled the crowd." The Court concluded, "Here again, as in *Edwards*, this evidence showed no more than that the opinions which…[the students] were peaceably expressing were sufficiently opposed to the views of the majority of the community to attract a crowd and necessitate police protection. Conceding this was so, the compelling answer…is that constitutional rights may not be denied simply because of hostility to their assertion or exercise."

Obscenity (*Miller* Test)

The government may prohibit obscene material. Material is obscene if (1) applying contemporary community standards, the average person would find that the material, taken as a whole, appeals to the prurient interest; (2) applying contemporary community standards, the material depicts patently offensive sexual conduct specifically defined by the applicable state law; and (3) applying national standards, the material, taken as a whole, lacks serious literary, artistic, political, or scientific value [*Miller v. California*, 413 U.S. 15 (1973)]. "Prurient interest" means the material appeals to a shameful or morbid interest in sex, rather than a normal interest. "Patently offensive" sexual conduct includes, for example, patently offensive representations or descriptions of ultimate sexual acts, masturbation, excretory functions, or lewd exhibition of the genitals.

- *Jenkins v. Georgia*, 418 U.S. 153 (1974). Jenkins, a theater manager, was convicted of violating Georgia's obscenity statute for showing the film *Carnal Knowledge* in a motion picture theater. The Court reversed the conviction. The Court held the film was not obscene because it did not depict sexual conduct in a patently offensive way. The Court explained, "While the subject matter of the picture is, in a broader sense, sex, and there are scenes in which sexual conduct including 'ultimate sexual acts' is to be understood to be taking place, the camera does not focus on the bodies of the actors at such times. There is no exhibition whatever of the actors' genitals, lewd or otherwise, during these scenes. There are occasional scenes of nudity, but nudity alone is not enough to make material legally obscene under the *Miller* standards."

- *Sable Communications v. FCC*, 492 U.S. 115 (1989). Section 223(b) of the Communications Act of 1934, as amended in 1998, banned both obscene and indecent interstate commercial telephone messages, commonly known as "dial-a-porn." The Court upheld the ban on obscene dial-a-porn, but invalidated the ban on indecent, nonobscene dial-a-porn. The Court explained, "there is no constitutional barrier to the ban on obscene dial-a-porn recordings. We have repeatedly held that the protection of the First Amendment does not extend to obscene speech." However, "Sexual expression which is indecent but not obscene is protected by the First Amendment."

- *Ashcroft v. Free Speech Coalition*, 535 U.S. 234 (2002). The Child Pornography Prevention Act of 1996 (CPPA) expanded the federal prohibition on child pornography. The CPPA prohibited not only pornographic images made using actual children, but also "any visual depiction, including any photograph, film, video, picture, or computer or computer-generated image or picture" that "is, or appears to be, of a minor engaging in sexually explicit conduct" ("virtual child pornography"). The Court invalidated the Act.

  The Court explained the CPPA "extends to images that appear to depict a minor engaging in sexually explicit activity without regard to the *Miller* requirements." First, "The materials need not appeal to the prurient interest. Any depiction of sexually explicit activity, no matter how it is presented, is proscribed. The CPPA applies to a picture in a psychology manual, as well as a movie depicting the horrors of sexual abuse." Second, "It is not necessary, moreover, that the image be patently offensive. Pictures of what appear to be 17-year-olds engaging in sexually explicit activity do not in every case contravene community standards." Third, "The CPPA prohibits speech despite its serious literary, artistic, political, or scientific value. The statute proscribes the visual depiction of an idea—that of teenagers engaging in sexual activity—that is a fact of modern society and has been a theme in art and literature throughout the ages."

Child Pornography

The government may prohibit the pandering, solicitation, sale, distribution, exhibition, and private possession of child pornography, even if it is not obscene under the *Miller* test.

- *New York v. Ferber*, 458 U.S. 747 (1982). A New York statute prohibited persons from knowingly promoting a sexual performance by a child under the age of sixteen by distributing material that depicts such a performance. Ferber was convicted under the statute for selling two films showing young boys masturbating. The Court upheld the statute and conviction. The Court explained child pornography may be prohibited even if it is not obscene under the *Miller* test, because "a State's interest in safeguarding the physical and psychological well-being of a minor is compelling." The Court noted, "The *Miller* standard, like all general definitions of what may be banned as obscene, does not reflect the State's particular and more compelling interest in prosecuting those who promote the sexual exploitation of children."

- *Osborne v. Ohio*, 495 U.S. 103 (1990). An Ohio statute prohibited any person from possessing or viewing any material or performance showing a minor who is not his child or ward in a state of nudity. Osborne was convicted under the statute for possessing in his home four photographs, each of which depicted a nude male adolescent posed in a sexually explicit position. The Court upheld the statute and reversed the conviction on other grounds. The Court explained, "Given the importance of the State's interest in protecting the victims of child pornography, we cannot fault Ohio for attempting to stamp out this vice at all levels in the distribution chain. According to the State, since the time of our decision in *Ferber*, much of the child pornography market has been driven underground; as a result, it is now difficult, if not impossible, to solve the child pornography problem by only attacking production and distribution. Indeed, 19 States have found it necessary to proscribe the possession of this material."

- *Ashcroft v. Free Speech Coalition*, 535 U.S. 234 (2002). The Child Pornography Prevention Act of 1996 (CPPA) expanded the federal prohibition on child pornography. The CPPA prohibited not only pornographic images made using actual children, but also "any visual depiction, including any photograph, film, video, picture, or computer or computer-generated image or picture" that "is, or appears to be, of a minor engaging in sexually explicit conduct" ("virtual child pornography"). The Court invalidated the Act.

  The Court explained, "In contrast to the speech in *Ferber*, speech that itself is the record of sexual abuse, the CPPA prohibits speech that records no crime and creates no victims by its production. Virtual child pornography is not 'intrinsically related' to the sexual abuse of children, as were the materials in *Ferber*. While the Government asserts that the images can lead to actual instances of child abuse, the causal link is contingent and indirect."

• *United States v. Williams*, 553 U.S. 285 (2008). The Prosecutorial Remedies and Other Tools to end the Exploitation of Children Today (PROTECT) Act of 2003 criminalized, in certain specified circumstances, the pandering or solicitation of child pornography. The Court upheld the Act. The Court explained, "The statute's definition of the material or purported material that may not be pandered or solicited precisely tracks the material held constitutionally proscribable in *Ferber* and *Miller*: obscene material depicting (actual or virtual) children engaged in sexually explicit conduct, and any other material depicting actual children engaged in sexually explicit conduct." It made no difference that the Act was not limited to "commercial" speech, because, "Offers to provide or requests to obtain unlawful material, whether as part of a commercial exchange or not, are similarly undeserving of First Amendment protection. It would be an odd constitutional principle that permitted the government to prohibit offers to sell illegal drugs, but not offers to give them away for free."

Private Possession

Except for child pornography, the government cannot prohibit private possession of obscene material in one's home [*Stanley v. Georgia*, 394 U.S. 557 (1969)]. However, the government may prohibit transportation of obscene material for private use [*United States v. Orito*, 413 U.S. 139 (1973)]; receiving obscene material through the mails [*United States v. Reidel*, 402 U.S. 351 (1971)]; importing obscene material from foreign countries [*United States v. 12 200-Foot Reels of Super 8MM. Film*, 413 U.S. 123 (1973)]; and public exhibition of obscene material, even if access is limited to consenting adults [*Paris Adult Theatre I v. Slaton*, 413 U.S. 49 (1973)].

Zoning

The government may use zoning ordinances to regulate the location of adult book stores and movie theaters, even if the material is not obscene under the *Miller* test.

- *Young v. American Mini-Theatres, Inc.*, 427 U.S. 50 (1976). Detroit's "Anti-Skid Row" zoning ordinances provided that an adult theater may not be located within 1,000 feet of any two other "regulated uses" such as adult book stores, cabarets, bars, taxi dance halls, and hotels, or within 500 feet of a residential area, even if the theater is not displaying obscene material. The Court upheld the ordinances.

  The Court explained the ordinances were not invalid as prior restraints on free speech because "the 1,000-foot restriction does not, in itself, create an impermissible restraint on protected communication. The city's interest in planning and regulating the use of property for commercial purposes is clearly adequate to support that kind of restriction applicable to all theaters within the city limits. In short, apart from the fact that the ordinances treat adult theaters differently from other theaters and the fact that the classification is predicated on the content of material shown in the respective theaters, the regulation of the place where such films may be exhibited does not offend the First Amendment."

- *Schad v. Borough of Mount Ephraim*, 452 U.S. 61 (1981). A Mount Ephraim zoning ordinance prohibited all live entertainment, whether a nude dance or some other form of live presentation, in any establishment in the borough. The Court invalidated the ordinance. The Court explained the ordinance was overbroad because, "By excluding live entertainment throughout the Borough, the Mount Ephraim ordinance prohibits a wide range of expression that has long been held to be within the protections of the First and Fourteenth Amendments. Entertainment, as well as political and ideological speech, is protected; motion pictures, programs broadcast by radio and television, and live entertainment, such as musical and dramatic works, fall within the First Amendment guarantee. Nor may an entertainment program be prohibited solely because it displays the nude human figure."

  The Court distinguished *Young* because the restriction in *Young* "did not affect the number of adult movie theaters that could operate in the city; it merely dispersed them. The Court [in *Young*] did not imply that a municipality could ban all adult theaters—much less all live entertainment or all nude dancing—from its commercial districts citywide."

- *City of Renton v. Playtime Theatres, Inc.*, 475 U.S. 41 (1986). A Renton ordinance prohibited adult motion picture theaters from locating within 1,000 feet of any residential zone, single or multiple-family dwelling, church, park, or school. The Court upheld the ordinance. First, the Court explained the ordinance was content neutral because it was aimed "not at the content of the films shown at 'adult motion picture theatres,' but rather at the secondary effects of such theaters on the surrounding community." Thus, "The ordinance by its terms is designed to prevent crime, protect the city's retail trade, maintain property values, and generally protect and preserve the quality of the city's neighborhoods, commercial districts, and the quality of urban life, not to suppress the expression of unpopular views."

  Second, the Court explained the ordinance served a substantial governmental interest in "attempting to preserve the quality of urban life." Finally, the ordinance allowed for reasonable alternative avenues of communication because "the ordinance leaves some 520 acres, or more than five percent of the entire land area of Renton, open to use as adult theater sites."

- *City of Los Angeles v. Alameda Books*, 535 U.S. 425 (2002). Los Angeles Municipal Code § 12.70(C) prohibited "the establishment or maintenance of more than one adult entertainment business in the same building, structure or portion thereof." The Court upheld the ordinance against a motion for summary judgment, without a majority opinion. Justice O'Connor wrote for the plurality and explained, "The city of Los Angeles may reasonably rely on a study it conducted some years before enacting the present version of § 12.70(C) to demonstrate that its ban on multiple-use adult establishments serves its interest in reducing crime. In 1977, the city of Los Angeles conducted a comprehensive study of adult establishments and concluded that concentrations of adult businesses are associated with higher rates of prostitution, robbery, assaults, and thefts in surrounding communities." Thus, "the city, at this stage of the litigation, has complied with the evidentiary requirement in *Renton*."

Media (Radio, Cable TV, and Internet)

The government may prohibit "indecent" language over the radio in the early afternoon, even if it is not obscene under the *Miller* test, because radio broadcasts are invasive into the home and children are more likely to be listening during this time.

Content-based regulation of cable TV and the Internet must satisfy strict scrutiny (i.e., the law must be neccessary to achieve a compelling state interest).

- *Federal Communications Commission v. Pacifica Foundation*, 438 U.S. 726 (1978). At about two o'clock in the afternoon a New York radio station owned by Pacifica Foundation broadcast satiric humorist George Carlin's twelve-minute monologue entitled "Filthy Words." In "Filthy Words," Carlin discussed "the words you couldn't say on the public, ah, airwaves, um, the ones you definitely wouldn't say, ever." The Federal Communications Commission (FCC) held the language as broadcast was indecent, though not necessarily obscene, and prohibited by 18 U.S.C. Section 1464 because it was "broadcast at a time when children were undoubtedly in the audience (i.e., in the early afternoon)." The Court held the FCC could prohibit such speech.

  First, the Court explained, "Patently offensive, indecent material presented over the airwaves confronts the citizen, not only in public, but also in the privacy of the home, where the individual's right to be left alone plainly outweighs the First Amendment rights of an intruder." Second, "broadcasting is uniquely accessible to children, even those too young to read. Although Cohen's written message [in *Cohen v. California*] might have been incomprehensible to a first grader, Pacifica's broadcast could have enlarged a child's vocabulary in an instant."

- *Denver Area Educational Telecommunications Consortium, Inc. v. Federal Communications Commission*, 518 U.S. 727 (1996). Section 10(a) of the Cable Television Consumer Protection and Competition Act of 1992 regulated "leased access channels" reserved under federal law for commercial lease by parties unaffiliated with the cable television system operator. Section 10(c) regulated "public access channels" required by local governments for public, educational, and governmental programming. Both section 10(a) and section 10(c) permitted the operator to allow or prohibit "programming" that it "reasonably believes...depicts sexual... activities or organs in a patently offensive manner."

Section 10(b) regulated leased access channels and required operators to segregate "patently offensive" programming on a single channel, block that channel from viewer access, and unblock it (or later to reblock it) within thirty days of a subscriber's written request.

The Court upheld section 10(a) and invalidated section 10(c) without a majority opinion, and invalidated section 10(b) with a majority opinion.

Regarding section 10(a), Justice Breyer wrote a plurality opinion stating, "The importance of the interest at stake here— protecting children from exposure to patently offensive depictions of sex; the accommodation of the interests of programmers in maintaining access channels and of cable operators in editing the contents of their channels; the similarity of the problem and its solution to those at issue in *Pacifica*; and the flexibility inherent in an approach that *permits* private cable operators to make editorial decisions, lead us to conclude that § 10(a) is a sufficiently tailored response to an extraordinarily important problem."

Regarding section 10(c), Justice Breyer wrote a plurality opinion stating that public access channels are normally subject to complex supervisory systems with both public and private elements, "making it unlikely that many children will in fact be exposed to programming considered patently offensive in that community." Hence, "the Government cannot sustain its burden of showing that § 10(c) is necessary to protect children or that it is appropriately tailored to secure that end."

Regarding section 10(b), Justice Breyer explained in a majority opinion, "The several up-to-30-day delays, along with single channel segregation, mean that a subscriber cannot decide to watch a single program without considerable advance planning and without letting the 'patently offensive' channel in its entirety invade his household for days, perhaps weeks, at a time." Also, "the 'written notice' requirement will further restrict viewing by subscribers who fear for their reputations should the operator, advertently or inadvertently, disclose the list of those who wish to watch the 'patently offensive' channel." Thus, "once one examines this governmental restriction, it becomes apparent that, not only is it not a 'least restrictive alternative' and is not 'narrowly tailored' to meet its legitimate objective, it also seems considerably 'more extensive than necessary.'"

- *Reno v. ACLU*, 521 U.S. 844 (1997). Provisions of the Communications Decency Act of 1996 (CDA) sought to protect minors from harmful material on the Internet. The CDA prohibited the "knowing" transmission of "obscene or indecent" messages to any recipient under eighteen years of age and the "knowing" sending or displaying to a person under eighteen of any message "that, in context, depicts or describes, in terms patently offensive as measured by contemporary community standards, sexual or excretory activities or organs." The Court invalidated the provisions.

   The Court explained the CDA was overbroad because, "the scope of the CDA is not limited to commercial speech or commercial entities. Its open-ended prohibitions embrace all nonprofit entities and individuals posting indecent messages or displaying them on their own computers in the presence of minors. The general, undefined terms 'indecent' and 'patently offensive' cover large amounts of nonpornographic material with serious educational or other value." Also, "the Internet is not as invasive as radio or television," because, "Unlike communications received by radio or television, the receipt of information on the Internet requires a series of affirmative steps more deliberate and directed than merely turning a dial." Finally, "unlike the conditions that prevailed when Congress first authorized regulation of the broadcast spectrum, the Internet can hardly be considered a 'scarce' expressive commodity. It provides relatively unlimited, low-cost capacity for communication of all kinds."

- *United States v. Playboy Entertainment Group, Inc.*, 529 U.S. 803 (2000). Section 505 of the Telecommunications Act of 1996 required cable television operators providing channels "primarily dedicated to sexually-oriented programming" either to "fully scramble or otherwise fully block" those channels or limit their transmission to hours when children are unlikely to be viewing, set by regulation as between 10 p.m. and 6 a.m. The Court invalidated the law.

First, the Court explained, "The speech in question is defined by its content; and the statute which seeks to restrict it is content based. Section 505 applies only to channels primarily dedicated to 'sexually explicit adult programming or other programming that is indecent.'" Thus, "Since § 505 is a content-based speech restriction, it can stand only if it satisfies strict scrutiny." Second, "the objective of shielding children does not suffice to support a blanket ban if the protection can be accomplished by a less restrictive alternative." The Court noted Section 504, which required cable operators to block undesired channels at individual households "upon request," was a plausible, less restrictive alternative. The Court concluded, "The Government has failed to show that § 505 is the least restrictive means for addressing a real problem."

- *Ashcroft v. ACLU*, 542 U.S. 656 (2004). In response to *Reno v. ACLU*, Congress passed the Child Online Protection Act (COPA). COPA prohibited the posting, for "commercial purposes," of World Wide Web content that was "harmful to minors," applying contemporary community standards. The Court upheld a preliminary injunction against enforcement of COPA.

  The Court explained that because COPA was content-based, "the burden is on the Government to prove that the proposed alternatives will not be as effective as the challenged statute." Internet content providers proposed that blocking and filtering software was a less restrictive alternative to COPA. For example, filters "impose selective restrictions on speech at the receiving end, not universal restrictions at the source." Also, filters may be more effective that COPA because "a filter can prevent minors from seeing all pornography, not just pornography posted to the Web from America. The District Court noted in its factfindings that one witness estimated that 40% of harmful-to-minors content comes from overseas. COPA does not prevent minors from having access to those foreign harmful materials." The Court concluded, "the Government has not shown that the less restrictive alternatives proposed by respondents should be disregarded. Those alternatives, indeed, may be more effective than the provisions of COPA. The District Court did not abuse its discretion when it entered the preliminary injunction."

Defamation

The First Amendment limits damages in defamation actions by public officials, public figures, and private figures.

Public Officials (New York Times Rule: Malice Needed)

A public official can recover damages for defamation if he proves by clear and convincing evidence that the defendant made a defamatory false statement of fact, relating to his official conduct, with malice.

"Public officials" include elected officials, candidates for public office, and government employees who have substantial responsibility for the conduct of governmental affairs.

Defamation liability may be based only on false statements of fact. However, an "opinion" may also be the basis of liability if it contains or implies a false assertion of fact [Milkovich v. Lorain Journal Co., 497 U.S. 1 (1990)]. For example, if a speaker says, "In my opinion John Jones is a liar," he implies knowledge of facts that may be proved false; the statement would be false if the speaker really did not think Jones had lied but said it anyway, or if Jones really had not lied. Thus, "Simply couching such statements in terms of opinion does not dispel these implications; and the statement, 'In my opinion Jones is a liar,' can cause as much damage to reputation as the statement, 'Jones is a liar.'" [Milkovich]. However, the statement, "In my opinion Mayor Jones shows his abysmal ignorance by accepting the teachings of Marx and Lenin," would not be actionable because it does not contain a "provably false factual connotation" [Milkovich].

Statements relating to "official conduct" include statements that relate to fitness for office.

"Malice" is defined as "knowledge that [the defamatory statement] was false" or "reckless disregard of whether it was false or not" [New York Times v. Sullivan, 376 U.S. 254 (1964)]. "Reckless disregard" of the truth requires proof the defendant had serious doubts about the statement's truth; mere negligence is not enough. Malice is required because "erroneous statement is inevitable in free debate, and . . . it must be protected if the freedoms of expression are to have the 'breathing space' that they 'need . . . to survive'" [New York Times].

- New York Times v. Sullivan, 376 U.S. 254 (1964). Alabama libel law required actual malice for punitive damages, but presumed malice for general damages. Sullivan, an elected official in Montgomery, Alabama, sued the *New York Times* for an advertisement containing false statements and criticizing the way Montgomery police treated civil rights demonstrators. Sullivan was awarded $500,000 in damages. The Court reversed the award.

First, the Court explained, "The constitutional guarantees require, we think, a federal rule that prohibits a public official from recovering damages for a defamatory falsehood relating to his official conduct unless he proves that the statement was made with 'actual malice'—that is, with knowledge that it was false or with reckless disregard of whether it was false or not." The Court noted the "profound national commitment to the principle that debate on public issues should be uninhibited, robust, and wide-open, and that it may well include vehement, caustic, and sometimes unpleasantly sharp attacks on government and public officials."

Second, the Court explained, "Since the trial judge did not instruct the jury to differentiate between general and punitive damages, it may be that the verdict was wholly an award of one or the other. But it is impossible to know, in view of the general verdict returned. Because of this uncertainty, the judgment must be reversed and the case remanded."

Third, the Court explained the evidence was constitutionally insufficient to support the award because "the evidence against the *Times* supports at most a finding of negligence in failing to discover the misstatements, and is constitutionally insufficient to show the recklessness that is required for a finding of actual malice."

Public Figures (New York Times Rule: Malice Needed)

The *New York Times* rule applies to "public figures" as well as "public officials." Thus, a public figure can recover damages for defamation if he proves the defendant made a defamatory false statement of fact with "malice" (knowledge of the falsity or reckless disregard of the truth). A public figure is a person who does not fit the definition of a public official but has "special prominence in the affairs of society." There are three types of public figures: (1) those who achieve such pervasive fame or notoriety that they become public figures for all purposes and in all contexts; (2) those who voluntarily thrust themselves to the forefront of particular public controversies to influence the resolution of the issues involved, and are therefore public figures with respect to those controversies; and (3) those who involuntarily become public figures with respect to particular controversies (exceedingly rare).

- *Curtis Publishing Co. v. Butts*, and companion case, *Associated Press v. Walker*, 388 U.S. 130 (1967). *Butts* involved the *Saturday Evening Post's* claim that Coach Wally Butts of the University of Georgia had conspired with Coach "Bear" Bryant of the University of Alabama to fix a football game between their respective schools. *Walker* involved an erroneous Associated Press account of former Major General Edwin Walker's participation in a University of Mississippi campus riot. Butts was paid by a private alumni association, and Walker had resigned from the Army; so neither could be classified as a "public official" under *New York Times*.

  However, Justice Harlan, writing for the plurality, explained, "both Butts and Walker commanded a substantial amount of independent public interest at the time of the publications; both, in our opinion, would have been labeled 'public figures' under ordinary tort rules. Butts may have attained that status by position alone and Walker by his purposeful activity amounting to a thrusting of his personality into the 'vortex' of an important public controversy, but both commanded sufficient continuing public interest and had sufficient access to the means of counterargument to be able 'to expose through discussion the falsehood and fallacies' of the defamatory statements."

- *Gertz v. Welch*, 418 U.S. 323 (1974). A Chicago policeman named Nuccio was convicted of murder. The victim's family retained Gertz, a reputable attorney, to represent them in civil litigation against Nuccio. *American Opinion*, a monthly outlet for the views of the John Birch Society, published an article alleging Nuccio's murder trial was part of a Communist conspiracy to discredit the local police and falsely stating Gertz had arranged Nuccio's "frame-up." The Court held the *New York Times* standard did not apply because Gertz was a private figure.

  The Court explained that although Gertz served briefly on housing committees appointed by the mayor of Chicago several years prior to the present incident, he was not a public official because "at the time of publication he had never held any remunerative governmental position." Gertz was not a public figure because "he had achieved no general fame or notoriety in the community. None of the prospective jurors called at the trial had ever heard of petitioner prior to this litigation, and respondent offered no proof that this response was atypical of the local population." Moreover, "he never discussed either the criminal or civil litigation with the press and was never quoted as having done so. He plainly did not thrust himself into the vortex of this public issue, nor did he engage the public's attention in an attempt to influence its outcome."

- *Time v. Firestone*, 424 U.S. 448 (1976). *Time* magazine falsely reported Mary Alice Firestone's divorce from a member of the wealthy Firestone family was granted on the grounds of extreme cruelty and adultery. Ms. Firestone sued for defamation. The Court held she was a private figure, not a public figure.

The Court explained that although she held a few press conferences during the divorce proceedings in an attempt to satisfy inquiring reporters, she "did not assume any role of especial prominence in the affairs of society, other than perhaps Palm Beach society, and she did not thrust herself to the forefront of any particular public controversy in order to influence the resolution of the issues involved in it." The Court added, "Dissolution of a marriage through judicial proceedings is not the sort of 'public controversy' referred to in *Gertz*, even though the marital difficulties of extremely wealthy individuals may be of interest to some portion of the reading public. Nor did respondent freely choose to publicize issues as to the propriety of her married life. She was compelled to go to court by the State in order to obtain legal release from the bonds of matrimony."

Private Figures (Gertz Rule)

A private figure can recover actual damages for defamation if he proves the defendant made a defamatory false statement of fact, about a matter of public concern, with negligence. States may require a higher degree of fault on the part of the defendant, such as "malice," but they cannot provide a lower one, such as liability without fault; at least negligence is required [*Gertz v. Welch*, 418 U.S. 323 (1974)]. "Actual damages" include out-of-pocket loss, impaired reputation and standing in the community, personal humiliation, and mental anguish and suffering. A matter of "public concern" is an issue in which the public has a legitimate interest.

A private figure can recover punitive damages and presumed damages (i.e., damages not supported by the evidence) for defamation involving a matter of public concern if he proves the defendant acted with "malice" (knowledge of the falsity or reckless disregard of the truth). If the defamation does not involve a matter of public concern, a private figure can recover punitive and presumed damages without proving malice.

- *Dun & Bradstreet, Inc. v. Greenmoss Builders, Inc.*, 472 U.S. 749 (1985). A credit reporting agency sent a report to five subscribers indicating that Greenmoss, a construction contractor, had filed a petition for bankruptcy. Greenmoss sued for defamation. The Court held the credit report did not involve a matter of public concern, so Greenmoss could recover actual and punitive damages without proving malice. Justice Powell, writing for the plurality, explained, "petitioner's credit report concerns no public issue. It was speech solely in the individual interest of the speaker and its specific business audience." Also, "since the credit report was made available to only five subscribers, who, under the terms of the subscription agreement, could not disseminate it further, it cannot be said that the report involves any strong interest in the free flow of commercial information."

- *Milkovich v. Lorain Journal Co.*, 497 U.S. 1 (1990). Milkovich, a high school wrestling coach, testified at an investigatory hearing about an altercation at a match between his team and another high school's team. After the hearing, Lorain Journal Company's newspaper published a column implying that Milkovich lied under oath in the hearing. The column stated, "Anyone who attended the meet, whether he be from Maple Heights, Mentor, or impartial observer, knows in his heart that Milkovich and Scott lied at the hearing after each having given his solemn oath to tell the truth. But they got away with it." Milkovich sued for defamation. Lorain Journal Company argued the alleged defamation was opinion, and therefore protected by the First Amendment. The Court held the alleged defamation was not protected by the First Amendment as "opinion" because it contained a factual statement that could be proved false.

The Court explained, "This is not the sort of loose, figurative, or hyperbolic language which would negate the impression that the writer was seriously maintaining that petitioner committed the crime of perjury. Nor does the general tenor of the article negate this impression. We also think the connotation that petitioner committed perjury is sufficiently factual to be susceptible of being proved true or false."

False Light

"False light" is a tort, similar to defamation, recognized in some states. It is generally defined as a publication placing another in a highly offensive false light. It is unclear whether the *New York Times* rule (requiring malice) applies in "false light" actions. The Court had held the plaintiff in a false light action involving a matter of public concern must satisfy the *New York Times* rule [*Time, Inc. v. Hill*, 385 U.S. 374 (1967)]. However, the Court later indicated this is an open question [*Gertz v. Welch*, 418 U.S. 323 (1974) (holding a private figure can recover actual damages for defamation if he proves the defendant was merely negligent); *Cantrell v. Forest City Publishing Co.*, 419 U.S. 245 (1974) (affirming a verdict for a plaintiff who proved malice in a false light action, but stating that because the parties did not object to jury instructions requiring malice, "this case presents no occasion to consider whether…the constitutional standard announced in *Time, Inc. v. Hill* [requiring malice] applies to all false-light cases"].

Intentional Infliction of Emotional Distress

The *New York Times* rule applies to actions for intentional infliction of emotional distress. Thus, a public official or public figure can recover damages if he proves the publication contains a false statement of fact made with malice (knowledge of the falsity or reckless disregard of the truth).

- *Hustler Magazine v. Falwell*, 485 U.S. 46 (1988). *Hustler* magazine published a parody of Jerry Falwell, a nationally known minister and commentator on politics and public affairs, and portrayed him as having engaged in a drunken incestuous rendezvous with his mother in an outhouse. At the bottom of the page, the ad contained the disclaimer "ad parody—not to be taken seriously." Falwell sued for intentional infliction of emotional distress. The Court held Falwell could not recover damages.

The Court explained, "Falwell is a 'public figure' for purposes of First Amendment law." However, the Court explained, "The jury found against respondent on his libel claim when it decided that the *Hustler* ad parody could not 'reasonably be understood as describing actual facts about [respondent] or actual events in which [he] participated.' The Court of Appeals interpreted the jury's finding to be that the ad parody 'was not reasonably believable,' and in accordance with our custom we accept this finding."

Public Disclosure of Private Facts

If information about a matter of public significance is lawfully obtained from public records and truthfully reported, liability for the tort of public disclosure of private facts may be imposed only when "narrowly tailored to a state interest of the highest order" [*Florida Star v. B.J.F.*, 491 U.S. 524 (1989)].

- *Cox Broadcasting Corp. v. Cohn*, 420 U.S. 469 (1975). During a news report of a rape case, a television reporter broadcast the deceased seventeen-year-old rape victim's name, which he obtained from indictments that were public records available for inspection in the courtroom. The victim's father sued for invasion of privacy. The Court held that the First Amendment prevented liability.

  The Court explained, "By placing the information in the public domain on official court records, the State must be presumed to have concluded that the public interest was thereby being served. Public records by their very nature are of interest to those concerned with the administration of government, and a public benefit is performed by the reporting of the true contents of the records by the media. The freedom of the press to publish that information appears to us to be of critical importance to our type of government in which the citizenry is the final judge of the proper conduct of public business. In preserving that form of government the First and Fourteenth Amendments command nothing less than that the States may not impose sanctions on the publication of truthful information contained in official court records open to public inspection."

- *Landmark Communications, Inc. v. Virginia*, 435 U.S. 829 (1978). A Virginia statute made it a crime to divulge information regarding proceedings before a state judicial review commission that was authorized to hear complaints about judges' disability or misconduct. The *Virginian Pilot*, a Landmark newspaper, published an article that accurately reported on a pending inquiry by the Virginia Judicial Inquiry and Review Commission and identified the state judge whose conduct was being investigated. Landmark was convicted of violating the statute. The Court invalidated the statute.

The Court explained, "The operation of the Virginia Commission, no less than the operation of the judicial system itself, is a matter of public interest, necessarily engaging the attention of the news media. The article published by Landmark provided accurate factual information about a legislatively authorized inquiry pending before the Judicial Inquiry and Review Commission, and in so doing clearly served those interests in public scrutiny and discussion of governmental affairs which the First Amendment was adopted to protect." The Court noted, "a major purpose of that Amendment was to protect the free discussion of governmental affairs."

- *Smith v. Daily Mail Publishing Co.*, 443 U.S. 97 (1979). A West Virginia statute made it a crime for a newspaper to publish, without written approval of the juvenile court, the name of any youth charged as a juvenile offender. Two newspapers published articles identifying by name a fourteen-year-old youth who had been arrested for allegedly killing another youth. The newspapers learned the juvenile's identity by using routine reporting techniques such as monitoring police band radio frequency and questioning witnesses, the police, and an assistant prosecuting attorney at the scene of the killing. The Court invalidated the statute.

The Court explained, "if a newspaper lawfully obtains truthful information about a matter of public significance then state officials may not constitutionally punish publication of the information, absent a need to further a state interest of the highest order." The state asserted an interest in protecting the anonymity of the juvenile offender, and argued confidentiality would further his rehabilitation and prevent him from losing future employment. However, the Court explained, "The magnitude of the State's interest in this statute is not sufficient to justify application of a criminal penalty to respondents." Also, "The statute does not restrict the electronic media or any form of publication, except 'newspapers,' from printing the names of youths charged in a juvenile proceeding. In this very case, three radio stations announced the alleged assailant's name before the *Daily Mail* decided to publish it. Thus, even assuming the statute served a state interest of the highest order, it does not accomplish its stated purpose."

- *Florida Star v. B.J.F.*, 491 U.S. 524 (1989). A Florida statute made it unlawful to "print, publish, or broadcast…in any instrument of mass communication" the name of the victim of a sexual offense. The *Florida Star*, a weekly newspaper, was found liable under the statute for publishing the name of a rape victim it obtained from a publicly released police report. The Court reversed and held the newspaper was not liable. The Court explained, "It is undisputed that the news article describing the assault on B. J. F. was accurate. In addition, appellant lawfully obtained B. J. F.'s name." Also, the article "involved a matter of paramount public import: the commission, and investigation, of a violent crime which had been reported to authorities."

- *Bartnicki v. Vopper*, 532 U.S. 514 (2001). During collective bargaining negotiations between a teachers union and a local school board, an unidentified person unlawfully intercepted and recorded a cell phone conversation between a union negotiator and union president. Vopper, a radio commentator, lawfully obtained the recording, knowing the source obtained it unlawfully, and played it on his public affairs talk show. Vopper was sued for damages under federal and state wiretapping laws. The Court held the government may not punish the publication of the recording by Vopper.

First, the Court explained Vopper's "access to the information on the tapes was obtained lawfully, even though the information itself was intercepted unlawfully by someone else." And, "the subject matter of the conversation was a matter of public concern." The government argued an interest in removing an incentive for parties to intercept private conversations. However, the Court explained, "The normal method of deterring unlawful conduct is to impose an appropriate punishment on the person who engages in it." The government also argued an interest in minimizing harm to persons whose conversations have been illegally intercepted. However, the Court explained "In this case, privacy concerns give way when balanced against the interest in publishing matters of public importance."

Symbolic Conduct (Nonverbal Speech: Four-Part *O'Brien* Test)

Symbolic conduct is conduct that communicates a message (e.g., burning a draft card, or wearing an armband). The First Amendment provides some protection for symbolic conduct because it is a form of expression. However, the government may regulate symbolic conduct if (1) the regulation is within the constitutional power of the government; (2) the regulation furthers an important or substantial governmental interest; (3) the governmental interest is unrelated to the suppression of free expression; and (4) the incidental restriction on alleged First Amendment freedoms is no greater than is essential to the furtherance of that interest [*United States v. O'Brien*, 391 U.S. 367 (1968)].

- *United States v. O'Brien*, 391 U.S. 367 (1968). A federal statute prohibited the knowing destruction of Selective Service registration certificates (draft cards). O'Brien burned his draft card on the steps of the South Boston Courthouse to influence others to adopt his antiwar beliefs, and was convicted under the statute. The Court upheld the statute and O'Brien's conviction.

    The Court explained, (1) the government's "broad and sweeping" constitutional power to raise and support armies and make all laws necessary and proper to that end includes the power to establish a registration system for individuals liable for training and service and "require such individuals within reason to cooperate in the registration system;" (2) "legislation to insure the continuing availability of issued certificates serves a legitimate and substantial purpose in the system's administration;" (3) the government's interests were unrelated to the suppression of free expression because the statute prohibited all draft card burning without regard to the message of the conduct; and (4) "We perceive no alternative means that would more precisely and narrowly assure the continuing availability of issued Selective Service certificates than a law which prohibits their willful mutilation or destruction" (i.e., the restriction was no greater than necessary).

- *Tinker v. Des Moines Independent Community School District*, 393 U.S. 503 (1969). School authorities adopted a regulation that any student wearing an armband to school would be asked to remove it, and if he refused would be suspended until he returned without the armband. Two public high school students and one junior high school student wore black armbands to their schools to publicize their objections to the hostilities in Vietnam. The Court invalidated the regulation because it was related to the suppression of free expression.

  The Court explained, "the action of the school authorities appears to have been based upon an urgent wish to avoid the controversy which might result from the expression, even by the silent symbol of armbands, of opposition to this Nation's part in the conflagration in Vietnam." The Court noted, "It is also relevant that the school authorities did not purport to prohibit the wearing of all symbols of political or controversial significance." Instead "a particular symbol—black armbands worn to exhibit opposition to this Nation's involvement in Vietnam—was singled out for prohibition."

- *Texas v. Johnson*, 491 U.S. 397 (1989). A Texas statute prohibited any person to "desecrate" or "mistreat" a flag "in a way that the actor knows will seriously offend one or more persons likely to observe or discover his action." Johnson burned a flag as part of a protest at the 1984 Republican National Convention and was convicted under the statute. The Court invalidated the statute.

  The Court explained that as "Johnson burned an American flag as part—indeed, as the culmination—of a political demonstration," his flag burning was conduct "sufficiently imbued with elements of communication to implicate the First Amendment." The state asserted an interest in "preserving the flag as a symbol of nationhood and national unity." However, the Court explained, "this interest is related to expression in the case of Johnson's burning of the flag. The State, apparently, is concerned that such conduct will lead people to believe either that the flag does not stand for nationhood and national unity, but instead reflects other, less positive concepts, or that the concepts reflected in the flag do not in fact exist, that is, that we do not enjoy unity as a Nation. These concerns blossom only when a person's treatment of the flag communicates some message, and thus are related 'to the suppression of free expression' within the meaning of O'Brien."

- *United States v. Eichman*, 496 U.S. 310 (1990). After *Texas v Johnson*, Congress passed the Flag Protection Act of 1989. The Act criminalized the conduct of anyone who "knowingly mutilates, defaces, physically defiles, burns, maintains on the floor or ground, or tramples upon" a U.S. flag, except conduct related to the disposal of a "worn or soiled" flag. The government prosecuted several people for violating the Act by knowingly setting fire to several U.S. flags on the steps of the U.S. Capitol while protesting various aspects of the government's domestic and foreign policy. The Court invalidated the Act.

  The government argued the Act was constitutional because, unlike the statute in *Johnson*, the Act did not target expressive conduct on the basis of the content of its message. However, the Court explained, "Although the Flag Protection Act contains no explicit contest-based limitation on the scope of prohibited conduct, it is nevertheless clear that the Government's asserted interest is related to the suppression of free expression, and concerned with the content of such expression." The Court noted, "the Government's desire to preserve the flag as a symbol for certain national ideals is implicated only when a person's treatment of the flag communicates a message to others that is inconsistent with those ideals." The Court concluded, "Although Congress cast the Flag Protection Act in somewhat broader terms than the Texas statute at issue in *Johnson*, the Act still suffers from the same fundamental flaw: it suppresses expression out of concern for its likely communicative impact."

- *Barnes v. Glen Theatre, Inc.*, 501 U.S. 560 (1991). Indiana's public indecency statute made it a misdemeanor to appear in a state of nudity in a public place, and effectively required female dancers to wear at least "pasties" and a "G-string" when they danced. Two Indiana establishments wished to present totally nude dancing as entertainment, and sought to enjoin enforcement of the statute. The Court upheld the statute.

  First, the Court explained, "The public indecency statute is clearly within the constitutional power of the State," because, "The traditional police power of the States is defined as the authority to provide for the public health, safety, and morals." Second, the statute furthered a substantial governmental interest in "protecting societal order and morality." Third, "This interest is unrelated to the suppression of free expression" because "we do not think that when Indiana applies its statute to the nude dancing in these nightclubs it is proscribing nudity because of the erotic message conveyed by the dancers." The Court noted, "the requirement that the dancers don pasties and G-strings does not deprive the dance of whatever erotic message it conveys." Fourth, "It is without cavil that the public indecency statute is 'narrowly tailored'; Indiana's requirement that the dancers wear at least pasties and G-strings is modest, and the bare minimum necessary to achieve the State's purpose."

- *City of Erie v. Pap's A.M.*, 529 U.S. 277 (2000). Erie, Pennsylvania, enacted an ordinance that prohibited public nudity. Pap's A.M. operated "Kandyland," an establishment featuring totally nude erotic dancing by women. To comply with the ordinance, dancers had to wear "pasties" and a "G-string." Pap's filed suit seeking an injunction against the ordinance's enforcement. The Court upheld the ordinance, without a majority opinion. Justice O'Connor wrote for the plurality.

First, the ordinance was within Erie's constitutional power because, "Erie's efforts to protect public health and safety are clearly within the city's police powers." Second, the ordinance furthered an important government interest in "combating the harmful secondary effects" on public health, safety, and welfare associated with nude dancing. Third, the government interest was unrelated to the suppression of free expression. Justice O'Connor explained, "The ordinance here, like the statute in *Barnes*, is on its face a general prohibition on public nudity. By its terms, the ordinance regulates conduct alone. It does not target nudity that contains an erotic message; rather, it bans all public nudity, regardless of whether that nudity is accompanied by expressive activity." Fourth, the restriction was no greater than essential to further the government interest because, "The ordinance regulates conduct, and any incidental impact on the expressive element of nude dancing is de minimis. The requirement that dancers wear pasties and G-strings is a minimal restriction in furtherance of the asserted government interests, and the restriction leaves ample capacity to convey the dancer's erotic message."

Commercial Speech (*Central Hudson* Test: Intermediate Scrutiny)

Commercial speech is expression that proposes a commercial transaction (e.g., advertising). Commercial speech that is false, misleading, or proposes an illegal activity is not protected by the First Amendment and may be prohibited [*Pittsburgh Press Co. v. Pittsburgh Commission on Human Relations*, 413 U.S. 376 (1973) (upholding an ordinance that prohibited newspapers from listing help-wanted advertisements in gender-designated columns such as "Jobs—Male Interest," "Jobs—Female Interest," and "Male-Female" because such advertisements propose illegal employment discrimination)].

Commercial speech that is truthful, not misleading, and concerns lawful activity is protected by the First Amendment but may be regulated if (1) there is a substantial government interest; (2) the law directly advances the government interest; and (3) the law is no more extensive than necessary to serve the government interest. The government need not use the absolutely "least restrictive alternative means" to achieve the government interest. So a "perfect fit" between the means (the law) and end (the government interest) is not required. For example, a law will not be invalidated simply because there is another means to achieve the government interest that is less restrictive of commercial speech. Instead, the law need only be "narrowly tailored" to achieve the government interest, with a "reasonable fit" between the means and end [*Central Hudson Gas v. Public Service Commission*, 447 U.S. 557 (1980); *Board of Trustees of the State University of New York v. Fox*, 492 U.S. 469 (1989)].

Finally, the overbreadth doctrine (used to invalidate laws regulating substantially more speech than the Constitution allows to be regulated) does not apply to commercial speech regulation. So a commercial speech regulation may not be challenged as being "overbroad." Normally, overbroad laws "chill" speech by causing people to refrain from expression rather than challenge the law. However, in commercial speech, the economic incentive to advertise is strong enough to overcome any chilling effect overbroad laws may have.

- *Lorillard Tobacco Co. v. Reilly*, 533 U.S. 525 (2001). Massachusetts adopted regulations that (1) prohibited outdoor advertising of smokeless tobacco and cigars within 1,000 feet of a school or playground; (2) prohibited indoor, point-of-sale advertising of smokeless tobacco or cigars lower than 5 feet from the floor of a retail establishment located within 1,000 feet of a school or playground; and (3) prohibited self-service displays of tobacco products and required retailers to place tobacco products behind counters so customers would have contact with a salesperson before handling such products. The Court invalidated the bans on outdoor and indoor advertising and upheld the ban on self-service displays.

  The Court explained the ban on outdoor advertising was unconstitutional because the state "failed to show that the outdoor advertising regulations for smokeless tobacco and cigars are not more extensive than necessary to advance the State's substantial interest in preventing underage tobacco use." The Court noted, "the regulations prohibit advertising in a substantial portion of the major metropolitan areas of Massachusetts." Also, "'Outdoor' advertising includes not only advertising located outside an establishment, but also advertising inside a store if that advertising is visible from outside the store. The regulations restrict advertisements of any size and the term advertisement also includes oral statements."

  The Court explained the ban on indoor, point-of-sale advertising was unconstitutional because it did not directly advance the state's interest. The Court noted, "the State's goal is to prevent minors from using tobacco products and to curb demand for that activity by limiting youth exposure to advertising. The 5 foot rule does not seem to advance that goal. Not all children are less than 5 feet tall, and those who are certainly have the ability to look up and take in their surroundings."

  Finally, the Court explained the ban on self-service displays was constitutional because, "the State has demonstrated a substantial interest in preventing access to tobacco products by minors and has adopted an appropriately narrow means of advancing that interest." The Court noted, "Unattended displays of tobacco products present an opportunity for access without the proper age verification required by law. Thus, the State prohibits self-service and other displays that would allow an individual to obtain tobacco products without direct contact with a salesperson. It is clear that the regulations leave open ample channels of communication. The regulations do not significantly impede adult access to tobacco products."

- *Thompson v. Western States Medical Center*, 535 U.S. 357 (2002). Drug compounding is a process by which a pharmacist or doctor combines, mixes, or alters ingredients to create a medication tailored to an individual patient's needs. The Food and Drug Administration Modernization Act of 1997 exempted "compounded drugs" from the Food and Drug Administration's standard drug approval process so long as drug providers did not advertise or promote compounded drugs. The Court invalidated the Act.

    The Court explained the government had substantial interests in (1) permitting small-scale drug compounding so patients with particular needs may obtain medications, and (2) preventing drug compounding from occurring on such a large scale that it would undermine the drug approval process. However, prohibiting advertising and promotion was more extensive than necessary. There were several nonspeech-related means available for drawing a line between small-scale drug compounding and large-scale drug manufacturing.

    For example, "the Government could ban the use of commercial scale manufacturing or testing equipment for compounding drug products. It could prohibit pharmacists from compounding more drugs in anticipation of receiving prescriptions than in response to prescriptions already received. It could prohibit pharmacists from offering compounded drugs at wholesale to other state licensed persons or commercial entities for resale. Alternately, it could limit the amount of compounded drugs, either by volume or by numbers of prescriptions, that a given pharmacist or pharmacy sells out of State."

Lawyer Advertising

- *Bates v. State Bar of Arizona*, 433 U.S. 350 (1977). The Supreme Court of Arizona imposed a disciplinary rule that prohibited attorneys from advertising in newspapers or other media. Two attorneys placed an advertisement in a newspaper for their "legal clinic," stating they were offering "legal services at very reasonable fees."

The advertisement listed their fees for services, including uncontested divorces, uncontested adoptions, simple personal bankruptcies, and changes of name. The attorneys were disciplined under the rule. The Court invalidated the rule.

The Court explained the state cannot prevent "the publication in a newspaper of appellants' truthful advertisement concerning the availability and terms of routine legal services." The state argued (1) price advertising adversely affected professionalism; (2) attorney advertising is inherently misleading because legal services are so individualized; (3) advertising may have the undesirable effect of "stirring up litigation;" (4) advertising increases the overhead costs of the profession and these costs would be passed along to consumers in the form of increased fees; (5) advertising would adversely affect the quality of service; and (6) the wholesale restriction on advertising was justified by problems of enforcement. However, the Court explained, "we are not persuaded that any of the preferred justifications rise to the level of an acceptable reason for the suppression of all advertising by attorneys."

- *In re Primus*, 436 U.S. 412 (1978). Primus, a South Carolina lawyer affiliated with the American Civil Liberties Union (ACLU), advised a gathering of women of their legal rights resulting from their having been sterilized as a condition of receiving public medical assistance. Primus informed one of the women in a subsequent letter that free legal assistance was available from the ACLU. The disciplinary board of the South Carolina Supreme Court determined the lawyer, by sending the letter, engaged in soliciting a client in violation of certain Disciplinary Rules of the State Supreme Court. The Court reversed that decision.

The Court explained the ACLU "engages in litigation as a vehicle for effective political expression and association, as well as a means of communicating useful information to the public." Moreover, "the efficacy of litigation as a means of advancing the cause of civil liberties often depends on the ability to make legal assistance available to suitable litigants." So, "The First and Fourteenth Amendments require a measure of protection for advocating lawful means of vindicating legal rights." The Court noted Primus did not engage in in-person solicitation for pecuniary gain, but instead sent a letter on behalf of a nonprofit organization. The

Court concluded, "The record does not support appellee's contention that undue influence, overreaching, misrepresentation, or invasion of privacy actually occurred in this case."

- *Ohralik v. Ohio State Bar*, 436 U.S. 447 (1978). Ohralik, an Ohio lawyer, visited an eighteen-year-old female in the hospital while she lay in traction after she was injured in a car accident in which she was a driver, and offered to represent her. After Ohralik visited her a second time in her hospital room, she signed a contingent-fee agreement. Ohralik also approached the driver's eighteen-year-old female passenger, who also had been injured, at her home on the day she was released from the hospital; she agreed orally to a contingent-fee arrangement. The disciplinary board of the Ohio Supreme Court found Ohralik violated disciplinary rules prohibiting solicitation. The Court upheld the disciplinary rules and held the state may prohibit in-person solicitation for pecuniary gain.

  The Court explained, "the State has a legitimate and indeed compelling interest in preventing those aspects of solicitation that involve fraud, undue influence, intimidation, overreaching, and other forms of vexatious conduct." Also, "The Rules were applied in this case to discipline a lawyer for soliciting employment for pecuniary gain under circumstances likely to result in the adverse consequences the State seeks to avert. In such a situation, which is inherently conducive to overreaching and other forms of misconduct, the State has a strong interest in adopting and enforcing rules of conduct designed to protect the public from harmful solicitation by lawyers whom it has licensed."

  The Court concluded, "The detrimental aspects of face-to-face selling even of ordinary consumer products have been recognized and addressed by the Federal Trade Commission, and it hardly need be said that the potential for overreaching is significantly greater when a lawyer, a professional trained in the art of persuasion, personally solicits an unsophisticated, injured, or distressed lay person."

- *Zauderer v. Office of Disciplinary Counsel*, 471 U.S. 626 (1985). Zauderer, an Ohio lawyer, ran a newspaper advertisement offering to represent women who had suffered injuries resulting from their use of a contraceptive known as the Dalkon Shield Intrauterine Device. The advertisement featured a drawing of the device and stated, "If there is no recovery, no legal fees are owed by our clients." The Board of Commissioners on Grievances and Discipline of the Ohio Supreme Court concluded the advertisement violated rules that (1) prohibited advertisements targeting specific legal problems; (2) prohibited the use of illustrations in advertising; and (3) required an attorney advertising his availability on a contingent-fee basis disclose that clients will have to pay costs, even if their lawsuits are unsuccessful.

First, the Court held the state could not discipline the attorney for running advertising geared to persons with a specific legal problem. The Court explained, "The advertisement's information and advice concerning the Dalkon Shield were, as the Office of Disciplinary Counsel stipulated, neither false nor deceptive: in fact, they were entirely accurate. The advertisement did not promise readers that lawsuits alleging injuries caused by the Dalkon Shield would be successful, nor did it suggest that appellant had any special expertise in handling such lawsuits other than his employment in other such litigation."

Second, the Court held the attorney could not be disciplined for using illustrations in advertising. The Court explained, "Given the possibility of policing the use of illustrations in advertisements on a case-by-case basis, the prophylactic approach taken by Ohio cannot stand; hence, appellant may not be disciplined for his use of an accurate and nondeceptive illustration."

Third, the Court held the state could require an attorney advertising his availability on a contingent-fee basis to disclose that clients will have to pay costs even if their lawsuits are unsuccessful. The Court explained, "The State's position that it is deceptive to employ advertising that refers to contingent-fee arrangements without mentioning the client's liability for costs is reasonable enough to support a requirement that information regarding the client's liability for costs be disclosed."

- *Shapero v. Kentucky Bar Association*, 486 U.S. 466 (1988). Shapero, a Kentucky lawyer, applied to Kentucky's Attorneys Advertising Commission for approval of a letter he proposed to send to potential clients who had a foreclosure suit filed against them. The commission declined to approve the letter based on a Kentucky Supreme Court rule. The rule prohibited lawyers from soliciting legal business for pecuniary gain by sending truthful and non-deceptive letters to potential clients known to face particular legal problems. The Court invalidated the rule. The Court explained, "Like print advertising, petitioner's letter—and targeted, direct-mail solicitation generally—poses much less risk of overreaching or undue influence than does in-person solicitation."

- *Peel v. Attorney Registration and Disciplinary Commission of Illinois*, 496 U.S. 91 (1990). Peel, an Illinois lawyer, stated on his letter-head he was certified by the National Board of Trial Advocacy as a "Civil Trial Specialist." The Illinois Supreme Court disciplined Peel for violating a state bar rule that prohibited an attorney from holding himself out as "certified" or a "specialist" in certain fields of law. The Court invalidated the rule.

  Justice Stevens explained in a plurality opinion, "Petitioner's letterhead was neither actually nor inherently misleading. There is no dispute about the bona fides and the relevance of NBTA certification. The Commission's concern about the possibility of deception in hypothetical cases is not sufficient to rebut the constitutional presumption favoring disclosure over concealment. Disclosure of information such as that on petitioner's letterhead both serves the public interest and encourages the development and utilization of meritorious certification programs for attorneys."

- *Florida Bar v. Went for It, Inc.*, 515 U.S. 618 (1995). Florida Bar rules prohibited personal injury lawyers from sending targeted direct-mail solicitations to victims and their relatives for thirty days following an accident or disaster. The Court upheld the rules. The Florida Bar asserted interests in (1) protecting "the privacy and tranquility of personal injury victims and their loved ones against intrusive, unsolicited contact by lawyers," and (2) protecting "the flagging reputations of Florida lawyers."

  First, the Court explained, "We have little trouble crediting the Bar's interest as substantial." Second, the rules directly advanced the government's interests. A two-year study of lawyer advertising and solicitation contained data "supporting the Bar's contentions that the Florida public views direct-mail solicitations in the immediate wake of accidents as an intrusion on privacy that reflects poorly upon the profession." Third, the law was no more extensive than necessary to serve the government's interests. The Court explained, "The Bar's rule is reasonably well tailored to its stated objective of eliminating targeted mailings whose type and timing are a source of distress to Floridians, distress that has caused many of them to lose respect for the legal profession."

The Court concluded, "We believe that the Florida Bar's 30-day restriction on targeted direct-mail solicitation of accident victims and their relatives withstands scrutiny under the three-pronged *Central Hudson* test that we have devised for this context."

"For Sale" Signs

- *Linmark Associates, Inc. v. Township of Willingboro*, 431 U.S. 85 (1977). A Willingboro ordinance prohibited the posting of real estate "For Sale" and "Sold" signs to stem what the township perceived as the flight of white home owners from a racially integrated community. The Court invalidated the ordinance. The Court explained promoting stable, racially integrated housing was an important governmental objective. However, the ordinance was not necessary to achieve that goal. For example, "the evidence does not support the Council's apparent fears that Willingboro was experiencing a substantial incidence of panic selling by white homeowners. A fortiori, the evidence does not establish that 'For Sale' signs in front of 2% of Willingboro homes were a major cause of panic selling. And the record does not confirm the township's assumption that proscribing such signs will reduce public awareness of realty sales and thereby decrease public concern over selling."

News Racks

- *City of Cincinnati v. Discovery Network, Inc.*, 507 U.S. 410 (1993). A Cincinnati ordinance prohibited the distribution of commercial handbills on public property. Cincinnati refused to allow Discovery to distribute their commercial publications in freestanding news racks on public property, based on the ordinance, but allowed the distribution of newspapers in news racks. The Court invalidated the ordinance.

  The Court explained the city had "legitimate interests in safety and esthetics." However, the ordinance was more extensive than necessary, and not "narrowly tailored," to serve the government interests. For example, "Not only does Cincinnati's categorical ban on commercial newsracks place too much importance on the distinction between commercial and noncommercial speech, but in this case, the distinction bears no relationship *whatsoever* to the particular interests that the city has asserted. It is therefore an impermissible means of responding to the city's admittedly legitimate interests."

The Court noted, "The city has asserted an interest in esthetics, but respondent publishers' newsracks are no greater an eyesore than the newsracks permitted to remain on Cincinnati's sidewalks. Each newsrack, whether containing 'newspapers' or 'commercial handbills,' is equally unattractive." The Court concluded "the city has not established the 'fit' between its goals and its chosen means that is required by our opinion in *Fox*."

Liquor Advertising

* *Rubin v. Coors Brewing Co.*, 514 U.S. 476 (1995). Section 5(e)(2) of the Federal Alcohol Administration Act prohibited beer labels from displaying alcohol content. The Court invalidated the Act. The Court explained, "the Government here has a significant interest in protecting the health, safety, and welfare of its citizens by preventing brewers from competing on the basis of alcohol strength, which could lead to greater alcoholism and its attendant social costs." However, the Act did not directly advance the government's interest because, "The failure to prohibit the disclosure of alcohol content in advertising, which would seem to constitute a more influential weapon in any strength war than labels, makes no rational sense if the Government's true aim is to suppress strength wars." Also, the Act was not narrowly tailored to achieve the government's interest because there were several alternatives, such as directly limiting the alcohol content of beers or prohibiting marketing efforts emphasizing high alcohol strength.

* *44 Liquormart, Inc. v. Rhode Island*, 517 U.S. 484 (1996). Rhode Island statutes banned the advertisement of retail liquor prices except at the place of sale. The Court invalidated the statutes. Justice Stevens, writing for a plurality, explained that even if it accepted the state had a substantial interest in promoting temperance, the statutes did not significantly advance the state's interest. For example, "the State has presented no evidence to suggest

that its speech prohibition will significantly reduce marketwide consumption." Also, the statutes were more extensive than necessary to achieve the state's interest. For, "It is perfectly obvious that alternative forms of regulation that would not involve any restriction on speech would be more likely to achieve the State's goal of promoting temperance. As the State's own expert conceded, higher prices can be maintained either by direct regulation or by increased taxation. Per capita purchases could be limited as is the case with prescription drugs. Even educational campaigns focused on the problems of excessive, or even moderate, drinking might prove to be more effective."

Lottery Advertising

* *United States v. Edge Broadcasting Co.*, 509 U.S. 418 (1993). Federal statutes prohibited lottery advertising by broadcasters in states that did not allow lotteries, but allowed lottery advertising by broadcasters in states that permitted lotteries. The Court upheld the statutes.

    First, the Court explained, "we are quite sure that the Government has a substantial interest in supporting the policy of nonlottery States, as well as not interfering with the policy of States that permit lotteries." Second, "We have no doubt that the statutes directly advanced the governmental interest at stake in this case." Third, the statutes were no more extensive than necessary to achieve the government interests. The Court explained, "We made clear in *Fox* that our commercial speech cases require a fit between the restriction and the government interest that is not necessarily perfect, but reasonable….We have no doubt that the fit in this case was a reasonable one."

Administration of Justice

The government may punish out-of-court statements by news media about pending cases if the statements pose a "clear and present" danger of harm to the legal system. The government may punish attorney speech about pending cases if it poses a "substantial likelihood of materially prejudicing an adjudicatory proceeding."

* *Bridges v. California*, 314 U.S. 252 (1941). The *Los Angeles Times* published an editorial about the pending sentencing of two union

members convicted of assaulting nonunion truck drivers, referring to the assailants as "thugs" and advocating prison sentences. The *Times* was held in contempt based on the editorial's "tendency" to interfere with the orderly administration of justice in an action then before a court for consideration. The Court overturned the contempt conviction.

The Court explained, "From the indications in the record of the position taken by the *Los Angeles Times* on labor controversies in the past, there could have been little doubt of its attitude toward the probation of Shannon and Holmes. In view of the paper's long-continued militancy in this field, it is inconceivable that any judge in Los Angeles would expect anything but adverse criticism from it in the event probation were granted. Yet such criticism after final disposition of the proceedings would clearly have been privileged. Hence, this editorial, given the most intimidating construction it will bear, did no more than threaten future adverse criticism which was reasonably to be expected anyway in the event of a lenient disposition of the pending case. To regard it, therefore, as in itself of substantial influence upon the course of justice would be to impute to judges a lack of firmness, wisdom, or honor—which we cannot accept as a major premise."

• *Gentile v. State Bar of Nevada*, 501 U.S. 1030 (1991). Nevada Supreme Court Rule 177 prohibited a lawyer from making extrajudicial statements to the press that he knows or reasonably should know will have a "substantial likelihood of materially prejudicing" an adjudicative proceeding. Gentile, a criminal defense attorney, gave a press conference hours after Nevada indicted his client. Gentile said his client was an innocent "scapegoat" and the state had not "been honest enough to indict the people who did it; the police department, crooked cops." Nevada brought disciplinary proceedings against Gentile under Rule 177. The Court upheld the rule. The Court explained, "We agree with the majority of the States that the 'substantial likelihood of material prejudice' standard constitutes a constitutionally permissible balance between the First Amendment rights of attorneys in pending cases and the State's interest in fair trials."

Political Speech

Political speech is speech about elections or the electoral process. The government may restrict political speech if strict scrutiny is satisfied (i.e., the law must be necessary to achieve a compelling state interest). Spending money in a political campaign is a form of political speech, so the government may not limit campaign expenditures; however, the government may limit campaign contributions to a candidate to limit the actuality or appearance of corruption.

- *Buckley v. Valeo*, 424 U.S. 1 (1976). The Federal Election Campaign Act of 1971, as amended in 1974, limited the amount of money an individual or group could contribute to a candidate for a federal elective office, and limited how much an individual, group, or candidate could spend in an election campaign. The Court upheld the contribution limits but invalidated the spending limits.

  The contribution limits, the Court explained, "constitute the Act's primary weapons against the reality or appearance of improper influence stemming from the dependence of candidates on large campaign contributions. The contribution ceilings thus serve the basic governmental interest in safeguarding the integrity of the electoral process without directly impinging upon the rights of individual citizens and candidates to engage in political debate and discussion."

  The spending limits, however, "place substantial and direct restrictions on the ability of candidates, citizens, and associations to engage in protected political expression, restrictions that the First Amendment cannot tolerate." Also, some of the spending limits applied to "expenditures for express advocacy of candidates made totally independently of the candidate and his campaign." The Court noted, "the independent advocacy restricted by the provision does not presently appear to pose dangers of real or apparent corruption comparable to those identified with large campaign contributions." Unlike contributions, "such independent expenditures may well provide little assistance to the candidate's campaign and indeed may prove counterproductive."

- *First National Bank of Boston v. Bellotti*, 435 U.S. 765 (1978). A Massachusetts criminal statute prohibited banks and business corporations from making contributions or expenditures "for the purpose of...influencing or affecting the vote on any question submitted to the voters, other than one materially affecting any of the property, business or assets of the corporation." The Court invalidated the statute.

The Court explained preserving the integrity of the electoral process, preventing corruption, sustaining the active role of the individual citizen in the electoral process, and preserving the individual citizen's confidence in government are interests of the highest importance. However, "there has been no showing that the relative voice of corporations has been overwhelming or even significant in influencing referenda in Massachusetts, or that there has been any threat to the confidence of the citizenry in government." Also, "To be sure, corporate advertising may influence the outcome of the vote; this would be its purpose. But the fact that advocacy may persuade the electorate is hardly a reason to suppress it: The Constitution protects expression which is eloquent no less than that which is unconvincing."

- *California Medical Association v. Federal Election Commission*, 453 U.S. 182 (1981). Provisions of the Federal Election Campaign Act of 1971 prohibited individuals and unincorporated associations from contributing more than $5,000 per calendar year to any multicandidate political committee, and made it unlawful for political committees knowingly to accept contributions exceeding the $5,000 limit. The Court upheld the provisions.

  The Court explained the contribution limit furthered the governmental interest in preventing the actual or apparent corruption of the political process as "it is clear that this provision is an appropriate means by which Congress could seek to protect the integrity of the contribution restrictions upheld by this Court in *Buckley*." Also, the First Amendment rights of a contributor are "not impaired by limits on the amount he may give to a multicandidate political committee."

- *Brown v. Hartlage*, 456 U.S. 45 (1982). Section 121.055 of the Kentucky Corrupt Practices Act prohibited a candidate from offering material benefits to voters in consideration for their votes. Brown, the challenger in a general election for Hartlage's office as a commissioner of Jefferson County, Kentucky, committed himself at a televised press conference to lowering commissioners' salaries if elected. When Brown won the election, Kentucky voided the election under the Act. The Court held voiding the election violated the First Amendment.

The Court explained, "States have a legitimate interest in preserving the integrity of their electoral processes." However, "It is clear that the statements of petitioner Brown in the course of the August 15 press conference were very different in character from the corrupting agreements and solicitations historically recognized as unprotected by the First Amendment. Notably, Brown's commitment to serve at a reduced salary was made openly, subject to the comment and criticism of his political opponent and to the scrutiny of the voters. We think the fact that the statement was made in full view of the electorate offers a strong indication that the statement contained nothing fundamentally at odds with our shared political ethic." The Court concluded "Like a promise to lower taxes, to increase efficiency in government, or indeed to increase taxes in order to provide some group with a desired public benefit or public service, Brown's promise to reduce his salary cannot be deemed beyond the reach of the First Amendment, or considered as inviting the kind of corrupt arrangement the appearance of which a State may have a compelling interest in avoiding."

- *FEC v. National Conservative PAC*, 470 U.S. 480 (1985). Section 9012(f) of the Presidential Election Campaign Fund Act made it a criminal offense for an independent "political committee" to expend more than $1,000 to further the election of a presidential candidate who elected public financing. The Court invalidated the statute. The Court explained, "preventing corruption or the appearance of corruption are the only legitimate and compelling government interests thus far identified for restricting campaign finances." However, "In *Buckley* we struck down the FECA's limitation on individuals' independent expenditures because we found no tendency in such expenditures, uncoordinated with the candidate or his campaign, to corrupt or to give the appearance of corruption. For similar reasons, we also find § 9012(f)'s limitation on independent expenditures by political committees to be constitutionally infirm."

- *Burson v. Freeman*, 504 U.S. 191 (1992). Section 2-7-111(b) of the Tennessee Code prohibited the solicitation of votes and the display or distribution of campaign materials within 100 feet of the entrance to a polling place. The Court upheld the statute, without a majority opinion. Justice Blackmun, writing for a plurality, explained Tennessee had "compelling interests in preventing voter intimidation and election fraud." The 100-foot boundary was narrowly drawn to achieve the state's interest because "some restricted zone around the voting area is necessary to secure the State's compelling interest," and "in establishing a 100-foot boundary, Tennessee is on the constitutional side of the line."

- *Nixon v. Shrink Missouri Government PAC*, 528 U.S. 377 (2000). A Missouri statute imposed limits ranging from $275 to $1,075 on contributions to candidates for state office. The Court upheld the statute. Shrink argued the $1,000 contribution limit upheld in *Buckley* should have been adjusted upward for inflation. However, the Court explained, "In *Buckley*, we specifically rejected the contention that $1,000, or any other amount, was a constitutional minimum below which legislatures could not regulate." The Court concluded, "There is no reason in logic or evidence to doubt the sufficiency of *Buckley* to govern this case in support of the Missouri statute."

- *Republican Party of Minnesota v. White*, 536 U.S. 765 (2002). The Minnesota Supreme Court adopted a canon of judicial conduct that prohibited a "candidate for a judicial office" from "announcing his or her views on disputed legal or political issues" (announce clause). The Court invalidated the clause. The state asserted interests in preserving the impartiality, and the appearance of the impartiality, of the state judiciary.

The Court explained, "One meaning of 'impartiality' in the judicial context—and of course its root meaning—is the lack of bias for or against either party to the proceeding." However, "We think it plain that the announce clause is not narrowly tailored to serve impartiality (or the appearance of impartiality) in this sense. Indeed, the clause is barely tailored to serve that interest at all, inasmuch as it does not restrict speech for or against particular parties, but rather speech for or against particular issues." The Court added, "It is perhaps possible to use the term 'impartiality' in the judicial context (though this is certainly not a common usage) to mean lack of preconception in favor of or against a particular legal view." However, "even if it were possible to select judges who did not have preconceived views on legal issues, it would hardly be desirable to do so. Proof that a Justice's mind at the time he joined the Court was a complete tabula rasa in the area of constitutional adjudication would be evidence of lack of qualification, not lack of bias."

- *Randall v. Sorrell*, 548 U.S. 230 (2006). A Vermont campaign finance statute limited both the amounts candidates for state office could spend on their campaigns (expenditure limitations) and the amounts individuals, organizations, and political parties could contribute to those campaigns (contribution limitations). The contribution limits for a "two-year general election cycle" were as follows: governor, lieutenant governor, and other statewide offices, $400; state senator, $300; and state representative, $200. The Court invalidated both limitations without a majority opinion.

  Justice Breyer explained in a plurality opinion, "Well-established precedent makes clear that the expenditure limits violate the First Amendment. The contribution limits are unconstitutional because in their specific details (involving low maximum levels and other restrictions) they fail to satisfy the First Amendment's requirement of careful tailoring. That is to say, they impose burdens upon First Amendment interests that (when viewed in light of the statute's legitimate objectives) are disproportionately severe."

- *Citizens United v. Federal Election Commission*, 130 S. Ct. 876 (2010). Federal law prohibited corporations and unions from using their general treasury funds to make independent expenditures for speech defined as an "electioneering communication" or for speech expressly advocating the election or defeat of a candidate. The Court invalidated the law. The Court explained "The Government may regulate corporate political speech through disclaimer and disclosure requirements, but it may not suppress that speech altogether." The Court noted "The law before us is an outright ban, backed by criminal sanctions."

  The Court overruled *Austin v. Michigan Chamber of Commerce*, 494 U. S. 652 (1990), which held that political speech may be banned based on the speaker's corporate identity. The Court concluded "We return to the principle established in *Buckley* and *Bellotti* that the Government may not suppress political speech on the basis of the speaker's corporate identity. No sufficient governmental interest justifies limits on the political speech of nonprofit or for-profit corporations."

Public Schools

School authorities may regulate speech to maintain discipline and order.

- *Tinker v. Des Moines Independent Community School District*, 393 U.S. 503 (1969). School authorities adopted a regulation that any student wearing an armband to school would be asked to remove it, and if he refused would be suspended until he returned without the armband. Two public high school students and one junior high school student wore black armbands to their schools to publicize their objections to the hostilities in Vietnam. The Court invalidated the regulation because it was related to the suppression of free expression.

  The Court explained, "There is no indication that the work of the schools or any class was disrupted. Outside the classrooms, a few students made hostile remarks to the children wearing armbands, but there were no threats or acts of violence on school premises." Rather, "the action of the school authorities appears to have been based upon an urgent wish to avoid the controversy which might result from the expression, even by the silent symbol of armbands, of opposition to this Nation's part in the conflagration in Vietnam."

- *Bethel School District No. 403 v. Fraser*, 478 U.S. 675 (1986). Fraser, a public high school student, delivered a speech at a voluntary assembly during school hours in which he nominated a fellow student for a student elective office. The assembly was attended by approximately 600 students, many of whom were fourteen-year-olds. During the entire speech, Fraser referred to his candidate in terms of an elaborate, graphic, and explicit sexual metaphor. The school district suspended the student. The Court upheld the suspension.

  The Court explained, "Surely it is a highly appropriate function of public school education to prohibit the use of vulgar and offensive terms in public discourse." Moreover, "The pervasive sexual innuendo in Fraser's speech was plainly offensive to both teachers and students—indeed to any mature person." The Court concluded, "We hold that petitioner School District acted entirely within its permissible authority in imposing sanctions upon Fraser in response to his offensively lewd and indecent speech. Unlike the sanctions imposed on the students wearing armbands in *Tinker*, the penalties imposed in this case were unrelated to any political viewpoint."

- *Morse v. Frederick*, 551 U.S. 393 (2007). At a school-sanctioned and school-supervised event, Morse, the high school principal, saw students unfurl a 14-foot banner stating "BONG HiTS 4 JESUS." Morse regarded the banner as promoting illegal drug use. Consistent with established school policy prohibiting such messages at school events, Morse directed the students to take down the banner. One student refused to do so, so Morse confiscated the banner and suspended the student. The Court upheld the confiscation of the banner and suspension of the student.

  The Court explained, "When Frederick suddenly and unexpectedly unfurled his banner, Morse had to decide to act—or not act—on the spot. It was reasonable for her to conclude that the banner promoted illegal drug use—in violation of established school policy—and that failing to act would send a powerful message to the students in her charge, including Frederick, about how serious the school was about the dangers of illegal drug use. The First Amendment does not require schools to tolerate at school events student expression that contributes to those dangers."

Speech of Public Employees

The government may not punish the speech of public employees if the speech involves a "matter of public concern" (e.g., political or social matters), unless the government's interest in promoting efficient public services outweighs the speech rights of the employee. This rule also applies to speech by government contractors [*Board of County Commissioners v. Umbehr*, 518 U.S. 668 (1996)].

- *Pickering v. Board of Education*, 391 U.S. 563 (1968). The board of education dismissed Pickering, a teacher, for writing and publishing in a newspaper a letter criticizing the board's allocation of school funds between educational and athletic programs. The Court held the firing violated the First Amendment. The Court explained, "What we do have before us is a case in which a teacher has made erroneous public statements upon issues then currently the subject of public attention, which are critical of his ultimate employer but which are neither shown nor can be presumed to have in any way either impeded the teacher's proper performance of his daily duties in the classroom or to have interfered with the regular operation of the schools generally. In these circumstances we conclude that the interest of the school administration in limiting teachers' opportunities to contribute to public debate is not significantly greater than its interest in limiting a similar contribution by any member of the general public."

- *Connick v. Myers*, 461 U.S. 138 (1983). Myers, an assistant district attorney, opposed a job transfer and prepared a questionnaire that she distributed to the other assistant district attorneys in the office concerning office transfer policy, office morale, the need for a grievance committee, the level of confidence in supervisors, and whether employees felt pressured to work in political campaigns. Connick, the district attorney, informed Myers she was being terminated for refusal to accept the transfer, and also told her distribution of the questionnaire was considered an act of insubordination. The Court upheld the termination.

  The Court explained, "In this case, with but one exception, the questions posed by Myers to her co-workers do not fall under the rubric of matters of 'public concern.'" The only question that touched upon a matter of public concern was whether assistant district attorneys "ever feel pressured to work in political campaigns on behalf of office supported candidates." The Court concluded, "Myers' questionnaire touched upon matters of public concern in only a most limited sense; her survey, in our view, is most accurately characterized as an employee grievance concerning internal office policy. The limited First Amendment interest involved here does not require that Connick tolerate action which he reasonably believed would disrupt the office, undermine his authority, and destroy close working relationships."

- *Givhan v. Western Line Consolidated School District*, 439 U.S. 410 (1979). Givhan, a teacher, was dismissed because of private encounters between Givhan and the school principal during which Givhan criticized the school district's policies and practices, which she believed to be racially discriminatory. The Court held the dismissal violated the First Amendment. The Court explained, "This Court's decisions in *Pickering, Perry,* and *Mt. Healthy* do not support the conclusion that a public employee forfeits his protection against governmental abridgment of freedom of speech if he decides to express his views privately rather than publicly." The Court concluded, "The First Amendment forbids abridgment of the 'freedom of speech.' Neither the Amendment itself nor our decisions indicate that this freedom is lost to the public employee who arranges to communicate privately with his employer rather than to spread his views before the public."

- *Rankin v. McPherson,* 483 U.S. 378 (1987). McPherson, a data-entry employee in a county constable's office, was discharged for remarking to a coworker, after hearing of an attempt on the president's life, "if they go for him again, I hope they get him." The Court held the discharge violated the First Amendment.

  First, the Court explained, "Considering the statement in context, as *Connick* requires, discloses that it plainly dealt with a matter of public concern. The statement was made in the course of a conversation addressing the policies of the President's administration. It came on the heels of a news bulletin regarding what is certainly a matter of heightened public attention: an attempt on the life of the President." The Court noted, "The inappropriate or controversial character of a statement is irrelevant to the question whether it deals with a matter of public concern."

  Second, the government's interest in promoting efficient public services did not outweigh the speech rights of the employee because, "While McPherson's statement was made at the workplace, there is no evidence that it interfered with the efficient functioning of the office. The Constable was evidently not afraid that McPherson had disturbed or interrupted other employees—he did not inquire to whom respondent had made the remark and testified that he 'was not concerned who she had made it to.'"

- *United States v. Treasury Employees,* 513 U.S. 454 (1995). Section 501(b) of the Ethics in Government Act prohibited federal employees from accepting compensation (honoraria) for making speeches or writing articles, even when the subject of the speech or article had no connection with the employee's official duties. Executive branch employees below grade GS-16 sued to invalidate Section 501(b). The Court invalidated the law. The Court explained, "the Government cites no evidence of misconduct related to honoraria in the vast rank and file of federal employees below grade GS-16."

- *Garcetti v. Ceballos* 547 U.S. 410 (2006). A deputy district attorney examined an affidavit used to obtain a search warrant in a pending criminal case, determined the affidavit contained serious misrepresentations, and wrote one of his supervisors a memo recommending dismissal of the case. The supervisors proceeded with the prosecution. The deputy sued, claiming his supervisors retaliated against him unconstitutionally for his memo by reassigning him from his calendar deputy position to a trial deputy position, transferring him to another courthouse, and denying him a promotion. The Court held the First Amendment did not insulate the deputy's communications from employer discipline.

  The Court explained, "The controlling factor in Ceballos' case is that his expressions were made pursuant to his duties as a calendar deputy. That consideration—the fact that Ceballos spoke as a prosecutor fulfilling a responsibility to advise his supervisor about how best to proceed with a pending case—distinguishes Ceballos' case from those in which the First Amendment provides protection against discipline. We hold that when public employees make statements pursuant to their official duties, the employees are not speaking as citizens for First Amendment purposes, and the Constitution does not insulate their communications from employer discipline." The Court added, "Contrast, for example, the expressions made by the speaker in *Pickering*, whose letter to the newspaper had no official significance and bore similarities to letters submitted by numerous citizens every day."

Loyalty Oaths

The government may require public employees to take an oath to uphold the country and its laws. However, the government may not require public employees to take an oath regarding group memberships unless the oath attempts to exclude from employment only active members of a subversive group with knowledge of its illegal objectives and specific intent to further those objectives.

- *Elfbrandt v. Russell*, 384 U.S. 11 (1966). An Arizona statute required state employees to take a loyalty oath. The statute also subjected to criminal penalties and discharge from employment any employee who took the oath and knowingly and willfully became or remained a member of the Communist Party of the United States, "or any other organization having for one of its purposes" the violent overthrow of the government of Arizona, if the employee had knowledge of such unlawful purpose of the organization. The Court invalidated the statute. The Court explained, "Those who join an organization but do not share its unlawful purposes and who do not participate in its unlawful activities surely pose no threat, either as citizens or as public employees. Laws such as this which are not restricted in scope to those who join with the 'specific intent' to further illegal action impose, in effect, a conclusive presumption that the member shares the unlawful aims of the organization."

- *Cole v. Richardson*, 405 U.S. 676 (1972). Richardson's employment at the Boston State Hospital was terminated when she refused to take the following oath required of all public employees in Massachusetts: "I do solemnly swear (or affirm) that I will uphold and defend the Constitution of the United States of America and the Constitution of the Commonwealth of Massachusetts and that I will oppose the overthrow of the government of the United States of America or of this Commonwealth by force, violence, or by any illegal or unconstitutional method." The Court upheld the oath and termination. The Court explained, "Since there is no constitutionally protected right to overthrow a government by force, violence, or illegal or unconstitutional means, no constitutional right is infringed by an oath to abide by the constitutional system in the future."

CHAPTER 19

Freedom of Speech— Public and Nonpublic Forums

THE FOLLOWING DESCRIBES GOVERNMENT REGULATION OF SPEECH IN PUBLIC FORUMS, nonpublic forums, and private property.

Public Forums ("Traditional" and "Designated")

There are two types of public forums: "traditional" public forums and "designated" public forums. Traditional public forums are places "which by long tradition or by government fiat have been devoted to assembly and debate," such as public streets, sidewalks, and parks [*Perry Education Association v. Perry Local Educators' Association*, 460 U.S. 37 (1983)].

A "designated" public forum is public property the government could close to speech activities, but voluntarily opens for use by the public as a place for speech (e.g., public schools and universities). If the government allows almost all speech and prohibits only some speech, then the government creates a designated public forum; however, the government may revoke this designation anytime and change a designated public forum to a nonpublic forum. If the government prohibits almost all speech and allows only some speech, then the forum remains a nonpublic forum, discussed later in this chapter.

Regulations

The government may regulate speech in traditional and designated public forums if the regulation is a reasonable "time, place, and manner" regulation that is (1) content neutral; (2) narrowly tailored to serve a significant government interest; and (3) leaves open adequate alternative channels for communication, "Narrowly tailored" means the regulation must not burden "substantially more speech than is necessary" to further the government's interests. However, the least restrictive alternative means need not be used (i.e., a regulation will not be invalid simply because the government's interest could be served by means that are less restrictive of speech).

Finally, if the regulation is content-based, it must satisfy strict scrutiny; the law must be necessary (the least-restrictive alternative) to achieve a compelling state interest.

- *Heffron v. International Society for Krishna Consciousness, Inc.*, 452 U.S. 640 (1981). Minnesota State Fair Rule 6.05 provided, "all persons, groups or firms which desire to sell, exhibit or distribute materials during the annual State Fair must do so only from fixed locations on the fairgrounds." The Court upheld the rule. First, the Court explained the rule was content neutral because, "the Rule applies evenhandedly to all who wish to distribute and sell written materials or to solicit funds." Second, the state had a substantial interest in "managing the flow of the crowd."

  Third, the rule allowed alternative forums of expression for the International Society for Krishna Consciousness (ISKCON) because, "the Rule has not been shown to deny access within the forum in question. Here, the Rule does not exclude ISKCON from the fairgrounds, nor does it deny that organization the right to conduct any desired activity at some point within the forum. Its members may mingle with the crowd and orally propagate their views. The organization may also arrange for a booth and distribute and sell literature and solicit funds from that location on the fairgrounds itself."

- *Frisby v. Schultz*, 487 U.S. 474 (1988). Brookfield, Wisconsin, adopted an ordinance completely banning picketing "before or about" any residence. The Court upheld the ordinance. First, the Court explained, "all public streets are held in the public trust and are properly considered traditional public fora. Accordingly, the streets of Brookfield are traditional public fora." Second, "the Brookfield ordinance is content neutral." Third, the ordinance served the significant government interest of "the protection of residential privacy." Fourth, the ordinance was narrowly tailored to serve that governmental interest because although its ban was complete, it targeted no more than the exact source of the "evil" it sought to remedy—offensive and disturbing picketing focused on a "captive" home audience.

  Finally, the ordinance preserved "ample alternative channels of communication." The ordinance permitted protestors to enter residential neighborhoods, go door-to-door to proselytize their views, and distribute literature, so long as they did not focus exclusively on a particular residence.

- *Widmar v. Vincent*, 454 U.S. 263 (1981). The University of Missouri at Kansas City (UMKC), a state university, made its facilities generally available for the activities of registered student groups (designated public forum). However, a University regulation prohibited the use of university buildings or grounds "for purposes of religious worship or religious teaching." The Court invalidated the regulation.

  First, the Court explained the regulation was content based because, "UMKC has discriminated against student groups and speakers based on their desire to use a generally open forum to engage in religious worship and discussion." Second, the regulation did not satisfy strict scrutiny. The university claimed a compelling interest in maintaining strict separation of church and state. However, the Court explained that although such an interest may be compelling, "It does not follow, however, that an 'equal access' policy would be incompatible with this Court's Establishment Clause cases."

- *United States v. Grace*, 461 U.S. 171 (1983). Title 40 U.S.C. Section 13k prohibited the "display [of] any flag, banner, or device designed or adapted to bring into public notice any party, organization, or movement" in the U.S. Supreme Court building or on its grounds, which were defined to include the public sidewalks constituting the outer boundaries of the grounds. The Court invalidated the statute. The statute was not a reasonable, time, place, and manner regulation.

First, the Court explained, "The public sidewalks forming the perimeter of the Supreme Court grounds, in our view, are public forums." Also, "it is clear that the prohibition is facially content-neutral."

However, the statue was not narrowly tailored. The purpose of the statute was to maintain "proper order and decorum." But the Court questioned "whether a total ban on carrying a flag, banner, or device on the public sidewalks substantially serves these purposes." The Court concluded, "A total ban on that conduct is no more necessary for the maintenance of peace and tranquility on the public sidewalks surrounding the building than on any other sidewalks in the city. Accordingly, § 13k cannot be justified on this basis."

- *Ward v. Rock Against Racism*, 491 U.S. 781 (1989). New York City adopted a use guideline for the Naumberg Acoustic Bandshell in New York City's Central Park that specified the city would furnish high-quality sound equipment and retain an independent, experienced sound technician for all performances. Rock Against Racism (RAR) wanted to use its own sound equipment and technicians. The Court upheld the guideline as a reasonable time, place, and manner regulation.

  First, the Court explained, "the bandshell was open, apparently, to all performers; and we decide the case as one in which the bandshell is a public forum for performances in which the government's right to regulate expression is subject to the protections of the First Amendment." Second, the guideline was content neutral because, "The principal justification for the sound-amplification guideline is the city's desire to control noise levels." And this justification had "nothing to do with content." Third, "It is undeniable that the city's substantial interest in limiting sound volume is served in a direct and effective way by the requirement that the city's sound technician control the mixing board during performances." Last, "The final requirement, that the guideline leave open ample alternative channels of communication, is easily met." For example, "the guideline continues to permit expressive activity in the bandshell, and has no effect on the quantity or content of that expression beyond regulating the extent of amplification."

- *Hill v. Colorado*, 530 U.S. 703 (2000). A Colorado statute made it unlawful, within 100 feet of the entrance to any health care facility, for any person to "knowingly approach" within eight feet of another person, without that person's consent, "for the purpose of passing a leaflet or handbill to, displaying a sign to, or engaging in oral protest, education, or counseling with such other person." The Court upheld the statute. The statute was a reasonable time, place, and manner regulation.

  First, the Court explained, "the public sidewalks, streets, and ways affected by the statute are 'quintessential' public forums for free speech." Second, the statute was content neutral because, "It places no restrictions on—and clearly does not prohibit—either a particular viewpoint or any subject matter that may be discussed by a speaker. Rather, it simply establishes a minor place restriction on an extremely broad category of communications with unwilling listeners." Third, the state had significant interests in "unimpeded access to health care facilities and the avoidance of potential trauma to patients associated with confrontational protests." Fourth, the statute was narrowly tailored because, "The 8-foot separation between the speaker and the audience should not have any adverse impact on the readers' ability to read signs displayed by demonstrators." Finally, the statute left open ample alternative channels for communication because, "the 8-foot restriction on an unwanted physical approach leaves ample room to communicate a message through speech. Signs, pictures, and voice itself can cross an 8-foot gap with ease."

- *United States v. Playboy Entertainment Group, Inc.*, 529 U.S. 803 (2000). Section 505 of the Telecommunications Act of 1996 required cable television operators providing channels "primarily dedicated to sexually-oriented programming" either to "fully scramble or otherwise fully block" those channels or limit their transmission to hours when children are unlikely to be viewing, set by regulation as between 10 p.m. and 6 a.m. The Court invalidated the law.

First, the Court explained, "The speech in question is defined by its content; and the statute which seeks to restrict it is content based. Section 505 applies only to channels primarily dedicated to 'sexually explicit adult programming or other programming that is indecent.'" Thus, "Since § 505 is a content-based speech restriction, it can stand only if it satisfies strict scrutiny." Second, "the objective of shielding children does not suffice to support a blanket ban if the protection can be accomplished by a less restrictive alternative." The Court noted Section 504, which required cable operators to block undesired channels at individual households "upon request," was a plausible, less restrictive alternative. The Court concluded, "The Government has failed to show that § 505 is the least restrictive means for addressing a real problem."

• *Watchtower Bible & Tract Society of New York, Inc. v. Village of Stratton*, 536 U.S. 150 (2002). A Village of Stratton ordinance prohibited "canvassers" from "going in and upon" private residential property to promote any "cause" without first obtaining a permit from the mayor's office. A congregation of Jehovah's Witnesses, a religious group whose religion mandated door-to-door canvassing, sued for injunctive relief against the Village. The Court invalidated the ordinance.

The Court explained, "The Village argues that three interests are served by its ordinance: the prevention of fraud, the prevention of crime, and the protection of residents' privacy. We have no difficulty concluding, in light of our precedent, that these are important interests." However, "The mere fact that the ordinance covers so much speech raises constitutional concerns. It is offensive—not only to the values protected by the First Amendment, but to the very notion of a free society—that in the context of everyday public discourse a citizen must first inform the government of her desire to speak to her neighbors and then obtain a permit to do so." The Court noted, "Even a spontaneous decision to go across the street and urge a neighbor to vote against the mayor could not lawfully be implemented without first obtaining the mayor's permission."

Also the ordinance was not tailored to the village's stated interests. The Court explained, "Even if the interest in preventing fraud could adequately support the ordinance insofar as it applies to commercial transactions and the solicitation of funds, that interest provides no support for its application to petitioners, to political campaigns, or to enlisting support for unpopular causes."

Injunctions

A content-neutral injunction that imposes "time, place, and manner" restrictions in a public forum must burden no more speech than necessary to serve a significant government interest. This is a more rigorous standard than for "time, place, and manner" regulations.

- *Madsen v. Women's Health Center, Inc.*, 512 U.S. 753 (1994). A state court issued an injunction enjoining protestors at an abortion clinic from blocking or interfering with clinic access and from physically abusing people entering or leaving the clinic. After the injunction, protestors still impeded access to the clinic. The trial court then issued a broader injunction enjoining protestors from (1) demonstrating within 36 feet of the clinic (buffer zone), and (2) approaching anyone "seeking the services of the Clinic" who is within 300 feet of the clinic unless the person "indicates a desire to communicate" (no approach zone).

  The Court upheld the 36-foot buffer zone. The Court explained significant state interests included ensuring public safety and order, promoting the free flow of traffic on streets and sidewalks, protecting property rights, and protecting a woman's freedom to seek pregnancy-related services. Also, the 36-foot buffer zone burdened no more speech than necessary to serve these interests. The trial court had few other options to protect access to the clinic; allowing protesters to remain on the sidewalks and in the clinic driveway was not a valid option because of their past conduct, and allowing them to stand in the street was impractical.

  The Court invalidated the 300-foot no approach zone. The Court explained, "it is difficult, indeed, to justify a prohibition on all uninvited approaches of persons seeking the services of the clinic, regardless of how peaceful the contact may be, without burdening more speech than necessary to prevent intimidation and to ensure access to the clinic. Absent evidence that the protesters' speech is independently proscribable (i.e., 'fighting words' or threats), or is so infused with violence as to be indistinguishable from a threat of physical harm, this provision cannot stand." The Court concluded, "The record before us does not contain sufficient justification for this broad a ban on picketing; it appears that a limitation on the time, duration of picketing, and number of pickets outside a smaller zone could have accomplished the desired result."

- *Schenck v. Pro-Choice Network of Western New York*, 519 U.S. 357 (1997). A federal district court issued a temporary restraining order (TRO) enjoining protestors at an abortion clinic from physically blockading the clinic. After the TRO, protestors continued to block or hinder people from entering and exiting the clinic. The district court then issued an injunction enjoining protestors from demonstrating (1) within 15 feet of doorway entrances, parking lot entrances, and driveway entrances of the clinic (fixed buffer zones), or (2) within 15 feet of any person or vehicle entering or leaving the clinic (floating buffer zones).

  The Court upheld the fixed buffer zones. The Court explained, "Given the factual similarity between this case and *Madsen*, we conclude that the governmental interests underlying the injunction in *Madsen*—ensuring public safety and order, promoting the free flow of traffic on streets and sidewalks, protecting property rights, and protecting a woman's freedom to seek pregnancy-related services—also underlie the injunction here, and in combination are certainly significant enough to justify an appropriately tailored injunction to secure unimpeded physical access to the clinics." Also, the fixed buffer zones burdened no more speech than necessary to serve these interests because they were "necessary to ensure that people and vehicles trying to enter or exit the clinic property or clinic parking lots can do so."

  The Court invalidated the floating buffer zones. The Court explained, "they burden more speech than is necessary to serve the relevant governmental interests." The floating buffer zones prevented protestors from communicating a message from a normal conversational distance or handing leaflets to people entering or leaving the clinic on public sidewalks. These are "classic forms of speech that lie at the heart of the First Amendment." Also, the sidewalk outside the clinic was only 17 feet wide so maintaining 15 feet of separation from persons or vehicles would be "hazardous."

Nonpublic Forums

A nonpublic forum is public property not open to the public, either by tradition or designation. The government can prohibit all speech activities in nonpublic forums, or it can allow certain speech. If the government prohibits almost all speech and allows only some speech, then the forum remains a nonpublic forum. (If the government allows almost all speech and prohibits only some speech, then the government creates a designated public forum, discussed previously.) The government may regulate speech in nonpublic forums based on subject matter and speaker identity if the regulation is reasonable and viewpoint neutral.

- *Greer v. Spock*, 424 U.S. 828 (1976). Fort Dix, a federal military reservation, had regulations that banned speeches and demonstrations of a partisan political nature, and prohibited the distribution of literature without prior approval of post headquarters. The Court upheld the regulations. The Court explained, "it is the primary business of armies and navies to fight or be ready to fight wars should the occasion arise. And it is consequently the business of a military installation like Fort Dix to train soldiers, not to provide a public forum." Also, the regulations were viewpoint neutral as there was "no claim that the military authorities discriminated in any way among candidates for public office based upon the candidates' supposed political views."

- *Members of the City Council of Los Angeles v. Taxpayers for Vincent*, 466 U.S. 789 (1984). Section 28.04 of the Los Angeles Municipal Code prohibited the posting of signs on public property. Taxpayers for Vincent, a group of supporters of a candidate for election to the Los Angeles City Council, entered into a contract with Candidates' Outdoor Graphics Service (COGS) to make and post signs with the candidate's name on them. COGS made cardboard signs and attached them to utility pole cross wires at various locations. The Court upheld the ordinance.

  The Court explained utility poles are a nonpublic forum because there was no traditional right of access to utility poles for communication "comparable to that recognized for public streets and parks." The ordinance served a legitimate government interest in esthetics and "proscribing intrusive and unpleasant formats for expression." And the ordinance was viewpoint neutral as, "The text of the ordinance is neutral—indeed it is silent—concerning any speaker's point of view."

- *Cornelius v. NAACP Legal Defense and Educational Fund, Inc.*, 473 U.S. 788 (1985). An executive order limited participation in the Combined Federal Campaign (CFC), a charity drive aimed at federal employees, to voluntary, tax-exempt, nonprofit charitable agencies that provided direct health and welfare services to individuals or their families. However, the order specifically excluded legal defense and political advocacy organizations. The Court upheld the order.

  The Court explained, "The Government's consistent policy has been to limit participation in the CFC to 'appropriate' voluntary agencies and to require agencies seeking admission to obtain permission from federal and local Campaign officials." Thus, "In light of the Government policy in creating the CFC and its practice in limiting access, we conclude that the CFC is a nonpublic forum."

  Also, excluding legal defense and political advocacy organizations was reasonable. The Court explained, "The reasonableness of the Government's restriction of access to a nonpublic forum must be assessed in the light of the purpose of the forum and all the surrounding circumstances. Here the President could reasonably conclude that a dollar directly spent on providing food or shelter to the needy is more beneficial than a dollar spent on litigation that might or might not result in aid to the needy. Moreover, avoiding the appearance of political favoritism is a valid justification for limiting speech in a nonpublic forum."

  As to whether the order was viewpoint neutral, the issue "was neither decided below nor fully briefed before this Court. We decline to decide in the first instance whether the exclusion of respondents was impermissibly motivated by a desire to suppress a particular point of view. Respondents are free to pursue this contention on remand."

- *Hazelwood School District v. Kuhlmeier*, 484 U.S. 260 (1988). A high school principal deleted from a school newspaper (*Spectrum*) two pages that included an article describing school students' experiences with pregnancy and another article discussing the impact of divorce on students at the school. The Court upheld the deletions.

  The Court explained *Spectrum* was a nonpublic forum as, "School officials did not evince either by policy or by practice any intent to open the pages of *Spectrum* to indiscriminate use by its student reporters and editors, or by the student body generally. Instead, they reserved the forum for its intended purpose, as a supervised learning experience for journalism students." Also, "Principal Reynolds acted reasonably" in requiring the deletions. For example, "The initial paragraph of the pregnancy article declared, '[a]ll names have been changed to keep the identity of these girls a secret.' The principal concluded that the students' anonymity was not adequately protected, however, given the other identifying information in the article and the small number of pregnant students at the school."

The Court concluded, "we cannot reject as unreasonable Principal Reynolds' conclusion that neither the pregnancy article nor the divorce article was suitable for publication in *Spectrum*. Reynolds could reasonably have concluded that the students who had written and edited these articles had not sufficiently mastered those portions of the Journalism II curriculum that pertained to the treatment of controversial issues and personal attacks, the need to protect the privacy of individuals whose most intimate concerns are to be revealed in the newspaper, and the legal, moral, and ethical restrictions imposed upon journalists within a school community that includes adolescent subjects and readers."

- *International Society for Krishna Consciousness, Inc. v. Lee*, 505 U.S. 672 (1992). The Port Authority of New York and New Jersey, which owned and operated three major airports in the New York City area and controlled certain terminal areas at the airports, adopted a regulation forbidding the repetitive solicitation of money within the terminals. The Court upheld the regulation.

The Court explained the airports were nonpublic forums because, "the tradition of airport activity does not demonstrate that airports have historically been made available for speech activity. Nor can we say that these particular terminals, or airport terminals generally, have been intentionally opened by their operators to such activity." Also, the regulation was reasonable. Solicitation impedes the normal flow of traffic and, "Delays may be particularly costly in this setting, as a flight missed by only a few minutes can result in hours worth of subsequent inconvenience." Moreover, "face-to-face solicitation presents risks of duress." And, "Compounding this problem is the fact that, in an airport, the targets of such activity frequently are on tight schedules. This in turn makes such visitors unlikely to stop and formally complain to airport authorities."

- *Lamb's Chapel v. Center Moriches Union Free School District*, 508 U.S. 384 (1993). A school board (District) issued regulations allowing social, civic, and recreational uses of its schools (Rule 10), but prohibiting use by any group for religious purposes (Rule 7). The District then refused two requests by an evangelical church and its pastor (Church) to use school facilities for a religious-oriented film series on family values and child rearing on the ground that the film series appeared to be church related. The Court held denying the Church access to school premises to exhibit the film series violated the freedom of speech clause. The Court explained the District's denial was not viewpoint neutral. Using school property to show a film series about family values and child rearing is a use for "social or civic purposes." So, the film series dealt with a subject that was otherwise permissible under Rule 10. But, "its exhibition was denied solely because the series dealt with the subject from a religious standpoint."

- *Arkansas Educational Television Commission v. Forbes*, 523 U.S. 666 (1998). The Arkansas Educational Television Commission (AETC), a state-owned public television broadcaster, sponsored a debate between the major party candidates for the 1992 election in Arkansas's Third Congressional District. When AETC denied the request of Forbes, an independent candidate with little popular support, for permission to participate in the debate, Forbes claimed he was entitled to participate under the First Amendment. The Court upheld AETC's exclusion of Forbes from the debate.

  The Court explained the debate was a nonpublic forum because, "AETC did not make its debate generally available to candidates for Arkansas' Third Congressional District seat. Instead, just as the Federal Government in *Cornelius* reserved eligibility for participation in the CFC program to certain classes of voluntary agencies, AETC reserved eligibility for participation in the debate to candidates for the Third Congressional District seat (as opposed to some other seat)." Also, Forbes's exclusion was reasonable and viewpoint-neutral because, "It is, in short, beyond dispute that Forbes was excluded not because of his viewpoint but because he had generated no appreciable public interest."

- *Good News Club v. Milford Central School*, 533 U.S. 98 (2001). Milford Central School enacted a policy authorizing district residents to use its building after school for instruction in education, learning, or the arts, and social, civic, recreational, and entertainment uses pertaining to the community welfare. The Good News Club, a private Christian organization for children ages 6 to 12, submitted a request to hold the Club's weekly afterschool meetings in the school to sing songs, hear Bible lessons, memorize scripture, and pray. Milford denied the request on the ground that the proposed use was the equivalent of religious worship prohibited by the community use policy. The Court invalidated the denial.

  The Court explained, "Like the church in *Lamb's Chapel*, the Club seeks to address a subject otherwise permitted under the rule, the teaching of morals and character, from a religious standpoint." The Court concluded "The only apparent difference between the activity of Lamb's Chapel and the activities of the Good News Club is that the Club chooses to teach moral lessons from a Christian perspective through live storytelling and prayer, whereas Lamb's Chapel taught lessons through films. This distinction is inconsequential. Both modes of speech use a religious viewpoint. Thus, the exclusion of the Good News Club's activities, like the exclusion of Lamb's Chapel's films, constitutes unconstitutional viewpoint discrimination."

- *Christian Legal Soc'y Chapter of the Univ. of Cal. v. Martinez*, 130 S. Ct. 2971 (2010). Hastings College of the Law, a school within the University of California public-school system, recognized student groups through its "Registered Student Organization" (RSO) program. Hastings required RSOs to accept "all comers" under its Nondiscrimination Policy ("open-access" policy), which barred discrimination on a number of bases, including religion and sexual orientation. Christian Legal Society (CLS), a national Christian association, excluded from its membership anyone who engaged in "unrepentant homosexual conduct" or held religious convictions different from those in a Statement of Faith that members were required to sign. Hastings rejected CLS's application for RSO status on the ground that CLS did not comply with the open-access policy because CLS barred students based on religion and sexual orientation. The Court upheld the open-access policy.

Hastings' open-access policy was reasonable because (1) it "ensures that the leadership, educational, and social opportunities afforded by [RSOs] are available to all students;" (2) it "helps Hastings police the written terms of its Nondiscrimination Policy without inquiring into an RSO's motivation for membership restrictions;" (3) Hastings "reasonably adheres to the view that an all-comers policy, to the extent it brings together individuals with diverse backgrounds and beliefs, encourages tolerance, cooperation, and learning among students;" and (4) Hastings' policy, "which incorporates. . .state-law proscriptions on discrimination, conveys the Law School's decision to decline to subsidize with public monies and benefits conduct of which the people of California disapprove."

The open-access policy was viewpoint neutral because "It is, after all, hard to imagine a more viewpoint-neutral policy than one requiring all student groups to accept all comers. In contrast to *Healy*, *Widmar*, and *Rosenberger*, in which universities singled out organizations for disfavored treatment because of their points of view, Hastings' all-comers requirement draws no distinction between groups based on their message or perspective. An all-comers condition on access to RSO status, in short, is textbook viewpoint neutral."

Private Property

The First Amendment does not provide the right to use the private property of others for speech [*Hudgens v. National Labor Relations Board*, 424 U.S. 507 (1976) (holding picketers did not have a First Amendment right to enter a privately owned shopping center for the purpose of advertising their strike against their employer)]. However, a state may create a state constitutional right to use privately owned shopping centers for speech [*PruneYard Shopping Center v. Robins*, 447 U.S. 74 (1980) (holding appellants' First Amendment rights were not infringed by the California Supreme Court's decision that the California Constitution gave appellees the right to solicit signatures on appellants' privately owned shopping center while exercising their state rights of free expression and petition)].

CHAPTER 20

Freedom of Association

THE FIRST AMENDMENT PROTECTS FREEDOM OF ASSOCIATION BECAUSE OF ITS CLOSE relationship to speech and assembly [*NAACP v. Alabama*, 357 U.S. 449 (1958) (stating, "Effective advocacy of both public and private points of view, particularly controversial ones, is undeniably enhanced by group association, as this Court has more than once recognized by remarking upon the close nexus between the freedoms of speech and assembly. It is beyond debate that freedom to engage in association for the advancement of beliefs and ideas is an inseparable aspect of the 'liberty' assured by the Due Process Clause of the Fourteenth Amendment, which embraces freedom of speech.")]. The First Amendment protection of freedom of association applies to the states through the Fourteenth Amendment [*Baggett v. Bullitt*, 377 U.S. 360 (1964)]. So freedom of association is protected from state and local interference as well as from federal interference.

PUNISHING GROUP MEMBERSHIP

The government may punish membership in a group if a person is an active member of a subversive group with knowledge of its illegal objectives and specific intent to further those objectives.

- *Scales v. United States*, 367 U.S. 203 (1961). The membership clause of the Smith Act made it a felony to acquire or hold membership in any organization that advocated the overthrow of the U.S. government by force or violence, knowing the purposes thereof. Scales, chairman of the North Carolina and South Carolina Districts of the Communist Party, was convicted of violating the clause. The indictment charged that from January 1946 to 1954 the Communist Party of the United States was such an organization and that, throughout that period, Scales was a member with knowledge of the party's illegal purpose and specific intent to accomplish overthrow of the government "as speedily as circumstances would permit." The Court upheld the membership clause and affirmed the conviction. The Court explained, "The clause does not make criminal all association with an organization which has been shown to engage in illegal advocacy. There must be clear proof that a defendant specifically intends to accomplish the aims of the organization by resort to violence."

- *Elfbrandt v. Russell*, 384 U.S. 11 (1966). An Arizona statute required state employees to take a loyalty oath. The statute subjected to criminal penalties and discharge from employment any employee who took the oath and knowingly and willfully became or remained a member of the Communist Party of the United States, "or any other organization having for one of its purposes" the violent overthrow of the government of Arizona, if the employee had knowledge of such unlawful purpose of the organization. The Court invalidated the statute. The statute punished group membership without proof the person had specific intent to further illegal objectives.

  The Court explained, "Those who join an organization but do not share its unlawful purposes and who do not participate in its unlawful activities surely pose no threat, either as citizens or as public employees. Laws such as this which are not restricted in scope to those who join with the 'specific intent' to further illegal action impose, in effect, a conclusive presumption that the member shares the unlawful aims of the organization." The Court concluded, "A law which applies to membership without the 'specific intent' to further the illegal aims of the organization infringes unnecessarily on protected freedoms. It rests on the doctrine of 'guilt by association' which has no place here."

- *Keyishian v. Board of Regents*, 385 U.S. 589 (1967). Sections 105 and 3022 of New York's teacher loyalty law made Communist Party membership prima facie evidence of disqualification for public school teachers. The Court invalidated the law. The Court explained the laws "are invalid insofar as they proscribe mere knowing membership without any showing of specific intent to further the unlawful aims of the Communist Party of the United States or of the State of New York."

- *Baird v. State Bar of Arizona*, 401 U.S. 1 (1971). The Arizona Bar Committee denied Baird admission to the bar because she refused to answer whether she had ever been a member of the Communist Party or any organization "that advocates overthrow of the United States Government by force or violence." The Court invalidated the denial. The Court explained, "The First Amendment's protection of association prohibits a State from excluding a person from a profession or punishing him solely because he is a member of a particular political organization or because he holds certain beliefs." The Court concluded, "This record is wholly barren of one word, sentence, or paragraph that tends to show this lady is not morally and professionally fit to serve honorably and well as a member of the legal profession. It was error not to process her application and not to admit her to the Arizona Bar."

- *Law Students Civil Rights Research Council v. Wadmond*, 401 U.S. 154 (1971). A two-part question on the New York Bar application asked whether the applicant had ever joined an organization he knew was advocating the overthrow of government by force or violence, and if so, whether the applicant had "the specific intent to further the aims of such organization." The Court upheld the bar question. The Court explained, "We have held that know-ing membership in an organization advocating the overthrow of the Government by force or violence, on the part of one sharing the specific intent to further the organization's illegal goals, may be made criminally punishable." The Court concluded, "Surely a State is constitutionally entitled to make such an inquiry of an applicant for admission to a profession dedicated to the peaceful and reasoned settlement of disputes between men, and between a man and his government."

Political Patronage

The government may not make decisions about hiring, firing, promotion, transfer, or recall after layoff of a public employee or contractor because of his political beliefs, unless the hiring authority can demonstrate party affiliation is an appropriate requirement for the effective performance of the public office involved.

- *Elrod v. Burns*, 427 U.S. 347 (1976). A newly elected Democratic sheriff in Cook County, Illinois, discharged noncivil-service employees who were Republicans because they were not affiliated with or sponsored by the Democratic Party. The Court invalidated the firings without a majority opinion. Justice Brennan explained in a plurality opinion, "it is doubtful that the mere difference of political persuasion motivates poor performance." Also, "less drastic means for insuring government effectiveness and employee efficiency are available to the State. Specifically, employees may always be discharged for good cause, such as insubordination or poor job performance, when those bases in fact exist." Justice Brennan concluded, "patronage dismissals severely restrict political belief and association. Though there is a vital need for government efficiency and effectiveness, such dismissals are on balance not the least restrictive means for fostering that end."

- *Branti v. Finkel*, 445 U.S. 507 (1980). A newly appointed Democratic public defender in Rockland County, New York, fired two assistant public defenders because they were members of the Republican Party and did not have the necessary Democratic sponsors. The Court invalidated the firings. The Court explained, "an employee's realization that he must obtain a sponsor in order to retain his job is very likely to lead to the same type of coercion as that described by the plurality in *Elrod*. While there was apparently no overt political pressure exerted on respondents in this case, the potentially coercive effect of requiring sponsorship was demonstrated by Mr. Finkel's change of party registration in a futile attempt to retain his position."

  Also, "whatever policymaking occurs in the public defender's office must relate to the needs of individual clients and not to any partisan political interests." The Court concluded, "it is manifest that the continued employment of an assistant public defender cannot properly be conditioned upon his allegiance to the political party in control of the county government. The primary, if not the only, responsibility of an assistant public defender is to represent individual citizens in controversy with the State."

- *Rutan v. Republican Party of Illinois*, 497 U.S. 62 (1990). The governor of Illinois, a Republican, issued an executive order that prohibited state officials from hiring any employee, filling any vacancy, creating any new position, or taking any similar action without the governor's express permission. Several persons alleged the governor had created a political patronage system to limit state employment and beneficial employment-related decisions to those who were supported by the Republican Party. The Court held the government may not make decisions about promotions, transfers, or recalls after layoffs for government employees based on political party affiliation.

    The Court explained, "The same First Amendment concerns that underlay our decisions in *Elrod* and *Branti* are implicated here. Employees who do not compromise their beliefs stand to lose the considerable increases in pay and job satisfaction attendant to promotions, the hours and maintenance expenses that are consumed by long daily commutes, and even their jobs if they are not rehired after a 'temporary' layoff." The Court concluded, "We hold that the rule of *Elrod* and *Branti* extends to promotion, transfer, recall, and hiring decisions based on party affiliation and support."

- *O'Hare Truck Service Inc. v. City of Northlake*, 518 U.S. 712 (1996). The city of Northlake maintained a list of companies to perform towing services at its request. The city removed O'Hare Truck Service, Inc., from the list after its owner, Gratzianna, refused to contribute to the mayor's reelection campaign and instead supported his opponent. The Court held the government may not retaliate against a contractor, or a regular provider of services, for the exercise of rights of political association or the expression of political allegiance.

    The Court explained, "Respondents insist the principles of *Elrod* and *Branti* have no force here, arguing that an independent contractor's First Amendment rights, unlike a public employee's, must yield to the government's asserted countervailing interest in sustaining a patronage system. We cannot accept the proposition, however, that those who perform the government's work outside the formal employment relationship are subject to what we conclude is the direct and specific abridgment of First Amendment rights described in this complaint. As respondents offer no justification for their actions, save for insisting on their right to condition a continuing relationship on political fealty, we hold that the complaint states an actionable First Amendment claim."

DISCLOSURE OF GROUP MEMBERSHIP

The government may require disclosure of group membership only if it meets strict scrutiny (i.e., the law must be necessary to achieve a compelling state interest).

- *NAACP v. Alabama ex. rel Patterson*, 357 U.S. 449 (1958). A civil contempt order was entered against the NAACP when it refused to comply with an order to produce to the state of Alabama a list of the names and addresses of all its Alabama members and agents. The Court invalidated the contempt order. The Court explained, "We think that the production order, in the respects here drawn in question, must be regarded as entailing the likelihood of a substantial restraint upon the exercise by petitioner's members of their right to freedom of association. Petitioner has made an uncontroverted showing that on past occasions revelation of the identity of its rank-and-file members has exposed these members to economic reprisal, loss of employment, threat of physical coercion, and other manifestations of public hostility."

  The state argued its interest in requesting the membership lists was to determine whether the NAACP was conducting intrastate business in violation of the Alabama foreign corporation registration statute. However, the Court explained, "whatever interest the State may have in obtaining names of ordinary members has not been shown to be sufficient to overcome petitioner's constitutional objections to the production order."

- *Shelton v. Tucker*, 364 U.S. 479 (1960). An Arkansas statute required every teacher, as a condition of employment in a state-supported school or college, to file annually an affidavit listing every organization to which he has belonged or regularly contributed within the preceding five years. The Court invalidated the statute.

  The Court explained, "there can be no question of the relevance of a State's inquiry into the fitness and competence of its teachers." However, "The scope of the inquiry required by [the statute] is completely unlimited. The statute requires a teacher to reveal the church to which he belongs, or to which he has given financial support. It requires him to disclose his political party, and every political organization to which he may have contributed over a five-year period. It requires him to list, without number, every conceivable kind of associational tie—social, professional, political, avocational, or religious. Many such relationships could have no possible bearing upon the teacher's occupational competence or fitness." The Court concluded, "The statute's comprehensive interference with associational freedom goes far beyond what might be justified in the exercise of the State's legitimate inquiry into the fitness and competency of its teachers."

- *Buckley v. Valeo*, 424 U.S. 1 (1976). The Federal Election Campaign Act of 1971, as amended in 1974, required political committees to keep detailed records of contributions and expenditures, including the name and address of each individual contributing in excess of $10. The Court upheld the Act. The Court explained, "The strict test established by *NAACP vs. Alabama* is necessary because compelled disclosure has the potential for substantially infringing the exercise of First Amendment rights." Also, "It is undoubtedly true that public disclosure of contributions to candidates and political parties will deter some individuals who otherwise might contribute."

  However, "disclosure provides the electorate with information as to where political campaign money comes from and how it is spent by the candidate." Also, "Congress could reasonably conclude that full disclosure during an election campaign tends to prevent the corrupt use of money to affect elections." Finally, "recordkeeping, reporting, and disclosure requirements are an essential means of gathering the data necessary to detect violations of the contribution limitations."

THE RIGHT NOT TO ASSOCIATE

The First Amendment also protects the right not to associate. Generally, the government may not force individuals to support ideas or activities they oppose or force groups to accept unwanted members. However, the government may prohibit groups from discriminating against unwanted members if there is a compelling state interest, unrelated to the suppression of ideas, that cannot be achieved through less restrictive means.

- *Abood v. Detroit Board of Education*, 431 U.S. 209 (1977). A Michigan statute authorized an "agency shop" arrangement in which every government employee represented by the union, even though not a union member, was required to pay to the union as a condition of employment a service fee equal in amount to union dues. Certain teachers alleged they were unwilling or had refused to pay union dues, and that the union used a substantial part of the agency shop fees to support ideological and political causes they opposed. The Court invalidated the use of service fees for political and ideological purposes to which an employee objected.

  The Court explained, "We do not hold that a union cannot constitutionally spend funds for the expression of political views, on behalf of political candidates, or toward the advancement of other ideological causes not germane to its duties as collective-bargaining representative. Rather, the Constitution requires only that such expenditures be financed from charges, dues, or assessments paid by employees who do not object to advancing those ideas and who are not coerced into doing so against their will by the threat of loss of governmental employment."

- *Roberts v. United States Jaycees*, 468 U.S. 609 (1984). A national organization of young men, the Jaycees, refused to grant full membership rights to women because of their sex, and challenged the Minnesota Human Rights Act, which prohibited such discrimination. The Court upheld the Act. The Court explained, "the Act reflects the State's strong historical commitment to eliminating discrimination and assuring its citizens equal access to publicly available goods and services. That goal, which is unrelated to the suppression of expression, plainly serves compelling state interests of the highest order." Also, "In applying the Act to the Jaycees, the State has advanced those interests through the least restrictive means of achieving its ends. Indeed, the Jaycees has failed to demonstrate that the Act imposes any serious burdens on the male members' freedom of expressive association."

- *Keller v. State Bar of California*, 496 U.S. 1 (1990). Members of the State Bar of California sued the bar, claiming it expended mandatory dues payments to advance ideological causes the members opposed. The Court held the bar may not use compulsory dues to finance political and ideological activities members opposed.

The Court explained, "the guiding standard must be whether the challenged expenditures are necessarily or reasonably incurred for the purpose of regulating the legal profession or improving the quality of the legal service available to the people of the State." For example, "Compulsory dues may not be expended to endorse or advance a gun control or nuclear weapons freeze initiative; at the other end of the spectrum petitioners have no valid constitutional objection to their compulsory dues being spent for activities connected with disciplining members of the bar or proposing ethical codes for the profession."

- *Hurley v. Irish-American Gay, Lesbian, and Bisexual Group of Boston*, 515 U.S. 557 (1995). Massachusetts's public accommodations statute prohibited discrimination based on sexual orientation in places of public accommodation. South Boston Allied War Veterans Council, an unincorporated association of individuals elected from various veterans groups, was authorized by the city of Boston to organize and conduct the St. Patrick's Day–Evacuation Day Parade. The Council refused access in the 1993 event to GLIB, an organization formed for the purpose of marching in the parade to express its members' pride in their Irish heritage as openly gay, lesbian, and bisexual individuals. The Court held the state could not compel the council to include GLIB in the parade.

The Court explained that a "parade" involves "marchers who are making some sort of collective point, not just to each other but to bystanders along the way." Parades are thus "a form of expression, not just motion." So compelling the council to include GLIB would essentially require petitioners "to alter the expressive content of their parade." But, "this use of the State's power violates the fundamental rule of protection under the First Amendment, that a speaker has the autonomy to choose the content of his own message." The Court added, "Considering that GLIB presumably would have had a fair shot (under neutral criteria developed by the city) at obtaining a parade permit of its own, respondents have not shown that petitioners enjoy the capacity to 'silence the voice of competing speakers.'"

- *Glickman v. Wileman Brothers & Elliott, Inc.*, 521 U.S. 457 (1997). Under regulations contained in marketing orders promulgated by the U.S. secretary of agriculture pursuant to the Agricultural

Marketing Agreement Act of 1937, producers and handlers of California nectarines, plums, and peaches were assessed for the cost of generic advertising of those fruits on radio and television and in newspapers. The Court upheld the mandatory assessments. The Court explained, "requiring respondents to pay the assessments cannot be said to engender any crisis of conscience. None of the advertising in this record promotes any particular message other than encouraging consumers to buy California tree fruit." The Court concluded, "(1) the generic advertising of California peaches and nectarines is unquestionably germane to the purposes of the marketing orders and, (2) in any event, the assessments are not used to fund ideological activities."

- *Board of Regents of the University of Wisconsin System v. Southworth*, 529 U.S. 217 (2000). The University required students at the University's Madison campus to pay a segregated activity fee used in part by the University to support student organizations engaging in political or ideological speech. The Court upheld the fee. The Court explained, "the University of Wisconsin may sustain the extracurricular dimensions of its programs by using mandatory student fees with viewpoint neutrality as the operational principle. The parties have stipulated that the program the University has developed to stimulate extracurricular student expression respects the principle of viewpoint neutrality. If the stipulation is to continue to control the case, the University's program in its basic structure must be found consistent with the First Amendment."

    The Court did not apply the "germaneness" test of *Abood* and *Keller* because, "If it is difficult to define germane speech with ease or precision where a union or bar association is the party, the standard becomes all the more unmanageable in the public university setting, particularly where the State undertakes to stimulate the whole universe of speech and ideas."

- *Boy Scouts of America v. Dale*, 530 U.S. 640 (2000). A New Jersey statute prohibited discrimination on the basis of sexual orientation in places of public accommodation. The Boy Scouts, a private not-for-profit organization engaged in instilling its system of values in young people, asserted homosexual conduct was inconsistent with those values and revoked Dale's position as assistant scoutmaster upon learning he was an avowed homosexual and gay rights activist. The Court held applying the statute to compel the Boy Scouts to retain Dale was unconstitutional.

The Court explained, "Here, we have found that the Boy Scouts believes that homosexual conduct is inconsistent with the values it seeks to instill in its youth members; it will not 'promote homosexual conduct as a legitimate form of behavior.' As the presence of GLIB in Boston's St. Patrick's Day parade would have interfered with the parade organizers' choice not to propound a particular point of view, the presence of Dale as an assistant scout-master would just as surely interfere with the Boy Scout's choice not to propound a point of view contrary to its beliefs." Also, "The state interests embodied in New Jersey's public accommodations law do not justify such a severe intrusion on the Boy Scouts' rights to freedom of expressive association."

- *United States v. United Foods, Inc.*, 533 U.S. 405 (2001). The Mushroom Promotion, Research, and Consumer Information Act mandated that fresh mushroom handlers pay assessments used primarily to fund advertisements promoting mushroom sales. The Court invalidated the mandatory assessments. The Court distinguished *Glickman* because there the mandatory assessments were part of a comprehensive regulatory scheme that bound producers together and required them to market their products according to cooperative rules, thereby displacing competition in favor of collective action. The Court noted, "the marketing orders [in *Glickman*] displaced competition to such an extent that they were expressly exempted from the antitrust laws."

But here, "The statutory mechanism as it relates to handlers of mushrooms is concededly different from the scheme in *Glickman*; here the statute does not require group action, save to generate the very speech to which some handlers object. In contrast to the program upheld in *Glickman*, where the Government argued the compelled contributions for advertising were part of a far broader regulatory system that does not principally concern speech, there is no broader regulatory system in place here. We have not upheld compelled subsidies for speech in the context of a program where the principal object is speech itself."

The Court concluded, "the expression respondent is required to support is not germane to a purpose related to an association independent from the speech itself; and the rationale of *Abood* extends to the party who objects to the compelled support for this speech."

CHAPTER 21

Freedom of Press

THE FIRST AMENDMENT PROTECTION OF FREEDOM OF PRESS APPLIES TO THE STATES through the Fourteenth Amendment [*Near v. Minnesota*, 283 U.S. 697 (1931)]. So freedom of press is protected from state and local interference as well as from federal interference.

TAXATION

The government may not single out the press for special taxes that apply only to the press unless it meets strict scrutiny (i.e., the law must be necessary to achieve a compelling state interest). However, the government may require the press to pay general taxes that apply to all businesses.

- *Grosjean v. American Press Co.*, 297 U.S. 233 (1936). A Louisiana statute imposed a tax on advertisements in publications with circulation of more than 20,000 copies per week. The Court invalidated the statute. The Court explained the tax "operates as a restraint in a double sense. First, its effect is to curtail the amount of revenue realized from advertising, and, second, its direct tendency is to restrict circulation." The Court concluded, "The tax here involved is bad not because it takes money from the pockets of the appellees. If that were all, a wholly different question would be presented. It is bad because, in the light of its history and of its present setting, it is seen to be a deliberate and calculated device in the guise of a tax to limit the circulation of information to which the public is entitled in virtue of the constitutional guaranties. A free press stands as one of the great interpreters between the government and the people. To allow it to be fettered is to fetter ourselves."

- *Minneapolis Star & Tribune Co. v. Minnesota Commissioner of Revenue*, 460 U.S. 575 (1983). A Minnesota tax statute imposed a special "use tax" on publications, assessing the tax on the cost of the ink and paper used in producing the publications. The Court invalidated the tax statute. The Court explained, "By creating this special use tax, which, to our knowledge, is without parallel in the State's tax scheme, Minnesota has singled out the press for special treatment." Moreover, "The main interest asserted by Minnesota in this case is the raising of revenue. Of course that interest is critical to any government. Standing alone, however, it cannot justify the special treatment of the press, for an alternative means of achieving the same interest without raising concerns under the First Amendment is clearly available: the State could raise the revenue by taxing businesses generally, avoiding the censorial threat implicit in a tax that singles out the press."

- *Arkansas Writers' Project, Inc. v. Ragland*, 481 U.S. 221 (1987). An Arkansas statute imposed a tax on receipts from sales of tangible personal property, but exempted newspapers and "religious, professional, trade, and sports journals and/or publications printed and published within this State" (magazine exemption). The Court invalidated the statute. The Court explained, "this case involves a more disturbing use of selective taxation than *Minneapolis Star*, because the basis on which Arkansas differentiates between magazines is particularly repugnant to First Amendment principles: a magazine's tax status depends entirely on its content." Also, Arkansas "advanced no compelling justification for selective, content-based taxation of certain magazines."

- *Leathers v. Medlock*, 499 U.S. 439 (1991). Arkansas's Gross Receipts Act imposed a tax on receipts from the sale of all tangible personal property and specified services, but expressly exempted certain receipts from newspaper and magazine sales. In 1987, Act 188 amended the

Gross Receipts Act to impose the tax on cable television. The Court upheld the amended Act.

The Court explained, "The Arkansas sales tax is a tax of general applicability," and, "The tax does not single out the press and does not therefore threaten to hinder the press as a watchdog of government activity." Moreover, "there is no indication in this case that Arkansas has targeted cable television in a purposeful attempt to interfere with its First Amendment activities. Nor is the tax one that is structured so as to raise suspicion that it was intended to do so. Unlike the taxes involved in *Grosjean* and *Minneapolis Star*, the Arkansas tax has not selected a narrow group to bear fully the burden of the tax." Finally, "Arkansas' sales tax is not content based. There is nothing in the language of the statute that refers to the content of mass media communications."

GENERALLY APPLICABLE LAWS

First Amendment freedom of press does not exempt the press from generally applicable laws (e.g., antitrust law, labor law, and contract law). The press has no special immunity from these laws.

- *Associated Press v. NLRB*, 301 U.S. 103 (1937). The Associated Press discharged Morris Watson, an employee in its New York office. The American Newspaper Guild, a labor organization, filed a charge with the National Labor Relations Board alleging Watson's discharge violated the National Labor Relations Act. The Associated Press claimed the Act, as applied to it, violated its constitutional rights, including freedoms of speech and press. The Court held the First Amendment does not exempt the press from the Act.

    The Court explained, "The business of the Associated Press is not immune from regulation because it is an agency of the press. The publisher of a newspaper has no special immunity from the application of general laws. He has no special privilege to invade the rights and liberties of others. He must answer for libel. He may be punished for contempt of court. He is subject to the anti-trust laws. Like others he must pay equitable and nondiscriminatory taxes on his business. The regulation here in question has no relation whatever to the impartial distribution of news."

- *Associated Press v. United States*, 326 U.S. 1 (1945). By-laws of the Associated Press (AP), a cooperative association engaged in gathering and distributing news in interstate and foreign commerce, prohibited service of AP news to nonmembers. A contract between AP and a Canadian press association obligated both to furnish news exclusively to each other. The government charged the bylaws and the contract violated the Sherman Antitrust Act. The Court held the First Amendment does not exempt the press from the Act.

  The Court explained, "The First Amendment, far from providing an argument against application of the Sherman Act, here provides powerful reasons to the contrary. That Amendment rests on the assumption that the widest possible dissemination of information from diverse and antagonistic sources is essential to the welfare of the public, that a free press is a condition of a free society." The Court concluded, "Freedom to publish is guaranteed by the Constitution, but freedom to combine to keep others from publishing is not."

- *Cohen v. Cowles Media Co.*, 501 U.S. 663 (1991). A newspaper breached a promise of confidentiality by publishing the identity of a source. The Court held the First Amendment does not exempt the press from state law that provides for damages under a promissory estoppel theory. The Court explained, "There can be little doubt that the Minnesota doctrine of promissory estoppel is a law of general applicability. It does not target or single out the press. Rather, insofar as we are advised, the doctrine is generally applicable to the daily transactions of all the citizens of Minnesota. The First Amendment does not forbid its application to the press."

CONFIDENTIAL SOURCES

The First Amendment does not exempt reporters from having to respond to relevant questions put to them in the course of a valid grand jury investigation or criminal trial [*Branzburg v. Hayes*, 408 U.S. 665 (1972) (holding, "the Constitution does not, as it never has, exempt the newsman from performing the citizen's normal duty of appearing and furnishing information relevant to the grand jury's task").

Also, the First Amendment does not exempt the press from valid searches of newsrooms pursuant to valid warrants [*Zurcher v. The*

Stanford Daily, 436 U.S. 547 (1978) (holding, "Properly administered, the preconditions for a warrant—probable cause, specificity with respect to the place to be searched and the things to be seized, and overall reasonableness—should afford sufficient protection against the harms that are assertedly threatened by warrants for searching newspaper offices")].

"Right-to-Reply" and "Must Carry" Laws

The government may require radio and television stations to allow reply time to answer personal attacks and political editorials, because broadcast frequencies are scarce and the right of viewers and listeners to access ideas and information is more important than the right of broadcasters (fairness doctrine) [*Red Lion Broadcasting Co. v. FCC*, 395 U.S. 367 (1969) (upholding Federal Communications Commission rules and regulations that required broadcasters to offer an individual personally attacked in broadcasts, or political opponents of those candidates who were endorsed by a station, a reasonable opportunity to respond over the licensee's facilities)].

However, the government may not require newspapers to give free reply space to political candidates whom they had attacked in their columns, because forcing newspapers to publish a reply intrudes on editorial discretion [*Miami Herald v. Tornillo*, 418 U.S. 241 (1974) (invalidating Florida's "right of reply" statute that granted a political candidate a right to equal space to answer criticism and attacks on his record by a newspaper)].

The government may require cable television companies to carry local broadcast stations ("must carry" laws) if intermediate scrutiny is satisfied [*Turner Broadcasting System, Inc. v. FCC*, 512 U.S. 622 (1994); *Turner Broadcasting System, Inc. v. FCC*, 520 U.S. 180 (1997) (upholding the "must carry" provisions of the Cable Television Consumer Protection and Competition Act of 1992, because the regulations were content neutral; they furthered important government interests in preserving free, over-the-air television broadcasts and promoting fair competition in television broadcasting; the government interests were unrelated to the suppression of free expression; and the regulations did not burden substantially more speech than necessary to further the government interests)].

ACCESS TO COURT PROCEEDINGS

Criminal Trials

The First Amendment provides the public and press a right of access to criminal trials, unless denial of access serves a compelling state interest and is narrowly tailored to serve that interest [*Richmond Newspapers v. Virginia*, 448 U.S. 555 (1980); *Globe Newspaper Co. v. Superior Court*, 457 U.S. 596 (1982) (invalidating a Massachusetts law that required trial judges to exclude the public and press from hearing the testimony of minor victims of sex crimes because although protecting minor victims from further trauma and embarrassment was a compelling state interest, requiring exclusion of the public and press in all cases was not narrowly tailored to serve that interest)].

Voir Dire Proceedings

The First Amendment provides the public and press a right of access to voir dire proceedings. The presumption of openness may be overcome only by an "overriding interest based on findings that closure is essential to preserve higher values and is narrowly tailored to serve that interest" [*Press-Enterprise Co. v. Superior Court*, 464 U.S. 501 (1984) (explaining, "public proceedings vindicate the concerns of the victims and the community in knowing that offenders are being brought to account for their criminal conduct by jurors fairly and openly selected")].

Pretrial Suppression Hearings

The Court has held the public and press may be excluded from a pretrial hearing to consider the suppression of a confession where the accused, the prosecutor, and the trial judge all agreed the proceeding should be closed to assure a fair trial [*Gannett Co., Inc. v. DePasquale*, 443 U.S. 368 (1979)].

ACCESS TO PRISONS

The First Amendment does not provide the press a right of access to prisons [*Pell v. Procunier*, 417 U.S. 817 (1974) (upholding a state prison regulation that prohibited "press and other media interviews with specific individual inmates," because "newsmen have no constitutional right of access to prisons or their inmates beyond that afforded the general public"); *Saxbe v. Washington Post Co.*, 417 U.S. 843 (1974) (upholding a Federal Bureau of Prisons policy statement prohibiting interviews between newsmen and individually designated inmates, because the case was "constitutionally indistinguishable from *Pell*")].

CHAPTER 22

Freedom of Religion

THE FIRST AMENDMENT CONTAINS TWO CLAUSES THAT PROTECT FREEDOM OF RELIGION: the establishment clause, and the free exercise clause. Both clauses apply to the states through the Fourteenth Amendment [*Everson v. Board of Education*, 330 U.S. 1 (1947) (establishment clause); *Cantwell v. Connecticut*, 310 U.S. 296 (1940) (free exercise clause)]. So freedom of religion is protected from state and local interference as well as from federal interference.

ESTABLISHMENT CLAUSE

Under the establishment clause, the government cannot pass laws that aid one religion or prefer one religion over another. The following describes discriminatory and nondiscriminatory law.

Discriminatory Law

The government may not discriminate among religious groups by preferring one religion or sect over others unless strict scrutiny is met (i.e., the law must be neccessary to achieve a compelling state interest).

- *Larson v. Valente*, 456 U.S. 228 (1982). Section 309.515, subdivision 1(b) of Minnesota's Charitable Solicitations Act provided only religious organizations that received more than half of their total contributions from members or affiliated organizations were exempt from the registration and reporting requirements of the Act. The Court invalidated the statute.

The Court explained, "The fifty per cent rule of § 309.515, subd. 1(b), clearly grants denominational preferences of the sort consistently and firmly deprecated in our precedents. Consequently, that rule must be invalidated unless it is justified by a compelling governmental interest, and unless it is closely fitted to further that interest."

The Court assumed, arguendo, the state had a compelling interest in "protecting its citizens from abusive practices in the solicitation of funds for charity." However, the statute was not closely fitted to further that interest. The Court explained, "Appellants' argument is based on three distinct premises: that members of a religious organization can and will exercise supervision and control over the organization's solicitation activities when membership contributions exceed fifty per cent; that membership control, assuming its existence, is an adequate safeguard against abusive solicitations of the public by the organization; and that the need for public disclosure rises in proportion with the percentage of nonmember contributions. Acceptance of all three of these premises is necessary to appellants' conclusion, but we find no substantial support for any of them in the record."

- *Board of Education of Kiryas Joel Village School District v. Grumet*, 512 U.S. 687 (1994). A New York statute created a special school district for a village inhabited exclusively by members of one religion. The district was created so children with disabilities could receive special education without having to attend a neighboring district's public schools with those outside their faith. The Court invalidated the statute. The Court explained the statute "singles out a particular religious sect for special treatment," and "it is clear that neutrality as among religions must be honored." The Court concluded, "the statute before us fails the test of neutrality."

Nondiscriminatory Law (*Lemon* Test)

If a law does not discriminate among religious groups and is religiously neutral on its face, then it must satisfy the three-part *Lemon* test: (1) it must have a secular purpose; (2) its primary effect must neither advance nor inhibit religion; and (3) it must not create excessive entanglement between government and religion (e.g., by requiring state monitoring) [*Lemon v. Kurtzman*, 403 U.S. 602 (1971)].

Religious Activities in Public Schools

- *McCollum v. Board of Education*, 333 U.S. 203 (1948). An Illinois school board permitted religious teachers to provide religious instruction in public school buildings during regular school hours once each week. Students who did not want religious instruction were required to leave their classrooms and go to some other place in the school building. The Court invalidated the program.

  The Court explained, "This is beyond all question a utilization of the tax-established and tax-supported public school system to aid religious groups to spread their faith. And it falls squarely under the ban of the First Amendment (made applicable to the States by the Fourteenth) as we interpreted it in *Everson v. Board of Education*." The Court concluded, "the First Amendment has erected a wall between Church and State which must be kept high and impregnable. Here not only are the State's tax-supported public school buildings used for the dissemination of religious doctrines. The State also affords sectarian groups an invaluable aid in that it helps to provide pupils for their religious classes through use of the State's compulsory public school machinery. This is not separation of Church and State."

- *Zorach v. Clauson*, 343 U.S. 306 (1952). New York City had a program that permitted its public schools, upon written request of the parents, to release students during the school day so they could leave the school buildings and school grounds and go to religious centers for religious instruction or devotional exercises at the expense of a duly constituted religious body. The program involved neither religious instruction in public schools nor the expenditure of public funds. The Court upheld the program.

  The Court explained, "There is a suggestion that the system involves the use of coercion to get public school students into religious classrooms. There is no evidence in the record before us that supports that conclusion. The present record indeed tells us that the school authorities are neutral in this regard and do no more than release students whose parents so request." The Court distinguished *McCollum* because, "In the *McCollum* case the classrooms were used for religious instruction and the force of the public school was used to promote that instruction. Here, as we have said, the public schools do no more than accommodate their schedules to a program of outside religious instruction."

- *Engel v. Vitale*, 370 U.S. 421 (1962). The state of New York adopted a program in which the following prayer was to be said aloud in public schools at the beginning of each school day: "Almighty God, we acknowledge our dependence upon Thee, and we beg Thy blessings upon us, our parents, our teachers and our Country." Observance of the prayer by students was voluntary. The Court invalidated the program. The Court explained, "There can be no doubt that New York's state prayer program officially establishes the religious beliefs embodied in the Regents' prayer."

- *Abington School District v. Schempp*, 374 U.S. 203 (1963). A Pennsylvania statute provided, "At least ten verses from the Holy Bible shall be read, without comment, at the opening of each public school on each school day. Any child shall be excused from such Bible reading, or attending such Bible reading, upon the written request of his parent or guardian." The exercises were held in the school buildings under the supervision and with the participation of teachers employed in those schools. The Board of School Commissioners of Baltimore City, Maryland, adopted a similar rule pursuant to statutory authority. The Court invalidated the laws.

  The Court explained, "It certainly may be said that the Bible is worthy of study for its literary and historic qualities. Nothing we have said here indicates that such study of the Bible or of religion, when presented objectively as part of a secular program of education, may not be effected consistently with the First Amendment. But the exercises here do not fall into those categories. They are religious exercises, required by the States in violation of the command of the First Amendment that the Government maintain strict neutrality, neither aiding nor opposing religion."

- *Epperson v. Arkansas*, 393 U.S. 97 (1968). Arkansas's "antievolution" statute made it unlawful for a teacher in any state-supported school or university "to teach the theory or doctrine that mankind ascended or descended from a lower order of animals," or "to adopt or use in any such institution a textbook that teaches" this theory. The Court invalidated the statute.

The Court explained, "Arkansas' law cannot be defended as an act of religious neutrality. Arkansas did not seek to excise from the curricula of its schools and universities all discussion of the origin of man. The law's effort was confined to an attempt to blot out a particular theory because of its supposed conflict with the Biblical account, literally read. Plainly, the law is contrary to the mandate of the First, and in violation of the Fourteenth, Amendment to the Constitution."

- *Stone v. Graham*, 449 U.S. 39 (1980). A Kentucky statute required the posting of a copy of the Ten Commandments, purchased with private contributions, on the wall of each public school classroom in the state. The Court invalidated the statute. The Court explained, "The pre-eminent purpose for posting the Ten Commandments on schoolroom walls is plainly religious in nature. The Ten Commandments are undeniably a sacred text in the Jewish and Christian faiths, and no legislative recitation of a supposed secular purpose can blind us to that fact."

- *Widmar v. Vincent*, 454 U.S. 263 (1981). The University of Missouri at Kansas City, a state university, had a regulation prohibiting the use of buildings or grounds "for purposes of religious worship or religious teaching." The university made its facilities generally available for the activities of registered student groups. However, the university closed its facilities, based on the regulation, to a registered student group seeking to use the facilities for religious worship and religious discussion. The Court invalidated the regulation.

The Court explained an "open forum" policy, opening facilities to religious groups, would not violate the establishment clause. For example, an open forum policy would have a secular purpose in providing "a forum in which students can exchange ideas." Also, "in the absence of empirical evidence that religious groups will dominate UMKC's open forum, we agree with the Court of Appeals that the advancement of religion would not be the forum's primary effect." Finally, an open forum policy would create less entanglement with religion than excluding "religious worship" and "religious speech" because excluding such activities would require "a continuing need to monitor group meetings to ensure compliance with the rule." The Court noted, "any religious benefits of an open forum at UMKC would be 'incidental' within the meaning of our cases."

- *Larkin v. Grendel's Den, Inc,* 459 U.S. 116 (1982). A Massachusetts statute gave schools and churches the power to prevent issuance of liquor licenses for premises within a 500-foot radius of the church or school. The Court invalidated the statute. The Court explained the purpose of the statute was to protect "spiritual, cultural, and educational centers from the hurly-burly associated with liquor outlets. There can be little doubt that this embraces valid secular legislative purposes."

  However, "The churches' power under the statute is standardless, calling for no reasons, findings, or reasoned conclusions. That power may therefore be used by churches to promote goals beyond insulating the church from undesirable neighbors; it could be employed for explicitly religious goals, for example, favoring liquor licenses for members of that congregation or adherents of that faith." Thus, "It does not strain our prior holdings to say that the statute can be seen as having a 'primary' and 'principal' effect of advancing religion." Finally, the statute "enmeshes churches in the processes of government and creates the danger of political fragmentation and divisiveness on religious lines. Ordinary human experience and a long line of cases teach that few entanglements could be more offensive to the spirit of the Constitution."

- *Wallace v. Jaffree,* 472 U.S. 38 (1985). Alabama statute section 16-1-20.1 authorized a one-minute period of silence in all public schools "for meditation or voluntary prayer." The Court invalidated the statute. The Court explained, "the enactment of § 16-1-20.1 was not motivated by any clearly secular purpose—indeed, the statute had no secular purpose. The sponsor of the bill that became § 16-1-20.1, Senator Donald Holmes, inserted into the legislative record—apparently without dissent—a statement indicating that the legislation was an 'effort to return voluntary prayer' to the public schools. Later Senator Holmes confirmed this purpose before the District Court. In response to the question whether he had any purpose for the legislation other than returning voluntary prayer to public schools, he stated: 'No, I did not have no other purpose in mind.' The State did not present evidence of any secular purpose."

- *Edwards v. Aguillard,* 482 U.S. 578 (1987). Louisiana's Creationism Act prohibited the teaching of the theory of evolution in public elementary and secondary schools unless accompanied by instruction in the theory of "creation science." The Court invalidated the Act. The Court explained, "In this case, the purpose of the Creationism Act was to restructure the science curriculum to conform with a particular religious viewpoint. Out of many possible science subjects taught in the public schools, the legislature chose to affect the teaching of the one scientific theory that historically has been opposed by certain religious sects. As in *Epperson*, the legislature passed the Act to give preference to those religious groups which have as one of their tenets the creation of humankind by a divine creator." The Court concluded, "Because the primary purpose of the Creationism Act is to advance a particular religious belief, the Act endorses religion in violation of the First Amendment."

• *Board of Education of Westside Community Schools v. Mergens*, 496 U.S. 226 (1990) The federal Equal Access Act prohibited public secondary schools that received federal assistance and maintained a "limited open forum" from denying "equal access" to students who wished to meet within the forum on the basis of the "religious, political, philosophical, or other content" of the speech at such meetings. The Court upheld the Act.

Justice O'Connor, writing for the plurality, explained, "We think the logic of *Widmar* applies with equal force to the Equal Access Act. As an initial matter, the Act's prohibition of discrimination on the basis of 'political, philosophical, or other' speech as well as religious speech is a sufficient basis for meeting the secular purpose prong of the *Lemon* test." Second, "To the extent that a religious club is merely one of many different student-initiated voluntary clubs, students should perceive no message of government endorsement of religion. Thus, we conclude that the Act does not, at least on its face and as applied to Westside, have the primary effect of advancing religion." Finally, the Act would not create excessive entanglement between government and religion because under the Act "faculty monitors may not participate in any religious meetings, and nonschool persons may not direct, control, or regularly attend activities of student groups."

Justice O'Connor added, "as the Court noted in *Widmar*, a denial of equal access to religious speech might well create greater entanglement problems in the form of invasive monitoring to prevent religious speech at meetings at which such speech might occur."

- *Lee v. Weisman*, 505 U.S. 577 (1992). The city of Providence, Rhode Island, had a policy that permitted its public high school and middle school principals to invite members of the clergy to offer invocation and benediction prayers as part of the schools' formal graduation ceremonies. The Court invalidated the policy.

  The Court explained, "The government involvement with religious activity in this case is pervasive, to the point of creating a state-sponsored and state-directed religious exercise in a public school. Conducting this formal religious observance conflicts with settled rules pertaining to prayer exercises for students, and that suffices to determine the question before us." The Court noted, "the fact that attendance at the graduation ceremonies is voluntary in a legal sense does not save the religious exercise," because "to say a teenage student has a real choice not to attend her high school graduation is formalistic in the extreme."

- *Lamb's Chapel v. Center Moriches Union Free School District*, 508 U.S. 384 (1993). A school board (District) issued regulations allowing social, civic, and recreational uses of its schools (Rule 10), but prohibiting use by any group for religious purposes (Rule 7). The District then refused two requests by an evangelical church and its pastor (Church) to use school facilities for a religious-oriented film series on family values and child rearing on the ground that the film series appeared to be church related. The Court held permitting District property to be used to exhibit the film series would not have been an establishment of religion.

  The Court explained, "The showing of this film series would not have been during school hours, would not have been sponsored by the school, and would have been open to the public, not just to church members." The Court concluded, "As in *Widmar*, permitting District property to be used to exhibit the film series involved in this case would not have been an establishment of religion under the three-part test articulated in *Lemon v. Kurtzman*: The challenged governmental action has a secular purpose, does not have the principal or primary effect of advancing or inhibiting religion, and does not foster an excessive entanglement with religion."

- *Rosenberger v. Rector and Visitors of the University of Virginia*, 515 U.S. 819 (1995). A state university adopted a program that authorized payment to outside contractors for the printing costs of a variety of student publications. The university withheld authorization for payments on behalf of a student group because their student paper "primarily promotes or manifests a particular belief in or about a deity or an ultimate reality." The Court held unconstitutional the university's refusal to authorize payment of printing costs.

   The Court explained, "The governmental program here is neutral toward religion. There is no suggestion that the University created it to advance religion or adopted some ingenious device with the purpose of aiding a religious cause." Moreover, "By paying outside printers, the University in fact attains a further degree of separation from the student publication, for it avoids the duties of supervision, escapes the costs of upkeep, repair, and replacement attributable to student use, and has a clear record of costs."

- *Santa Fe Independent School District v. Doe*, 530 U.S. 290 (2000). Before the litigation, a student elected as Santa Fe High School's student council chaplain delivered a prayer over the public address system before each home varsity football game. When the practice was challenged in court, the school district adopted a policy authorizing two elections. The first election would determine whether "invocations" should be delivered at games, and the second election would select the spokesperson to deliver them. The students held elections authorizing such prayers and selecting a spokesperson. The Court invalidated the district's policy.

   The district claimed the secular purposes of the policy were to "foster free expression of private persons…as well [as to] solemnize sporting events, promote good sportsmanship and student safety, and establish an appropriate environment for competition." However, the Court explained, "the District's approval of only one specific kind of message, an 'invocation,' is not necessary to further any of these purposes. Additionally, the fact that only one student is permitted to give a content-limited message suggests that this policy does little to 'foster free expression.' Furthermore, regardless of whether one considers a sporting event an appropriate occasion for solemnity, the use of an invocation to foster such solemnity is impermissible when, in actuality, it constitutes prayer sponsored by the school." The Court concluded, "The policy is invalid on its face because it establishes an improper majoritarian election on religion, and unquestionably has the purpose and creates the perception of encouraging the delivery of prayer at a series of important school events."

Public Aid to Sectarian Educational Institutions

- *Everson v. Board of Education*, 330 U.S. 1 (1947). Acting under a New Jersey statute, a township board of education authorized the reimbursement of parents for fares paid for the transportation by public carrier of children attending public and Catholic schools. The Court upheld the statute. The Court explained, "The State contributes no money to the schools. It does not support them. Its legislation, as applied, does no more than provide a general program to help parents get their children, regardless of their religion, safely and expeditiously to and from accredited schools. The First Amendment has erected a wall between church and state. That wall must be kept high and impregnable. We could not approve the slightest breach. New Jersey has not breached it here."

- *Board of Education v. Allen*, 392 U.S. 236 (1968). New York statute section 701 required local public school authorities to lend textbooks free of charge to all students in grades 7 through 12, including students attending private parochial schools. The Court upheld the statute. The Court explained, "The express purpose of § 701 was stated by the New York Legislature to be furtherance of the educational opportunities available to the young. Appellants have shown us nothing about the necessary effects of the statute that is contrary to its stated purpose. The law merely makes available to all children the benefits of a general program to lend school books free of charge. Books are furnished at the request of the pupil and ownership remains, at least technically, in the State. Thus no funds or books are furnished to parochial schools, and the financial benefit is to parents and children, not to schools." Moreover, "the language of § 701 does not authorize the loan of religious books, and the State claims no right to distribute religious literature."

- *Lemon v. Kurtzman*, 403 U.S. 602 (1971). A Pennsylvania statute provided financial support to nonpublic elementary and secondary schools by way of reimbursement for the cost of teachers' salaries, textbooks, and instructional materials in specified secular subjects. Under a Rhode Island statute, the state paid directly to teachers of secular subjects in nonpublic elementary schools a supplement of 15 percent of their annual salary. Under each statute, state aid was given to church-related educational institutions. The Court invalidated both statutes.

   The Court explained, "Inquiry into the legislative purposes of the Pennsylvania and Rhode Island statutes affords no basis for a conclusion that the legislative intent was to advance religion. On the contrary, the statutes themselves clearly state that they are intended to enhance the quality of the secular education in all schools covered by the compulsory attendance laws." However, "the cumulative impact of the entire relationship arising under the statutes in each State involves excessive entanglement between government and religion." Pervasive restrictions and comprehensive, discriminating, and continuing state surveillance would be required to "ensure that teachers play a strictly nonideological role." The Court noted, "Unlike a book, a teacher cannot be inspected once so as to determine the extent and intent of his or her personal beliefs and subjective acceptance of the limitations imposed by the First Amendment."

- *Committee for Public Education v. Nyquist*, 413 U.S. 756 (1973). A New York law established three financial aid programs for nonpublic elementary and secondary schools: (1) direct money grants from the state to nonpublic schools for the maintenance and repair of school facilities and equipment; (2) tuition reimbursements to parents of children attending elementary or secondary nonpublic schools; and (3) tax relief to those who failed to qualify for tuition reimbursement. The Court invalidated the law.

   The Court explained the law had a secular purpose because each program was "adequately supported by legitimate, nonsectarian state interests." However, the Court invalidated the direct money grants for maintenance and repair because, "No attempt is made to restrict payments to those expenditures related to the upkeep of facilities used exclusively for secular purposes, nor do we think it possible within the context of these religion-oriented institutions to impose such restrictions." Thus, "Absent appropriate restrictions on expenditures for these and similar purposes, it simply cannot be denied that this section has a primary effect that advances religion in that it subsidizes directly the religious activities of sectarian elementary and secondary schools."

The Court explained the tuition reimbursement program "also fails the 'effect' test, for much the same reasons that govern its maintenance and repair grants. The state program is designed to allow direct, unrestricted grants of $50 to $100 per child (but no more than 50% of tuition actually paid) as reimbursement to parents in low-income brackets who send their children to nonpublic schools, the bulk of which is concededly sectarian in orientation."

Finally, the Court invalidated the tax relief program because, "In practical terms there would appear to be little difference, for purposes of determining whether such aid has the effect of advancing religion, between the tax benefit allowed here and the tuition grant allowed under § 2. The qualifying parent under either program receives the same form of encouragement and reward for sending his children to nonpublic schools. The only difference is that one parent receives an actual cash payment while the other is allowed to reduce by an arbitrary amount the sum he would otherwise be obliged to pay over to the State."

- *Tilton v. Richardson*, 403 U.S. 672 (1971). The Higher Education Facilities Act of 1963 provided federal construction grants for college and university facilities, excluding "any facility used or to be used for sectarian instruction or as a place for religious worship." The United States retained a twenty-year interest in any facility constructed with funds under the Act, opening the facility to use for any purpose at the end of that period.

The Court upheld the construction grants. The Court explained the grants reflected a secular purpose in accommodating the "rapidly growing numbers of youth who aspire to a higher education." Also, the grants did not have the primary effect of advancing or inhibiting religion because "The Act itself was carefully drafted to ensure that the federally subsidized facilities would be devoted to the secular and not the religious function of the recipient institutions." Finally, there was no excessive government entanglement with religion because "inspection as may be necessary to ascertain that the facilities are devoted to secular education is minimal and indeed hardly more than the inspections that States impose over all private schools within the reach of compulsory education laws. The entanglement between church and state is also lessened here by the nonideological character of the aid that the Government provides."

However, the Court invalidated the twenty-year interest period because "If, at the end of 20 years, the building is, for example, converted into a chapel or otherwise used to promote religious interests, the original federal grant will in part have the effect of advancing religion."

- *Roemer v. Board of Public Works of Maryland*, 426 U.S. 736 (1976). Maryland enacted a statute that authorized payment of state funds to any private institution of higher learning within the state that refrained from awarding "only seminarian or theological degrees." The Court upheld the statute. The Court explained, "the purpose of Maryland's aid program is the secular one of supporting private higher education generally, as an economic alternative to a wholly public system." Also, the statute did not have the primary effect of advancing religion because the colleges were not "pervasively sectarian," and, "The statute in terms forbids the use of funds for "sectarian purposes."

  Finally, the statute did not create excessive entanglement between government and religion because the colleges performed "essentially secular educational functions." So, "There is no danger, or at least only a substantially reduced danger, that an ostensibly secular activity—the study of biology, the learning of a foreign language, an athletic event—will actually be infused with religious content or significance. The need for close surveillance of purportedly secular activities is correspondingly reduced."

- *Committee for Public Education and Religious Liberty v. Regan*, 444 U.S. 646 (1980). A New York statute authorized the use of public funds to reimburse church-sponsored and secular nonpublic schools for performing various testing and reporting services mandated by state law. The Court upheld the statute. The Court explained, "there is clearly a secular purpose behind the legislative enactment: To provide educational opportunity of a quality which will prepare New York citizens for the challenges of American life in the last decades of the twentieth century." Also, there was "no substantial risk that the examinations could be used for religious educational purposes." So, "Reimbursement for the costs of so complying with state law, therefore, has primarily a secular, rather than a religious, purpose and effect."

Finally, "The reimbursement process, furthermore, is straight forward and susceptible to the routinization that characterizes most reimbursement schemes. On its face, therefore, the New York plan suggests no excessive entanglement, and we are not prepared to read into the plan as an inevitability the bad faith upon which any future excessive entanglement would be predicated."

- *Mueller v. Allen*, 463 U.S. 388 (1983). A Minnesota statute allowed state taxpayers to deduct expenses incurred in providing "tuition, textbooks and transportation" for their children attending a public or private elementary or secondary school. The Court upheld the statute. The Court explained, "An educated populace is essential to the political and economic health of any community, and a State's efforts to assist parents in meeting the rising cost of educational expenses plainly serves this secular purpose of ensuring that the State's citizenry is well educated."

Also, the statute did not have the primary effect of advancing religion because "the deduction is available for educational expenses incurred by all parents, including those whose children attend public schools and those whose children attend nonsectarian private schools or sectarian private schools." The Court noted, "Just as in *Widmar v. Vincent*, where we concluded that the State's provision of a forum neutrally 'available to a broad class of nonreligious as well as religious speakers' does not 'confer any imprimatur of state approval,' so here: 'the provision of benefits to so broad a spectrum of groups is an important index of secular effect.'"

Finally, "Turning to the third part of the *Lemon* inquiry, we have no difficulty in concluding that the Minnesota statute does not 'excessively entangle' the State in religion. The only plausible source of the 'comprehensive, discriminating, and continuing state surveillance' necessary to run afoul of this standard would lie in the fact that state officials must determine whether particular textbooks qualify for a deduction." However, "Making decisions such as this does not differ substantially from making the types of decisions approved in earlier opinions of this Court."

- *Witters v. Washington Department of Services for the Blind*, 474 U.S. 481 (1986). A Washington statute authorized the Commission for the Blind to "[provide] for special education and/or training in the professions, business or trades" so as to "assist visually handicapped persons to overcome vocational handicaps and to obtain the maximum degree of self-support and self-care." Witters, a blind person studying at a Christian college and seeking to become a pastor, missionary, or youth director, applied to the commission for vocational rehabilitation services under the statute. The Court held extending aid under the vocational rehabilitation program to finance Witter's training at the Christian college would not violate the establishment clause.

  The Court explained, "all parties concede the unmistakably secular purpose of the Washington program. That program was designed to promote the well-being of the visually handicapped through the provision of vocational rehabilitation services, and no more than a minuscule amount of the aid awarded under the program is likely to flow to religious education."

  Also, the program did not have the primary effect of advancing religion because "vocational assistance provided under the Washington program is paid directly to the student, who transmits it to the educational institution of his or her choice. Any aid provided under Washington's program that ultimately flows to religious institutions does so only as a result of the genuinely independent and private choices of aid recipients. Washington's program is made available generally without regard to the sectarian-nonsectarian, or public-nonpublic nature of the institution benefited."

- *Zobrest v. Catalina Foothills School District*, 509 U.S. 1 (1993). A public school district refused to provide a sign-language interpreter for a deaf student at a Roman Catholic high school. The Court held the establishment clause did not bar the school district from providing the interpreter. The Court explained, "The service at issue in this case is part of a general government program that distributes benefits neutrally to any child qualifying as 'handicapped' under the IDEA [Individuals with Disabilities Act], without regard to the sectarian-nonsectarian, or public-nonpublic nature of the school the child attends. By according parents freedom to select a school of their choice, the statute ensures that a government-paid interpreter will be present in a sectarian school only as a result of the private decision of individual parents." Also, "Nothing in this record suggests that a sign-language interpreter would do more than accurately interpret whatever material is presented to the class as a whole."

- *Agostini v. Felton*, 521 U.S. 203 (1997). The city of New York implemented a program, under Title I of the Elementary and Secondary Education Act of 1965, in which the city sent public school teachers into parochial schools during regular school hours to provide remedial education to disadvantaged children. The Court upheld the program. The Court explained the program did not have the primary effect of advancing religion because "there is no reason to presume that, simply because she enters a parochial school classroom, a full-time public employee such as a Title I teacher will depart from her assigned duties and instructions and embark on religious indoctrination, any more than there was a reason in *Zobrest* to think an interpreter would inculcate religion by altering her translation of classroom lectures." Also, "The services are available to all children who meet the Act's eligibility requirements, no matter what their religious beliefs or where they go to school."

  The Court treated the "entanglement" factor as an aspect of the inquiry into the program's effect. The Court then explained the program did not create excessive entanglement between government and religion because "after *Zobrest* we no longer presume that public employees will inculcate religion simply because they happen to be in a sectarian environment. Since we have abandoned the assumption that properly instructed public employees will fail to discharge their duties faithfully, we must also discard the assumption that pervasive monitoring of Title I teachers is required."

  The Court then overruled *Aguilar v. Felton* [473 U.S. 402 (1985)], and partially overruled *Grand Rapids School District v. Ball* [473 U.S. 373 (1985)], both of which invalidated similar programs.

- *Mitchell v. Helms*, 530 U.S. 793 (2000). Chapter 2 of the Education Consolidation and Improvement Act of 1981 distributed federal funds through state educational agencies to local educational agencies. The local agencies in turn loaned educational materials and equipment such as library and media materials and computer software and hardware to public and private elementary and secondary schools to implement "secular, neutral, and nonideological" programs. The Court upheld Chapter 2, without a majority opinion.

  In a plurality opinion, Justice Thomas explained, "we see no basis for concluding that Jefferson Parish's Chapter 2 program 'has the effect of advancing religion.' Chapter 2 does not result in governmental indoctrination, because it determines eligibility for aid neutrally, allocates that aid based on the private choices of the parents of schoolchildren, and does not provide aid that has an impermissible content. Nor does Chapter 2 define its recipients by reference to religion."

  The District Court held Chapter 2 had a secular purpose and did not create an excessive entanglement, and those holdings were not challenged. The Court then overruled *Meek v. Pittenger* [421 U.S. 349 (1975)] and *Wolman v. Walter* [433 U.S. 229 (1977)], both of which invalidated similar programs.

- *Zelman v. Simmons-Harris*, 536 U.S. 639 (2002). Ohio enacted a program that provided tuition aid for students to attend participating public or private schools of their parent's choosing. The Court upheld the program. The Court explained "There is no dispute that the program challenged here was enacted for the valid secular purpose of providing educational assistance to poor children in a demonstrably failing public school system." Also, the program did not have the primary effect of advancing or inhibiting religion because, "We believe that the program challenged here is a program of true private choice, consistent with *Mueller*, *Witters*, and *Zobrest*, and thus constitutional. As was true in those cases, the Ohio program is neutral in all respects toward religion. It is part of a general and multifaceted undertaking by the State of Ohio to provide educational opportunities to the children of a failed school district."

Public Aid to Religious Institutions

- *Bradfield v. Roberts*, 175 U.S. 291 (1899). Providence Hospital was a religiously affiliated hospital incorporated by an act of Congress. Congress appropriated $30,000 to the hospital for the construction of hospital buildings. The Court upheld the appropriation. The Court explained, "the allegation is that the church exercises great and perhaps controlling influence over the management of the hospital." However, "There is no allegation that its hospital work is confined to members of that church or that in its management the hospital has been conducted so as to violate its charter in the smallest degree. It is simply the case of a secular corporation being managed by people who hold to the doctrines of the Roman Catholic Church, but who nevertheless are managing the corporation according to the law under which it exists. The charter itself does not limit the exercise of its corporate powers to the members of any particular religious denomination, but on the contrary those powers are to be exercised in favor of any one seeking the ministrations of that kind of an institution."

- *Bowen v. Kendrick*, 487 U.S. 589 (1988). The Adolescent Family Life Act (AFLA) authorized federal grants to public or nonprofit private organizations or agencies for services and research in the area of premarital adolescent sexual relations and pregnancy. The Court upheld the Act. The Court explained, "it is clear from the face of the statute that the AFLA was motivated primarily, if not entirely, by a legitimate secular purpose—the elimination or reduction of social and economic problems caused by teenage sexuality, pregnancy, and parenthood."

  The Act allowed religious institutions to participate as recipients of federal funds. However, the Act did not have the primary effect of advancing religion because "a fairly wide spectrum of organizations is eligible to apply for and receive funding under the Act, and nothing on the face of the Act suggests it is anything but neutral with respect to the grantee's status as a sectarian or purely secular institution." Also, "The facially neutral projects authorized by the AFLA—including pregnancy testing, adoption counseling and referral services, prenatal and postnatal care, educational services, residential care, child care, consumer education, etc.—are not themselves 'specifically religious activities,' and they are not converted into such activities by the fact that they are carried out by organizations with religious affiliations."

The government would have to review the educational materials that a grantee proposed to use, and visit the clinics or offices where AFLA programs were being carried out. But, "in our view, this type of grant monitoring does not amount to 'excessive entanglement,' at least in the context of a statute authorizing grants to religiously affiliated organizations that are not necessarily 'pervasively sectarian.'"

Sunday Closing Laws

- *McGowan v. Maryland*, 366 U.S. 420 (1961). A Maryland statute (Sunday Closing Law) prohibited the sale on Sunday of all merchandise except the retail sale of tobacco products, confectioneries, milk, bread, fruit, gasoline, oils, greases, drugs, medicines, newspapers, and periodicals. The Court upheld the statute. The Court explained, "despite the strongly religious origin of these laws, beginning before the eighteenth century, nonreligious arguments for Sunday closing began to be heard more distinctly and the statutes began to lose some of their totally religious flavor." The Court concluded, "the statutes' present purpose and effect is not to aid religion but to set aside a day of rest and recreation."

- *Estate of Thornton v. Caldor*, 472 U.S. 703 (1985). A Connecticut statute provided, "No person who states that a particular day of the week is observed as his Sabbath may be required by his employer to work on such day. An employee's refusal to work on his Sabbath shall not constitute grounds for his dismissal." The Court invalidated the statute. The Court explained, "In essence, the Connecticut statute imposes on employers and employees an absolute duty to conform their business practices to the particular religious practices of the employee by enforcing observance of the Sabbath the employee unilaterally designates." The Court concluded, "the statute goes beyond having an incidental or remote effect of advancing religion. The statute has a primary effect that impermissibly advances a particular religious practice."

Religious Displays and Ceremonies

- *Marsh v. Chambers*, 463 U.S. 783 (1983). The Nebraska legislature began each of its sessions with a prayer by a chaplain paid by the state with the legislature's approval. The Court upheld the chaplaincy practice. The Court explained, "In light of the unambiguous and unbroken history of more than 200 years, there can be no doubt that the practice of opening legislative sessions with prayer has become part of the fabric of our society. To invoke Divine guidance on a public body entrusted with making the laws is not, in these circumstances, an 'establishment' of religion or a step toward establishment; it is simply a tolerable acknowledgment of beliefs widely held among the people of this country." Moreover, "The content of the prayer is not of concern to judges where, as here, there is no indication that the prayer opportunity has been exploited to proselytize or advance any one, or to disparage any other, faith or belief."

- *Lynch v. Donnelly*, 465 U.S. 668 (1984). The city of Pawtucket, Rhode Island, annually erected a Christmas display in a park owned by a nonprofit organization and located in the heart of the city's shopping district. The display included a Santa Claus house, a Christmas tree, a banner that read "SEASONS GREETINGS," and a crèche or Nativity scene. The Court upheld the display.

  The Court explained, "The display is sponsored by the city to celebrate the Holiday and to depict the origins of that Holiday. These are legitimate secular purposes." Moreover, the display did not have the primary effect of advancing religion because "whatever benefit there is to one faith or religion or to all religions, is indirect, remote, and incidental; display of the crèche is no more an advancement or endorsement of religion than the Congressional and Executive recognition of the origins of the Holiday itself as 'Christ's Mass,' or the exhibition of literally hundreds of religious paintings in governmentally supported museums."

  Finally, the display did not create excessive entanglement between religion and the government because, "There is nothing here, of course, like the 'comprehensive, discriminating, and continuing state surveillance' or the 'enduring entanglement' present in *Lemon*."

- *County of Allegheny v. American Civil Liberties Union*, 492 U.S. 573 (1989). The government of Allegheny County, Pennsylvania, permitted a crèche to be placed on the Grand Staircase of the Allegheny County Courthouse, and a Chanukah menorah to be placed just outside the City-County Building, next to a Christmas tree and a sign saluting liberty. The Court invalidated the display of a crèche but upheld the display of a menorah.

  The Court explained the crèche was by itself, so "unlike in *Lynch*, nothing in the context of the display detracts from the crèche's religious message. The *Lynch* display comprised a series of figures and objects, each group of which had its own focal point. Santa's house and his reindeer were objects of attention separate from the crèche, and had their specific visual story to tell." Here, in contrast "the crèche stands alone: it is the single element of the display on the Grand Staircase." The Court concluded, "In sum, *Lynch* teaches that government may celebrate Christmas in some manner and form, but not in a way that endorses Christian doctrine. Here, Allegheny County has transgressed this line. It has chosen to celebrate Christmas in a way that has the effect of endorsing a patently Christian message."

  Justice Blackmun explained in a separate opinion the menorah was accompanied by other religious and secular symbols. Thus, "the relevant question for Establishment Clause purposes is whether the combined display of the tree, the sign, and the menorah has the effect of endorsing both Christian and Jewish faiths, or rather simply recognizes that both Christmas and Chanukah are part of the same winter-holiday season, which has attained a secular status in our society. Of the two interpretations of this particular display, the latter seems far more plausible and is also in line with *Lynch*."

- *Van Orden v. Perry*, 545 U.S. 677 (2005). Among twenty-one historical markers and seventeen monuments surrounding the Texas State Capitol was a 6-foot-high monolith inscribed with the Ten Commandments. The Court, without a majority opinion, held the monolith did not violate the establishment clause. Chief Justice Rehnquist explained in a plurality opinion, "Such acknowledgments of the role played by the Ten Commandments in our Nation's heritage are common throughout America. We need only look within our own Courtroom. Since 1935, Moses has stood, holding two tablets that reveal portions of the Ten Commandments written in Hebrew, among other lawgivers in the south frieze." Also, "Our opinions, like our building, have recognized the role the Decalogue plays in America's heritage." Finally, "The placement of the Ten Commandments monument on the Texas State Capitol grounds is a far more passive use of those texts than was the case in Stone [v. Graham], where the text confronted elementary school students every day. Indeed, Van Orden, the petitioner here, apparently walked by the monument for a number of years before bringing this lawsuit."

The Chief Justice concluded, "Texas has treated its Capitol grounds monuments as representing the several strands in the State's political and legal history. The inclusion of the Ten Commandments monument in this group has a dual significance, partaking of both religion and government. We cannot say that Texas' display of this monument violates the Establishment Clause of the First Amendment."

- *McCreary County v. ACLU*, 545 U.S. 844 (2005). Two Kentucky counties posted a version of the Ten Commandments in their courthouses. When the American Civil Liberties Union (ACLU) sued, alleging establishment clause violations, each county adopted a resolution calling for a more extensive exhibit meant to show the Commandments were Kentucky's "precedent legal code." The Court invalidated the displays.

Regarding the first display, the Court explained, "The display in *Stone* [v. Graham] had no context that might have indicated an object beyond the religious character of the text, and the Counties' solo exhibit here did nothing more to counter the sectarian implication than the postings at issue in *Stone*. Actually, the posting by the Counties lacked even the *Stone* display's implausible disclaimer that the Commandments were set out to show their effect on the civil law."

When the counties were sued they changed the exhibits. However, "The [second] display's unstinting focus was on religious passages, showing that the Counties were posting the Commandments precisely because of their sectarian content. That demonstration of the government's objective was enhanced by serial religious references and the accompanying resolution's claim about the embodiment of ethics in Christ."

When the counties changed lawyers, they mounted a third display. However, "the sectarian spirit of the common resolution found enhanced expression in the third display, which quoted more of the purely religious language of the Commandments than the first two displays had done." The Court concluded, "No reasonable observer could swallow the claim that the Counties had cast off the objective so unmistakable in the earlier displays."

Tax Exemptions

- *Walz v. Tax Commission*, 397 U.S. 664 (1970). A New York statute provided tax exemptions for property used exclusively for religious, educational, or charitable purposes. The Court upheld the statute. The Court explained, "The legislative purpose of the property tax exemption is neither the advancement nor the inhibition of religion; it is neither sponsorship nor hostility. New York, in common with the other States, has determined that certain entities that exist in a harmonious relationship to the community at large, and that foster its 'moral or mental improvement,' should not be inhibited in their activities by property taxation or the hazard of loss of those properties for nonpayment of taxes. It has not singled out one particular church or religious group or even churches as such; rather, it has granted exemption to all houses of religious worship within a broad class of property owned by nonprofit, quasi-public corporations which include hospitals, libraries, playgrounds, scientific, professional, historical, and patriotic groups."

  Also, the tax exemption did not create excessive entanglement between government and religion. Rather, eliminating the exemption "would tend to expand the involvement of government by giving rise to tax valuation of church property, tax liens, tax foreclosures, and the direct confrontations and conflicts that follow in the train of those legal processes."

- *Texas Monthly, Inc. v. Bullock*, 489 U.S. 1 (1989). A Texas statute exempted from sales taxes "[p]eriodicals that are published or distributed by a religious faith and that consist wholly of writings promulgating the teaching of the faith and books that consist wholly of writings sacred to a religious faith." The Court invalidated the statute. The Court explained that unlike the tax exemptions in *Walz* that benefited a wide variety of religious and nonreligious groups, the Texas sales tax exemption was available only to religious groups and lacked a secular purpose. The tax exemption thus effectively endorsed religious belief. The Court noted, "If the State chose to subsidize, by means of a tax exemption, all groups that contributed to the community's cultural, intellectual, and moral betterment, then the exemption for religious publications could be retained, provided that the exemption swept as widely as the property tax exemption we upheld in *Walz*."

Exemptions from Military Service

- *Gillette v. United States*, 401 U.S. 437 (1971). Section 6(j) of the Military Selective Service Act of 1967 provided no person shall be subject to "service in the armed forces of the United States who, by reason of religious training and belief, is conscientiously opposed to participation in war in any form." Two persons conscientiously objected to participation in the Vietnam conflict as an "unjust" war; one sought exemption from the draft, and the other sought discharge from the Army. Their requests were denied. The Court upheld the Act.

  As a preliminary matter, the Court held that "Congress intended to exempt persons who oppose participating in all war—'participation in war in any form'—and that persons who object solely to participation in a particular war are not within the purview of the exempting section, even though the latter objection may have such roots in a claimant's conscience and personality that it is 'religious' in character."

  Regarding the establishment clause issue, the Court first explained the petitioners' position: "petitioners' contention is that the special statutory status accorded conscientious objection to all war, but not objection to a particular war, works a de facto discrimination among religions. This happens, say petitioners, because some religious faiths themselves distinguish between personal participation in 'just' and in 'unjust' wars, commending the former and forbidding the latter, and therefore adherents of some religious faiths—and individuals whose personal beliefs of a religious nature include the distinction—cannot object to all wars consistently with what is regarded as the true imperative of conscience."

However, the Court explained, "Section 6 (j) serves a number of valid purposes having nothing to do with a design to foster or favor any sect, religion, or cluster of religions. There are considerations of a pragmatic nature, such as the hopelessness of converting a sincere conscientious objector into an effective fighting man." Thus, "we conclude not only that the affirmative purposes underlying § 6 (j) are neutral and secular, but also that valid neutral reasons exist for limiting the exemption to objectors to all war, and that the section therefore cannot be said to reflect a religious preference."

FREE EXERCISE CLAUSE

The government may not deny the free exercise of religion by burdening "sincerely held" religious beliefs. The following describes protected beliefs, neutral law, and nonneutral law.

Protected Religious Beliefs

The Court determines only if a person's religious belief is "sincerely held." The Court does not determine whether a person's belief is "true" or "false;" whether the person asserting the belief is a member of an organized church, sect, or denomination; whether the belief is asserted by a formal religious organization; or whether it is the dominant view within the religion.

- *United States v. Ballard*, 322 U.S. 78 (1944). Members of the "I Am" movement were indicted for mail fraud. The indictment alleged the members solicited funds through the mails by falsely claiming they were divine messengers with supernatural powers to cure diseases. The District Court instructed the jury to find whether "defendants honestly and in good faith believe those things," but did not instruct the jury to find whether the defendants' religious beliefs were true or not. The Circuit Court of Appeals held the question of whether the defendants' religious beliefs were true or not should have been submitted to the jury. The U.S. Supreme Court held, "we do not agree that the truth or verity of respondents' religious doctrines or beliefs should have been submitted to the jury."

The Court explained, "Men may believe what they cannot prove. They may not be put to the proof of their religious doctrines or beliefs. Religious experiences which are as real as life to some may be incomprehensible to others. Yet the fact that they may be beyond the ken of mortals does not mean that they can be made suspect before the law."

- *Thomas v. Review Board of the Indiana Employment Security Division*, 450 U.S. 707 (1981). Thomas, a Jehovah's Witness, worked in a foundry. When the foundry closed, he was transferred to a department that fabricated turrets for military tanks. Thomas asked to be laid off because all the employer's remaining departments to which he might have been transferred were engaged directly in the production of weapons. When his request was denied, he quit and asserted his religious beliefs prevented him from participating in the production of weapons. He then applied for unemployment compensation benefits. The hearing referee found Thomas had terminated his employment because of his religious convictions, but denied benefits because his voluntary termination was not based on a "good cause [arising] in connection with [his] work." The Indiana Supreme Court denied Thomas benefits, holding he quit voluntarily for personal reasons and his belief was more "personal philosophical choice" than religious belief.

The U.S. Supreme Court held the state's denial of unemployment compensation benefits violated the First Amendment right to free exercise of religion. The Court explained, "In reaching its conclusion, the Indiana court seems to have placed considerable reliance on the facts that Thomas was 'struggling' with his beliefs and that he was not able to 'articulate' his belief precisely." However, "Courts should not undertake to dissect religious beliefs because the believer admits that he is 'struggling' with his position or because his beliefs are not articulated with the clarity and precision that a more sophisticated person might employ." Moreover, "The Indiana court also appears to have given significant weight to the fact that another Jehovah's Witness had no scruples about working on tank turrets." However, "the guarantee of free exercise is not limited to beliefs which are shared by all of the members of a religious sect. Particularly in this sensitive area, it is not within the judicial function and judicial competence to inquire whether the petitioner or his fellow worker more correctly perceived the commands of their common faith. Courts are not arbiters of scriptural interpretation."

- *Frazee v. Illinois Department of Employment Security*, 489 U.S. 829 (1989). Frazee was denied unemployment compensation benefits because he refused a temporary retail position that would have required him to work on Sunday in violation of his personal religious beliefs. He was not a member of an established religious sect or church. The Court invalidated the denial of benefits.

  The Court explained, "Undoubtedly, membership in an organized religious denomination, especially one with a specific tenet forbidding members to work on Sunday, would simplify the problem of identifying sincerely held religious beliefs, but we reject the notion that to claim the protection of the Free Exercise Clause, one must be responding to the commands of a particular religious organization. Here, Frazee's refusal was based on a sincerely held religious belief. Under our cases, he was entitled to invoke First Amendment protection."

Neutral Law

A law that is religiously neutral (i.e., does not have the purpose of burdening religious beliefs) and generally applicable (i.e., applies to everyone, regardless of religion) must satisfy only the rational basis test, even if the law has the incidental effect of burdening a particular religious practice [*Employment Division v. Smith*, 494 U.S. 872 (1990)]. Generally, the Court will not grant a person a religious exemption to a religiously neutral and generally applicable criminal law. However, the Court has allowed religious exemptions in unemployment compensation and compulsory education.

- *Reynolds v. United States*, 98 U.S. (8 Otto) 145 (1878). A Federal statute prohibited polygamy. The defendant argued it was his duty, as a member of the Mormon Church, to practice polygamy. He was convicted of bigamy. The Court upheld the statute. The Court explained, "the only question which remains is, whether those who make polygamy a part of their religion are excepted from the operation of the statute. If they are, then those who do not make polygamy a part of their religious belief may be found guilty and punished, while those who do, must be acquitted and go free. This would be introducing a new element into criminal law." The Court concluded, "Can a man excuse his practices to the contrary because of his religious belief? To permit this would be to make the professed doctrines of religious belief superior to the law of the land, and in effect to permit every citizen to become a law unto himself. Government could exist only in name under such circumstances."

- *Braunfeld v. Brown*, 366 U.S. 599 (1961). A Pennsylvania criminal statute prohibited the retail sale on Sundays of clothing and home furnishings. Merchants sued to enjoin enforcement of the statute because their Orthodox Jewish Faith required the closing of their places of business and total abstention from all work from nightfall each Friday until nightfall each Saturday. They claimed the statute interfered with the free exercise of their religion by imposing serious economic disadvantages upon them. The Court upheld the statute.

  The Court explained, "the statute before us does not make criminal the holding of any religious belief or opinion, nor does it force anyone to embrace any religious belief or to say or believe anything in conflict with his religious tenets." The merchants argued the state should have provided an exception from the Sunday labor prohibition for those people who, because of religious conviction, observe a day of rest other than Sunday. However, the Court explained, "reason and experience teach that to permit the exemption might well undermine the State's goal of providing a day that, as best possible, eliminates the atmosphere of commercial noise and activity. Although not dispositive of the issue, enforcement problems would be more difficult since there would be two or more days to police rather than one and it would be more difficult to observe whether violations were occurring."

- *Sherbert v. Verner*, 374 U.S. 398 (1963). Sherbert, a member of the Seventh-Day Adventist Church, was discharged by her South Carolina employer because she would not work on Saturday, the Sabbath Day of her faith. The employment commission denied her claim for unemployment compensation benefits because her refusal to work Saturdays caused other employers to refuse to hire her and disqualified her for failure to accept "suitable work." The Court invalidated the denial of benefits.

The Court explained, "not only is it apparent that appellant's declared ineligibility for benefits derives solely from the practice of her religion, but the pressure upon her to forego that practice is unmistakable. The ruling forces her to choose between following the precepts of her religion and forfeiting benefits, on the one hand, and abandoning one of the precepts of her religion in order to accept work, on the other hand. Governmental imposition of such a choice puts the same kind of burden upon the free exercise of religion as would a fine imposed against appellant for her Saturday worship."

- *Gillette v. United States*, 401 U.S. 437 (1971). Section 6(j) of the Military Selective Service Act of 1967 provided no person shall be subject to "service in the armed forces of the United States who, by reason of religious training and belief, is conscientiously opposed to participation in war in any form." Two persons conscientiously objected to participation in the Vietnam conflict as an "unjust" war; one sought exemption from the draft, and the other sought discharge from the Army. Their requests were denied. The Court upheld the Act.

As a preliminary matter, the Court held that "Congress intended to exempt persons who oppose participating in all war—'participation in war in any form'—and that persons who object solely to participation in a particular war are not within the purview of the exempting section, even though the latter objection may have such roots in a claimant's conscience and personality that it is 'religious' in character."

Regarding the free exercise clause issue, the Court explained, "the impact of conscription on objectors to particular wars is far from unjustified. The conscription laws, applied to such persons as to others, are not designed to interfere with any religious ritual or practice, and do not work a penalty against any theological position. The incidental burdens felt by persons in petitioners' position are strictly justified by substantial governmental interests that relate directly to the very impacts questioned. And more broadly, of course, there is the Government's interest in procuring the manpower necessary for military purposes, pursuant to the constitutional grant of power to Congress to raise and support armies."

- *Wisconsin v. Yoder*, 406 U.S. 205 (1972). A Wisconsin compulsory school-attendance law required children to attend public or private school until reaching age sixteen. Members of the Old Order Amish religion declined to send their children, ages fourteen and fifteen, to public or private school after they completed the eighth grade, and were convicted of violating the law. They claimed the compulsory school-attendance law interfered with the free exercise of their religion. The Court invalidated the convictions and granted the Amish a religious exemption to the compulsory school-attendance law.

  The Court explained, "the record in this case abundantly supports the claim that the traditional way of life of the Amish is not merely a matter of personal preference, but one of deep religious conviction." Moreover, "The impact of the compulsory-attendance law on respondents' practice of the Amish religion is not only severe, but inescapable, for the Wisconsin law affirmatively compels them, under threat of criminal sanction, to perform acts undeniably at odds with fundamental tenets of their religious beliefs." The state asserted an interest in compelling school attendance of children to age sixteen. However, "an additional one or two years of formal high school for Amish children in place of their long-established program of informal vocational education would do little to serve those interests."

  The Court concluded, "enforcement of the State's requirement of compulsory formal education after the eighth grade would gravely endanger if not destroy the free exercise of respondents' religious beliefs."

- *United States v. Lee*, 455 U.S. 252 (1982). Lee, a self-employed farmer and carpenter and member of the Old Order Amish religion, sued for a refund of social security taxes paid by him on account of his employment of other members of that religion on his farm and in his carpentry shop. He claimed imposition of the taxes violated his First Amendment free exercise rights and those of his employees. Lee argued the Amish believed there was a religious obligation to provide for their fellow members the same kind of assistance contemplated by the social security system, and both payment and receipt of social security benefits was forbidden by the Amish faith. The Court upheld the taxes.

  The Court explained, "The social security system is by far the largest domestic governmental program in the United

States today, distributing approximately $11 billion monthly to 36 million Americans. The design of the system requires support by mandatory contributions from covered employers and employees. This mandatory participation is indispensable to the fiscal vitality of the social security system." Also, "Unlike the situation presented in *Wisconsin v. Yoder*, it would be difficult to accommodate the comprehensive social security system with myriad exceptions flowing from a wide variety of religious beliefs." For example, if "a religious adherent believes war is a sin, and if a certain percentage of the federal budget can be identified as devoted to war-related activities, such individuals would have a similarly valid claim to be exempt from paying that percentage of the income tax. The tax system could not function if denominations were allowed to challenge the tax system because tax payments were spent in a manner that violates their religious belief."

- *Bob Jones University v. United States*, 461 U.S. 574 (1983). The Internal Revenue Service (IRS) denied tax-exempt status under 26 U.S.C.S. section 501(c)(3) to two private schools under an IRS ruling that interpreted 26 U.S.C.S. subsection 170 and 501(c)(3) as prohibiting tax-exempt status for private schools having a racially discriminatory policy. The Court upheld the IRS ruling. The Court explained, "the Government has a fundamental, over-riding interest in eradicating racial discrimination in education—discrimination that prevailed, with official approval, for the first 165 years of this Nation's constitutional history. That governmental interest substantially outweighs whatever burden denial of tax benefits places on petitioners' exercise of their religious beliefs."

- *Goldman v. Weinberger*, 475 U.S. 503 (1986). An Air Force regulation prohibited members of the Air Force from wearing headgear while indoors, except for headgear for armed security police in the performance of their duties. Pursuant to the regulation, Goldman, an Orthodox Jew and ordained rabbi, was ordered not to wear a yarmulke while on duty and in uniform as a commissioned officer in the Air Force at March Air Force Base. The Court upheld the regulation.

The Court explained, "Quite obviously, to the extent the regulations do not permit the wearing of religious apparel such as a yarmulke, a practice described by petitioner as silent devotion akin to prayer, military life may be more objectionable for petitioner and probably others. But the First Amendment does not require the military to accommodate such practices in the face of its view that they would detract from the uniformity sought by the dress regulations. The Air Force has drawn the line essentially between religious apparel that is visible and that which is not, and we hold that those portions of the regulations challenged here reasonably and evenhandedly regulate dress in the interest of the military's perceived need for uniformity. The First Amendment therefore does not prohibit them from being applied to petitioner even though their effect is to restrict the wearing of the headgear required by his religious beliefs."

- *Hobbie v. Unemployment Appeals Commission of Florida*, 480 U.S. 136 (1987). After 2 1/2 years, Hobbie informed her employer she was joining the Seventh-day Adventist Church and that, for religious reasons, she would no longer be able to work at the employer's store on her Sabbath. She was discharged when she refused to work scheduled shifts on Friday evenings and Saturdays. So she filed a claim for unemployment compensation. Under Florida law, unemployment compensation benefits were available to persons who became "unemployed through no fault of their own." Her claim was denied on the ground that she was "disqualified for benefits" because she had been discharged for "misconduct connected with [her] work." The Court invalidated the denial of benefits.

    The Court explained, "The First Amendment protects the free exercise rights of employees who adopt religious beliefs or convert from one faith to another after they are hired. The timing of Hobbie's conversion is immaterial to our determination that her free exercise rights have been burdened; the salient inquiry under the Free Exercise Clause is the burden involved. In *Sherbert, Thomas,* and the present case, the employee was forced to choose between fidelity to religious belief and continued employment; the forfeiture of unemployment benefits for choosing the former over the latter brings unlawful coercion to bear on the employee's choice."

- *O'Lone v. Estate of Shabazz*, 482 U.S. 342 (1987). Prison inmates and members of the Islamic faith contended two policies adopted by New Jersey prison officials prevented them from attending

Jumu'ah, a Muslim congregational service held on Friday afternoons. The first policy required inmates in certain custody classifications to work outside the buildings in which they were housed and in which Jumu'ah was held; the second policy prohibited inmates assigned to outside work from returning to those buildings during the day. The Court upheld the policies.

The Court explained, "a regulation must have a logical connection to legitimate governmental interests invoked to justify it. The policies at issue here clearly meet that standard. The requirement that full minimum and gang minimum prisoners work outside the main facility was justified by concerns of institutional order and security." Moreover, "The subsequent policy prohibiting returns to the institution during the day also passes muster under this standard. Prison officials testified that the returns from outside work details generated congestion and delays at the main gate, a high risk area in any event." Finally, "The record establishes that respondents are not deprived of all forms of religious exercise, but instead freely observe a number of their religious obligations. The right to congregate for prayer or discussion is virtually unlimited except during working hours."

- *Lyng v. Northwest Indian Cemetery Protective Association*, 485 U.S. 439 (1988). The U.S. Forest Service planned to construct a road through, and harvest timber in, a portion of a national forest traditionally used for religious purposes by members of three American Indian tribes in northwestern California. The Court upheld the plans.

  The Court explained, "It is undisputed that the Indian respondents' beliefs are sincere and that the Government's proposed actions will have severe adverse effects on the practice of their religion." However, the affected individuals would not "be coerced by the Government's action into violating their religious beliefs." Nor would the governmental action "penalize religious activity by denying any person an equal share of the rights, benefits, and privileges enjoyed by other citizens." The Court concluded, "However much we might wish that it were otherwise, government simply could not operate if it were required to satisfy every citizen's religious needs and desires."

- *Jimmy Swaggart Ministries v. Board of Equalization of California*, 493 U.S. 378 (1990). A religious organization claimed the

California tax board's imposition of sales and use tax liability on its sale of religious materials violated the free exercise clause. The Court upheld the tax. The Court explained the generally applicable tax "represents only a small fraction of any retail sale, and applies neutrally to all retail sales of tangible personal property made in California. California imposes its sales and use tax even if the seller or the purchaser is charitable, religious, non-profit, or state or local governmental in nature. Thus, the sales and use tax is not a tax on the right to disseminate religious information, ideas, or beliefs per se; rather, it is a tax on the privilege of making retail sales of tangible personal property and on the storage, use, or other consumption of tangible personal property in California."

Moreover, "There is no evidence in this case that collection and payment of the tax violates appellant's sincere religious beliefs. California's nondiscriminatory sales and use tax law requires only that appellant collect the tax from its California purchasers and remit the tax money to the State. The only burden on appellant is the claimed reduction in income resulting from the presumably lower demand for appellant's wares (caused by the marginally higher price) and from the costs associated with administering the tax." The Court concluded, "At bottom, though we do not doubt the economic cost to appellant of complying with a generally applicable sales and use tax, such a tax is no different from other generally applicable laws and regulations—such as health and safety regulations—to which appellant must adhere."

- *Employment Division v. Smith*, 494 U.S. 872 (1990). Two persons were fired by a private drug rehabilitation organization because they ingested peyote, a hallucinogenic drug, for sacramental purposes at a ceremony of their Native American Church. Oregon denied their applications for unemployment compensation under a state law that disqualified employees discharged for work-related "misconduct." The Court upheld the law and denial of benefits.

The Court explained, "the right of free exercise does not relieve an individual of the obligation to comply with a valid and neutral law of general applicability on the ground that the law proscribes (or prescribes) conduct that his religion prescribes (or proscribes)." The Court concluded, "There being no contention that Oregon's drug law represents an attempt to regulate religious beliefs, the communication of religious beliefs, or the raising of one's children in those beliefs, the rule to which we have adhered ever since *Reynolds* plainly controls."

Nonneutral Law

A law that is not religiously neutral or "generally applicable" must satisfy strict scrutiny (i.e., necessary to achieve a compelling governmental interest). A law is not neutral if its object is to infringe on or restrict practices because of their religious motivation.

* *Church of the Lukumi Babalu Aye, Inc. v. Hialeah*, 508 U.S. 520 (1993). A church and its congregants practiced the Santeria religion, which employed animal sacrifice as one of its principal forms of devotion. The church applied for and received licensing, inspection, and zoning approvals to establish a church in the city. In response, the city council passed ordinances that prohibited animal sacrifice. The Court invalidated the ordinances.

    The Court explained, "The city does not argue that Santeria is not a 'religion' within the meaning of the First Amendment." Also, "Neither the city nor the courts below, moreover, have questioned the sincerity of petitioners' professed desire to conduct animal sacrifices for religious reasons." However, the ordinances were not religiously neutral because, "The ordinances had as their object the suppression of religion. The pattern we have recited discloses animosity to Santeria adherents and their religious practices; the ordinances by their own terms target this religious exercise; the texts of the ordinances were gerrymandered with care to proscribe religious killings of animals but to exclude almost all secular killings."

    Moreover, the ordinances suppressed more religious conduct than necessary to achieve the legitimate ends asserted in their defense. The Court explained, "The legitimate governmental interests in protecting the public health and preventing cruelty to animals could be addressed by restrictions stopping far short of a flat prohibition of all Santeria sacrificial practice." For example, "If improper disposal, not the sacrifice itself, is the harm to be prevented, the city could have imposed a general regulation on the disposal of organic garbage." And, "With regard to the city's interest in ensuring the adequate care of animals, regulation of conditions and treatment, regardless of why an animal is kept, is the logical response to the city's concern, not a prohibition on possession for the purpose of sacrifice."

CHAPTER 23

The Second Amendment

THE SECOND AMENDMENT STATES, "A WELL REGULATED MILITIA, BEING NECESSARY to the security of a free State, the right of the people to keep and bear Arms, shall not be infringed." The Second Amendment protects the right of the people to keep and bear arms for the purpose of self-defense [*District of Columbia v. Heller*, 128 S. Ct. 2783 (2008)]. The Second Amendment right to keep and bear arms applies to the states through the Fourteenth Amendment [*McDonald v. Chicago*, 130 S. Ct. 3020 (2010)]. So the right to keep and bear arms is protected from state and local interference as well as from federal interference.

- *District of Columbia v. Heller*, 128 S. Ct. 2783 (2008). A District of Columbia law banned handgun possession in the home, and required that any lawful firearm in the home be disassembled or bound by a trigger lock at all times, rendering it inoperable. The Court invalidated the law.

    The District argued that the Second Amendment protected only the right to possess and carry a firearm in connection with militia service. However, the Court noted that four states adopted provisions similar to the Second Amendment "in the period between independence and the ratification of the Bill of Rights. Two of them—Pennsylvania and Vermont—clearly adopted individual rights unconnected to militia service." Three important "founding-era legal scholars" interpreted the Second Amendment in published writings, and "All three understood it to protect an individual right unconnected with militia service." The 19th-century cases that interpreted the Second Amendment "universally support an individual right unconnected to militia service." It was "plainly the understanding in the post-Civil War Congress that the Second Amendment protected an individual right to use arms for self-defense." And, "Every late-19th-century legal scholar that we have read interpreted the Second Amendment to secure an individual right unconnected with militia service." The Court concluded, "There seems to us no doubt, on the basis of both text and history, that the Second Amendment conferred an individual right to keep and bear arms."

After concluding "the inherent right of self-defense has been central to the Second Amendment right," the Court invalidated the handgun ban because it "amounts to a prohibition of an entire class of 'arms' that is overwhelmingly chosen by American society for that lawful purpose. The prohibition extends, moreover, to the home, where the need for defense of self, family, and property is most acute. Under any of the standards of scrutiny that we have applied to enumerated constitutional rights, banning from the home the most preferred firearm in the nation to keep and use for protection of one's home and family would fail constitutional muster."

The Court invalidated the requirement that firearms in the home be rendered and kept inoperable at all times because, "This makes it impossible for citizens to use them for the core lawful purpose of self-defense and is hence unconstitutional."

The Court noted, however, "Like most rights, the right secured by the Second Amendment is not unlimited." Thus, "nothing in our opinion should be taken to cast doubt on longstanding prohibitions on the possession of firearms by felons and the mentally ill, or laws forbidding the carrying of firearms in sensitive places such as schools and government buildings, or laws imposing conditions and qualifications on the commercial sale of arms."

Case Index

A

Abington School District v. Schempp, 374
U.S. 203 (1963), 277

Abood v. Detroit Board of Education, 431
U.S. 209 (1977), 262

Aetna Life Insurance Co. v. Haworth,
300 U.S. 227 (1937), 5, 6–7, 8

Agins v. Tiburon, 447 U.S. 255
(1980), 140

Agostini v. Felton, 521 U.S. 203
(1997), 289

Aguilar v. Felton 473 U.S. 402
(1985), 289

A.L.A. Schechter Poultry Corporation v.
United States, 295 U.S. 495
(1935), 101

Alden v. Maine, 527 U.S. 706 (1999),
30–31

Allen v. Wright, 468 U.S. 737 (1984), 12

Allied Structural Steel Co. v. Spannaus,
438 U.S. 234 (1978), 147

Ambach v. Norwick, 441 U.S. 68
(1979), 167

Anderson v. Martin, 375 U.S. 399
(1964), 150–151

Application of Griffiths, 413 U.S. 717
(1973), 166

Arkansas Educational Television
Commission v. Forbes, 523 U.S.
666 (1998), 252

Arkansas Writers' Project, Inc. v.
Ragland, 481 U.S. 221 (1987), 268

ASARCO Inc. v. Kadish, 490 U.S. 605
(1989), 15

Ashcroft v. ACLU, 542 U.S. 656
(2004), 205

Ashcroft v. Free Speech Coalition, 535
U.S. 234 (2002), 197, 198–199

Associated Industries of Missouri v.
Lohman, 511 U.S. 641 (1994), 85

Associated Press v. NLRB, 301 U.S. 103
(1937), 269

Associated Press v. United States, 326
U.S. 1 (1945), 270

Associated Press v. Walker, 388 U.S. 130
(1967), 208

Austin v. Michigan Chamber of Commerce,
494 U. S. 652 (1990), 234

B

Bacchus Imports, Ltd. v. Dias, 468 U.S.
263 (1984), 91–92

Baggett v. Bullitt, 377 U.S. 360 (1964),
177, 255

Bailey v. Drexel Furniture Co., 259 U.S.
20 (1922), 52

Baird v. State Bar of Arizona, 401 U.S. 1
(1971), 257

Baker v. Carr, 369 U.S. 186 (1962), 23, 25

Baldwin v. Fish and Game Commission of
Montana, 436 U.S. 371 (1978), 88

Bank of Marin v. England, 385 U.S. 99
(1966), 8

Barenblatt v. United States, 360 U.S. 109
(1959), 111

Barnes v. Glen Theatre, Inc., 501 U.S.
560 (1991), 217–218

Barrows v. Jackson, 346 U.S. 249 (1953), 17

Bartnicki v. Vopper, 532 U.S. 514 (2001), 214–215

Bates v. State Bar of Arizona, 433 U.S. 350 (1977), 221–222

Bell v. Burson, 402 U.S. 535 (1971), 133

Berman v. Parker, 348 U.S. 26 (1954), 143

Bernal v. Fainter, 467 U.S. 216 (1984), 167–168

Bethel School District No. 403 v. Fraser, 478 U.S. 675 (1986), 235–236

Bibb v. Navajo Freight Lines, 359 U.S. 520 (1959), 76

Blake v. McClung, 172 U.S. 239 (1898), 87

Blatchford v. Native Village of Noatak, 501 U.S. 775 (1991), 29

Board of Airport Commissioners of Los Angeles v. Jews for Jesus, Inc., 482 U.S. 569 (1987), 179

Board of County Commissioners v. Umbehr, 518 U.S. 668 (1996), 236

Board of Education of Kiryas Joel Village School District v. Grumet, 512 U.S. 687 (1994), 275

Board of Education of Westside Community Schools v. Mergens, 496 U.S. 226 (1990), 280–281

Board of Education v. Allen, 392 U.S. 236 (1968), 283

Board of Regents of the University of Wisconsin System v. Southworth, 529 U.S. 217 (2000), 264

Board of Regents v. Roth, 408 U.S. 564 (1972), 131, 132

Board of Trustees of the State University of New York v. Fox, 492 U.S. 469 (1989), 219

Bob Jones University v. United States, 461 U.S. 574 (1983), 304

Bolling v. Sharpe, 347 U.S. 497 (1954), 149

Bowen v. Kendrick, 487 U.S. 589 (1988), 291–292

Bowers v. Hardwick, 478 U.S. 186 (1986), 118

Bowsher v. Synar, 478 U.S. 714 (1986), 105–106

Boy Scouts of America v. Dale, 530 U.S. 640 (2000), 264–265

Bradfield v. Roberts, 175 U.S. 291 (1899), 291

Brandenburg v. Ohio, 395 U.S. 444 (1969), 190–191

Braniff Airways, Inc. v. Nebraska State Board of Equalization and Assessment, 347 U.S. 590 (1954), 82–83

Branti v. Finkel, 445 U.S. 507 (1980), 258

Branzburg v. Hayes, 408 U.S. 665 (1972), 270

Braunfeld v. Brown, 366 U.S. 599 (1961), 301

Bridges v. California, 314 U.S. 252 (1941), 228–229

Brig Amy Warwick, 67 U.S. (2 Black) 635 (1863), 50

Broadrick v. Oklahoma, 413 U.S. 601 (1973), 178

Brown v. Board of Education, 347 U.S. 483 (1954), 150

Brown v. Hartlage, 456 U.S. 45 (1982), 231–232

Buckley v. Valeo, 424 U.S. 1 (1976), 104, 150, 230, 261

Burson v. Freeman, 504 U.S. 191 (1992), 232–233

Burton v. Wilmington Parking Authority, 365 U.S. 715 (1961), 42–43

Butler v. Michigan, 352 U.S. 380 (1957), 178

C

Caban v. Mohammed, 441 U.S. 380 (1979), 159–160

Cabell v. Chavez-Salido, 454 U.S. 432 (1982), 167

Calder v. Bull, 3 U.S. (3 Dall.) 386 (1798), 169

Califano v. Aznavorian, 439 U.S. 170 (1978), 120

Califano v. Webster, 430 U.S. 313 (1977), 158–159

California Medical Association v. Federal Election Commission, 453 U.S. 182 (1981), 231

Cantrell v. Forest City Publishing Co., 419 U.S. 245 (1974), 211

Cantwell v. Connecticut, 310 U.S. 296 (1940), 194, 274

Carey v. Population Services International, 431 U.S. 678 (1977), 123

Carroll v. President and Commissioners of Princess Anne, 393 U.S. 175 (1968), 7

Central Hudson Gas v. Public Service Commission, 447 U.S. 557 (1980), 219

Champion v. Ames, 188 U.S. 321 (1903), 55–56

Chaplinsky v. New Hampshire, 315 U.S. 568 (1942), 192

Chew v. Colding, 344 U.S. 590 (1953), 131

Chicago & G.T.R. Co. v. Wellman, 143 U.S. 339 (1892), 9

Chisholm v. Georgia, 2 Dall. 419 (1793), 28

Christian Legal Soc'y Chapter of the Univ. of Cal. v. Martinez, 130 S. Ct. 2971 (2010), 253–254

Church of the Lukumi Babalu Aye, Inc. v. Hialeah, 508 U.S. 520 (1993), 308–309

Citizens United v. Federal Election Commission, 130 S. Ct. 876 (2010), 234–235

City of Boerne v. Flores, 521 U.S. 507 (1997), 66

City of Cincinnati v. Discovery Network, Inc., 507 U.S. 410 (1993), 226–227

City of Cleburne, Texas v. Cleburne Living Center, Inc., 473 U.S. 432 (1985), 156–157

City of Erie v. Pap's A.M., 529 U.S. 277 (2000), 218–219

City of Lakewood v. Plain Dealer Publishing Co., 486 U.S. 750 (1988), 184

City of Los Angeles v. Alameda Books, 535 U.S. 425 (2002), 201

City of Los Angeles v. Lyons, 461 U.S. 95 (1983), 11

City of Philadelphia v. New Jersey, 437 U.S. 617 (1978), 73–74

City of Renton v. Playtime Theatres, Inc., 475 U.S. 41 (1986), 201

Clark v. Jeter, 486 U.S. 456 (1988), 160–161

Cleveland Board of Education v. Loudermill, 470 U.S. 532 (1985), 134

Clinton v. Jones, 520 U.S. 681 (1997), 114

Coates v. Cincinnati, 402 U.S. 611 (1971), 177

Cohens v. Virginia, 19 U.S. (6 Wheat.) 264 (1821), 29

Cohen v. California, 403 U.S. 15 (1971), 192–193

Cohen v. Cowles Media Co., 501 U.S. 663 (1991), 270

Coleman v. Miller, 307 U.S. 433 (1939), 21–22, 24–25

Cole v. Richardson, 405 U.S. 676 (1972), 240

College Savings Bank v. Florida Prepaid Postsecondary Education Expense Board, 527 U.S. 666 (1999), 31

Committee for Public Education and Religious Liberty v. Regan, 444 U.S. 646 (1980), 286–287

Committee for Public Education v. Nyquist, 413 U.S. 756 (1973), 284–285

Commonwealth Edison v. Montana, 453 U.S. 609 (1981), 84–85, 86

Commonwealth of Massachusetts v. Mellon, 262 U.S. 447 (1923), 16

Complete Auto Transit, Inc. v. Brady, 430 U.S. 274 (1977), 82

Connally v. General Construction Co., 269 U.S. 385 (1926), 177

Connecticut v. Doehr, 501 U.S. 1 (1991), 136–137

Connick v. Myers, 461 U.S. 138 (1983), 237

Container Corp. v. Franchise Tax Board, 463 U.S. 159 (1983), 84

Cornelius v. NAACP Legal Defense and Educational Fund, Inc., 473 U.S. 788 (1985), 250

County of Allegheny v. American Civil Liberties Union, 492 U.S. 573 (1989), 294

Cox Broadcasting Corp. v. Cohn, 420 U.S. 469 (1975), 212

Cox v. Louisiana, 379 U.S. 536 (1965), 195–196

Cox v. New Hampshire, 312 U.S. 569 (1941), 182

Craig v. Boren, 429 U.S. 190 (1976), 151, 158

Cruzan v. Director, Missouri Department of Health, 497 U.S. 261 (1990), 129

Curtis Publishing Co. v. Butts, 388 U.S. 130 (1967), 208

D

Dandridge v. Williams, 397 U.S. 471 (1970), 155

Daniels v. Williams, 474 U.S. 327 (1986), 130

Davis v. Bandemer, 478 U.S. 109 (1986), 27

Dean Milk Co. v. City of Madison, 340 U.S. 349 (1951), 72–73

DeFunis v. Odegaard, 416 U.S. 312 (1974), 7–8

Delaware v. Prouse, 440 U.S. 648 (1979), 35

Denver Area Educational Telecommunications Consortium, Inc. v. Federal Communications Commission, 518 U.S. 727 (1996), 202–203

DeShaney v. Winnebago County Department of Social Services, 489 U.S. 189 (1989), 130

District of Columbia v. Heller, 128 S. Ct. 2783 (2008), 310–311

Dobbert v. Florida, 432 U.S. 282 (1977), 170–171

Doe v. Bolton, 410 U.S. 179 (1973), 88

Doe v. McMillan, 412 U.S. 306 (1973), 110

Dolan v. City of Tigard, 512 U.S. 374 (1994), 141–142

Doremus v. Board of Education of Hawthorne, 342 U.S. 429 (1952), 15, 16

Dun & Bradstreet, Inc. v. Greenmoss Builders, Inc., 472 U.S. 749 (1985), 210

E

Edelman v. Jordan, 415 U.S. 651 (1974), 30, 31

Edmonson v. Leesville Concrete Co., 500 U.S. 614 (1991), 45

Edwards v. Aguillard, 482 U.S. 578 (1987), 279–280

Edwards v. South Carolina, 372 U.S. 229 (1963), 195

Eisenstadt v. Baird, 405 U.S. 438 (1972), 123

Elfbrandt v. Russell, 384 U.S. 11 (1966), 240, 256

El Paso v. Simmons, 379 U.S. 497 (1965), 146

Elrod v. Burns, 427 U.S. 347 (1976), 258

Employment Division v. Smith, 494 U.S. 872 (1990), 66, 300, 307–308

Energy Reserves Group v. Kansas Power & Light, 459 U.S. 400 (1983), 145

Engel v. Vitale, 370 U.S. 421 (1962), 277

Epperson v. Arkansas, 393 U.S. 97 (1968), 277–278

Estate of Thornton v. Caldor, 472 U.S. 703 (1985), 292

Evans v. Newton, 382 U.S. 296 (1966), 41

Everson v. Board of Education, 330 U.S. 1 (1947), 274, 283

Evitts v. Lucey, 469 U.S. 387 (1985), 8

Ex parte McCardle, 74 U.S. (7 Wall.) 506 (1869), 5

Ex Parte State of New York, 256 U.S. 490 (1921), 29

Ex Parte Young, 209 U.S. 123 (1908), 30

Exxon Corp. v. Governor of Maryland, 437 U.S. 117 (1978), 77

F

FEC v. National Conservative PAC, 470 U.S. 480 (1985), 232

Federal Communications Commission v. League of Women Voters, 468 U.S. 364 (1984), 187

Federal Communications Commission v. Pacifica Foundation, 438 U.S. 726 (1978), 202

Federal Maritime Commission v. South Carolina State Ports Authority, 535 U.S. 743, 753 (2002), 28, 31

Feiner v. New York, 340 U.S. 315 (1951), 194–195

First National Bank of Boston v. Bellotti, 435 U.S. 765 (1978), 230–231

Fitzpatrick v. Bitzer, 427 U.S. 445 (1976), 32

Flagg Brothers, Inc. v. Brooks, 436 U.S. 149 (1978), 41–42

Flast v. Cohen, 392 U.S. 83 (1968), 14–15

Fletcher v. Peck, 10 U.S. (6 Cranch) 87 (1810), 3

Florida Bar v. Went for It, Inc., 515 U.S. 618 (1995), 225–226

Florida Lime & Avocado Growers, Inc. v. Paul, 373 U.S. 132 (1963), 70

Florida Prepaid Postsecondary Education Expense Board v. College Savings Bank, 527 U.S. 627 (1999), 32

Florida Star v. B.J.F., 491 U.S. 524 (1989), 212, 214

Foley v. Connelie, 435 U.S. 291 (1978), 166–167

Ford Motor Co. v. Department of Treasury of the State of Indiana, 323 U.S. 459 (1945), 29

Forsyth County v. The Nationalist Movement, 505 U.S. 123 (1992), 184

44 Liquormart, Inc. v. Rhode Island, 517 U.S. 484 (1996), 91, 227–228

Frazee v. Illinois Department of Employment Security, 489 U.S. 829 (1989), 300

Freedman v. Maryland, 380 U.S. 51 (1965), 183

Free Enter. Fund v. Pub. Co. Accounting Oversight Bd., 177 L. Ed. 2d 706 (2010), 107–108

Frisby v. Schultz, 487 U.S. 474 (1988), 243

Frothingham v. Mellon, 262 U.S. 447 (1923), 13–14

G

Gannett Co., Inc. v. DePasquale, 443 U.S. 368 (1979), 272

Garcetti v. Ceballos 547 U.S. 410 (2006), 239

Garcia v. San Antonio Metropolitan Transit Authority, 469 U.S. 528 (1985), 97–98

General Motors Corp. v. Romein, 503 U.S. 181 (1992), 148

Gentile v. State Bar of Nevada, 501 U.S. 1030 (1991), 229

Georgia v. McCollum, 505 U.S. 42 (1992), 45–46

Gertz v. Welch, 418 U.S. 323 (1974), 208–210, 211

Gibson v. Florida Legislative Investigation Committee, 372 U.S. 539 (1963), 111

Gillette v. United States, 401 U.S. 437 (1971), 297–298, 302

Gitlow v. New York, 268 U.S. 652 (1925), 174

Givhan v. Western Line Consolidated School District, 439 U.S. 410 (1979), 237–238

Glickman v. Wileman Brothers & Elliott, Inc., 521 U.S. 457 (1997), 263–264

Globe Newspaper Co. v. Superior Court, 457 U.S. 596 (1982), 272

Goldberg v. Kelly, 397 U.S. 254 (1970), 132, 134

Goldman v. Weinberger, 475 U.S. 503 (1986), 304–305

Goldwater v. Carter, 444 U.S. 996 (1979), 26–27

Gonzales v. Carhart, 550 U.S. 124 (2007), 126

Gonzales v. Raich, 545 U.S. 1 (2005), 61–62

Good News Club v. Milford Central School, 533 U.S. 98 (2001), 253

Goss v. Lopez, 419 U.S. 565 (1975), 133, 135

Graham v. Richardson, 403 U.S. 365 (1971), 30, 165

Grand Rapids School District v. Ball, 473 U.S. 373 (1985), 289

Granholm v. Heald, 544 U.S. 460 (2005), 75, 92

Gratz v. Bollinger, 539 U.S. 244 (2003), 163–164

Gravel v. United States, 408 U.S. 606 (1972), 108–109

Greer v. Spock, 424 U.S. 828 (1976), 249

Griffin v. School Board of Prince Edward County, 377 U.S. 218 (1964), 152–153

Griswold v. Connecticut, 381 U.S. 479 (1965), 17–18, 122

Grosjean v. American Press Co., 297 U.S. 233 (1936), 267–268

Grutter v. Bollinger, 539 U.S. 306 (2003), 164–165

Guinn v. United States, 238 U.S. 347 (1915), 152

H

Haig v. Agee, 453 U.S. 280 (1981), 119

Hans v. Louisiana, 134 U.S. 1 (1890), 29

Harlow v. Fitzgerald, 457 U.S. 800 (1982), 115

Harman v. Forssenius, 380 U.S. 528 (1965), 33

Harper v. Virginia State Board of Elections, 383 U.S. 663 (1966), 129

Hauenstein v. Lynham, 100 U.S. (10 Otto) 483 (1879), 48

Havens Realty Corp. v. Coleman, 455 U.S. 363 (1982), 18–19

Hawaii Housing Authority v. Midkiff, 467 U.S. 229 (1984), 143

Hawker v. New York, 170 U.S. 189 (1898), 170

Hazelwood School District v. Kuhlmeier, 484 U.S. 260 (1988), 250–251

Heart of Atlanta Motel Inc. v. United States, 379 U.S. 241 (1964), 59–60

Heffron v. International Society for Krishna Consciousness, Inc., 452 U.S. 640 (1981), 242

Helvering v. Davis, 301 U.S. 672 (1937), 52

Herb v. Pitcairn, 324 U.S. 117 (1945), 34

Hess v. Indiana, 414 U.S. 105 (1973), 191

Hicklin v. Orbeck, 437 U.S. 518 (1978), 89

Hillsborough County, Florida v. Automated Medical Laboratories, Inc., 471 U.S. 707 (1985), 69

Hill v. Colorado, 530 U.S. 703 (2000), 245

Hines v. Davidowitz, 312 U.S. 52 (1941), 68–69, 70

Hipolite Egg Co. v. United States, 220 U.S. 45 (1911), 56

Hisquierdo v. Hisquierdo, 439 U.S. 572 (1979), 70

Hobbie v. Unemployment Appeals Commission of Florida, 480 U.S. 136 (1987), 305

Hoke v. United States, 227 U.S. 308 (1913), 56

Home Building & Loan Association v. Blaisdell, 290 U.S. 398 (1934), 145–146

Hostetter v. Idlewild Bon Voyage Liquor Corp., 377 U.S. 324 (1964), 91

Houston, East & West Texas Railway Company v. United States, 234 U.S. 342 (1914), 57–58

Houston v. Hill, 482 U.S. 451 (1987), 179

Hudgens v. National Labor Relations Board, 424 U.S. 507 (1976), 41, 254

Hughes v. Alexandria Scrap Corp., 426 U.S. 794 (1976), 79–80

Hughes v. Oklahoma, 441 U.S. 322 (1979), 74

Humphrey's Executor v. United States, 295 U.S. 602 (1935), 105

Hunter v. Underwood, 471 U.S. 222 (1985), 153

Hunt v. United States, 278 U.S. 96 (1928), 63–64

Hunt v. Washington State Apple Advertising Commission, 432 U.S. 333 (1977), 19, 73

Hurley v. Irish-American Gay, Lesbian, and Bisexual Group of Boston, 515 U.S. 557 (1995), 263

Hustler Magazine v. Falwell, 485 U.S. 46 (1988), 211–212

Hutchinson v. Proxmire, 443 U.S. 111 (1979), 110–111

Hutto v. Finney, 437 U.S. 678 (1978), 30, 32

I

Idaho v. Coeur d'Alene Tribe of Idaho, 521 U.S. 261 (1997), 30

Immigration and Naturalization Service v. Chadha, 462 U.S. 919 (1983), 103

In re Primus, 436 U.S. 412 (1978), 222–232

International Society for Krishna Consciousness, Inc. v. Lee, 505 U.S. 672 (1992), 251–252

J

Jackson v. Metropolitan Edison Co., 419 U.S. 345 (1974), 41, 44

James v. Dravo Contracting Co., 302 U.S. 134 (1937), 94

Japan Line, Ltd. v. County of Los Angeles, 441 U.S. 434 (1979), 62

Jenkins v. Georgia, 418 U.S. 153 (1974), 196

Jimmy Swaggart Ministries v. Board of Equalization of California, 493 U.S. 378 (1990), 306–307

Johnson v. Maryland, 254 U.S. 51 (1920), 95

Jones v. Alfred H. Mayer Co., 392 U.S. 409 (1968), 36

Jones v. Helms, 452 U.S. 412 (1981), 119

Jones v. Rath Packing Co., 430 U.S. 519 (1977), 67

K

Kassel v. Consolidated Freightways Corp., 450 U.S. 662 (1981), 78

Katzenbach v. McClung, 379 U.S. 294 (1964), 60

Keller v. State Bar of California, 496 U.S. 1 (1990), 262–263

Kelo v. City of New London, 545 U.S. 469 (2005), 143–144

Kennecott Copper Corp. v. State Tax Commission, 327 U.S. 573 (1946), 31

Kentucky v. Graham, 473 U.S. 159 (1985), 29

Kentucky Whip & Collar Co. v. Illinois Central R. Co., 299 U.S. 334 (1937), 56

Keyishian v. Board of Regents, 385 U.S. 589 (1967), 257

Keystone Bituminous Coal Association v. DeBenedictis, 480 U.S. 470 (1987), 140–141, 147–148

Kirchberg v. Feenstra, 450 U.S. 455 (1981), 160

Kleppe v. New Mexico, 426 U.S. 529 (1976), 63

Korematsu v. United States, 323 U.S. 214 (1944), 161

Kunz v. New York, 340 U.S. 290 (1951), 182

L

Laird v. Tatum, 408 U.S. 1 (1972), 5–6, 10–11

Lalli v. Lalli, 439 U.S. 259 (1978), 159

Lamb's Chapel v. Center Moriches Union Free School District, 508 U.S. 384 (1993), 252, 281–282

Landmark Communications, Inc. v. Virginia, 435 U.S. 829 (1978), 212–213

Lapides v. Board of Regents of University System of Georgia, 535 U.S. 613 (2002), 31

Larkin v. Grendel's Den, Inc., 459 U.S. 116 (1982), 279

Larson v. Valente, 456 U.S. 228 (1982), 274–275

Lawrence v. State Tax Commission, 286 U.S. 276 (1932), 34

Lawrence v. Texas, 539 U.S. 558 (2003), 118–119

Law Students Civil Rights Research Council v. Wadmond, 401 U.S. 154 (1971), 257

Leathers v. Medlock, 499 U.S. 439 (1991), 268–269

Lebron v. National Railroad Passenger Corp., 513 U.S. 374 (1995), 38–39

Lee v. Weisman, 505 U.S. 577 (1992), 281

Legal Services Corporation v. Velazquez, 531 U.S. 533 (2001), 188

Lemon v. Kurtzman, 403 U.S. 602 (1971), 276, 284

Lincoln County v. Luning, 133 U.S. 529 (1890), 30

Linmark Associates, Inc. v. Township of Willingboro, 431 U.S. 85 (1977), 226

Loretto v. Teleprompter Manhattan CATV Corp., 458 U.S. 419 (1982), 139

Lorillard Tobacco Co. v. Reilly, 533 U.S. 525 (2001), 220

Lovell v. Griffin, 303 U.S. 444 (1938), 181–182

Loving v. United States, 116 S. Ct. 1737 (1996), 102

Loving v. Virginia, 388 U.S. 1 (1967), 120

Lucas v. South Carolina Coastal Council, 505 U.S. 1003 (1992), 140

Lugar v. Edmonson Oil Co., 457 U.S. 922 (1982), 44–45

Lujan v. Defenders of Wildlife, 504 U.S. 555 (1992), 9, 11

Luther v. Borden, 48 U.S. (7 How.) 1 (1849), 23–24

Lynch v. Donnelly, 465 U.S. 668 (1984), 293

Lyng v. Northwest Indian Cemetery Protective Association, 485 U.S. 439 (1988), 306

M

Mackey v. Montrym, 443 U.S. 1 (1979), 135

Madsen v. Women's Health Center, Inc., 512 U.S. 753 (1994), 247–248

Maine v. Taylor, 477 U.S. 131 (1986), 74

Malloy v. South Carolina, 237 U.S. 180 (1915), 170

Marbury v. Madison, 5 U.S. (1 Cranch) 137 (1803), 2, 3

Marsh v. Alabama, 326 U.S. 501 (1946), 40

Marsh v. Chambers, 463 U.S. 783 (1983), 293

Martin v. Hunter's Lessee, 14 U.S. (1 Wheat.) 304 (1816), 3

Maryland v. Baltimore Radio Show, 338 U.S. 912 (1950), 4

Maryland v. Louisiana, 451 U.S. 725 (1981), 20–21

Massachusetts Board of Retirement v. Murgia, 427 U.S. 307 (1976), 156

Massachusetts v. Mellon, 262 U.S. 447 (1923), 20

Massachusetts v. United States, 435 U.S. 444 (1978), 96–97

Mathews v. Diaz, 426 U.S. 67 (1976), 168

Mathews v. Eldridge, 424 U.S. 319 (1976), 133, 134–135

Mayo v. United States, 319 U.S. 441 (1943), 95

McCleskey v. Kemp, 481 U.S. 279 (1987), 153–154

McCollum v. Board of Education, 333 U.S. 203 (1948), 276

McCray v. United States, 195 U.S. 27 (1904), 52

McCreary County v. ACLU, 545 U.S. 844 (2005), 295–296

McCulloch v. Maryland, 17 U.S. (4 Wheat.) 316 (1819), 93–94

McDonald v. Chicago, 130 S. Ct. 3020 (2010), 310

McGowan v. Maryland, 366 U.S. 420 (1961), 292

McKesson Corporation v. Division of Alcoholic Beverages and Tobacco, Department of Business Regulation of Florida, 496 U.S. 18 (1990), 29

Medtronic, Inc. v. Lohr, 518 U.S. 470 (1996), 67

Meek v. Pittenger, 421 U.S. 349 (1975), 290

Members of City Council of City of Los Angeles v. Taxpayers for Vincent, 466 U.S. 789 (1984), 176, 249–250

Memphis Light, Gas & Water Division v. Craft, 436 U.S. 1 (1978), 133, 135–136

Metropolitan Life Insurance Co. v. Ward, 470 U.S. 869 (1985), 79, 156

Miami Herald v. Tornillo, 418 U.S. 241 (1974), 271

Michael M. v. Superior Court, 450 U.S. 464 (1981), 160

Michigan v. Long, 463 U.S. 1032 (1983), 35

Milkovich v. Lorain Journal Co., 497 U.S. 1 (1990), 206, 210–211

Miller v. California, 413 U.S. 15 (1973), 196

Miller v. Florida, 482 U.S. 423 (1987), 171

Miller v. Johnson, 515 U.S. 900 (1995), 163

Minneapolis Star & Tribune Co. v. Minnesota Commissioner of Revenue, 460 U.S. 575 (1983), 268

Minnesota v. Clover Leaf Creamery Co., 449 U.S. 456 (1981), 77–78

Missouri v. Holland, 252 U.S. 416 (1920), 48–49

Mistrette v. United States, 488 U.S. 361 (1989), 101–102

Mitchell v. Helms, 530 U.S. 793 (2000), 290

Moore v. Charlotte-Mecklenburg Board of Education, 402 U.S. 47 (1971), 9

Moore v. Ogilvie, 394 U.S. 814 (1969), 7

Moorman Manufacturing Co. v. Bair, 437 U.S. 267 (1978), 83–84

Moose Lodge Number 107 v. Irvis, 407 U.S. 163 (1972), 43–44

Morrison v. Olson, 487 U.S. 654 (1988), 104–105, 106

Morse v. Frederick, 551 U.S. 393 (2007), 236

Mt. Healthy City School District Board of Education v. Doyle, 429 U.S. 274 (1977), 30

Mueller v. Allen, 463 U.S. 388 (1983), 287–288

Murphy v. Hunt, 455 U.S. 478 (1982), 7

Muskrat v. United States, 219 U.S. 346, (1911), 8

N

NAACP v. Alabama, 357 U.S. 449 (1958), 255

NAACP v. Alabama ex rel. Patterson, 357 U.S. 449 (1958), 34, 260

NAACP v. Claiborne Hardware Co., 458 U.S. 886 (1982), 191–192

Nash v. Florida Industrial Commission, 389 U.S. 235 (1967), 70–71

Near v. Minnesota, 283 U.S. 697 (1931), 180, 267

Nebraska Press Association v. Stuart, 427 U.S. 539 (1976), 181

Nevada v. Hall, 440 U.S. 410 (1979), 31

New Energy Co. of Indiana v. Limbach, 486 U.S. 269 (1988), 85

New England Power Co. v. New Hampshire, 455 U.S. 331 (1982), 80–81

New Motor Vehicle Bd. v. Orrin W. Fox Co., 439 U.S. 96 (1978), 33

New Orleans v. Dukes, 427 U.S. 297 (1976), 155–156

New York Times v. Sullivan, 376 U.S. 254 (1964), 206–207

New York Times v. United States, 403 U.S. 713 (1971), 180

New York v. Ferber, 458 U.S. 747 (1982), 197–198

New York v. United States, 326 U.S. 572 (1946), 96

New York v. United States, 505 U.S. 144 (1992), 98

Nixon v. Administrator of General Services, 433 U.S. 425 (1977), 114, 173

Nixon v. Condon, 286 U.S. 73 (1932), 37, 39

Nixon v. Fitzgerald, 457 U.S. 731 (1982), 114

Nixon v. Herndon, 273 U.S. 536 (1927), 37

Nixon v. Shrink Missouri Government PAC, 528 U.S. 377 (2000), 233

Nixon v. United States, 506 U.S. 224 (1993), 27–28

NLRB v. Jones & Laughlin Steel Corp., 301 U.S. 1 (1937), 58

Nollan v. California Coastal Commission, 483 U.S. 825 (1987), 141

O

O'Hare Truck Service Inc. v. City of Northlake, 518 U.S. 712 (1996), 259–260

Ohio v. Akron Center for Reproductive Health, 497 U.S. 502 (1990), 127

Ohio v. Helvering, 292 U.S. 360 (1934), 96

Ohralik v. Ohio State Bar, 436 U.S. 447 (1978), 223

O'Lone v. Estate of Shabazz, 482 U.S. 342 (1987), 305–306

Orr v. Orr, 440 U.S. 268 (1979), 159

Osborne v. Ohio, 495 U.S. 103 (1990), 198

P

Pacific Gas & Electric Co. v. Public Utilities Commission, 475 U.S. 1 (1986), 186

Pacific States Telephone & Telegraph Co. v. Oregon, 223 U.S. 118 (1912), 24

Paris Adult Theatre I v. Slaton, 413 U.S. 49 (1973), 199

Paul v. Davis, 424 U.S. 693 (1976), 132

Peel v. Attorney Registration and Disciplinary Commission of Illinois, 496 U.S. 91 (1990), 225

Pell v. Procunier, 417 U.S. 817 (1974), 272

Penn Central Transportation Co. v. City of New York, 438 U.S. 104 (1978), 139–140

Pennhurst State School and Hospital v. Halderman, 451 U.S. 1 (1981), 53

Pennhurst State School and Hospital v. Halderman, 465 U.S. 89 (1984), 30

Pennsylvania v. Nelson, 350 U.S. 497 (1956), 69

Perez v. Campbell, 402 U.S. 637 (1971), 71

Perez v. United States, 402 U.S. 146 (1971), 60

Perry Education Association v. Perry Local Educators' Association, 460 U.S. 37 (1983), 241

Personnel Administrator of Massachusetts v. Feeney, 442 U.S. 256 (1979), 153

Pickering v. Board of Education, 391 U.S. 563 (1968), 236–237

Pierce v. Society of Sisters, 268 U.S. 510 (1925), 121

Pittsburgh Press Co. v. Pittsburgh Commission on Human Relations, 413 U.S. 376 (1973), 219

Planned Parenthood v. Casey, 505 U.S. 833 (1992), 124–125, 127, 128

Planned Parenthood v. Danforth, 428 U.S. 52 (1976), 127, 128

Plessy v. Ferguson 163 U.S. 537 (1896), 150

Plyler v. Doe, 457 U.S. 202 (1982), 168

Poe v. Ullman, 367 U.S. 497 (1961), 6

Polk County v. Dodson, 454 U.S. 312 (1981), 38

Port Authority Trans-Hudson Corp. v. Feeney, 495 U.S. 299 (1990), 31

Poulos v. New Hampshire, 345 U.S. 395 (1953), 182–183

Powell v. McCormack, 395 U.S. 486 (1969), 26

Press-Enterprise Co. v. Superior Court, 464 U.S. 501 (1984), 272

Principality of Monaco v. Mississippi, 292 U.S. 313 (1934), 29

Printz v. United States, 521 U.S. 898 (1997), 98

Prize Cases 67 U.S. (2 Black) 635 (1863), 48

Prudential Insurance Co. v. Benjamin, 328 U.S. 408 (1946), 78–79

PruneYard Shopping Center v. Robins, 447 U.S. 74 (1980), 185, 254

Pumpelly v. Green Bay & Mississippi Canal Co., 80 U.S. (13 Wall.) 166 (1871), 138–139

Q

Quern v. Jordan, 440 U.S. 332 (1979), 32

Quill Corporation v. North Dakota, 504 U.S. 298 (1992), 83

Quinn v. Millsap, 491 U.S. 95 (1989), 11

R

Railroad Commission v. Pullman Co., 312 U.S. 496 (1941), 33

Railway Express Agency v. New York, 336 U.S. 106 (1949), 155

Raines v. Byrd, 521 U.S. 811 (1997), 22

Randall v. Sorrell, 548 U.S. 230 (2006), 234

Rankin v. McPherson, 483 U.S. 378 (1987), 238

R.A.V. v. City of St. Paul, Minnesota, 505 U.S. 377 (1992), 175–176, 193

Red Lion Broadcasting Co. v. FCC, 395 U.S. 367 (1969), 271

Reeves, Inc. v. Stake, 447 U.S. 429 (1980), 80

Regan v. Taxation with Representation of Washington, 461 U.S. 540 (1983), 186–187

Regan v. Wald, 468 U.S. 222 (1984), 120

Regents of University of California v. Bakke, 438 U.S. 265 (1978), 161–162

Reid v. Covert, 354 U.S. 1 (1957), 48

Reitman v. Mulkey, 387 U.S. 369 (1967), 42, 43

Rendell-Baker v. Kohn, 457 U.S. 830 (1982), 42, 45

Reno v. ACLU, 521 U.S. 844 (1997), 204

Reno v. Condon, 528 U.S. 141 (2000), 57, 99

Republican Party of Minnesota v. White, 536 U.S. 765 (2002), 233–234

Reynolds v. United States, 98 U.S. (8 Otto) 145 (1878), 300–301

Richmond Newspapers v. Virginia, 448 U.S. 555 (1980), 272

Richmond v. J.A. Croson Co., 488 U.S. 469 (1989), 162–163

Roberts v. United States Jaycees, 468 U.S. 609 (1984), 262

Roemer v. Board of Public Works of Maryland, 426 U.S. 736 (1976), 286

Roe v. Wade, 410 U.S. 113 (1973), 7, 123–124

Romer v. Evans, 517 U.S. 620 (1996), 157–158

Rosenberger v. Rector and Visitors of the University of Virginia, 515 U.S. 819 (1995), 282

Rubin v. Coors Brewing Co., 514 U.S. 476 (1995), 227

Ruckelshaus v. Monsanto Co., 467 U.S. 986 (1984), 142–143

Rumsfeld v. Forum for Academic & Institutional Rights, Inc., 547 U.S. 47 (2006), 189

Rust v. Sullivan, 500 U.S. 173 (1991), 187–188

Rutan v. Republican Party of Illinois, 497 U.S. 62 (1990), 259

S

S. v. D., 410 U.S. 614 (1973), 10, 13

Sable Communications v. FCC, 492 U.S. 115 (1989), 196–197

Saenz v. Roe, 526 U.S. 489 (1999), 90–91

Saia v. New York, 334 U.S. 558 (1948), 182

San Antonio Independent School District v. Rodriguez, 411 U.S. 1 (1973), 155

Sandin v. Conner, 515 U.S. 472 (1995), 131

Santa Fe Independent School District v. Doe, 530 U.S. 290 (2000), 282–283

Santosky v. Kramer, 455 U.S. 745 (1982), 121–122, 131

Saxbe v. Washington Post Co., 417 U.S. 843 (1974), 273

Scales v. United States, 367 U.S. 203 (1961), 256

Schad v. Borough of Mount Ephraim, 452 U.S. 61 (1981), 179, 200–201

Schall v. Martin, 467 U.S. 253 (1984), 136

Schenck v. Pro-Choice Network of Western New York, 519 U.S. 357 (1997), 248

Scheuer v. Rhodes, 416 U.S. 232 (1974), 30

Schlesinger v. Reservists Committee to Stop the War, 418 U.S. 208 (1974), 21

Screws v. United States, 325 U.S. 91 (1945), 37–38

Selective Service System v. Minnesota Public Interest Research Group, 468 U.S. 841 (1984), 173

Seminole Tribe of Florida v. Florida, 517 U.S. 44 (1996), 32

Shapero v. Kentucky Bar Association, 486 U.S. 466 (1988), 224–255

Shapiro v. Thompson, 394 U.S. 618 (1969), 119

Shaughnessy v. United States ex rel. Mezei, 345 U.S. 206 (1953), 131

Shelley v. Kraemer, 334 U.S. 1 (1948), 42

Shelton v. Tucker, 364 U.S. 479 (1960), 260–261

Sherbert v. Verner, 374 U.S. 398 (1963), 301

Shuttlesworth v. City of Birmingham, 394 U.S. 147 (1969), 183–184

Sibron v. New York, 392 U.S. 40 (1968), 7, 8

Sierra Club v. Morton, 405 U.S. 727 (1972), 10

Simon & Schuster, Inc. v. Members of New York State Crime Victims Board, 502 U.S. 105 (1991), 175

Simon v. Eastern Kentucky Welfare Rights Organization, U.S. 26 (1976), 12

Skinner v. Oklahoma, 316 U.S. 535 (1942), 120–121

Slaughter-House Cases, 83 U.S. (16 Wall.) 36 (1873), 90

Smith v. Allwright, 321 U.S. 649 (1944), 39–40

Smith v. Daily Mail Publishing Co., 443 U.S. 97 (1979), 213–214

Smith v. Goguen, 415 U.S. 566 (1974), 178

Smith v. Reeves, 178 U.S. 436 (1900), 29

Sosna v. Iowa, 419 U.S. 393 (1975), 8

South Carolina State Highway Department v. Barnwell, 303 U.S. 177 (1938), 75–76

South Carolina v. Baker, 485 U.S. 505 (1988), 97

South Carolina v. Katzenbach, 383 U.S. 301 (1966), 66

South-Central Timber Development, Inc. v. Wunnicke, 467 U.S. 82 (1984), 81–82

South Dakota v. Dole, 483 U.S. 203 (1987), 52, 53, 54

South Dakota v. North Carolina, 192 U.S. 286 (1904), 29

Southern Pacific Co. v. Arizona, 325 U.S. 761 (1945), 76

Speiser v. Randall, 357 U.S. 513 (1958), 186

Sperry v. Florida, 373 U.S. 379 (1963), 95

Stanley v. Georgia, 394 U.S. 557 (1969), 199

Stanley v. Illinois, 405 U.S. 645 (1972), 131

Stenberg v. Carhart, 530 U.S. 914 (2000), 125–126

Stone v. Graham, 449 U.S. 39 (1980), 278

Strauder v. West Virginia, 100 U.S. (10 Otto) 303 (1879), 150

Sugarman v. Dougall, 413 U.S. 634 (1973), 166

Supreme Court of New Hampshire v. Piper, 470 U.S. 274 (1985), 88, 89–90

T

Terry v. Adams, 345 U.S. 461 (1953), 40–41

Texas Monthly, Inc. v. Bullock, 489 U.S. 1 (1989), 296–297

Texas v. Johnson, 491 U.S. 397 (1989), 216–217

Thomas v. Review Board of the Indiana Employment Security Division, 450 U.S. 707 (1981), 299

Thompson v. Western States Medical Center, 535 U.S. 357 (2002), 221

Tileston v. Ullman, 318 U.S. 44 (1943), 16–17

Tilton v. Richardson, 403 U.S. 672 (1971), 285–286

Time, Inc. v. Hill, 385 U.S. 374 (1967), 211

Time v. Firestone, 424 U.S. 448 (1976), 209

Tinker v. Des Moines Independent Community School District, 393 U.S. 503 (1969), 216, 235

Toomer v. Witsell, 334 U.S. 385 (1948), 87–88

Trafficante v. Metropolitan Life Insurance Co., 409 U.S. 205 (1972), 10

Troxel v. Granville, 530 U.S. 57 (2000), 122

Turner Broadcasting System, Inc. v. FCC, 512 U.S. 622 (1994), 271

Turner Broadcasting System, Inc. v. FCC, 520 U.S. 180 (1997), 271

U

United Bldg. & Constr. Trades v. Mayor and Council of the City of Camden, 465 U.S. 208 (1984), 87

United Public Workers v. Mitchell, 330 U.S. 75 (1947), 6

United States ex rel. Knauff v. Shaughnessy, 338 U.S. 537 (1950), 131

United States Trust Co. v. New Jersey, 431 U.S. 1 (1977), 146

United States v. 564.54 Acres of Land, More or Less, Situated in Monroe and Pike Counties, Pennsylvania, 441 U.S. 506 (1979), 144

United States v. American Library Association, Inc., 123 S.Ct. 2297 (2003), 54

United States v. American Library Association, Inc., 539 U.S. 194 (2003), 188–189

United States v. Ballard, 322 U.S. 78 (1944), 298–299

United States v. Brewster, 408 U.S. 501 (1972), 109

United States v. Brown, 381 U.S. 437 (1965), 172–173

United States v. Carolene Products Co., 304 U.S. 144 (1938), 117–118

United States v. Causby, 328 U.S. 256 (1946), 139

United States v. Constantine, 296 U.S. 287 (1935), 52

United States v. Curtiss-Wright Export Corp., 299 U.S. 304 (1936), 47

United States v. Darby, 312 U.S. 100 (1941), 57, 58–59

United States v. Edge Broadcasting Co., 509 U.S. 418 (1993), 228

United States v. Eichman, 496 U.S. 310 (1990), 217

United States v. Gillock, 445 U.S. 360 (1980), 108

United States v. Grace, 461 U.S. 171 (1983), 243–244

United States v. Guest, 383 U.S. 745 (1966), 119

United States v. Helstoski, 442 U.S. 477 (1979), 109, 110

United States v. Johnson, 319 U.S. 302 (1943), 9

United States v. Klein, 80 U.S. (13 Wall.) 128 (1871), 5

United States v. Lee, 455 U.S. 252 (1982), 303–304

United States v. Lopez, 514 U.S. 549 (1995), 55, 60–61

United States v. Lovett, 328 U.S. 303 (1946), 172

United States v. Mississippi, 380 U.S. 128 (1965), 29

United States v. Morrison, 529 U.S. 598 (2000), 36, 61

United States v. Munsingwear, Inc., 340 U.S. 36 (1950), 6

United States v. New Mexico, 455 U.S. 720 (1982), 94

United States v. Nixon, 418 U.S. 683 (1974), 114

United States v. O'Brien, 391 U.S. 367 (1968), 215

United States v. Orito, 413 U.S. 139 (1973), 199

United States v. Paradise, 480 U.S. 149 (1987), 162

United States v. Pink, 315 U.S. 203 (1942), 49

United States v. Playboy Entertainment Group, Inc., 529 U.S. 803 (2000), 204–205, 245–246

United States v. Reidel, 402 U.S. 351 (1971), 199

United States v. Richardson, 418 U.S. 166 (1974), 15

United States v. South-Eastern Underwriters Association, 322 U.S. 533 (1944), 57

United States v. Students Challenging Regulatory Agency Procedures, 412 U.S. 669 (1973), 10

United States v. Texas, 143 U.S. 621 (1892), 29

United States v. Treasury Employees, 513 U.S. 454 (1995), 238–239

United States v. 12 200-Foot Reels of Super 8MM. Film, 413 U.S. 123 (1973), 199

United States v. United Foods, Inc., 533 U.S. 405 (2001), 265–266

United States v. Virginia, 518 U.S. 515 (1996), 151

United States v. Williams, 553 U.S. 285 (2008), 199

United States v. W.T. Grant Co., 345 U.S. 629 (1953), 7

V

Vacco v. Quill, 521 U.S. 793 (1997), 129

Valley Forge Christian College v. Americans United for Separation of Church and State, Inc., 454 U.S. 464 (1982), 15

Vance v. Bradley, 440 U.S. 93 (1979), 156

Van Orden v. Perry, 545 U.S. 677 (2005), 294–295

Veazie Bank v. Fenno, 75 U.S. (8 Wall.) 533 (1869), 51

Village of Arlington Heights v. Metropolitan Housing Development Corp., 429 U.S. 252 (1977), 152

Village of Hoffman Estates v. Flipside, Hoffman Estates, Inc., 455 U.S. 489 (1982), 178

Virginia v. Black, 538 U.S. 343 (2003), 193–194

W

Wallace v. Jaffree, 472 U.S. 38 (1985), 279

Walz v. Tax Commission, 397 U.S. 664 (1970), 296

Ward v. Rock Against Racism, 491 U.S. 781 (1989), 244–245

Warth v. Seldin, 422 U.S. 490 (1975), 9, 13, 18

Washington v. Glucksberg, 521 U.S. 702 (1997), 129

Watchtower Bible & Tract Society of New York, Inc. v. Village of Stratton, 536 U.S. 150 (2002), 246

Watkins v. United States, 354 U.S. 178 (1957), 111

Weaver v. Graham, 450 U.S. 24 (1981), 171

Webb's Fabulous Pharmacies, Inc. v. Beckwith, 449 U.S. 155 (1980), 142

Webster v. Reproductive Health Services, 492 U.S. 490 (1989), 128

Weinstein v. Bradford, 423 U.S. 147 (1975), 7

West Coast Hotel v. Parrish, 300 U.S. 379 (1937), 117

West v. Atkins, 487 U.S. 42 (1988), 38

West Virginia State Board of Education
v. Barnette, 319 U.S. 624 (1943),
184–185

White v. Massachusetts Council of
Construction Employers, 460 U.S.
204 (1983), 81

Whitman v. American Trucking
Associations, 531 U.S. 457
(2001), 102

Whitney v. Robertson, 124 U.S. 190
(1888), 49

Wickard v. Filburn, 317 U.S. 111
(1942), 59

Widmar v. Vincent, 454 U.S. 263
(1981), 243, 278

Williamson v. Lee Optical, 348 U.S. 483
(1955), 118

Williams v. Zbarez, 448 U.S. 358
(1980), 128

Wisconsin v. Yoder, 406 U.S. 205
(1972), 303

Witters v. Washington Department of
Services for the Blind, 474 U.S. 481
(1986), 288

Wolman v. Walter, 433 U.S. 229
(1977), 290

Woods v. Cloyd W. Miller Co., 333
U.S. 138 (1948), 50

Wood v. Chesborough, 228 U.S. 672
(1913), 34

Wooley v. Maynard, 430 U.S. 705
(1977), 185

Wyoming v. Oklahoma, 502 U.S. 437
(1992), 20

Y

Yick Wo v. Hopkins, 118 U.S. 356
(1886), 152

Youngberg v. Romeo, 457 U.S. 307
(1982), 129

Youngstown Sheet & Tube Co. v. Sawyer,
343 U.S. 579 (1952), 112–113

Young v. American Mini-Theatres, Inc.,
427 U.S. 50 (1976), 200

Z

Zauderer v. Office of Disciplinary Counsel,
471 U.S. 626 (1985), 223–224

Zelman v. Simmons-Harris, 536 U.S. 639
(2002), 290

Zobrest v. Catalina Foothills School
District, 509 U.S. 1 (1993),
288–289

Zorach v. Clauson, 343 U.S. 306 (1952),
276–277

Zurcher v. The Stanford Daily, 436 U.S.
547 (1978), 270–271

Subject Index

A

Abortion, 123–128
  government funding, 128
  informed consent, 127
  parental notification and consent, 127
  reporting and recording, 128
  spousal notification and consent, 128
  twenty-four-hour waiting period, 127
  viability tests, 127–128
Absolute immunity, in executive
  immunity, 114
Abstention doctrine, 32–33
Acts and motives, legislative, 108–109
Acts and promises, political, 109–110
Adequate state grounds, 34
Administration of justice, 228–229
Adolescent Family Life Act (AFLA),
  291–292
Advertising. *See* Commercial speech
Advisory opinions, 8
Advocacy of unlawful conduct, 190–192
Agricultural Adjustment Act of 1938,
  59, 62, 70
Agricultural Marketing Agreement Act
  of 1937, 263–264
Airport and Airway Revenue Act,
  96–97
Alienage classification, 165–168
  federal discrimination, 168
  state discrimination, 165–168
Alien Registration Act of 1940, 68
Ambassadors, 47–48
Ambiguous cases, 35
Appointment power (appointments
  clause), 103–105

Ashurst-Sumners Act of 1935, 56
Association standing, 18–20
  suing on behalf of members, 19–20
  suing on own behalf, 18–19

B

Balanced Budget and Emergency Deficit
  Control Act of 1985, 105–106
Bankruptcy Act, 71
Beachfront Management Act, 140
Bills of attainder, 172–173
Bituminous Mine Subsidence and Land
  Conservation Act, 140–141, 147
Brady Handgun Violence Prevention
  Act, 98

C

Cable Television Consumer Protection
  and Competition Act of 1992,
  202–203, 271
Case or controversy rule, 5
Causation, 11–12
Central Hudson test, 219–228. *See also*
  Commercial speech
Certiorari (discretionary) appellate
  jurisdiction, 4–5
  federal court of appeals cases, 4
  state cases, 4–5
Charitable Solicitations Act, 274–275
Child care, custody, and control, 121–122
Child Labor Amendment, 21–22
Child Online Protection Act
  (COPA), 205
Child pornography, 197–199

Child Pornography Prevention Act
(CPPA) of 1996, 197–199
Children's Internet Protection Act
(CIPA), 188
Children's rights, in procedural due
process, 136
Citizen standing, 21
Civil rights, congressional power to
enforce, 65–66
Civil Rights Act of 1964, 59–60
Civil Rights Act of 1968, 10, 32
Civil Rights Attorney's Fees Awards
Act of 1976, 32
Class actions, 8
Classification, in equal protection
clause, 150–154
facially discriminatory law, 150–151
facially neutral law, 151–154
Clean Air Act, 102
Collateral consequences exception, 8
Collusive cases, 9
Commander in chief, 48
Commerce clause
federal commerce power and, 55–62
foreign nations and, 62
Indian tribes and, 62
purpose of, 55, 72
See also Dormant commerce clause;
Interstate commerce
Commercial speech, 219–228
"For Sale" and "Sold" signs, 226
lawyer advertising, 221–226
liquor advertising, 227–228
lottery advertising, 228
news racks, 226–227
Communications Act of 1934, 196–197
Communications Decency Act (CDA)
of 1996, 204
Confidential sources, freedom of press
and, 270–271
Conflict preemption, 69–70
Congressional approval, as exception
in state regulation of interstate
commerce, 78–79
Congressional power, 49
to enforce civil rights, 65–66
to investigate, 111–112
war power, 50
Consumer Credit Protection Act, 60

Content-based regulation, 175–176
Content-neutral regulation, 176
Contraceptives, 122–123
Contract clause, 145–148
Controlled Substances Act (CSA),
61–62
Court injunctions, 180–181
Court proceedings, freedom of press
and, 272
criminal trials, 272
pretrial suppression hearings, 272
voir dire proceedings, 272
Creationism Act, 279–280
Creditor's claims, in procedural due
process, 136–137
Criminal trials, freedom of press
and, 272

D

Dalkon Shield Intrauterine Device,
223–224
Declaratory judgments, 8
Defamation, 206–211
private figures (Gertz rule), 209–211
public figures (New York Times rule,
malice needed), 207–209
public officials (New York Times rule,
malice needed), 206–207
Delegation of legislative power
(nondelegation doctrine),
100–102
Deportation, liberty and, 131
Dial-a-porn, 196–197
Direct appeal, in appellate jurisdiction, 4
Discriminatory law, 274–275
in state regulation of interstate
commerce, 72–75
District of Columbia Redevelopment
Act of 1945, 143
Dormant commerce clause, 72–86
state regulation of interstate
commerce, 72–82
state taxation of interstate
commerce, 82–86
Driver's license, in procedural due
process, 132–133, 135
Driver's Privacy Protection Act, 57, 99
Due process, 116–137

procedural, 130–137
substantive, 116–129

E

Economic state discrimination (strict scrutiny), 165–166
Education Consolidation and Improvement Act of 1981, 290
Elementary and Secondary Education Act of 1965, 14, 289
Eleventh Amendment, 28–32
  background, 28
  congressional authorization, 31–32
  federal court, 30–31
  private suits, 29
  rule, 29–32
  state defendant (protecting state treasury), 29–30
  waiver, 31
Eminent domain. *See* Taking clause
Endangered Species Act, 11
Equal Access Act, 280
Equal protection clause, 149–168
  classification, 150–154
  tests, 154–168
Establishment clause, 274–298
  discriminatory law, 274–275
  nondiscriminatory law (*Lemon* test), 275–298
Ethics in Government Act, 104–105, 106, 238–239
Exclusion, liberty and due process clause, 131
Executive agreements, 49
Executive immunity, in separation of powers doctrine, 114–115
  official acts (absolute immunity), 114
  other executive officials (qualified immunity), 115
  unofficial acts (no immunity), 114–115
Executive power, 47–49
  ambassadors, 47–48
  commander in chief, 48
  executive agreements (Senate approval not required), 49
  treaties (Senate approval required), 48–49
  war power, 50

Executive power, in separation of powers doctrine, 112–115
  executive immunity, 114–115
  executive privilege, 114
  lawmaking power, 112–113
  war power, 113–114
Executive privilege, in separation of powers doctrine, 114
Ex post facto laws, 169–171
Express preemption, 67–68

F

Facially discriminatory law, 150–151
Facially neutral law, 151–154
Fair Housing Act, 18–19
Fair Labor Standards Act (FLSA), 56, 58–59, 97–98
Fairly apportioned tax in state regulation of interstate commerce, 83–84
Fairly related tax in state regulation of interstate commerce, 85–86
False light, 211
Federal Alcohol Administration Act, 227
Federal commerce power, 55–62
  commerce with foreign nations and Indian tribes, 62
  interstate commerce, 55–62
Federal court of appeals cases, 4
Federal discrimination (rational basis test), 168
Federal Election Campaign Act of 1971, 104, 230, 261
Federal Insecticide, Fungicide, and Rodenticide Act (FIFRA), 142–143
Federal judicial power, 2–35
  abstention doctrine, 32–33
  adequate state grounds, 34
  advisory opinions, 8
  ambiguous cases, 35
  case or controversy rule, 5
  collusive cases, 9
  declaratory judgments, 8
  independent state grounds, 34–35
  mootness doctrine, 6–8
  political question doctrine, 22–28
  ripeness doctrine, 5–6

scope of, 2–3
source of, 2
sovereign immunity and Eleventh
    Amendment, 28–32
standing, 9–22
Federal Lottery Act of 1895, 55–56
Federal Meat Inspection Act (FMIA),
    67–68
Federal property power, 63–64
    Article I, 63
    Article IV, 63–64
Federal regulation of state governments,
    97–99
Federal taxation of state governments,
    96–97
Federal taxpayers, 13–15
    exception (*Flast* "Nexus" Test), 14–15
    general rule (no standing), 13–14
Federal Trade Commission Act, 105
Field preemption, 68–69
Fifth Amendment, 144, 149–150
Filled Milk Act of 1923, 117–118
Flag Protection Act of 1989, 217
Flast "Nexus" Test, 1415
Food and Drug Administration
    Modernization Act of 1997, 221
Foreign affairs, 47–50
    congressional power, 49
    executive power, 47–49
    judicial power, 49
    war power, 50
Foreign nations, federal commerce
    power and, 62
Foreign Service Act of 1946, 156
"For Sale" and "Sold" signs, 226
Four-part *O'Brien* test, 215–219
Fourteenth Amendment, 6, 26, 31–32,
    36, 43, 44–45, 65–66, 118, 120,
    129, 133, 150, 166, 174, 255, 267,
    274, 278, 310
Free exercise clause, 298–309
    neutral law, 300–308
    nonneutral law, 308–309
    protected religious beliefs, 298–300
Freedom of association, 255–266
    disclosure of group membership,
        260–261
    punishing group membership,
        255–260

right not to associate, 261–266
Freedom of press, 267–273
    confidential sources, 270–271
    court proceedings, access to, 272
    generally applicable laws, 269–270
    prisons, access to, 272–273
    "right of reply" and "must carry"
        laws, 271
    taxation, 267–269
Freedom of religion, 274–309
    establishment clause, 274–298
    free exercise clause, 298–309
Freedom of speech, general
        considerations, 174–189
    content-based regulation (presumed
        invalid), 175–176
    content-neutral regulation
        (intermediate scrutiny), 176
    overbreadth doctrine, 178–179
    prior restraints (presumed invalid),
        180–184
    right not to speak, 184–186
    unconstitutional condition doctrine,
        186–189
    void for vagueness doctrine,
        176–178
Freedom of speech, public and
        nonpublic, 241–254
    nonpublic forums, 249–254
    private property, 254
    public forums (traditional and
        designated), 241–248
Freedom of speech, restricted speech,
        190–240
    administration of justice, 228–229
    advocacy of unlawful conduct,
        190–192
    commercial speech (*Central Hudson*
        test, intermediate scrutiny),
        219–228
    defamation, 206–211
    false light, 211
    imminent and uncontrolled violence,
        194–196
    intentional infliction of emotional
        distress, 211–212
    loyalty oaths, 239–240
    obscenity (*Miller* test), 196–205
    political speech, 230–235

profane, obscene, lewd, libelous, insulting words, 192–194

public disclosure of private facts, 212–215

public schools, 235–236

speech of public employees, 236–239

symbolic conduct (non-verbal speech, four-part *O'Brien* test), 215–219

Fundamental rights, regulation of, 119–129

abortion, 123–128

child care, custody, and control, 121–122

contraceptives, 122–123

international travel, 120

interstate travel, 119

involuntary commitment, 129

marriage, 120

medical care, refusing, 129

procreation, 120–121

suicide, 129

voting, 129

G

Generally applicable laws, freedom of press and, 269–270

Gertz rule, 209–211

Government action required (state action doctrine rule), 37–39

Government employment, in procedural due process, 132, 134

Gross Receipts Act, 268–269

Group membership, disclosure of, 260–261

Group membership, punishing, 255–260

political patronage, 258–260

Gun-Free School Zones Act of 1990, 60–61

H

Habitual Criminal Sterilization Act, 120–121

Hatch Act, 6

Higher Education Facilities Act of 1963, 285–286

Housing and Rent Act of 1947, 50

I

Immigration and Nationality Act, 103

Imminent and uncontrolled violence, 194–196

Immunities clause

privileges *and*, 86–90

privileges *or*, 90–91

Implied preemption, 68–71

conflict preemption, 69–70

field preemption, 68–69

interference preemption, 70–71

Independent state grounds, 34–35

Indian tribes, federal commerce power and, 62

Individuals with Disabilities Act (IDEA), 289

Injunctions, in public forums, 247–248

Injury, 10–11

Intentional infliction of emotional distress, 211–212

Interference preemption, 70–71

Intergovernmental immunity, 93–99

federal regulation of state governments, 97–99

federal taxation of state governments, 96–97

state regulation of federal government, 95–96

state taxation of federal government, 93–94

Intermediate scrutiny, 158–161

Central Hudson test, 219–228

undocumented aliens, 168

International travel, 120

Interstate commerce, 55–62

channels and instrumentalities of, 55–57

intrastate activities having substantial effect on, 57–62

Interstate commerce, state regulation of, 72–82

congressional approval, as exception, 78–79

discriminatory law, 72–75

market participant exception,
79–82
nondiscriminatory ("even handed")
law, 75–78
Interstate commerce, state taxation of,
82–86
fairly apportioned tax, 83–84
fairly related tax, 85–86
nondiscriminatory tax, 84–85
substantial nexus of taxed activity,
82–83
Interstate travel, 119
Involuntary commitment, 129

J

Judicial power, 49
Just compensation, 144
Jus Tertii standing. *See* Third-party
standing

K

Kentucky Corrupt Practices Act, 231

L

Labor-Management Reporting and
Disclosure Act, 172–173
Land Reform Act of 1967, 143
Lawmaking power, in separation of
powers doctrine, 112–113
Lawyer advertising, 221–226
Legal incidence test, 93–94
Legal Services Corporation Act, 188
Legislative immunity, 108–111
legislative acts and motives
(protected), 108–109
political acts and promises (not
protected), 109–110
republication of materials (not
protected), 110–111
Legislative power, in separation of
powers doctrine, 100–112
appointment power (appointments
clause), 103–105
congressional power to investigate,
111–112

delegation of (nondelegation
doctrine), 100–102
legislative immunity, 108–111
legislative veto (unconstitutional), 103
removal power, 105–108
Legislative veto (unconstitutional), 103
Legislator standing, 21–22
Lemon test. *See* Nondiscriminatory law
(*Lemon* test)
Liberty, in procedural due process,
130–132
deportation and exclusion, 131
parental rights, 131
prisoners, 131
reputation, 132
Licensing systems, 181–184
Line Item Veto Act, 22
Liquor advertising, 227–228
Lottery advertising, 228
Low-Level Radioactive Waste Policy
Amendment Act, 98
Loyalty oaths, 239–240

M

Market participant exception, 79–82
Marriage, 120
Maternity Act of 1921, 14–15
Mathews test, 133–137
children's rights, 136
creditor's claims, 136–137
driver's license, 135
government employment, 134
public education, 135
public utilities, 135–136
social security benefits, 134–135
welfare benefits, 134
McCarran Act, 78–79
Media (radio, cable, TV, Internet),
202–205
Medical care, refusing, 129
Merit System of Personnel
Administration Act, 178
Military Selective Service Act, 173
Military Selective Service Act of 1967,
297, 302
Military service exemptions, 297–298
Miller test. *See* Obscenity (*Miller* test)
Minnesota Human Rights Act, 262

Mootness doctrine, 6–8
  class actions, 8
  collateral consequences exception, 8
  repetition exception, 7–8
  voluntarily cessation, 7
Motor Vehicle Safety Responsibility
  Act, 71
Municipal taxpayers, 16
Mushroom Promotion, Research, and
  Consumer Information Act, 265
"Must carry" laws, freedom of press
  and, 271

N

National Industrial Recovery Act, 101
National Labor Relations Act of 1935,
  58, 70, 269
Negative commerce clause. See
  Dormant commerce clause
Neutral law, 300–308
News racks, 226–227
New York Family Court Act, 121
New York Times rule, 206–209, 211
  public figures (malice needed),
    207–209
  public officials (malice needed),
    206–207
No immunity, in executive immunity,
  114–115
Nondelegation doctrine, 100–102
Nondiscriminatory law (Lemon test),
  275–298
  military service exemptions, 297–298
  public aid to religious institutions,
    291–292
  public aid to sectarian educational
    institutions, 283–290
  religious activities in schools,
    276–283
  religious displays and ceremonies,
    293–296
  Sunday closing laws, 292
  tax exemptions, 296–297
Nondiscriminatory ("even handed")
  law, in state regulation of
  interstate commerce, 75–78
Nondiscriminatory tax in state regulation
  of interstate commerce, 84–85

Nonfundamental rights, regulation of,
  117–119
Nonneutral law, 308–309
Nonpublic forums, 249–254
Non-verbal speech, four-part O'Brien
  test, 215–219

O

Obscenity (Miller test), 196–205
  child pornography, 197–199
  media (radio, cable, TV, Internet),
    202–205
  private possession, 199
  zoning, 199–201
Official acts (absolute immunity), in
  executive immunity, 114
Oregon Compulsory Education Act, 121
Other executive officials (qualified
  immunity), in executive
  immunity, 115
Overbreadth doctrine, 178–179

P

Parens patriae, 20–21
Parental rights, liberty and, 131
Partial-Birth Abortion Ban Act
  of 2003, 126
Penal tax, 52
Pennsylvania Abortion Control Act of
  1982, 124
Pennsylvania Alien Registration Act of
  1939, 68–69
Pennsylvania Sedition Act, 69
Pentagon Papers, 180
Personal standing, 9–13
  causation, 11–12
  injury, 10–11
  redressability, 12–13
Political function exception (rational
  basis test), 166–168
Political patronage, 258–260
Political question doctrine, 22–28
  Baker Test, 23
  examples, 23–28
Political speech, 230–235
Possessory taking, 138–139
Preemption, 67–71

express preemption, 67–68
implied preemption, 68–71
Presidential Election Campaign Fund
  Act, 232
Presidential Recordings and Materials
  Preservations Act, 173
Pretrial suppression hearings, freedom of
  press and, 272
Prior restraints (presumed invalid),
  180–184
  court injunctions, 180–181
  licensing systems, 181–184
Prisoners, liberty and, 131
Prisons, freedom of press and, 272–273
Private figures, defamation of, 209–211
Private Pension Benefits Protection
  Act, 147
Private possession, 199
Private property, 142–143, 254
Privileges *and* immunities clause, 86–90
  citizens, 87
  closely related to substantial state
    interest and less discriminatory
    means not available, 89–90
  fundamental rights, 87–88
Privileges *or* immunities clause, 90–91
Procedural due process, 130–137
  government deprivation,
    intentional, 130
  liberty, 130–132
  life, deprivation of, 130
  notice, hearing, and decision maker
    requirements, 133–137 (*See also*
    Mathews test)
  property, 132–133
Procreation, 120–121
Profane, obscene, lewd, libelous,
  insulting words, 192–194
Property, in procedural due process,
  132–133
  driver's license, 132–133
  government employment, 132
  public education, 133
  public utilities, 133
  welfare benefits, 132
Prosecutorial Remedies and Other
  Tools to end the Exploitation of
  Children Today (PROTECT) Act
  of 2003, 199

Protected religious beliefs, 298–300
Public Broadcasting Act of 1967, 187
Public disclosure of private facts,
  212–215
Public education, in procedural due
  process, 133, 135
Public figures, defamation of, 207–209
Public forums (traditional and
  designated), 241–248
  injunctions, 247–248
  regulations, 242–247
Public function exception, 39–42
Public Health Service Act, 69, 187
Public officials, defamation of, 206–207
Public schools, 235–236
Public use, 143–144
Public utilities, in procedural due
  process, 133, 135–136
Pullman Sleeper, 33
Pure Food and Drug Act of 1906, 56

Q

Qualified immunity, in executive
  immunity, 115

R

Race and national origin classification,
  161–165
Railroad Retirement Act of 1974
Rational basis test, 117–119, 154–158
  federal discrimination, 168
  political function exception,
    166–168
Redressability, 12–13
Regulations, in public forums, 242–247
Regulatory taking, 139–142
Religious activities in schools, 276–283
Religious displays and ceremonies,
  293–296
Religious Freedom Restoration Act
  (RFRA), 66
Religious institutions, public aid to,
  291–292
Removal power, legislative, 105–108
Repetition exception, 7–8
Republication of materials, 110–111
Reputation, liberty and, 132

Revenue Act of 1932, 96
Right not to associate, 261–266
Right not to speak, 184–186
"Right of reply," freedom of press and, 271
Ripeness doctrine, 5–6

S

Sarbanes-Oxley Act of 2002, 107
Second Amendment, 310–311
Sectarian educational institutions,
    public aid to, 283–290
Senate Concurrent Resolution No. 3,
    22, 25
Sentencing Reform Act of 1984,
    101–102
Separation of powers doctrine, 100–115
    executive power, 112–115
    legislative power, 100–112
Sherman Antitrust Act, 270
Smith Act of 1940, 69, 256
Social Security Act, 120, 158, 168
Social security benefits, in procedural
    due process, 134–135
Soil Conservation and Domestic
    Allotment Act, 95
South Carolina Act, 170
Sovereign immunity, 28–32. See also
    Eleventh Amendment
Speech of public employees, 236–239
Spending power (Dole Test), 52–54
    general welfare, 52
    independent constitutional bar, 54
    related conditions, 53
    unambiguous conditions, 53
Standing, 9–22
    association, 18–20
    citizen, 21
    legislator, 21–22
    personal, 9–13
    state, 20–21
    taxpayer, 13–16
    third-party, 16–18
Standing taxpayer, 13–16
State action doctrine, 36–46
    general rule (government action
        required), 37–39
    public function exception, 39–42
    state involvement exception, 42–46

State cases, 4–5
State discrimination
    economic (strict scrutiny),
        165–166
    political function exception (rational
        basis test), 166–168
    undocumented aliens (intermediate
        scrutiny), 168
State involvement exception, 42–46
State power, 67–92
    dormant commerce clause, 72–86
    preemption, 67–71
    privileges and immunities clause,
        86–90
    privileges or immunities clause,
        90–91
    Twenty-first Amendment, 91–92
State regulation of federal government,
    95–96
State standing, 20–21
    suing on behalf of citizens (parens
        patriae), 20–21
    suing on own behalf, 20
State taxation of federal government,
    93–94
State taxpayers, 15
Strict scrutiny, 161
    alienage classification, 165–168
    economic discrimination, 165–166
    race and national origin
        classification, 161–165
Strict scrutiny test. See Fundamental
    rights, regulation of
Substantial nexus of taxed activity
    in state regulation of interstate
    commerce, 82–83
Substantive due process, 116–129
    fundamental rights, regulation of,
        119–129
    nonfundamental rights, regulation of,
        117–119
Suicide, 129
Sunday closing laws, 292
Supreme Court jurisdiction, 3–5
    appellate jurisdiction, 3–5
    certiorari (discretionary), 4–5
    direct appeal (mandatory), 4
    limiting, by Congress, 5
    original jurisdiction, 3

Symbolic conduct (non-verbal speech, four-part O'Brien test), 215–219

T

Taking clause, 138–144
  just compensation, 144
  possessory taking, 138–139
  private property, 142–143
  public use, 143–144
  regulatory taking, 139–142
Taxation
  exception (Flast "Nexus" Test), 14–15
  federal, of state governments, 96–97
  freedom of press, 267–269
  general rule, 13–14
  penal, 52
  state, of federal government, 93–94
  state, of interstate commerce, 82–86
Taxation of interstate commerce, state, 82–86
  fairly apportioned tax, 83–84
  fairly related tax, 85–86
  nondiscriminatory tax, 84–85
  substantial nexus of taxed activity, 82–83
Tax exemptions, nondiscriminatory law and, 296–297
Taxing power, 51–52
Taxpayers
  federal, 13–15
  municipal, 16
  state, 15
Taxpayer standing, 13–16
  federal taxpayers, 13–15
  municipal taxpayers, 16
  state taxpayers, 15
Telecommunications Act of 1996, 204, 245
Tests, in equal protection clause, 154–168
  intermediate scrutiny, 158–161
  rational basis test, 154–158
  strict scrutiny, 161
Third-party standing, 16–18
  exception, 17–18
  general rule (no standing), 16–17

Trademark Remedy Clarification Act, 32
Treaties (Senate approval required), 48–49
Twenty-first Amendment, 91–92

U

Unconstitutional condition doctrine, 186–189
Undocumented aliens (intermediate scrutiny), 168
Unofficial acts (no immunity), in executive immunity, 114–115
Urgent Deficiency Appropriation Act, 173

V

Violence Against Women Act of 1994, 61
Void for vagueness doctrine, 176–178
Voir dire proceedings, freedom of press and, 272
Voluntarily cessation, 7
Voter initiative and referendum, 24
Voting, 129
Voting Rights Act of 1965, 66, 163

W

War power, 50
  congressional, 50
  executive, 50
War power, in separation of powers doctrine, 113–114
War Powers Resolution, 50, 113–114
Welfare benefits, in procedural due process, 132, 134
"White Primary Case," 37, 39
White Slave Act of 1910, 56
Wholesome Meat Act, 67–68
Wild Free-roaming Horses and Burros Act, 63–64

Z

Zoning, 199–201